THE RUSSIA I BELIEVE IN

THE RUSSIA I BELIEVE IN

The Memoirs of

SAMUEL N. HARPER · 1902–1941

EDITED BY PAUL V. HARPER

WITH THE ASSISTANCE OF RONALD THOMPSON

UNIVERSITY OF CHICAGO PRESS · CHICAGO · ILLINOIS

26055

University of Chicago Press · Chicago 37
Agent: Cambridge University Press · London

THIS BOOK IS DEDICATED TO THE CHILDREN OF MY
BROTHER'S MANY FRIENDS, WHO CALLED HIM
"UNCLE SAM," AND PARTICULARLY TO HIS NEPHEW
WHO BEARS HIS NAME, SAMUEL HARPER OVERTON

FOREWORD

WHEN PRESIDENT WILLIAM RAINEY HARPER OF THE UNIVERSITY OF CHI-cago visited Russia with Mr. Charles R. Crane in 1900, Russia had not yet awakened from that obscure period known as "the Twilight," which has been so wonderfully described by Chekhov. This makes it all the more remarkable that President Harper should have launched his son Samuel on this subject, and Russia has been in the limelight ever since.

Samuel had just completed his preparation in time for the First Duma, Russia's first essay in parliamentary life. Neither he nor I were correspondents bound to the telegraph office but students of contemporary history. I suggested that we should live and work together for a week, and this developed into a life-partnership, whether direct or indirect. We worked out a procedure of our own. We visited anyone who took a prominent part in the hectic public life of that time—but never as interviewers; and as all confidences were respected, he would tell us his whole story—how he started, his views, his objects, and the part that he had played. Usually we went together: one of us handled the conversation, and the other committed it to memory; and the results we always recorded before we went to bed. Usually the work of each of us is recorded in the handwriting of the other. All these materials are now to be preserved at the University of Chicago; and the light that they will throw on that period for students will be, in a sense, unique. Suppose we were seeing, say, the fifth person present at some historical meeting; we could ourselves suggest corrections in his account, so that it was almost as if we were helping him to revise his memoirs before they appeared in print. To take an outstanding example, Professor Milyukov, one of the most central figures in that period, gave us no less than ten "sittings" to cover his whole career. Our friends were mostly among the liberals, who at that time held the center of the stage; but we had intimate friends in all parties and kept ourselves rigorously out of all of them.

We took far more interest in the Russian people than in Russian politics; and in the vacations of the Duma we traveled systematically over great areas of the country, always with a prepared program and never leaving a place until we had done all that we wanted to do in it. Samuel was at all times a delightful comrade, with the zest and spirit of a great boy. The Russians loved him—perhaps most of all the children—for he carried the pleasure of living with him wherever we went; and the whole of our work was like an enthralling adventure. But he was also more practical than I, particularly in the tracing and capturing of out-of-the-way materials of political history, which we hunted up over the country.

For a time we worked together in the University of Liverpool, but his own university claimed him as professor of Russian language and institutions. He limited himself to those subjects in which he was a first-class scholar, but he certainly carried out in full the assignment he had received from his father—to become the first authority in the United States on things Russian. As such, he was recognized by the State Department, which frequently sought his opinion and at one time absorbed him in its work. Without question, this book, which owes so much to the care and devotion of his brother, is the first source in America for the history of the years which it covers.

Harper rendered a great service to many others besides Americans when, in spite of obstacles, he returned to the new Russia after the break caused by the Revolution. He was the first expert of his standing to do so, and personally I consider that his study of the Soviet period is even more valuable than the work which we did together earlier. I gained enormously from his short crisp letters, which always told me far more than they expressed in words. In 1939 I witnessed in London a part of his last great journey of study; this time I was a spectator and rejoiced in his mastery and success. It was on his advice that I came to America, in December, 1942. I had three more concise letters, giving me all the advice I asked for. I was on my way to Chicago for a duet with my old partner on the University of Chicago Round Table when the end came, so suddenly.

Each of his students whom I saw afterward knew exactly at what he was aiming. For three wonderful days I sat with his brother in the old home, where one of the best of these students, Ronald Thompson, brought to us Samuel's full personal record of all his studies in type—the draft of his memoirs, together with some brief memoranda which he had prepared on questions that must come up at the peace settlement. Was ever a task more fully discharged?

BERNARD PARES

UNIVERSITY OF TORONTO
January 17, 1945

viii

PREFACE

THE UNFINISHED MEMOIRS OF MY BROTHER, SAMUEL NORTHRUP HARPER, which are the basis of this book, were found upon his death among his Russian documents—a collection of notes, letters, and papers accumulated during a period of more than forty years of Russian travel and study. In the dark years of 1940 and 1941, when everyone was scowling at the mention of the word Russia, I knew that my brother was finding great solace in preparing his memoirs, even though he never showed them to anyone.

As I read the manuscript, I was impressed by its clear, frank disclosure of my brother's character and of the unusually vital life he had made out of his academic career, as well as by its informal and personal approach to the heroic struggles of Russia over these forty-odd years. As it stood, the material was not ready for publication. Had the memoirs been designed for the academic world, as were most of my brother's publications, I should not have dared to attempt their further editing. But he obviously meant the book to be as much about himself in relation to Russia as about Russia itself. It can also be said to be about us all, for my brother's observations on public opinion with respect to Russia throughout these years are sensitive and often penetrating.

Through the very able efforts of Ronald Thompson, a graduate student who came to the University of Chicago to study under my brother in the field of Russia, my brother's Russian papers were sorted out and put in chronological order. In the course of a year of meticulous and scholarly work Mr. Thompson brought into usable shape the full collection of travel notes, records of interviews with leaders of thought, original studies, and reports, lectures, and memoranda covering many phases of Russia and the Russians. There were also my brother's copies of translations of records, newspaper articles, and reports documenting the early revolutionary Bolshevik days during the period of 1918–21—a period still not well known—which were prepared by him while he was attached to the State Department during these years. To me the most interesting collection was the very complete file of his correspondence, including his letters to the family written while he was on his travels, as well as his lively exchanges, largely concerning Russia, with an unusually wide and varied group.

With this wealth of material available I undertook in some trepidation to edit the memoirs for their present publication. I make no pretense of having reviewed all the material at hand. That is a long task for trained students and scholars, and for their benefit this collection will be lodged with the Library of the University of Chicago. In my editing I have followed certain principles. The dating of Russian documents and events has been adjusted to our own calendar. I have deliberately retained many colloquialisms which my brother used in the preliminary development of his memoirs, because they harmonize with the informality of his family letters and reflect his characteristic conversational tone. Contemporary letters and notes have been used to some extent, principally in the earlier years, to replace or to supplement observations and descriptions of facts and situations appearing in the original memoir manuscript; but care has been taken to preserve my brother's conclusions as expressed at the time of writing of the manuscript. Use has been made of his other writings, his written lectures and notes, and his correspondence, to clarify and amplify parts of his manuscript. In substantially all cases my brother's own words and expressions, taken from this outside material, have been followed, although introductory phrases and transitions have been used which, I wish frankly to state, have been placed on the lips of my brother for the sake of readability. Subject to this, and to general literary editing of the memoirs and other writings, the memoirs as published in this book are the words of my brother; and his original basic organization of the material has been carefully followed. The material in Part IX, covering the years 1937–41, was fragmentary and unorganized; and this portion necessarily is given special treatment. What is presented represents a brief summary of certain more important matters of this period, being a compilation of the related material found, in the main, in parts of the memoirs, in a series of memoranda on Soviet foreign policy, a special report on my brother's 1939 survey of Europe, and other notes of the period. For this compilation particularly, I am indebted to the able and careful work of Mr. Thompson. I am also indebted to Sarah M. Harris for assistance in preparing the present manuscript for the press.

My treatment in editing these memoirs may not be the treatment which my brother would have given to them if he had lived to review his work. All developments since the days of Stalingrad, when my brother died, have necessarily been ignored, and the work is to that extent "dated." This is the best I have been able to do. If I have violated any academic principles in editing this material or have made other mistakes, this must be charged against me. Even with this possibility in mind, I believe the completing of the book is worth the risk.

I wish to express my special appreciation for help and encouragement in preparing this book to my brother's colleagues, Sir Bernard Pares and Professor Louis Gottschalk, and to the staff of the University of Chicago Press. To Mrs. Horace Martin and to my brother's Washington friends, Loy Henderson, W. Chapin Huntington, Victor Clark, and Mortimer Graves, to all of whom I have been somewhat of a burden, I express my thanks for their interest and help. To many other friends mentioned personally by my brother in portions of the original manuscript which could not be included in this book, I express my regrets.

I have been moved in all this by sentiment for the memory of my brother, a man of character who carried through successfully an unusual career. I hope that this book may lead other young men in the future toward the serious study of foreign lands and peoples. I am influenced as well by the thought that an informal glimpse of Russia during the last forty years, through the eyes of an American, a trained and very human student, struggling to understand, will serve a public purpose in these days of general lack of knowledge and understanding of the U.S.S.R.

PAUL V. HARPER

CHICAGO, ILLINOIS
January 17, 1945

xi

TABLE OF CONTENTS

PART VII. SOVIET RUSSIA EMERGING: 1926–36

PART VIII. THE PRESS

PART IX. THE NEXT FIVE YEARS
1937—JUNE 22, 1941

PART I

THE BEGINNINGS

CHAPTER I

LIFE WITH MY FATHER

IN MY EARLY YEARS IT WAS INTERESTING BUT OFTEN DIFFICULT TO BE the son of a man who has been called "a dynamo in trousers." My father was president of the recently established University of Chicago; and his continual planning for some new activity in the field of education reached to the family, his cousins and brothers, of whom the house was always full, as well as to us children. Not physically strong as a child, and handicapped by weak eyes, I felt—often with anxiety—the constant pressure, from which it was difficult to escape. But this pressure was part of our training, which was always on my father's mind; and our direct association with one or another of the activities often centered in the home was a deliberate policy.

We had to come to meals on time, even breakfast, for these were the hours that father would be at home. Frequently there were house guests, visiting professors from abroad, spending the whole summer with us. We were to be allowed to benefit from close association and friendship with such men as George Adam Smith, of Edinburgh, and Gaston Bonnet-Maury, of Paris. These foreign guests were of particular interest to me and probably influenced my selection of a foreign field of study, though there was one definite drawback to their entertainment. I had to shine the shoes they always left, according to European custom, outside their door at night, unless I wanted to see my mother get up half an hour earlier to do it. American maids refused to perform this service, and our French butler was Americanized by the time he came to us.

We children were regularly encouraged to undertake small enterprises. One of my brothers was helped to organize a renting library, my father purposely drawing up the contract in a careless way which would get the boy into trouble. He was to learn by experience to make more careful contracts. I was persuaded to sign a contract under which I was responsible for making father take an hour of exercise, usually a bicycle ride, before breakfast. I could not use force to get him up and

1

dressed and started. He could try to persuade me to let him have another hour of sleep; failure on my part to get him up entailed a monetary penalty deducted from the weekly honorarium agreed upon in the contract. The second week I lost money, and the lesson was learned of the need of care in signing any agreement involving finances.

As a youngster at Chautauqua, I sold the *Assembly Herald*, thus earning my first money. In New Haven, at a large Baptist convention, I acted as page boy at the age of eight, sitting on the edge of the platform near the speaker, to carry notes or messages as directed. Under the influence of these practices within the family, one brother started a shoe-shining project at his high school. It was the publicity to which this activity led that brought a kindly paternal reprimand; for always we were enjoined to behave ourselves so as not to embarrass father in his work. Yet once when I raised the question of whether some activity which did not appeal to me would be "dignified" in the son of a president of a university, I received one of the few real scoldings which my father ever gave me. With much vigor he declared that he never wanted to hear that word from me again, either as an alibi or in such a distinctly snobbish sense.

As we grew older, the lessons in getting along in the world involved more responsibility. Our house was practically a hotel. Father made my sister and me help in handling the problem of meals. There was a fixed budget for the table, with ample provision for guests. Father insisted that, as good housekeepers, we should not be disturbed by the last-minute addition of three or four guests at a lunch or dinner; and he would often bring home from his office the people with whom he had been conferring when the lunch or dinner hour arrived. This constant flow of guests at meals or living in the house was arranged to save my father's time, and also it gave him recreation and us children the opportunity of meeting and listening to all sorts of people.

At times we were asked to provide adequate refreshments for a gathering of some importance. After the occasion there would be a post-mortem and an evaluation of the capacity we had shown under responsibility, resulting in the suggestion to us of certain rules. My father evolved quite a number of slogans for his own work as well as for our training. One such slogan has stuck with me throughout my life: "Don't let your machinery rattle." He first applied it to me, after I had handled the arrangements for a particular party well but with so much tenseness on my part that I caused nervousness in others. Often at dinner my father would tell of his day's work in order to illustrate the application of the rules he suggested. This rule about the rattling of machinery he made graphic by a detailed picture of a senate meeting at the university, where the faculty had been led to make a certain decision without suspecting that it was a decision over which my father had worked and worried for many weeks.

Of his rules, there were two that appeared, on the surface, to be poor guides for life. The first was never to do anything you could get someone else to do, because, he insisted, the other person could probably do it better than you could, and your task was to find this other person and give him the opportunity. The second rule, which at first glance suggests the opposite of my father's practice, was never to do today what could be postponed until tomorrow. He interpreted this in the sense that a decision made prematurely and on a snap judgment would fail to take into consideration all the factors, particularly eleventh-hour developments. With this interpretation we were told that the rule did not imply sheer procrastination.

Despite, perhaps rather than because of, the high pressure under which the household lived, a phrase that constantly came out as father worked, or talked, or played and joked with us, was: "Cultivate repose." Just as he constantly took short naps, sitting in his chair, even at formal conferences, so he would often make us sit down, fold our hands, and keep silent for a short time. I believe this practice was developed from the one he saw in Russia, where, always before leaving the house to catch a train or start on any serious journey, all sit in silence for a few minutes.

My father suggested, rather than ordered, that we children could help him in his work if we did not get too chummy with the children of any faculty family. He himself made no particular members of the university his most intimate friends. His "playmates" he selected outside the faculty in the downtown group—for various reasons, one of which was the avoidance of any suggestion that this or that person was in special favor, a kind of pet of the president's. And he constantly took what steps he dared to discourage the forming of cliques within the group of scholars which he had brought together from all sorts of institutions to this completely new environment without traditions. Friendships and loyalty to friendships were not to be eliminated from personal life, but the interests of the larger group were to be constantly recognized and fostered. For example, when a faculty club was formed, he insisted that all members of the faculty were to be eligible, although some pressure to this end had to be put on the initiators of the organization, who were inclined to look on themselves as the chosen social leaders because of their former relation to famous eastern schools.

Because the university was a new enterprise in the community, we were told that as a family we had to be particularly cautious. We were never to put ourselves under special obligations to anybody, lest that person try to utilize the relationship to the detriment of the work of the university. More serious consequences of real indiscretion were explained to us, with specific instances—the names I still recall—of persons who, through their children's behavior, had been "caught in the toils" of a blackmailer. Several times I was asked to sit in the corner of the library as a polite witness and read while my father received a stranger who had been alarmingly insistent on an interview.

My father could and did get angry with us children, as well as with others, for trying to "work a racket" because of our special position or for any dishonesty in thought or action. He could be unforgiving when somebody had played him false or had even tried to use him in a way that caused him embarrassment. There were several names of persons with whom he had been closely associated which he purposely avoided mentioning; but if the names came up, there was no hesitancy, within the family group, in characterizing these persons as he believed they deserved. Gossip was taboo in his presence, however, and most of the scoldings he gave us were precisely on this score. When personalities were discussed, another of the precepts laid down for us was to work with the good in a person and not to exaggerate the bad, which each of us has. If he talked openly to the family, it was perhaps to let off steam in a safe place. But, as I look back on it, I believe the main purpose of his confidential accounts of his troubles with this or that co-worker was to train us to analyze people's motives, to look below the surface manner to the actual performance, and to learn to judge people. In my mother, because of her quiet but perceptive way of observing a situation or an individual, he sought and found his greatest aid in evaluating people.

In spite of these various considerations, however, all of us children had many friends of our own ages. They were always welcome in the house and at meals, no matter what guests were present. Often these friends were slightly subdued at being mixed up, as we were, with the older people. Some of them, on coming for the first time, were overawed by father himself, but not after they met him. He took great pains to talk to them about themselves and their plans and their ideas about the university. Apparently, it never occurred to father that any of us preferred the company of these youngsters to that of his contemporaries. I felt this particularly on the occasion of my twentieth birthday. As the date approached, I was reminded that I had a twin: one of my father's publications, the *Biblical World*, started on the Easter Sunday on which I was born. So on April 9, 1902, a birthday luncheon was arranged. To note my special interest, already beginning to develop, the luncheon was to be of Russian style—without the vodka. But the guests were the friends of my twin—theologians, professors, clergymen, and divinity students. The only fun I got out of it was to show them how to handle the several dozen kinds of hors d'œuvres—Russian *zakuska*—which I had helped prepare.

In his last years my father often took me on his trips east, to the yearly budget sessions at 26 Broadway, Mr. Rockefeller's office, to conventions or congresses, or to a particular lecture. I acted as secretary and valet for him, sometimes for several co-travelers as well, and in this way grew to know Butler of Columbia, Faunce of Brown, Butterick of the General Education Board, and others—friendships which later stood me in good stead. My father's companions on pleasure trips were usually outside the academic group. Charles R. Crane, A. C. Bartlett, and H. H. Kohlsaat, of Chicago, were among his most intimate friends. Traveling around with such men gave me an intimate insight into the methods of various fields of activity. Some of my first notions of economics and politics were acquired at dinner with these men, where again I served as major-domo but was allowed to listen to, and to participate in, their discussion.

My father enjoyed such evenings of talk around a table where a fine dinner with proper wine was being served. He was familiar with all the best restaurants in Chicago and New York and was well known for his good taste in food. Every Christmas he received large boxes of delicacies from such purveyors as De Jonhge and Jevnes in Chicago. Many times he was called upon by some of the city's great hostesses to plan a special dinner for them. My mother's table, to her dying day, was outstanding.

In these travels, or on the walks which he finally consented to take after the doctors had fixed a definite limit to the time on which he could count, my father shared with me some of the thoughts about his work, which he was co-ordinating in those last months. He had told us earlier that he would probably kill himself by the pace he set, but that his work, the building of a new university, had to be done rapidly in order to be well done. Dawdling along was contrary to his temperament and, he believed, inimical to the success of any job. He confessed to me one day that much of what he had done he had accomplished on sheer bluff. He immediately qualified the general statement by saying that in his work as a student and teacher there had never been any bluffing. "In scholarship a bluff won't work," he said. This was a subtle warning to me, for we were discussing my graduate studies, of which I had just completed the second year in Paris.

What I have sought to bring out here is the rather unusual training which it was my good fortune to have in my early years. I learned to meet and to enjoy meeting all sorts of people. I learned much about human nature and how to appraise people and situations. I saw new traditions being deliberately worked out in a new institution and was thus enabled to appreciate a similar process, the advent of Bolshevism in Russia, that took place in the country I later selected to study.

CHAPTER II

WHY DID I STUDY RUSSIA?

THE INFLUENCES WHICH CONTRIBUTED TO MY DECISION TO SELECT Russia as an area of study began to operate as early as 1900, when I was eighteen years old. In that year Mr. Charles R. Crane persuaded my father to accompany him on one of his periodic trips to Russia. The son of the founder of the Crane Company of Chicago, Mr. Crane was not much interested in business except in its broadest implications. He became a traveler and student in foreign countries almost immediately after he had completed his formal education, and he seemed to concentrate on those countries about which there was little informed opinion in America. The three peoples he visited most frequently were the Chinese, the Arabs, and the Slavs, and, among the latter, particularly the Russians. I do not know in which group his interest first developed; he shifted later from one to the other. It seemed to me that he always came back to the Russians, despite the fact that developments in Russia often tended to go counter to those aspects of life in which he was most interested.

During his lifetime Mr. Crane made twenty-three trips to Russia. The first, I believe, was early in the 1890's. He was one of the first foreigners to penetrate Soviet Russia in 1922. His last trip was made in 1937. Apparently casual in his manner of drifting from place to place and person to person, Mr. Crane actually had a particular design in his travels: to note the most important manifestations of life in any given community. While he probably deserved the criticism that he was careless in respect to statistics, his remarkable ability to "feel" a political situation became known and useful to many.

My father's long letters from Russia told how in the daytime Mr. Crane's party, including the Martin Ryersons and Charles L. Hutchinsons—all close Chicago friends—did the usual round of museums, churches, and other places of interest in regular tourist style. Then, after the Ryersons and Hutchinsons had been put to bed, father and Mr. Crane made the rounds of Crane's many Russian friends, dropping in informally, often in the middle of the night, now in one home and now in another. They talked with the outstanding creator of church murals, visited the workshop where the best Russian lacquer work was produced, and spent much time listening to the training of the Cathedral Choir. They attended the famous opera and ballet under the personal guidance of the director, Prince Volkonsky, whom they later brought to the University of Chicago to lecture on Russian literature.

Although most of these visits were informal, some had to be formal. The travelers were received in audience by Emperor Nicholas II, who impressed my father as a very gracious and kindly person, deeply interested in the things cultural to which the conversation was directed. Their visit to Tolstoy was less satisfactory, because the great writer, for some reason, showed an interest in how an endowed institution could be run, and later expressed disappointment that an American educator had talked so much about raising money.

Some of the best-known Russian professors of history and the social sciences were intimate friends of Mr. Crane's. Among those whom my father met were Thomas Masaryk, of Prague, whose field of study was Russian religious philosophic thought; Maxim Kovalevsky, founder of the modern school of Russian sociologists; and Paul Milyukov, professor of Russian history at the University of Moscow. The two Russians became important political figures during the revolution of 1905. and already in 1900 they were having difficulty continuing their academic work under tsarist censorship. All three of these authorities on Russian history and thought later lectured at the University of Chicago, under a special fund for Russian studies which Mr. Crane established. These lectures represented the beginning of work at the university in the Russian field.

My father returned from this trip with a tremendous enthusiasm for all things Russian, and I believe that the many stories he told me about Russian life were the ultimate source of my own interest in that country. Perhaps even more important in shaping my immediate program was an incident which occurred as the Crane party passed through Paris on the way to St. Petersburg. One of Mr. Crane's friends very frankly expressed surprise that my father, a student and teacher of many ancient languages, had only English at his command for conversation— "The president of a university, and you cannot speak French!" This remark so chagrined my father that he determined I should learn French at once; and he cabled me to leave by the first boat for Paris, where he had got me a job as one of the American Guards at the Paris Exposition. After the day's work I was to study French in a French home, to which I would return in time for dinner—a strange apartment on the second floor of an inside cobblestoned courtyard, at No. 5 Rue de l'Odéon. My room was over a mule's stable. My father arranged for these lessons to be supervised by Gaston Bonnet-Maury, professor of church history at the Sorbonne, who had once been a visiting professor at Chicago. Needless to say, I accepted this command with alacrity. During the six months that I served at the Exposition I did little toward compensating for my father's lack of facility in French; but I did learn to get about easily in a foreign country and to live, after a fashion, on my own earnings.

Sixty young men constituted the American Guards at the Paris Exposition. We were in uniform, attached to the main American sections of the Exposition. About half of us were college students; and the others, somewhat older, were political appointees, two of them prize fighters. When a reunion of the group was attempted in 1910, several could not attend because they were in penitentiaries, while two sent regrets from the Far East, where they were engaged in missionary work. My post, with one of the future missionaries at the American pavilion, was one of the most strenuous but also the most interesting. The only unpleasant feature of the job was the need to explain constantly to French mothers that they could not nurse their babies in the comfortable lounge rooms of the pavilion.

The work at the Exposition and the association with this rather closely knit corps of Guards were useful training. I learned to "work the rackets," to use a modern expression for practices even then fully developed in the competitive system of our democratic capitalism. For example, the manager of the American restaurant in the basement of the pavilion was not, at first, fully co-operative when it was suggested to him that the Guards on the main floor should have luncheons for a nominal price of forty-five cents. When he overheard us recommending the other American restaurant, however, he became agreeable. The concessionaire for the soda-water fountain in the basement was easily persuaded that we should be allowed free drinks. By similar tactics we were able to provide ourselves with a supply of playing cards and other small articles of American style. For the sideshows our technique was very simple. A group of six or more of us in uniform, staying over for an evening of fun, would walk up to the gate of a sideshow on the assumption that we would, of course, be admitted free, and stand there, stubbornly refusing to understand French and blocking other admissions, until we were passed.

When the Crane party returned to Paris from Moscow, I was given detailed accounts of the trip every evening for a full week. Some of these evenings were spent at the homes of Russians living in Paris, whom I frequently visited during the following year. Because it was clear that I had not learned French thoroughly, my father decided that the whole family should spend the winter in Paris. The others arrived while I was still serving as Guard and, by an odd coincidence, stopped in a pension on the Avenue d'Iéna, overlooking the courtyard of the Guards' barracks. From their window, shortly after their arrival on the early morning boat train from Cherbourg, they discovered me changing into uniform.

With the closing of the Exposition, we rented an apartment, near the Luxembourg, from the opera singer Geraldine Farrar. My brother and I entered the Ecole alsacienne, where I qualified for the Senior class. During part of the year I lived in the home of one of the teachers of the school while I prepared for the regular examinations, which were to give me the Bachelor's degree from the Sorbonne.

Returning home in the summer of 1901, I found my father still full of the impressions and ideas he had got during his Russian trip. Of the famous restaurants of which he often spoke when discussing the "art of eating," Testov's, in Moscow, was now put at the head of the list. He brought Masaryk to Chicago to lecture during the following academic year, and he prevailed upon a young Russian who was completing his work at the university to offer a course in the Russian language. The latter was a famous two-mile runner with a charming personality and the extraordinary name, always given in full, of Xenophon de Blumenthal Kalamatiano. Despite the fact that he was himself a student, Kalamatiano attracted about five of us to take his announced course in the spring of 1902, the last quarter of my Senior year; and for three months we struggled with this most difficult of modern Western languages. All Russians are proverbially bad teachers of Russian, and I am afraid that Kalamatiano was no exception—at least, I did not learn very much about the language. But my interest in Russia, first aroused by my father and Mr. Crane, and continually encouraged by them, was further stimulated by this course.

After completing my undergraduate work that spring, I began to think seriously of selecting Russian history and culture as a field for advanced study. What course that study might take, I could then hardly foresee. At that time little attention was being given in American universities to the analysis of events, historical or contemporary, east of the line of Vienna. Archibald Coolidge and Leo Wiener, at Harvard, were perhaps the only recognized workers in the field. The only book on Russia written by an American that had secured wide currency by that date was George Kennan's *The Siberian Exile System*, which, of course, gave full details of this worst feature of tsarism but also introduced to American readers the leaders of Russian liberalism and revolutionary thought whom Kennan was allowed to interview on his journeys through Siberia. The American press saw in Russia mainly a source for bloody and hair-raising stories; and American judges, in their decisions, would sometimes refer to "tsarist absolutism" as they defined American institutions by contrast. Russian music and Russian literature, in translation, were just beginning to attain a certain reach and appeal in this country. There seemed to be, therefore, a promising open field.

Mr. Crane took every occasion to discuss Russia with me and invited me many times to sit in on conversations or conferences he was having with others on this subject. He frankly urged me toward the Russian program. If I decided in favor of Russia, the immediate step was clearly laid out before me: to break the back of the problem of learning the difficult language. This meant attending the School of Oriental Languages in Paris, which included a Russian course, not because Russian was considered one of the Oriental languages, but because it resembled these in the difficulty of acquisition. The head of the Russian work at this school was Professor Paul Boyer, already recognized at that time as one of the outstanding teachers of Russian. Both the British and French foreign offices and various European war departments depended on him to train men wishing to specialize in the Russian field. I had already been introduced to him by Mr. Crane in 1900.

The novel character of Russian studies was perhaps one of the factors that attracted me, for at that time Russia was generally considered the land of bombs, Cossack knouts, pogroms, and other terrors. Kipling's characterization of the Russian as "the bear that walked like a man" had taken deep root in American thought.

I finally made the decision in favor of Russia and set off in October, 1902, to begin my studies at the School of Oriental Languages. I found that my friends tended to see in my action an element of the heroic.

PART II

*BREAKING THE BACK OF THE RUSSIAN
LANGUAGE: 1902–5*

CHAPTER III

L'ECOLE DES LANGUES ORIENTALES; PARIS

THE OPENING OF MY CAREER AS A STUDENT OF RUSSIA WAS RECORDED
in my diary: "Finally got off on 11:30 Michigan Central, traveling on
a cut-rate ticket under name of F. C. Hatch. Mother and Miss Wallace
came to train. Had 230 pounds of luggage. Went right to bed." From
New York I sailed second-class on the "Vaderland," and spent most of
the voyage being chased off the first-class deck. My only objection to
second-class cabins was the limited deck space provided with them, so
that I was unable to walk off my meals and hesitated to eat as much as
I wanted to.

In Paris I registered as a regular student at the School of Oriental
Languages and set up a small apartment with Charles Burroughs. Burroughs had, in fact, preceded me by a few weeks and had our place all
ready for my arrival. He held a traveling fellowship from the University of Chicago and was specializing in French history. One of the many
Iowa boys who came to Chicago, he had been an outstanding student,
the hundred-yard champion in the Western Conference, and the president of my fraternity. I felt indeed fortunate to have found such a partner for my first formal graduate studies. No sooner had I begun my
work at the school, however, than poor Burroughs fell ill, having caught
typhoid fever from eating French oysters. Despite the best of care,
he died after a month. The whole experience saddened and confused
my early weeks in Paris.

George Norlin, who had taught me Greek, persuaded me to move to
his pension. He, too, was in Paris as a traveling fellow, and I had several other friends there from Chicago who were studying architecture.
I was invited to use the table set apart for this last group at the Café
Panthéon, the bright spot of the Latin Quarter for those students of all

nationalities (including the French) whose allowances were generous enough to permit the use of it.

The students of the School of Oriental Languages were sent to the Sorbonne, the Ecole des Sciences politiques, and the Ecole des hautes Etudes for courses in history and political science as well as in literature and philology. I worked under such men as Louis Paul Leger, Alfred Meillet, and Émile Haumant. My classmates were for the most part French, with a small sprinkling of foreigners. Gradually the latter dropped out, and I remained the only foreigner in my particular class. Some of the French students were preparing for the diplomatic service; some for business or journalism; and others, like myself, for academic work. My fellow-student, André Mazon, has since succeeded to Meillet's chair in Slavic philology. Fortunately, I had sufficient knowledge of French to keep from being a burden to the others. I was not even much handicapped in having to learn Russian through another foreign language.

The school had for each of its language sections, supplementing the French professor in charge, one or more so-called *repetiteurs indigènes*, or "native rehearsers." For Russian, this post was held by Nicholas Gay, the son of the famous Russian painter and a close friend of Tolstoy. Young Gay was, in fact, an adopted son of Tolstoy's and had spent much of his life on the Tolstoy estate. This was during Tolstoy's period of "going to the people," not only for outlook, but, as he himself said, for direct style and expression of ideas which he found in the peasant as opposed to the intellectual. We students often remarked that Gay had adapted himself well to Tolstoy's special bias of the moment, for in manners, as well as in appearance, he was very much of a peasant. His long beard, his loping walk, and also his somewhat casual methods of work I later came to recognize as distinct Muzhik traits. Professor Boyer, who was writing a manual for students of Russian based on selections from a primer which Tolstoy had arranged and used in teaching peasant children, had brought Gay to Paris especially to help him with this work.

Early in March, Boyer proposed that I prepare an English edition of this manual, which presented the method of teaching for which he had become well known. As this method was very similar to the "inductive method" for the study of languages which my father had introduced for Hebrew and for Latin and Greek and which I had used, I had some background for the task. The translation of the French text involved the most exacting study of Russian grammar and structure, under the direct and very personal guidance of my teacher; and I recognized it at once as an invaluable opportunity. I was also helped in this work by Ellis Minns, a former pupil of Boyer's, then on the staff of Pembroke College, Cambridge. In the summer of 1903 I spent two months at Cambridge, living "in quarters," practically as a member of Pembroke

12

College, by courtesy of Minns. Without his assistance I could hardly have handled the English edition of Boyer's work at that early stage in my knowledge of Russian.

During this first year I was often discouraged at what seemed to me the insurmountable difficulties of the Russian language, and frequently dismayed at my reactions to the Russians I met in Paris. Compared to my gay American friends and my courteous and hospitable French professors, they seemed, indeed, an uninteresting lot; and there were times when I almost dreaded going to their country. Then I would throw myself into the student life of Paris with the greatest abandon in the world; make expeditions to St. Denis, Versailles, Fontainebleau; join in champagne suppers and visit the opera, the theaters, the Moulin-Rouge. At such periods I became an indefatigable caller, drank tea with my French acquaintances, and accepted all their dinner invitations. Or I would drop in three or four times a day to see my American friends and play ping-pong or penny-ante poker with them. Most of all I enjoyed the Bal Bullier, where American dancing was much in vogue and where I went whenever I could find an American partner. French or Russian girls seemed to me singularly inept at this particular pastime.

I remember well my first experience at the Bal Bullier. It was Mardi gras, and my friend Norlin was to leave Paris the next day. In the afternoon we had a farewell tea in my room and drove up to see the crowds on the boulevards. He was to dine with two girls from Philadelphia. I was quietly reading in the evening when a *petit bleue* from Norlin told me to be at Bullier at ten-thirty, where a *bal masque* was in progress. We joined in and danced. I did not know I enjoyed dancing so much. My first good American whirl since I had left home! Other Americans there followed our example. We went in for a good time; and the girls were very good—that is, they adapted themselves to the rough and tumble of it. When the cakewalk came, we made the hit of the evening, and the crowd cried out: "Donnez place aux américains!" We left at an early hour and marched down Boule Miche, singing and shouting and joining always in the fun. A crowd of Americans who had been celebrating even more completely than ourselves insisted on accompanying us, and we sang "Ain't It a Shame" until our voices were gone.

The absolute independence of my life in Paris, after the strict regimen at home, was perhaps a little demoralizing; and it took some time for me to achieve a fully balanced program. Soon enough, however, after such a spree as this, I would be filled with a sense of time's urgency and would become once more the recluse, attacking the Russian verb with renewed determination and limiting my recreation to weekly visits to the Concert Rouge. Music diverted without distracting me, and the programs there were excellent.

I had thought of going to Russia in the summer of 1903; but my father persuaded me to postpone this initial visit until the following winter, when I might be expected to have a better command of the Russian language, meanwhile to accompany him on a sort of Cook's tour of Germany. He and my mother were traveling with our Chicago friends, the Bartletts; and I served as escort for young Miss Bartlett and her chum. We visited Wiesbaden, Frankfurt, Nürnberg, Carlsbad, and Munich and came back to France by way of Switzerland. At Carlsbad, an almost ideal watering place, we spent three weeks. Here were miles and miles of walks through wild forests, always within a few minutes' reach of big restaurants, fine concerts and theater. Here, too, were all the "swells" of Europe, solemnly taking the Carlsbad treatment in preparation for next winter's dissipation. Undoubtedly, this tour was the sort of vacation that my father needed; and he enjoyed it fully, going every night to the theater or opera and dining elaborately afterward. But after my year of freedom, I found it peculiarly irksome to dress for dinner so regularly; and I was restless and eager to get back to work—so much so, indeed, that my father took occasion to lecture me severely on my "boorishness."

In November, 1903, I returned to Paris for my second year at the School of Oriental Languages; and in an effort to get more practice in the use of everyday Russian, I settled in the home of a Russian family where there were some twenty Russian boarders. The house was in a dirty street back of the Panthéon; and my room was small, cold, dreary, and next to the sitting-room, where a girl was eternally playing scales. When it was not the piano, it was the Russians jabbering; but I was determined to make whatever sacrifices might be required to learn the language before leaving for Russia in February. The Russians in this house constituted a radical group with frank revolutionary plans, voluntary exiles who had found it impossible to carry on with any safety under the increasingly repressive measures of that personification of the tsarist police—Plehve. They had set up here, for purposes of economy, an eating commune; and I joined the group for meals.

In addition to practice in conversation, I gained some acquaintance with the thinking and methods of these Russian revolutionists. One day there was a meeting in memory of one of the exiles of prominence, who presumably had died. I allowed myself to remark on the great loss the cause had suffered, but was told not to be too concerned, because the comrade had not really died but had returned to Russia for underground work. The memorial meeting was held to deceive the local agents of the Russian police, who were known to be operating in Paris.

Many evenings were spent addressing envelopes in which small pamphlets of revolutionary content were sent to individuals in Russia. These pamphlets were printed on rice paper and folded like personal letters, for letters got through the strict censorship more easily than did printed matter.

After two months of this relationship I somewhat alienated the group by trying to explain the Jim Crow laws and practices in our southern states. I tried to get out of the jam in which my effort to put the facts had got me by suggesting that perhaps my inadequate control of the Russian language had led to the misunderstanding, but from then on the revolutionaries regarded me with considerable skepticism. As conversation was anything but comfortable under these circumstances and as my American friends had frequently protested at the unhygienic conditions in which I lived there, I finally decided to spend January in an ordinary pension and to build up my health for my Russian trip. The pension had a lovely address: "Impasse de la Visitation."

As the time for my departure approached, I was filled with great excitement. I engaged a tutor, a poor Russian student, as entertaining as he was intelligent, who considerably brightened my whole outlook on the possibilities of my field of study. We frequently lunched together, speaking only Russian on such occasions; and I learned from him many things about the new life which I was soon to experience. I was still far from proficient in the language, but I felt confident that in Russia I would improve rapidly. In preparation for the trip I collected an impressive number of letters of introduction from Boyer, Crane, and others and a vast amount of advice —particularly, as I remember, about drinking. It was the universal opinion among my friends that in Russia one must drink to excess or else not touch a drop; and to manage the latter course gracefully, I was advised to wink slyly and say that I had been overindulgent and that my doctor had insisted that I let up a little!

The newspapers were full of rumors of war between Russia and Japan; but nevertheless I set off for Moscow on February 4, 1904, arriving there on the very day of the Japanese assault on Port Arthur, which opened one of the first "undeclared wars" of our period. Stopping at Moscow's Grand Hotel, opposite and overlooking the Kremlin, I found myself in the midst of excitement, although popular demonstrations—one way or the other—were very limited, carefully organized, and strictly policed.

I had arrived in this second capital of the Russian Empire without knowing a single soul. Professor Boyer had lists of Russian families available for his students; and I soon established myself in the home of one of these, a Professor Melgunov of the University of Moscow. It was not a very good choice, for the habits of the members of this family were irregular and they took their assumed obligations toward me in a most casual manner. However, my room was warm in those winter days when the temperature frequently dropped to thirty below. I supplemented the language work which I received from the family by instruction from private tutors, students at the Moscow University, of whom the overwhelming majority lived by giving lessons. With these tutors I talked Russian four hours a day and read another four.

15

Through my letters of introduction I was able to make acquaintances and gradually to build up a series of friendships. At first it seemed to me that I could hardly have chosen a less opportune moment to appear in Moscow. Everything was confused because of the war, and America was thought to be in league with England in encouraging the Japanese attack. I expected to be less heartily received on this account and felt somewhat embarrassed when all conversations turned inevitably to the war. Nevertheless, I set out purposefully each day—conventionally got up in frock coat, small nine-dollar astrakhan hat, and enormous snow boots—to present at least one of my letters or to pay a call. Even with the boots, I had difficulty in making my way through the heavy black slush that covered the city; and I frequently resorted to the little sleighs or cab-sleds that could be hired, after the customary dickering with the driver, for as little as fifteen cents a ride.

Actually, however, I met a great many people and was welcomed everywhere with the traditional Russian hospitality. The fact that I was an American seemed to create interest rather than distrust. I was questioned eagerly about America's real attitude toward the war and about conditions in my country, and everyone seemed gratified to have a real flesh-and-blood American at hand, to contrast with the unfriendly specters raised by our belligerent press. Even so, it was a great comfort to me when Secretary Hay finally and publicly upbraided American newspapermen for their biased treatment of Russia.

Professor Maxim Kovalevsky, whom I had met in Paris, had given me letters to the Ozerovs. Professor Ozerov was an economist, and his wife was an active social worker in Moscow. Their large apartment was a gathering place for academic and literary people, and I spent many evenings at their long table, where tea was served from seven to twelve whenever guests dropped in. In those days nine o'clock was the fashionable hour for calls. These long evenings listening to Russian helped me with my still unfinished task of learning the language. Here I came to learn, too, of the rising movement of opposition to the government, in which university men later were to play such a prominent part.

The American consul at Moscow, Mr. Samuel Smith, was a distant cousin of Mr. Crane's and had lived in Russia practically all of his life. He and his wife and his brother, Thomas Smith, who knew my father, were particularly kind to me, explaining Russian social customs and political situations in great detail, introducing me to many useful people, and fortifying me against homesickness with American luncheons of clam chowder or baked beans.

I was much impressed with Russian hospitality and pleased at the prospect of repaying some of it at home the following summer, when several of my Russian friends planned to come to America for the St. Louis Exposition. In fact, I took great pains to warn my family that we should have Russians dropping in on us and that, when a Russian called, it meant an invitation to a meal. I was also full of ideas about converting our third floor into a Russian salon, planning to set up a samovar and initiate my Chicago friends into the mysteries of Russian living.

Another home at which I was received, through a letter from a brother living in Paris, was that of Shchukin, one of the richest merchants of Moscow. He and his brother had spent much of their wealth on modern European paintings. He owned one of the large "merchant palaces" and gave gorgeous parties. This palace is now the Museum of Western Art. To the Shchukin collection the Soviet government added the paintings expropriated from the bourgeoisie in 1917. The enlarged collection is probably one of the best in Europe today.

Like all students of language, I made extensive use of the theater, though at first I found this somewhat difficult to do in Moscow. Tickets for most performances were sold well in advance, and I always encountered long lines of valets waiting in the snow for hours before the box offices opened. The famous Moscow Art Theatre, however, being in part an educational project supported by several rich individuals, made special arrangements for students and had stalls reserved for us at a ridiculously low price. Thus I came to visit this theater often and to know some of its leading workers. Much of my previous study had been of the Russian classical plays, and these I was able to see and hear now for the first time. One of the first plays I saw in Moscow was *Julius Caesar* in Russian, very well translated and richly set up; and I remember being elated at how much of it I understood, particularly parts which I had once known by heart in English. I also visited the big vaudeville theater, Omon, said to be one of the most elaborate in the world, though of questionable character. Here, as was customary in Russian theaters, all-night suppers were served to the patrons after the performances.

By the middle of March my frock coat had begun to show signs of wear and I had almost got used to walking in my snow boots. The snows were melting, but the boots were more essential than ever, for the streets had become veritable swimming pools. The layers of refuse that had been deposited under successive snows during the winter all appeared on the surface now and gave off odors beyond description. An additional hazard was provided by the throngs of drunken Russians who seemed to be constantly churning an uncertain course through these quagmires. I had become accustomed to seeing many drunks on the streets, for during the bitter winter months the Russian workingman usually found it cheaper to buy vodka than wood, and warmed himself from within rather than from without. But the impressive increase in the spring surprised me. I soon discovered that it was the Russian manner of observing Lent: to abstain from solids but not from liquids.

The celebration of Easter was perhaps the most dramatic experience of this first trip to Russia. It began with the traditional church service at three o'clock on the morning before Easter, the entire congregation parading around the church with lighted candles in their hands. Then at twelve o'clock that night, every bell in Moscow was rung and Easter Sunday was triumphantly ushered in. At midnight I went to the Shchukins for the ceremonial dinner, when, after six weeks of the strictest fasting, the Greek Orthodox returns not only to meat but to butter and eggs and to the most famous dishes of the Russian cuisine. I inquired into the preparation of many of these dishes and determined to amaze my father with a true Russian dinner when I returned to Chicago.

Soon after Easter I prepared to return to Chicago, stopping in Paris for my examinations at the School of Oriental Languages. I was eager to talk to Boyer in Russian and to discover from him what progress I had made in the language, for I knew that my Russian friends in Moscow had become used to my accent and had probably learned to interpret even my rather inadequate *r*-sound generously. Then, too, I was eager to talk to almost anyone in French or English. It had been something of a strain to use Russian constantly, requiring the most careful attention from me at all times; and when I actually found myself dreaming in Russian, I began to look forward to the relaxation of a more familiar tongue. The many Russian books which I had bought, after what I considered rather expert haggling at the Sunday fairs, I shipped off to Chicago, planning to spend the summer at home browsing through them and to return to Moscow for the opening of the university in the fall. For this return trip I made all arrangements, and then departed for Paris, my bags bulging with little jars of caviar, which I earnestly hoped to smuggle into France. I was not sorry to be leaving Russia for six months, but I did hate to leave the fresh caviar.

Once back in Chicago, I began to realize that I had chosen to study a subject about which there was not only little knowledge in the United States but also a great deal of prejudice and emotionalism. American public opinion was definitely on the side of "little Japan" and against Russia in the war. In the prelude to the Russo-Japanese conflict, Russian diplomacy had, in fact, been devious and dilatory, although I have often wondered whether it was, as generally believed, worse in its methods than the diplomacy of other countries. In some respects it was very direct, and for that very reason, perhaps, aroused the criticism that it did. I resorted then, as I often did afterward, to the words of E. J. Dillon, an Irishman writing under the name of "Lanin," who had taught at Moscow University. On the basis of long years of residence and work in Russia he hit off their characteristic directness by declaring that "the Russian people lack the cement of hypocrisy." Perhaps it is because I have seen the factor of compromise, necessary to the functioning of our Western democratic system, degenerate so frequently into sheer hypocrisy that I consider this comment on the Russians so important to our understanding of them.

18

The regime of absolutism in Russia was, of course, the basis for the unfavorable attitude in America toward political Russia. And the manifestation of this absolutism which most shocked America was Russian anti-Semitism, which had produced in the nineties a whole series of pogroms. Many of the immigrants to America from Russia were these persecuted Russian Jews, often of the intellectual group; and they quite naturally contributed to the anti-Russian sentiment in America. At this time, and also in other periods, the Jewish question in Russia proved to be one of my most difficult problems. I tried to convince Americans that the position of the Russian Jew was but a single symptom of a generally grave social and economic situation. Frequently I found myself quoting H. G. Wells, whose writings about a first visit to Russia were criticized because he failed to mention the pogroms or the condition of the Jews. Wells answered this criticism rather vehemently by pointing out that there were other sides to Russia than this Jewish question and that he was tired of hearing about Russia exclusively "from a peculiar people who suffer from peculiar grievances."

☙ ☙ ☙

CHAPTER IV

THE UNIVERSITY OF MOSCOW

IN OCTOBER, 1904, I SET OFF AGAIN FOR RUSSIA, SAILING FROM NEW YORK to Hamburg. On board ship were two Russians—a farm-implement manufacturer from Odessa and a wealthy hardware merchant—who had been traveling together for some months and were obviously bored with each other. They sought diversion in conversation with me, since none of the other passengers spoke Russian; and I learned all about the Russian iron industry, not to mention serving as interpreter for an American salesman aboard, who managed, through me, to sell the hardware magnate some stoves. It was good practice for me and gave me confidence about proceeding to Russia. Nevertheless, I lingered in Berlin two days longer than I had intended, as though I rather dreaded breaking away from civilization. But once on the train for Moscow, I became reconciled, jabbered away with the Russians, and was more or less happy.

I noticed that the country around Brest Litovsk, which had been covered with snow when I passed through it the winter before, now had its fall tinge of brown. Although the trees were small and scattered, the region was less desolate than I expected to find it. Contrary to what was reported, the soil, too, seemed well cultivated. The low wooden houses with their enormous straw roofs were very pretty from a distance, though I presumed they were dirty enough. But the peasants at the station, what filth and rags!

Once in Moscow, I determined to waste no more time with dilatory Russian families. I took a room in a small hotel for fifteen dollars a month, including samovar twice a day, and planned to prepare my own breakfasts and suppers of coffee or tea, bread and butter, and Russian *kasha*, a kind of buckwheat cereal eaten with milk. Across the street from the hotel was an excellent boarding place, where I arranged to have my dinners with a congenial group of young people. I began at once to make my first calls and to renew acquaintance with the Smiths, the Ozerovs, the Shchukins, and others.

I was admitted to the University of Moscow as an "unregistered listener" and attended courses in Russian language, literature, and history. Of these courses, the most important for me was that of Professor Klyuchevsky in Russian history. I happened to sit between two students at the first lecture of this course who immediately adopted me and agreed to give me private tutoring.

One of my first impressions of the University of Moscow was the prevalence of uniforms. The students wore a semimilitary uniform. The attendants who took charge of our coats were also in uniform, and there was a goodly supply of these attendants. I soon learned that the uniform was obligatory for the students, enforced by police regulation to insure surveillance of this group, which was considered one of the most politically untrustworthy. The attendants were police officials, who exercised the surveillance and prevented illegal meetings or gatherings of the students. During the preceding year, student demonstrations had become chronic in practically all Russian universities, organized in support of workmen's strikes, in protest against the conduct of the war, or simply for propaganda purposes, to stir up thought. Such activity was definitely political and represented one of the few forms of political activity possible under tsarism. These student demonstrations almost always ended in street fighting with the police. From my student tutors I learned much about the radical views of the younger intelligentsia.

But this dissatisfaction was by no means limited to the young people of Russia. Almost immediately after I came to Moscow that October, I began to feel the political tenseness that had developed with ten months of unsuccessful war against Japan. These months had shown clearly the complete ineffectiveness and constant blundering of the Russian bureaucracy, which stubbornly refused to allow any popular movement in aid of the war lest such a movement break the bureaucratic monopoly of administration. Everywhere in Russia opposition to bureaucratic absolutism was rising from underground, the liberals were becoming more outspoken, and the revolutionaries were urging direct action. By underground routes we learned of renewed activity in the exile centers in Switzerland and Paris. I knew these groups from my

Paris days, for it was there that I had met and talked with the frankly revolutionary elements of the movement.

The evenings at the Ozerovs' were almost entirely given up to political discussion. The Shchukins, my wealthy merchant friends, were nervous. Like so many of the merchant group, they supported with money and in views the liberal movement, because they themselves were subject to restrictions under the semifeudalistic social system of tsarism; but they wished to avoid revolution. The foreign colony, which included many German and British merchants and manufacturers, discussed more frankly the danger of an outbreak; naturally, they were not particularly in favor of any revolutionary movement either.

Soon after my arrival, Plehve, the hated head of the Russian secret police, was assassinated by the revolutionaries. Although the intrinsic value of such acts of political terrorism was hotly debated within the revolutionary group and generally denied by the liberal reform elements, yet, in the atmosphere that prevailed in Russia at that moment, the removal of this symbol of ruthless repression was welcomed even in conservative circles. Plehve was generally believed to have recommended "a little war" with Japan as a good means of meeting the threatening internal situation; and, in fact, there is some evidence to support this view. In this instance the use of terrorism proved to be politically expedient, for it did actually bring concessions. Plehve's successor, Svyatopolk-Mirsky, was well known as one of the most liberal men of the higher bureaucracy, and he set out immediately to try to establish relations of trust between government and public. In line with this policy Mirsky did not prevent the Zemstvo Congress from meeting in November, 1904.

The Zemstvo Congress, a meeting of representatives from the various zemstvos, or district assemblies of Russia—the first such meeting in Russian history—met in the capitol of St. Petersburg. But in Moscow, too, the fact of the meeting, and its eleven-point petition for greater cooperation between the zemstvos and the central government, was the subject of great discussion in the groups in which I circulated. This congress was the prelude to the 1905 revolution. It was what the Russian leaders later called the "spring" of that political movement which came to a head in 1905. At the time it was difficult to guess whether concessions or reaction would result from the eleven-point petition, but certainly it was a period of great excitement. The atmosphere in even the most casual social gathering was charged with political intensity in those last months of 1904. On Coronation Day, I went to the Imperial Opera, half expecting some sort of violence to develop during the performance of Glinka's *Life for the Tsar*. Such gorgeous costumes, scenery, and dancing, I have seldom seen; but there was no demonstration. The only hint of the general tension was the weak applause which greeted the national hymn, handsomely sung in full chorus.

Yet on every hand men spoke openly against the government and made statements for which they would have been sent to Siberia six months past. The papers printed the most rabid attacks on the bureaucracy, the war, and the government. Even the cabmen took a lively interest in the situation. The students, as usual, were the leaders in the revolt; but now they were joined by the older men—professors, lawyers, and representatives of the zemstvos and other elective administrative bodies—in entering protests freely and forcibly. Members of particular professions met at banquets for the purpose of indorsing the Zemstvo Congress petition, and at these meetings there was free expression of liberal thought. Commenting on one such occasion, a Russian friend remarked to me in astonishment that not a single arrest had been made by the police at the banquet.

In this atmosphere it was not easy to follow the rigid program of studies which with Professor Boyer's help I had outlined for myself. I was still engaged in reading proof for the English edition of Boyer's book, to which I tried to devote three or four hours every morning; and I attended two lectures daily at the university, besides having two hours a day of private tutoring. But this purely academic side of my work rather paled in comparison with the social side. My circle of acquaintances widened continuously, and my expense book became one long record of candy, flowers, cab fare, and tips to servants. The last was quite an item, for it was customary to fee servants generously on leaving any house, no doubt because tippling guests so frequently required assistance in getting into their carriages, but sober guests were not exempt. Everywhere I went I found new expressions of the same political excitement. The routine business of paying calls to improve my conversational Russian rapidly developed into a much more serious effort to collect material on Russian history in the making. Often I remained at one evening gathering or another until three o'clock, and the boy who brought the breakfast samovar to my room literally had to pull me out of bed at ten in the morning.

Even though I missed only half an hour of daylight by keeping these heathenish hours, my conscience was somewhat uneasy until I encountered a genial doctor who justified this situation for me. He explained that 2:00 A.M. in Russia was only 8:00 P.M. in America and that, since for some twenty years I had been accustomed to being up at 8:00 P.M., I naturally found myself wide awake at this time. Similarly, 10:00 A.M. in Russia was equivalent to 4:00 A.M. at home, an hour at which I would reasonably resent being waked! On the basis of this comforting theory, I arranged a new schedule for myself and henceforth felt very virtuous when I awoke at noon.

About this time I became good friends with the son of a British merchant long resident in Moscow, who knew the language and the people better than I; and the two of us worked out a rather remarkable scheme for making contacts with the lower-middle-class merchants of Moscow, a group that had previously been inaccessible to me. At that date, American ragtime and cakewalking were in high fashion all over Europe and had penetrated even to Russia. This young Englishman and I both enjoyed dancing and had occasionally performed together at small parties at his parents' or friends' homes. So we conceived the idea of doing a little professional work. With the help of the Negro porter at the famous Moscow restaurant, Yar, which was chiefly frequented by small businessmen, we registered as entertainers for supper parties, and were regularly called in, like the gipsy choirs, to perform in the private dining-rooms. Like the gipsies, we were given our fee and also food and wine. We generally revealed our identity to our hosts; and I followed up several of the acquaintances made in this way, thus penetrating to that particular group of the Russian community.

One of these merchants agreed to help me with a pressing personal problem, the selection of a fur coat. I had decided early in November that my ordinary overcoat was no protection against the bitter cold of Moscow in winter, but I rather hesitated to invest in furs without some expert guidance. Consequently, I met my friend, as arranged, at a coffee shop. He was talking with some rich Russian clients, to whom he introduced me, explaining that we were going to hunt for a fur coat. One of the gentlemen at the table immediately offered me a pawn ticket and proposed that I take a look at a coat which he had bought at a bargain some five months before and then pawned. Russians always pawned their furs during the summer at the government pawnshops, where they were well taken care of. He declared that he had paid $250 for the coat and that I might have it for $100. My merchant friend and I looked at the coat, and it was a beauty. It was a little too big for me, but it was fashionable to wear them loose. My friend advised me to take it. In fact, he offered to buy the pawn ticket for $50 out of his own pocket, give it to me to redeem for another $50, and in a month I could repay him the $50 he had advanced.

"This way," he said, "you are guaranteed, for you are paying out nothing. You can pawn the coat tomorrow for $50, and not pay me if you find that we have worked a game on you."

He wouldn't even take a note from me. So we clapped hands together, said "on my word of honor" in true Russian fashion, I drew $50, and redeemed the coat. At once I went to the biggest fur-dealer in Moscow and, asking to buy another coat like the one I was wearing, discovered that it was indeed worth $250. I was incredulous. I had cleared $150.

A week or so later my merchant friend turned up with another proposition—a beautiful fur coat valued at $300, to be had for $115. He explained that he got these chances by accepting pawn tickets in payment of debts. I began to wonder what chance I would have of selling such furs in America. Would my father advance the money? Should I invest my small savings? For a time I was mightily taken with the idea of buying out the Moscow pawnshops and selling the coats at a great profit in Chicago. My father, with considerable tact, managed to dissuade me from this course, pointing out the many perils of speculation in general and of speculation in furs in particular. My own coat, however, proved practically indestructible, and I believe it is still doing service for some member of the family.

Toward the end of November, rumors reached Moscow of an abrupt change in the attitude of the political police. In St. Petersburg, it was said, the university students held a meeting, like those being held in every corner of Russia, to indorse the zemstvo petition. Afterward, they started home; and as there was only one bridge to the center of town, for which most of them were bound, they were obliged to walk "together" across this bridge. Russian students were prohibited by law from walking in mass formation, but this was certainly an informal and unavoidable procession. A squad of mounted police ordered them to disperse and immediately charged on them. The students were panic-stricken, and threw themselves over the bridge. Many were hurt; and public indignation ran high, further aroused by the fact that no official account of the affair was allowed to circulate.

A few days later, the man who killed Plehve was sentenced to life-imprisonment. The students of Moscow University did not attend class that day. The next day, during Klyuchevsky's lecture, a note was passed along under the desks at which we sat, giving the time and place for a student demonstration. As a foreigner I was not expected to participate in this protest, but I determined to be an interested onlooker if possible. On the way to my boarding place I picked up several handbills announcing the demonstration, which were strongly worded indeed. They amounted, in fact, to a call to arms. I showed these proclamations to a friend at dinner, who took one glance at them and then quickly burned them in the fireplace.

"If you are homesick for America," he said quietly, "show such papers to that gentleman over there."

And he pointed to a minor administrative official who regularly dined across the room from us. A few nights before, my friend told me, his room had been entered by the police and thoroughly searched for just such documents. I thought soberly of the pages of notes I had made on the current Russian situation, and determined to destroy most of them. It was rather early in my career to be barred from Russia entirely.

Nevertheless, on the day appointed for the student demonstration, I arranged to meet Samuel Smith, the American consul, at Philipov's coffee shop, where the floor-length windows gave a clear view of the open square before the prefecture of police. Here several hundred students gathered in small groups and, raising the red flag, began to sing. Immediately the courtyard doors of all the large houses on the square opened, and mounted Cossacks rode out, brandishing their whips. They were followed by an army of policemen, who charged on the students, slashing right and left with the flat of their swords. One student broke away and tried to run to safety. Ten policemen instantly fell on him and hacked away. Then they surrounded the rest, divided them into groups, and drove some of them into the courtyards, which had already been prepared for their reception. Others were hustled off to a near-by police station with ruthless kicking and slashing. Nine students were brutally killed, some sixty wounded, and many others thrown into prison. My room, which was just two blocks away, was used as a refuge by one of my tutors for several days.

Two days later, when Professor Klyuchevsky appeared in his class-room to lecture, he found on his desk a petition from the class, asking that the lecture be suspended because so many of his students had been arrested and could not be present. After reading the petition, he re-marked in a friendly voice that, if the students didn't want to hear him, he didn't want to lecture; and he gathered up his notes and retired. The university was closed by the police that same afternoon and did not open again until September, 1905.

As a protest against the oppression of the government, the student demonstration more than achieved its purpose, for all of Moscow rang with indignation. The Council of Professors of the university protested angrily to the police, as did the Duma, the local organ of municipal legis-lation. It appeared that the expected turn of events had come and that it was not to be concession this time but severe reprisals and a tighten-ing of the reins of autocracy. Yet there were still rumors of a manifesto to be delivered by Nicholas II in answer to the zemstvo petition, abolishing political arrests and granting complete freedom of the press. For many Russians seemed to believe that the Tsar himself was less auto-cratic than his government. The only official answer that was forth-coming, however, stated that zemstvos and dumas were overstepping their jurisdiction in petitioning concerning internal affairs, thus inciting the young people of Russia to revolt, and that persons engaged in such practices would be prosecuted henceforth.

In December the temperature regularly dropped to thirty below zero, and a kind of fog appeared to settle over everything because of the ex-treme cold. The horses pulling the open sleighs against the bitter wind were covered with frost, and their drivers looked like Santa Clauses with their frosted beards. The suffering in Moscow was intense and did little to resign the Russians to the defeat of their political hopes. Ru-mors of revolution persisted, and the general tension increased. With the closing of the university, I, too, began to feel somewhat restless and decided to spend the approaching Christmas holidays in St. Petersburg.

My own Christmas day—December 12 in Russia because of the dif-ference in calendars—had left me feeling a bit gloomy in spite of the fine Christmas tree which an artist friend had decorated for me. She was a Russian girl about my own age, whom I had met through Mr. Crane and with whom I had supper two or three times a week as long as she was in Moscow. We took turns being host and presiding at the chafing dish, and on one memorable occasion I shared with her a can of baked beans (Heinz) which Mrs. Smith, the consul's wife, had graciously presented to me.

In St. Petersburg, as the guest of Mr. W. E. Smith, another cousin of Mr. Crane's, who was director of the Russian Westinghouse Company, I saw much of the social life of the capital—Russian as well as foreign. The Smiths had two daughters; and the three of us were soon involved in a holiday round of dancing parties, picnics to the islands, snowshoeing, and sleighing behind racing horses on the frozen Neva. Nor were these the only events on my social calendar; for when I first arrived in Petersburg, I presented myself at the American embassy, the peculiar conditions prevailing in Russia at that time suggesting the advisability of so doing. Ambassador McCormick was very cordial and invited me to tea to meet the other members of the staff. The date which he set was Sunday, January 22, when the Christmas holidays would be over; and I looked forward to the affair with some eagerness.

For all the Christmas gaiety in the capital, the atmosphere was still anxious and strained. In addition to the political excitement, which was as intense there as in Moscow, the workmen were striking again and the employers were threatening shutouts. Through my host, Mr. Smith, I learned of the attitude and anxieties of the owners of large industrial enterprises. St. Petersburg, because it was situated at the one western-sea outlet of the country, was the industrial center of the Empire. Christmas and January first passed quietly because the strike movement could be looked upon by both sides and by the government as an extension of the long holiday usual under the Orthodox religious calendar. But with the end of the holidays, the continuation of unrest in workmen's groups began to cause distinct worry.

Then there appeared upon the scene the famous Father Gapon. The background and character of Father Gapon were at the time, and still are, full of questions. He had police connections; but the revolutionaries had finally come to have confidence in him, perhaps because they saw that he had secured a large and loyal workman following. Caught in the political atmosphere of the moment, Gapon determined to bring his organization, which he had built up with police permission, into the general movement. As zemstvo members had petitioned the Tsar, and professional groups meeting at banquets had expressed their views, it seemed reasonable that the workmen, too, should have their say. Some of the members of this group had joined in the strikes of that time and had been dismissed by their employers for so doing. When the employers refused to reinstate them, Gapon's whole organization of some eleven thousand decided to take their grievance direct to Nicholas II. A petition was prepared in which political demands were inserted at the suggestion of the socialist leaders with whom Gapon was in consultation. Gapon informed his police friends that on the following Sunday he would lead his followers, and any other workmen who cared to join them, to the Winter Palace Square to present their petition in person to the Tsar.

That Sunday morning, January 22, 1905, from my hotel, which was only half a block from the Winter Palace Square, I watched the gathering of these groups. The workers carried religious banners and sang religious songs. Men moved among them, trying to persuade them to disperse; but the workers answered simply that they wanted their "Little Father" to talk to them and promise them help. Still the Tsar did not appear. Other workers continued to arrive; and when several thousand were congregated in the enormous square, they began to crowd toward the palace. It was then that military units and Cossack regiments, concentrated in surrounding courtyards and in the large park of the Admiralty, moved in and opened fire. At least five hundred men, women, and children were killed by the charge, and many more were wounded. I did my own fastest running that day before an advancing Cossack troop and was glad that the hotel was only a short distance away.

When things had quieted down somewhat, I slipped out to keep my appointment at the American embassy. During tea I gave my eyewitness account of the events of that morning, and the ambassador suggested that we young men make the rounds of the central portion of the city to see if anything was still going on. Among the group were some with whom I was to work in later years: Basil Miles, who organized the Russian Division of the State Department in 1918; Joseph Grew; and Robert Bliss. We wandered around the Winter Palace Square, to which we were not admitted, and tried to talk with the military guards stationed all about, in most instances huddling around the fires built on the sidewalk against the severe cold. It was my first experience with the practice which I was to continue for almost forty years, of making informal reports to our diplomatic representatives.

The day, January 22, 1905, has since gone down in history as "Bloody Sunday." As it drew to a close, the streets of the capital were quiet except for the orderly parading of squads of Cossacks. But there was no rest in St. Petersburg. Fantastic stories swept the city. The workers were making dynamite! They had been paid forty million rubles by the Japanese to create a disturbance! The chief of police had been court-martialed! Father Gapon had fled to Moscow! Father Gapon was dead! Sevastopol was in flames! Moscow was ready to revolt! And most persistent of all was the story that Nicholas II, who could so easily have placated the workers by simply greeting them and hearing their petition, had left his palace immediately on learning of Gapon's plans and had given orders that "bullets are not to be spared." For workers and intellectuals alike, this tragedy put an end to the distinction that had previously been made between the bureaucracy and the Tsar. All with whom I talked agreed that this day marked the beginning, and not the end, of the opposition movement.

PART III
I BECOME A STUDENT OF POLITICS
THE EARLY DUMAS: 1906–10

For the convenience of the reader:

1. The Tsar established the new constitution, providing for the Duma, by manifesto of October 30, 1905.

2. The first Duma opened May 10, 1906, and was prorogued July 22 of that year.

3. The second Duma opened March 5, 1907, and was prorogued June 16 of that year.

4. The Tsar changed the election laws under assumed rights of prerogative by the imperial decree of June 16, 1907.

5. The third Duma, elected under the new election law, opened November 14, 1907, and continued to function until 1912.

6. The fourth Duma, elected in 1912, continued to function until the third year of World War I, when the revolution of March, 1917, resulted in the abdication of the Tsar.

MAJOR POLITICAL PARTIES: 1905–12

Nationalist	Extreme rightist party
Octobrist	Next most conservative—a constitutionalist party whose platform was based on the October 30, 1905, manifesto
Constitutional Democrat (C.D. or "Cadets")	Liberal center party
Social Revolutionary (S.R.)	This party was an active force in the Peasant Union and represented an organization of the elemental but sporadic agrarian disturbance groups. It was largely underground but had representation in the Duma as the "Group of Toil"
Social Democrat (S.D.) Menshevik Bolshevik	Socialist party, the Mensheviks, representing the right wing and the Bolsheviks the left wing
There were also Polish and various minor special parties	

CHAPTER V

THE FIRST DUMA: HISTORY IN THE MAKING

ON FEBRUARY 3, 1905, I WAS CALLED HOME BECAUSE OF THE SERIOUS illness of my father. I managed to make a record trip from Moscow to Chicago for that period and the existing means of transportation. Missing the boat at Hamburg, I was able to catch it at Cherbourg by taking the Berlin-Paris express. The ship was one of the fast North German Lloyd liners, and I reached Chicago on the eleventh day.

That first year of Russia's Revolution was a troubled one for me, full of new cares and responsibilities; and, though at my father's insistence I went to Paris for a few months during the summer to complete the year's work at the School of Oriental Languages, the gravity of his condition made it impossible for me to return to Russia. As well as I could, however, I followed the course of the Revolution as it deployed after Bloody Sunday.

American interest in the Revolution was keen at the outset. Russian revolutionaries were able to collect large sums of money for their cause from prosperous Americans, particularly of the gentler sex; at one meeting I actually heard a mild Chicago matron offer her thousand dollars with the hope that they would reach the "Bloody Tsar!" But as acts of violence increased in Russia, an element of doubt developed in this country. The bombing of grand dukes was all right, and perhaps even the peasant attacks on landlords were understandable. But when terrorism got completely out of hand and reached ordinary policemen, when the workmen's strikes took on a political character and mutinies broke out in the army and navy, many expressed the thought that the Russians were going pretty far. The general strike of October, 1905, and the setting up of a Soviet of Workmen Deputies—which proved to be the prototype of the later Soviet system—were interpreted in the American press as "dangerous trends." Thus I found that, while there had been sympathy for the Revolution before it came, it caused concern when it in fact developed.

The failure of the Revolution to upset the existing government obscured to many its one really significant result—the creation, by the manifesto of October 30, 1905, of the Imperial Duma, an elected body with legislative powers, which marked the beginnings of constitutionalism in Russia. Only a few thoughtful writers pointed out the constructive side of the upheaval. Among these were several British interpreters of Russia, particularly Bernard Pares, Harold Williams, and Maurice Baring, whose work I came to know and respect.

During the year I taught a course in elementary Russian at the University of Chicago; and on the basis of this experience and of my past record, Mr. Crane offered, at the end of 1905, to support the continuation of my work. It was arranged that I should spend six months of each year at the University of Chicago, giving courses in the Russian language and in Russian political institutions, and that I should devote the remaining six months to further study and travel in Russia.

My association with Mr. Crane—perhaps the most important outside influence in my academic life—was fortunate and lasting, and I believe that the care with which it was established contributed much to its success. There was danger, under the somewhat extraordinary procedure of his individual support of my studies, that a feudal relationship might develop. Mr. Crane, for his part, promised that he would never interfere in any way with the objectivity of my work or make any effort to influence its direction. He was always free to ask me to do this or that particular thing, but I was always free to refuse when I felt it interfered with my main work. To these conditions we both adhered rigidly at all times. On his advice I laid down for myself many principles, some of them rather unusual. For example, I was never to have an investment in the country which I was studying; I was never to accept employment from a foreign government; and I was to remain abroad not longer than one year at a time without returning to America.

Throughout my life I kept in close touch with Mr. Crane, and through him I met many people important to my studies. I profited greatly by his remarkable insight in political matters. Furthermore, it was Mr. Crane who suggested that perhaps teaching, writing, and lecturing were not the only means of establishing a real understanding of Russia in America. I therefore adopted an additional method which became an important part in my educational program, and with his help established a number of centers here for informal periodic reporting, selecting representative publishers, educators, businessmen, and others influencing policy and opinion, with whom to discuss events in Russia at regular intervals.

It was during the last few months of my father's life that these wise and farseeing arrangements with Mr. Crane for the continuance of my Russian studies were made. When my father died, on January 10, 1906, I lost the chief close supporter of the unusual life I had planned for myself. Fortunately, I had completed before his death the fundamental training period; I was well equipped with the language. It was now my task, at the age of twenty-three, to chart my course on my own responsibility.

Leaving the administration of my father's estate in the hands of my brother-in-law, Charles Scribner Eaton, I started abroad in April, 1906, stopping in Paris for my final oral examinations at the School of Oriental Languages, and then moved on immediately to St. Petersburg for the opening of the first Imperial Duma. Something of the trepidation, as well as of the excitement and enthusiasm, with which I undertook the study of this new representative body is reflected, I think, in my letters and notes of this period.

30

S.S. "Bergensfiord," April 9, 1906

DEAR MOTHER: A note to you on my birthday—24. I am very lonely. The last year has been almost more than I could bear.

ST. PETERSBURG, April 16, 1906

DEAR MOTHER: Here I am at last in St. Petersburg. I got through the customs without any difficulty. Baron Schlippenbach's letter brought all the officials to their knees, and they couldn't be too polite. I shall use that letter on every occasion. Hechmann's books were glanced at, but my trunk was just opened and nothing touched.

I couldn't get a sleeper from the frontier on, and arrived this morning dirty as a pig. I stopped at my old hotel, took a bath, and went to the Smiths'. They were most cordial. They were just starting out for a drive, and I went along and saw more of St. Petersburg in those two hours than I had ever seen before. I lunched with the Smiths and went calling with one of the girls. Saw some of Crane's friends and gave them news. Then I set out to find permanent quarters. I think I have a room, but it is horribly expensive, $18 a month. It is right in the center of things, near the Smiths', and in case of trouble, handy to the embassy. I have about decided to take it in spite of the price. I dined with the Smiths and gossiped until eleven, and have just returned to my hotel.

I am afraid to try to tell you all I heard today. The anxiety in general —all sorts of rumors about. Nobody puts faith in the Duma; but, contrary to what we are told in our papers, everybody is intensely interested in the Duma. The liberals are rallying to use it as a means for further reforming the institutions of their country along Western democratic lines. The revolutionaries are, of course, bitterly disappointed in the meagerness of their victory and are boycotting the Duma. And the Emperor and his bureaucracy are regretting already the concessions which were forced from them by the general strike of last October, the Moscow uprising of December, and the extensive peasant rioting and mutinies in the army this past winter. It is considered quite probable that bombs will be thrown at the first Duma meeting. I think I am going to get my entrance ticket, but I may not want to use it!

The weather is delightfully cool. I am surprised at the cleanliness here. I believe I am going to like it better than Moscow. I have just figured up my accounts and find that the trip from Chicago here amounted to just a little over $150. Not bad, considering the distance.

This is Monday night, and I shall send my weekly letter on Mondays. If I don't write more often, you must understand that it is because of the rush. I start making official calls tomorrow. I am a little tired, but feeling wonderfully well after such a long trip.

ST. PETERSBURG
Saturday, April 21, 1906

DEAR MOTHER: Here I am in my new quarters. I am almost ashamed of myself, for I have taken a very luxurious room on a fashionable street

31

and am paying $23 a month for it. I could find absolutely nothing for less than $18 and decided it would pay to take this better one. I am trying to comfort myself with the thought that I really must have a respectable place to receive people in. I am frightfully discouraged over the money side of this trip. Everything is going up in price. I may have to draw more than I had planned to; but I feel that, once here, I ought to get the most possible out of it.

I never expected to get into society here as I have these last two days. Everybody seems interested in me and ready to do anything to help. I lunch with the ambassador in an hour; tomorrow luncheon with a member of the Imperial Council, who, by the way, has already asked me to spend a week with him in the country this summer. I was at a Russian "evening" until two o'clock this morning and met a lot of students who asked to call on me. Kovalevsky, the great Russian sociologist, takes me to luncheon Tuesday, Professor Paul Milyukov on Wednesday, and one of the best-known political leaders is going to supply me with reading material. Two professors have opened their libraries to me. The Smiths have made me promise to come in for meals whenever and as often as I wish. I shall be a wreck in a month or so.

I am to get a definite answer from the ambassador today as to ticket. If he fails me, I have two other strings to pull. The newspapermen are being very cordial to me because of my credentials from the *Chicago Tribune*. I have explained to them that I have no intention of sending back regular correspondence and am not in any sense a competitor; that the credentials I hold are mainly to give me the entree of the "press." I want access to their day-by-day observations as well as their general interpretations. In my task of tracing the course of the 1905 revolution and following at firsthand its institutional product, the Duma, I may often pick up spot-news items, which I plan to hand out to the correspondents, thereby cementing our close relationship.

Also, I frequent the hotels and restaurants where the newspapermen generally gather. It is a most interesting group and includes British and French, as well as American, journalists and writers. There are also two American socialists, who are frankly here to get inspiration from the workmen and the revolutionary aspect of the movement, which they feel sure is only beginning instead of gradually dying out. I have not observed any Germans in the group, no doubt because they feel themselves much superior. The German journalists do, indeed, know Russia much more thoroughly than the rest of us.

I just measured my room—24 × 22—and it is so cheerful. I shall not dread coming home at night as I usually do when abroad. I'll finish this when I return from lunch.

Sunday morning, April 22, 1:00 A.M.

Just returned from another Russian "evening." The ambassador has filed a petition for me, and Mr. Smith is going to move things a little from another direction. I visited the Tauride Palace, where the Duma is to meet. I shall *honestly* be surprised if I get in. We counted the seats, and there are only thirty-four for both Russian and foreign correspondents. I shall send on an article for the *Chicago Tribune* in a day or so; it will not be signed. Please remind Keeley by note when the material is sent to him that my name is not to appear under any circumstances.

How delightful to return to my cheerful room tonight. I don't feel the least bit lonely. Three people called on me today in my absence. I made my own supper out of a hunk of bread, a slice of ham, and a glass of tea.

By the way, remember there is a good chance of trouble here in three weeks now, and you are not to worry. If it is a serious outbreak, I'll cable so that you will know I am safe and sound.

ST. PETERSBURG
Sunday evening, April 29, 1906

DEAR PEOPLE: Well, another week is over. I have been seeing a great many people, reading a great many papers and books, and I don't know whether I am discouraged or not. Disgusted I know I am—everybody seems to be so, and I follow in. It appears that a conflict between the Duma and the government is inevitable. Such seeming blunders on the part of the powers that be! I am all dressed and waiting to go out to spend the evening with a member of the Council of State, that body which is responsible for the Fundamental Laws (the new constitution), which you must have heard about. Last night I dined with the private secretary of the Empress. Crane will tell you his name. We were just the two of us, and he cross-examined me on America's attitude toward the Russian situation. I had a hard time to answer gracefully. It was a mean trick on his part to put me in such an embarrassing position.

My hopes of getting a ticket for the Duma are a bit higher. I shall try to get my friend tonight to put in a good word for me.

For breakfast I am having a cup of tea and two oranges. Is forty cents for ten expensive? They are measly little oranges at that. My, how money does go. I have to use cabs so much; the streetcars are so limited in number. I drew ten pounds last week. You have probably heard of it by this time.

I sent a letter direct to Keeley yesterday. Read the *Tribune* carefully and perhaps you will find it. Will you ask Shailer Matthews for me if he will give me $50 for an article on the opening of the Duma for his *The World Today?* Tell him the *Outlook* has offered me that.

Monday night, April 30

I was in high society last night. Princes and counts on every side. I had a long talk with a general and only afterward learned that he was a member of the imperial family. Today has been a hard one. I got some books out of the library, and then spent all afternoon pushing my appli-

33

cation for a seat in the Duma. It looks more favorable. I am surprised I have not more letters. Where are Paul and the rest of them? You must write me often, because I feel so frightfully lonely over here this year.

ST. PETERSBURG
Saturday, May 5, 1906

DEAR MOTHER: Glad you went to Atlantic City. You must excuse this short letter, but I am all fagged out. We have been having insufferably hot weather, and I have been attending political meetings. I am getting on fine—meeting people by the dozens every day. I knock off work tomorrow afternoon and go out into the country with the Smiths. Went driving with them from six to eight o'clock today. The parks are beautiful and make me restless. The dust here in St. Petersburg is terrible. I am getting thinner and thinner, for I have no appetite these hot days. But I am feeling very, very well.

I never knew I enjoyed meeting people so much before. Many influential men seem interested in me. In this short day I talked with sixteen different people, many of them important political leaders. My brain is all in a muddle; so I am off to bed. I may have to send you just short letters for a week or so.

Monday morning, May 7

It was great yesterday to feel nice soft grass underfoot. The Smiths have an ideal place on the gulf. I am hoping they open it up this summer so that I can run out there on Sundays. Got enough fresh air to last through this week. We are going to have an interesting time. Probably I will get into the Winter Palace for the throne speech, but not into the Duma. There are only eight places for foreign correspondents, one for each country. The bomb-throwing at Moscow yesterday was the most unfortunate thing that could have happened. But at Milyukov's party's meeting last night they (the Constitutional Democrats) *applauded* the news. The anxiety and excitement are great. This afternoon the foreign correspondents get together to fight for their eight places. Yesterday the Russians had their fight for their places. Professor Kovalevsky, after the meeting which lasted from two to ten, said he never had gone through such a mill. I have a pleasant afternoon ahead of me. My knowing Russian is going to be a strong argument in my favor. Will finish tonight. Troops are already coming in in anticipation of Thursday.

Wednesday morning, May 9

I have decided to hold this letter. I seem to have lost out on the Duma, but probably will get into the Imperial Council. Also, I have a good chance to be at the Winter Palace. Spent all day yesterday and a good many rubles besides to work this last.

Things are coming to a head. Two meetings attended by members of the Duma and Council were broken up by police—no bloodshed. The publication of the Fundamental Laws has provoked a loud, emphatic protest.

Thursday night: A New Era, May 10

If anybody deserves a good night's rest, it is your humble servant. I won't tell you what happened today, for you know it already. I am sending on a description, to the *Tribune*. I got into the Winter Palace and was not twenty yards from the Emperor during the whole throne speech. It was a disappointment. I stood outside the Duma, and it was more interesting there than inside. Tomorrow I go to the opening of the Imperial Council. Am getting tired of wearing my dress suit in the mornings.

On the morning of the opening of the Duma, the foreign correspondents to be admitted gathered for breakfast at the Hotel France, just across the square from the Winter Palace. Under instructions, we were in full dress, with tails and white tie, according to the custom of Continental Europe. We all felt very silly, and the British group was particularly annoyed at having to wear evening dress in the morning. We trouped across to the Winter Palace, where, under guard, we were escorted to a balcony of one of the largest reception rooms, which was capable of holding some fifteen hundred people, who later filled it. We were ordered to remain standing and were told not to raise our hands from the sides of our legs. There were guards behind us to enforce the instructions.

As we looked down on the gathering below us, we were all impressed by the contrast of the five hundred Duma members on one side in plain civilian clothes, some two hundred of them in peasant costumes, and on the other side the glittering uniforms of official Russia, civilian and military.

The Emperor read a short speech from the throne, which, because of its formal wording and the manner of reading, could hardly be called one of welcome. It was clear that he did not enjoy the new role of constitutional monarch which had been forced upon him, and his subsequent action was in line with the attitude he showed that important morning. The Duma group representing the new Russia showed its disappointment by the restraint of its applause. The uniformed old Russia applauded vociferously, but we all knew that it was as unhappy over developments as was the Emperor. The gulf between these two groups was clear during that short opening ceremony and was to be made wider and deeper during the next days when the new assembly began to try to function.

The Duma deputies were taken from the Winter Palace to the Tauride Palace up the Neva on boats, but we foreign observers had to go home first and change our costumes. Thus we missed an incident which symbolized the place and role of the Duma. For, as the boats carrying the deputies passed a prison on the banks of the river, the inmates, against all regulations, waved handkerchiefs and other articles through the bars and shouted appeals to the popular representatives; and a very considerable percentage of these prisoners were political prisoners, arrested for participation in strikes, soviets, or workmen's organizations.

Friday morning, 12:00 noon, May 11

DEAR MOTHER: The disappointment is not very strongly expressed in the morning paper, but all agree that nothing really definite has been done except the calling of the Duma. What the Duma's relation to the government is going to be is still an *open* question. I must get into a dress suit now, have lunch, and go to the opening of the Council. The Duma has a meeting tomorrow, and there is a slight chance of my getting in.

Saturday morning, 1:30 A.M., May 12

The Council meeting was a frost. They are a crowd of old dotards, and I understand why everybody wants that institution abolished. I got something out of the meeting, however. I knew a member, and he took us to a tearoom during intermission. At a table not five feet from me were Witte, the prime minister, and Durnovo, the minister of the interior. I saw all the old "pillars" of the Empire.

Have just finished my story for the *Tribune*. That is why I am up so late. I have almost reached my limit of endurance, but tomorrow is the last day of the week and I'll sleep all day Sunday. I'm almost sure to get into the Duma tomorrow. I got Leroy Beaulieu (the great French scholar and publicist) into the meeting today, and he was very grateful. I am making many close friends here.

I finally gained admission not only to the press box in the assembly room of the Tauride Palace (which had been reconstructed for the new national assembly) but also to the lobby, committee rooms, and restaurants. For the next sixty days, the duration of this first Duma, I spent most of my time there, listening to speeches and debates, meeting and talking with deputies, exchanging views with other foreign students and correspondents, using the lobby gardens and restaurants as a kind of club. Here it was possible to talk with individuals from every part of the Empire, representatives of the various nationalities as well as of the various social groups.

The system of elections which the government worked out for this first elective representative body was based on the old class divisions which still prevailed from the period of serfdom which had terminated only in 1861. Under this system of elections, all classes, as well as all national groups, had direct representation, although there had been an attempt so to gerrymander the procedure of elections, which were indirect, as to give the more conservative and Russian elements weighted representation. Thus there was a very large group of peasants, who were considered conservative by the government. One of the outstanding leaders of the peasant group was Alexis Aladin, who was of peasant origin but had managed to do some university work and had acquired the background of the intelligentsia.

The Russian peasant is hard to reach because of the attitude of suspicion which his conditions have developed, particularly toward intellectuals. In the lobby of the Duma I often watched the Russian liberal try to talk with his colleague, the peasant deputy; and the difficulty he was having was clearly apparent. But some of us foreigners who knew the language were able to allay the suspicions of these peasants much more easily than the Russians, who did not seem able to avoid a condescending approach. I found it useful to mention in my talks with peasants that my grandfather had been an Ohio farmer and that I myself had lived on a farm for a time in my youth. Another of the foreign group often seen in the lobby who seemed able to reach the peasant was the Englishman, Maurice Baring. He was much more successful at this than such an outstanding liberal leader as Professor Milyukov, whose pedantic manner in lobby talks, as well as from the Duma tribune, greatly reduced his usefulness.

It was in the lobby of the Duma that I first met Professor Bernard Pares, of the University of Liverpool. A lecturer on European history, he had decided, as early as 1900, to extend his studies to eastern Europe. He had acquired a working knowledge of Russian and had already traveled considerably in Russia. Pares and I soon discovered that our aims were very closely related. We both wanted to promote the study of Russian history and institutions in our respective countries, and both of us had decided that frequent trips to Russia were essential to the success of our efforts. Pares later became the pioneer in promoting Russian studies in England. He was somewhat eccentric in his enthusiastic and energetic approach to this problem. On the other hand, he had the peculiar ability to feel and interpret a political situation which I had already noted in Charles Crane. Mr. Crane, to the end of his life, considered Pares one of the Westerners who best understood the Russian people.

On the basis of our common interest, Pares and I decided to work together in a systematic way. Thus we shared interviews which we had held separately, and often arranged to interview a Russian leader together. When we used this second method, one of us asked questions, always according to a previously prepared outline, and the other listened or, when advisable, took notes. Important interviews were immediately written up in duplicate by the person who listened. Later, Pares and I traveled together to provincial towns, to estates of friends, and to peasant villages. Such traveling was easier, sometimes safer, and certainly more pleasant in companionship. I doubt if either of us would have done so much of it if we had had to go alone.

This arrangement with Pares was of particular value to me, for he had been longer in Russia and had a better historical background than I had. I believe, however, that I had a better knowledge of the language, or at least more facility in speaking it. There were times when we got on each other's nerves; but, as I look back, these instances seem very rare in view of the many difficult physical, as well as political, situations in which we found ourselves. Coming from a conservative British family, Pares was somewhat more conservative in his general political outlook than I. Even while he was professionally combating the traditional British-Russian distrust, he was, of course, always thinking of the interests of the British Empire. As an American, I was more definitely the objective student interested in a particular field of study. Because of this difference, we sometimes found ourselves in disagreement, which probably contributed much to our respective thinking.

The Duma, as a first step in constitutional government, was an important one; and we Western observers were, of course, pleased that our institutions were being introduced in another country. The leadership of the Duma was in the hands of the liberals, organized in the Constitutional Democratic party, which was one of Milyukov's achievements and under his direction was modeled, as far as possible, on features of the Western parliamentary systems. We could not fail to note, however, that the large contingent of peasant deputies was politically unprepared for this system. The peasants showed this immediately by organizing what they called a "nonparty peasant party." Also, we felt a little concerned at the immaturity displayed by these first Russian legislators, although we recognized that their task was made difficult by the stubborn attitude of the bureaucracy which controlled completely the executive branch of the government.

We were pleased when the Russian constitutionalists tried to secure "ministerial responsibility" and a new press law modeled on our Western concept of freedom of the press. But I believe we were sobered considerably when the all-important land question was forced to the fore by the pressure from peasant deputies, by peasant deputations arriving daily, and by reports of restlessness in rural Russia caused by the Duma's slowness in satisfying the peasants' land hunger. When the Duma proposed forcible confiscation of private property to meet this situation, with only nominal provision for compensation to the owners, Pares and I were forced to realize more clearly the peculiar social-economic conditions under which our Western institutions were being introduced.

It must be remembered that the serfdom of the peasants had ended only under the great Reform of 1861, shortly after Russia's defeat in the Crimean War. Even under the system of serfdom, the peasants always had a traditional but peculiar viewpoint about the land. They regarded themselves, to be sure, as belonging to their landlords; but the land they tilled they always thought of as their own. Under the Reform, the large landowners were required to give up half of their land, which was then given, not to the peasants individually, but collectively to a village community, the so-called *mir*. This *mir* was collectively responsible for the redemption compensation to the original owners and for all taxes. This collective responsibility of the *mir*, or commune had thus continued even after the original owners had been paid off. A peasant could not leave the commune at will because he would be withdrawing a taxpayer. Needless to say, the land originally apportioned to the *mirs* was not generally the best land and was circumscribed in many ways from water and roads, etc. The dissatisfaction over this system made up the great Russian agrarian problem.

It was over the extremist proposals to work out this agrarian problem that the first Duma was finally prorogued. During the interval between its dissolution and the assembly of the second Duma in 1907, Stolypin, the new premier, set out to remove what he considered the main causes of the agricultural crisis. He hoped to avert the danger of agrarian disorders, which were the aspect of the revolutionary movement that had caused the greatest concern to the authorities, most of whom were themselves landlords. Using the emergency clause in the constitution, Stolypin enacted a series of land-reform measures and put them into force without the sanction of the Duma. These measures provided easier conditions for the purchase of state land by the peasants, government subsidy to those migrating to Siberia, and government assistance to those peasants who wished to leave the commune and establish themselves as individuals on the basis of private ownership of land.

This last measure was a sweeping one, directed against the communal system of land tenure. Stolypin wished to break up the commune primarily because it acted as a brake on peasant initiative. But political considerations also directed this new policy, for it was believed that the peasants as private landowners would show more respect for the principle of private property and thus abstain from attack on neighboring landlords and that private ownership would raise in their ranks opposition to expropriation proposals. Under these enactments the communal land could be sold and mortgaged—a fact which would lead to sharp economic differentiation in the peasantry, to the development of a rich peasant group. Stolypin saw and wanted this feature. He was going to gamble on the economically stronger element in the peasant.

CHAPTER VI

SIDE LIGHTS ON THE DAYS OF THE FIRST DUMA

MY NOTES AND LETTERS THROW MANY SIDE LIGHTS ON THE HISTORIC period of the first Duma.

ST. PETERSBURG
May 18, 1906. 1:45 A.M.

DEAR MOTHER:

A spectacular moment is coming. The Duma has accepted the project of an answer to the throne speech by paragraphs. The committee is incorporating the few changes made, and in an hour or so we will see the Duma accept it unanimously (we hope). I have been here in the Palace since 10:30 this morning. I am all done up but want to stay to the end. As I look out over the river, I can see the beginning of twilight. We have only two or three hours of real night now. Then for a four-mile drive home, and in the morning I must write my "impressions" for Matthews.

I won't need to travel this summer, for I can find right here representatives of all Russia. I spend a good deal of time in the lobby interviewing the deputies.

The speeches have been very radical tonight. I am not prophesying, but I don't see how the Duma's answer to the Emperor can fail to make trouble. I believe, after all, there will be excitement soon. I was almost arrested the other day for addressing a crowd on the street. They saw me coming out of the Duma and asked me what had been done. I was just finishing my account when an officer came up and told me I was breaking the law. I was just too late for the Cossack charges on the Nevsky last Monday night. Saturday is the Emperor's birthday. I don't know what we are to see, but I go out to the country to clear my brain.

4:00 A.M.

Just home. Answer accepted unanimously by the Duma after six rightists had left the room. Then we clapped and started home. There was not much expression of joy, whether because all were tired or because a conflict is feared. Our cabman insisted we would see bloodshed soon. But I am getting accustomed to such pessimism. I am off to bed— a pretty good day's work, considering that I started at seven yesterday morning. No meeting until Tuesday, I am glad to say, and I am going to rest.

Friday, 3:30 P.M.

I never woke until twelve o'clock. I had an extra large breakfast to celebrate—sent out for a roll to supplement my orange and glass of tea.

The heat outside today is intolerable, so the maid tells me. I dread going out, but I have to take dinner with some Russians at five and I must get dressed. I am more or less encouraged about my work, but still everything is so unsettled. I find it hard to do my research work. Perhaps it's just as well. I shall never again have this chance of seeing a new era of history begin.

ST. PETERSBURG
May 24, 1906

DEAR PAUL:

I am not satisfied with what I am accomplishing. But it is hard to see results, perhaps, when everything is in such a mix-up. I sent off an article to Shailer Matthews yesterday. I am a little ashamed of it; but it's hard to write now, and all the men here are desperate. They don't know what to write.

I have got hold of a valuable man, Bernard Pares, a lecturer on Russian history at the University of Liverpool. His work here is almost the the same as mine. He is writing a book and wants to bring it up to date. He has asked me to write four or five chapters for him—of course over my own name. I may do it. Just now we are going to share all the material we collect, and he is going to let me use some documents he has been collecting for the last two years. I have much to gain by the co-operation. He has promised to spend a week in the country with me "doing" a small district, i.e., seeing every type from peasant to landed proprietor. This is just what I want to do for a month or so this summer, and it will be a great help to be initiated by an old hand at that kind of business.

No use of my trying to give you political news. There may be some kind of indication in a week or so, but just now everything is hopelessly in the air. I am busy interviewing the peasant deputies. I want to write an article on them—a psychological study, if I can.

[*From the notes*]
May 27, 1906

Had a long talk with the deputy Remiet, a Constitutional Democrat, or "Cadet." He thought Russia must be very much like America—not like France or Germany—made for large-scale cultivation, similar in climate and character. He felt that the present course of the Duma was suicidal. At the very most, it could only be a temporary palliative. The agrarian problem should be worked out gradually. The artificial methods of Premier Witte are absurd. He considered the Duma as fundamentally sound, but with only a few men of really strong convictions —Aladin, Milyukov, and a few others—and that a break was bound to come soon, but no telling how soon.

Also interviewed a Cossack from Orenburg. He had worked a great deal in a newspaper office; extreme leftist. He said the Cossacks of his territory really want to become Russians and to be freed from the military caste position in which they are placed. In many cases they have refused to do police duty. They are all liberals, and pretty well educated because they have obligatory free instruction for both sexes. There are many cases of intermarriage with Russians. It is also possible for an outsider to enter Cossack ranks.

The Cossacks did not want to be represented in the Duma by officers. They sent him as a deputy because he is a common soldier. At first he received threatening letters from officers. He gets many letters of congratulation from his fellow-soldiers. They devour papers and letters eagerly. He said Cossacks of his territory mostly cultivate the land, but a few are workmen.

He thinks the Cadets (Constitutional Democrats) are playing a cowardly role, and he would have little confidence in their ministry as presently represented. To him it's all very well to talk about "in the long run," but meanwhile people are being shot. He read a telegram reporting that some of his own comrades had been shot, and cried for half an hour.

He said the zemstvos did not bring about the Revolutionary movement: it was the war with Japan. Today the Revolution is the only issue on his mind. To him the Cadets are all of the old regime; the new, young generation has to carry through the movement. He thinks the present tactics will lead to nothing and that more forceful measures must be adopted. The position cannot be made worse.

St. Petersburg
June 2, 1906

Dear Mother: Perhaps you are right, that I am worrying too much about money matters. But I can't help it. I drew $50 today, which means that I have spent $120 in seven weeks. After all, perhaps that is really not so bad. And to my delight the *Outlook* published a short editorial I wrote them, and sent me $15. I was planning to move up nearer the Duma tomorrow. Am practically packed. But when I saw what miserable, dirty rooms there were for $15, and then came back to my fine, homelike room, I decided that, inasmuch as I have made $15, that will cover the difference. So here I stay in a respectable place where I am not ashamed to receive anybody.

The work at the Duma is most tiring. I come out, after a seven-hour session, completely exhausted. I spend much time talking with the deputies. I am getting together considerable material for informal talks. The material for my university course is being collected, but I decided it would be better not to work it up just now. More profit in following the present stage—of getting an intimate knowledge of the men, etc. The weather has been most trying—damp, rainy. I never go out without a coat.

About the situation, it is very critical. Both sides have made enormous blunders—the government in not going halfway to meet the demands of the Duma, the Duma perhaps in not making its first protest more emphatic. The government has concluded that it does not need to listen to "hotheaded men blowing off steam." The moderates do not want a conflict, but many think an open break is the only possible issue. The country is quiet for the present, but there are sure to be local disturbances before long. My summer trip in the country may be spoiled, but I can find plenty to keep me busy until September 15. If politics can't be studied, I always have literature to fall back on. I am off to dinner, will finish later. . . . .

I have worked all evening with my English collaborator, and we are getting a clearer and clearer insight into things. An interview shows that a change can be expected in not less than two, not more than six, weeks. The present ministry will go out, and one containing rights and Cadets will be substituted. The Cadets may balk at this, but it is the only solution and is a great step forward. It will mean the ultimate evolution of reform without the long-promised revolution. I was given this in confidence and wish I could hand it over to the "telegraph men," the correspondents who "wire" their news. I am sending it to you as an experiment. I want to verify my judgment—a good thing to practice in this country where one has to take everything with a bit of salt.

I am getting in with the radicals through some Social Revolutionists—but am careful to keep at a safe distance, for even now papers are confiscated. I have already four papers which I have been able to mark "confiscated" before filing away.

It is 12:45 A.M., and I just sat on my window sill and read a newspaper. How can one sleep when there is no night? But I'm off to bed. I feel more happy after a hard evening's work.

[*From the notes*]
June 9, 1906

K. D. is a girl of good family and well known. There is a price on her head. She has a shop here in St. Petersburg under another name, and her friends do not recognize in her the prominent leader. The family knows that she is a liberal but has no idea that she is a terrorist. The man with her was the typical Jewish revolutionary, with long hands and a nervous way. He started out with her on her revolutionary career. She shrank when she saw a horse fall and struggle in harness, yet had stood behind barricades.

I had considerable difficulty getting into revolutionary headquarters. I was told that the man I asked for was not there, but at last I was admitted. A peasant woman with a fascinating face came in and shook hands all around. K. D. and the man and I went out up some steps to a kind of w. c. door, and she gave a peculiar knock and we were admitted. That was the central bureau. Two girls of good family—one noble, both rich—lived there. They said that Dvornin, a Social Democrat, lived with them. (In St. Petersburg the Social Democrats and Social

Revolutionaries are now at cross-purposes, as they were in Moscow.) They received visitors, both soldiers and sailors. When they saw that everything was all right, they signaled at the window, and others came up. The girls have so many visitors that they were told by the police to take out yellow tickets (the common method for being absolutely free, and it is quite likely that free love goes with free comradeship in a common cause). Soldiers and sailors fill their boots and blouses with pamphlets. A man can carry away as many as five hundred. One of the girls went out with a soldier, to be taken into the barracks as a peasant woman. There she was to hold a meeting while he sat outside on guard.

A comrade came in dressed as a sailor, to be smuggled on board a ship and there hold a meeting. Word had already been sent to the boat to expect her, and the disguise brought. Because of an article in which an S.R. (Social Revolutionist) had mentioned that the work was going on well in Kronstadt, sailors are not allowed to go ashore there; so meetings are held on the boats. (There was considerable consternation at this point when it was learned that I was not a Russian, but this gradually declined.) The girl said that at the last meeting she held, she went on board after leaving her papers to be destroyed if she didn't come back. She knew well that this might be her last piece of work, but she held the meeting between the decks at midnight and came out all right.

They claim that 15,000 out of 20,000 seamen, all the artillery, part of the infantry, and many officers are sympathetic. They say that one girl went as a governess for one of the officers, who proposed this in order to help her do her propaganda work. The program now consists in wet-blanketing the sailors, making them hold back until the proper time. Alcohol will be destroyed before the movement is started. Vodka caused the failure of the uprising before.

St. Petersburg
June 9, 1906

DEAR MOTHER: I came to the same conclusion as you, that there's no use "writing" to newspapers and trying to compete with telegraph men, who, by the way, are giving you simple drivel. So I have sent nothing to the *Tribune* for some time, and don't know as I will. I have concluded that it's better, after all, to stick to scholarship and let the money advantages of corresponding go. I shall forthwith stop worrying about money, though it will be hard. I have to take these men to lunch in order to get at them, and that adds up.

Crane cabled two days ago that he thought I might be taken on the embassy staff for the summer. That would interfere absolutely with my work, as the ambassador is very hard on his secretaries. So I shall not even ask if I might be used. I'll write to Crane more in detail about the matter in a day or so.

It is wonderful the amount of time one can waste in this country. I began this letter at six this afternoon in the Duma, started toward home at seven, and stepped in to say goodbye to a man who is being sent to a post in Siberia because of his free expression of liberal sentiments, when, like so many others, he thought that at last the government had raised the lid. I stopped in for dinner at our little correspondents' hangout and found the famous financier, Flint, there. Then I got into a conversation with the *New York Sun*'s correspondent, who, by the way, is the clearest-headed one here, and met a certain Durland, of some fame as a magazine writer, whom I brought to my room. He is in with the revolutionists and gave me some interesting information. And now it is 12:00 P.M. and time to think of going to bed.

I am rather glad I find this "popular" writing hard because it means that I will be satisfied with the purely scientific approach to any question, and soon the sensational approach will be completely overworked. I am not even using my camera. Well, I'll write up my notes for the day and turn in. I had hoped to go to the country tomorrow, but I must make some social calls and will go at it early.

[*From the notes*]
June 11, 1906

Scene in lobby of the Duma.

Little squabbles going on all over the lobby. Peasants laughingly divide the ministries. Aladin wants the Ministry of Marine. Another man spoke for the Finance Ministry as the most profitable. Considerable hilarity.

McGowan and Alkin talking. McGowan had written to the *Standard* that the Tartars do not understand literary Russian. He had seen them vote both ways on one question. Alkin was remonstrating with him. The article had been reprinted in a Kazan paper. Alkin asked McGowan if he had ever talked with any Tartars, and McGowan admitted that he had not. Alkin finally appeased by McGowan's promise to publish a letter from him to the editor.

ST. PETERSBURG
June 15, 1906

DEAR MOTHER: I have acquired a reputation at the Duma for chumming with the peasants. Some way I have become very intimate with several, and that has given me an entree to the others. I shall tell you someday how I took tea with a crowd of them one night.

William Jennings Bryan has been here two days. I had a long talk with him and interpreted for him in a conversation with a peasant. He wants me to come to see him in America and tell him more about my work. If he is our next president, I have not spent the morning in vain, for I devoted it to him and Mrs. Bryan.

I go to Finland Sunday (only an hour by train) to a political meeting.

There is no danger, though. No political meeting in this "constitutional" country!

The news of a new Jewish massacre made the state of excitement at the Duma all the more tense today. In addition, in answer to an interpellation, the Duma was told that the question did not concern it. Then a member of the Duma was threatened with prosecution because of an article in a newspaper. Four newspapers were confiscated yesterterday. The fourteen workmen deputies were accused of revolutionary propaganda because of a resolution which they sent out. The minister of war appeared yesterday and as much as said that military death sentences would go on, and was followed by cries of "Hangman!" and "Murderer!" as he left the hall. What is the government driving at? Nobody knows, everybody is afraid to imagine—and so we sit back and wait. The peasant disorders are beginning; and, of course, the revolutionists say, "It's come at last." I don't believe that, though. We are promised a grand strike here in less than ten days on account of the affair of the fourteen workmen deputies. I fortunately have at last come to look on these pessimistic prophecies as an interesting indication of the general psychology of this poor people. My side partner and I find it a great help to control our judgment by frequent comparisons of impressions, and thus insure a purely objective idea of the whole situation.

My, it is 1:00 A.M., but quite light outside. I have chosen 1:30–10:00 for sleep these last days. It seems the most convenient time, and it really makes no difference when one sleeps.

As I said before, I am not sending on any "correspondence" and feel much happier with that off my mind. One can't write about the Russian situation for a popular public that wants to know what's coming.

I'll think of you in the wilds of Wisconsin while I swelter away here. The heat is not intense; but it's damp and smelly (from the canals), dirty (from the streets), and noisy (from the cobblestones).

ST. PETERSBURG
June 24, 1906

DEAR PAUL: Had a fine time last Sunday at the revolutionary meeting in Finland. You should have seen me rowing with a crowd of well-known revolutionists under a red flag. I hope no secret service man got our picture. We had over eighty spies with us. But it was a farce as far as revolution goes—they only squabbled with each other. We have been giving these revolutionists too much credit for the reform movement. The air was great, though; and I sat on the sand until the sun began to set, and then came home to noisy St. Petersburg.

Word that the *Tribune* had sent checks cheered me up, and I wrote a letter to Keeley until two-thirty this morning. My work is going on very well. I have collected some interesting material from individuals and will be well supplied to give talks on Russia if I am invited to.

The weather has been ideal this last week, and I have done a lot of work. I lunch with the third secretary at the embassy today, and then come back to do some more writing. I am way behind in my correspondence and must catch up. . . . .

The situation continues the same. This Bialystok massacre (a pogrom) was an awful thing. I saw pictures of it that almost turned me sick. You will no doubt hear some wild stories about it, but here is the truth. It was started by the police. They were probably not put up to it by the government, but knew they would not be punished and would perhaps be rewarded. That is the way all these massacres have come about; formerly with more organized stimulus from the government. This one was probably the last echo of the former system. But so long as this system is not completely renovated, there can be no assurance against recurrence. That is why the Duma demands that the ministers get out.

It is a little disconcerting to note the rapid spread of anarchy all over the country. But a newspaperman told me that a great many of these reports were stories, not of facts, but of what ought to be done. In other words, newspapers are being used for propaganda purposes.

The tension continues to draw very tightly. The least rumor causes a small panic. I am assured this morning that the workmen are to break out in St. Petersburg tomorrow. One gets used to these scares. But at times, when such reports are received from someone whose judgment you have thought to trust, you cannot help hoping that at last it is coming. Not that I am for a revolution now—but I would like something to happen. This ridiculous situation has gone on for six weeks now. Newspapers are confiscated every day, and I have to pay my little boy extra for hiding a copy under his coat for me. The revolutionists are, of course, trying to discredit the Duma; the government is helping them do this. But if the moderate element can hang on a little longer, there is a possibility of a peaceful solution.

We have fresh bread again. The bakers struck four days ago, and the bread we got was becoming a little too stale. Well, I must go to bed, I suppose, or the birds will begin to sing and keep me awake. It's almost time for them to start.

St. Petersburg
June 30, 1906

Dear Mother: I am getting on beautifully with my work, only it's getting too interesting and I am getting more than I can handle. (Excuse all the "gettings." I am very tired.) W. E. Curtin of the *Record Herald* is here. I am writing five articles for him for which I get credit together with my English collaborator. Curtin wanted to pay us, but we decided to use him as our advertising agent. He is to write a column on the work this Englishman and I are doing here. Curtin offered to get me a job as correspondent for the *Daily News* at $250 a month. But it would have stopped my other work, which is too important.

I can't tell you what valuable material we are getting, and nobody else is going into the work the way we are. It's a shame, because there is so much more than we can handle. With all reserve, this movement will someday be of as great historical importance as the French Revolution. And it will be an honor to have lived through it and studied it.

I don't dare tell you all I am doing. I have done the first really risky thing tonight. A workman on the street, one of 43,000 unemployed in St. Petersburg, asked me for money. We brought him to my room and heard his story. It was not reassuring. But he was a little drunk, fortunately. He may be a spy, but we took our precautions against that. He is to take us to the headquarters of the workers' organization on Wednesday and give us copies of all their proclamations, etc. We are going to get these materials and then drop this line of investigation, as it might lead to trouble. Don't mention this, please, in answer. They say the censor is at work again, although I don't believe it.

It's not little that they say these days. But everyone is far from normal—the nervous strain is getting slightly disagreeable. I am glad the bakers have stopped their strike and that I can get my cookies to serve with tea.

If nothing else, I am advertising myself. Helped a certain Flint, well-known promoter of grand business schemes, who was very grateful to me for a lot of things and people I put him on to. Curtin is to arrange for me to give a lecture at the Historical Association in Washington. I am almost tempted to stay on here until January 1. No, as I think of it when I see this date before me, you can expect me back September 30, as planned.

About the situation, nobody knows what is coming. I personally think the deadlock can continue another month, perhaps even two. And the prospects of a peaceful issue are good, I feel sure. If, however, many more mistakes are made, there will be trouble, and you can be sure it will be a frightful breakup. Then little Sammie rushes across the frontier, which, fortunately, is not many miles off. The rebellion in the Emperor's own battalion is the most serious thing that happened last week. The stories of discontent in the army have been exaggerated; but this is a fact, only too true, I am afraid.

I am becoming really intimate with several prominent Duma members. You read of Aladin, perhaps. I went boating with him one day and often drink tea with him. Petrunkevitch always stops to say good day and promises to give me another interview any time I want one. Milyukov is getting a little impressed with his own importance, but Kovalevsky is always cordial and jovial and takes the trouble to talk with me for a minute or so every day. The peasants are almost a nuisance with their friendliness. Tomorrow, Sunday, is to be an easier day for me, though I have an appointment with the priest, Gregory Petrov, the liberal priest of the movement, who was pointed out as the probable religious reformer of Russia two years ago. I must go to bed. It is almost two o'clock.

St. Petersburg
July 7, 1906

Dear Paul: I wish I could begin to tell you what I have done today. I got hold of some documents which I shall publish if I can find a magazine that will take them. They will prove that the massacres these last years were organized. But I must get my mind off all this business. I think nothing but politics these days. Had dinner with Judge Anderson of the Supreme Court. Mother will know him. He is from Cambridge. Recognized me by resemblance. Is here sight-seeing. I told him of my work, and he was much interested. Showed him all the prominent men when he came to Duma. Tonight I gave him a two-hour account of the Russian reform movement. He is going to arrange another lecture for me in Washington while I am there to speak at the Historical Society meeting next winter. Hurrah! That makes four lectures I am already booked to give.

Things look a little more serious. I did my investigating among unemployed workmen and got out all right. But I shan't monkey around with them any more. The revolutionists are doing their level best to force an issue and start bloodshed. The government, in its continued blindness, does everything to help them. The Duma is still buffeting off both sides—though showing distinct signs of weakening. These blamed Russians lack backbone and stamina. They can't stand a little punishment, though perhaps they have stood all they are physically and mentally capable of standing. Milyukov and his party are in a blue funk— they are playing a ticklish game, trying to keep in with the radicals and yet not become radical themselves. If they would only stand up and be honest instead of seeming to countenance the revolutionary tendency with a view to bringing it back to reasonableness. Here I am off again— I must go to bed because it is raining and delightfully dark.

St. Petersburg
July 15, 1906

Dear Charlie: Things are getting rather serious. And for the first time I begin to see real danger ahead. I don't think it will come before I leave, but there is no telling. I go to the country in ten days for a week or so.

Am continuing to see many interesting people. Spent the evening with Aladin, about whom the papers speak so much. Often see the revolutionists, people whose last name one never asks. But I recognize their emptiness and irresponsibility more clearly every day and dread to think

49

what will happen if they succeed in their mad plan of getting up a genuine bloody revolution.

The moderates are losing their hold more and more, it would seem. The government is doing its best to help the revolutionists and kill the reformers. It makes me boil over to see how utterly blind our "Grand Master" is. If he isn't careful, he will lose the respect of the peasants. But there will be no real disorders, I am sure, until autumn.

[*From the notes*]
July 20, 1906

Labor group very much put out. Are going to draw up their own appeal to the people. So are the Cadets. But printing shops have all received word that resolutions of the Duma are not to be printed. Duma press telephones that the matrix of the resolutions got spoiled. General feeling of unrest, but no anxiety. Astrof tells me, however, that this is the last day. Cadets still strutting around. Milyukov and Cadets have been defeated. No longer have authority inside or out. In the evening Ratchinsky says that he was told for sure that the Duma will be dissolved.

[*From the diary*]
July 21, 1906

Agrarian Commission meets.

St. Petersburg
July 22, 1906

Dear People: The Duma is dismissed. It has been expected these last three days, but we never believed the government would go that far. Martial law declared here—city full of soldiers. There will probably be a Constituent Assembly in Finland tomorrow. I shall go, and am off to the appointed place tonight. This means revolution, of course. I shall not go to the country, but stay here in St. Petersburg. Don't worry over the reports of the next weeks. I shall be careful.

[*From the diary*]
July 22, 1906

The ukase of dissolution issued. Parties all meet secretly. The labor-group men's rooms are searched. Stakhovitch turns pale when news comes, and decides to go to Finland and try to hold them back. Labor group takes morning boat for Viborg. Cadets hold meeting and decide to go to Finland; also, Social Democratic Poles send delegation. All get off without trouble. *Veslo* says that it was decided Tuesday night. Emperor says keep order, don't spare victims. Goremykin (successor to Witte as premier) could not stand for the game, nor Stishinsky, and went out. Stolypin becomes premier. Rodzyanko goes to Peterhof. Attempt to bomb the latter Saturday night.

Meeting opened at 8:00 A.M., 176 present. 47 Cadets against appeal. Milyukov brings them around. Commission of six, two from each principal group; Constitutional Democrats, Social Democrats, and labor group draw up appeal. Governor sends word that meeting must stop or martial law. This did not have the effect on decision that the newspapers stated. Wonderful display of harmony and common sense at this meeting. Everybody showed his best side. Little of the petty wrangling which characterized the last meeting of the Duma, though the Social Democrats and labor group of course wanted something more radical. Poles sent delegates to say that they sympathized but could not join in because they were instructed to work for autonomy and must draw up an appeal apart for their constituents.

Heyden and Stakhovich came on but saw they could do nothing to influence decision and went home. No "nonparty" peasants. They asked who was the *starshima* (elder) in St. Petersburg and were told the *gradonachalnik* (mayor), and went to him. Asked that the Emperor be told they were going home. Lithuanian Poles did not take part in conference (but two days later drew up their own communication to their constituents). 176 signed appeal. Ride home quite calm. No demonstration at station. Many copies of appeal printed and brought in.

Perhaps those who signed the appeal (216 in all after the list was brought to St. Petersburg) will be prosecuted and their trial delayed during the next elections, so as to exclude them.

We foreign students and correspondents made the journey to Viborg with the deputies and traveled back with them, some of us bringing in a batch of the deputies' appeals as printed under the free conditions at Viborg. This was one of the few occasions when I was forced by circumstances to become, in fact, involved in Russian politics. I admit I shared the nervousness of the returning deputies; but the Russian authorities touched neither them nor us, and the people paid no attention to the appeal.

Nor did the agrarian disorders begin, as we had all anticipated. On my return home that autumn it was interesting to read in the *Chicago Tribune*, which I was supposed to represent but to which I rarely sent dispatches, how blood flowed in the streets of St. Petersburg those next days. Actually, there were only a few drunken brawls, though we all expected trouble. Russian bureaucracy had gauged the situation better than had the Russian liberals or we outsiders.

CHAPTER VII

THE REACTION; TRAVELS IN RUSSIA

I RETURNED TO CHICAGO IN SEPTEMBER AND BEGAN MY FORMAL TEACHING at the university that autumn quarter. During the academic years 1906–9 I was first assistant instructor, then associate, in Russian language and institutions, and for administrative purposes I was put in the Department of Comparative Philology. The response to my course in elementary Russian was reasonably encouraging. Even several colleagues who wanted to acquire a reading knowledge of Russian took this course. But the courses in Russian political institutions which I offered with the idea of developing a more general interest in my field were, on the whole, poorly attended. A few outside organizations invited me to lecture on Russian affairs, but the number of these was relatively small. It was difficult to explain to Western minds the peculiar social-economic conditions of this country of eastern Europe and Asia. Also, few seemed particularly interested. Although an active interest in things Russian had developed during President Roosevelt's mediation in the Russo-Japanese War and during the spectacular events of the 1905 revolution, it was now definitely waning.

As my three-year term at the university was drawing to a close, President Judson, with his usual outspokenness, expressed his doubts as to the future of Russian studies in America in general, and particularly at Chicago. With his conservative outlook, he had decided that the Russians were a nuisance and had nothing constructive to offer to the progress of the world. When I explained this situation to Mr. Crane, he agreed that it might be wise temporarily to discontinue the Russian studies at the university; and this I did in 1909.

Meanwhile I set off for Russia each April, joined up with Pares to continue our co-operative study, and returned in the autumn to resume my teaching. During the three springs and summers of 1907, 1908, and 1909 Pares and I would first go to St. Petersburg to attend the Duma and then start out on trips to the provinces and the peasant villages.

The second Duma convened in March, 1907, and, like the first, was dissolved after sixty-odd days. From the point of view of the government, it was a less satisfactory body than the first. It was also less effective in its legislative work. The liberals who had led the first group were disfranchised for signing the Viborg appeal. They were all under trial at the time of the second elections and were therefore ineligible to take part. In fact, their trial was still pending when the third Duma was elected, and they were deprived of their civil rights a second time. This group included the cream of the liberal parties, which were consequently less well represented in the later Dumas—in quality as well as quantity.

Many other liberals were excluded by new interpretations of certain articles in the electoral law, after the dissolution of the first Duma. These interpretations were all directed toward limiting the franchise, and the most important was that which redefined the peasant voter. In the first election, all of peasant origin voted as peasants. One example will be sufficient to show what the new definition meant. Alexis Aladin, one of the ablest members of the first Duma, was of peasant origin, though he had been a student of the university, a workman in London, a newspaperman, and a socialist worker. He came back from exile after the October manifesto, went down to the village where he was still a member of the village commune, was elected night watchman so that he would be in paid civil service, and thus was eligible for election. But for the second elections, it was decided that a peasant must not only belong to a peasant commune but must also be a *householder* in that commune to be entitled to a vote. This consequently excluded all the peasant "intelligents"—village schoolteachers, agricultural experts, village doctors, men of peasant origin, and men living with the peasants and knowing their conditions of life—but not actual peasants, in the sense of cultivators of the soil. The peasants had elected many such "intelligents" to the first Duma, realizing that these men would represent peasant interests and would be better fitted to advocate them in a national assembly. Thousands were disfranchised by this interpretation. Other such interpretations limited the vote of the small landowner and the workman; there were wholesale and individual exclusions on separate and various charges. Professor Kovalevsky was excluded because his janitor gave the wrong date of the signing of the lease for his apartment. The mistake was corrected, but only after the election lists had been finally confirmed.

The Socialists, including the Bolsheviks, who had boycotted the first Duma, had decided that the institution could be used for propaganda purposes; there were forty-five Social Democrats in the second Duma. Conservatives and reactionaries, calling themselves "Russian Nationalists," also decided to go into the Duma in order to disrupt from within this "Western" institution which they believed to be alien to Russian thought and life. Non-Russian elements, such as the Poles, found themselves able to determine votes by siding now with the left, now with the right or center. The government continued to boycott the Duma, or to scold it, when the ministers condescended to answer the interpellations addressed to them.

The sessions of the Duma were marked by constant storms, many deliberately provoked from the extreme left or from the extreme right. One evening the physician of the Duma, himself a member, remarked to Pares and me, with whom he was dining, that his whole supply of bromides had been used up that afternoon. Pares and I had watched this performance of nerves from the press box with more discouragement than amusement.

One of the stormy meetings of this second session of the Russian parliament was over the eternal Russian-Polish question. Some of us foreigners felt a certain responsibility for what happened that afternoon. The Polish leader Roman Dmowsky had invited us all to a luncheon, and he had felt it necessary to honor each of the nationalities represented by serving what he thought was the national drink of each country. We were having a very pleasant time when a message from the Duma called Dmowsky to participate in the debate which someone had started over the Polish question. The picture of the group driving madly to the Tauride Palace in rattling Russian cabs was very amusing; it was a hot day, and the drive did not sober us. Dmowsky, on arrival, had to ascend the rostrum immediately; and it was on this occasion that he explained the difficulty of Polish-Russian relations with the unfortunate statement: "Your government is Asiatic."

The second Duma, like the first, was dissolved as unworkable. This time the date for new elections was set, but it was announced that the election law would be changed. Such a change, under the new Fundamental Laws, would require the vote of the Duma; but a change in the election laws was the last thing to be expected from the Duma as constituted. In this deadlock the Tsar resorted to "prerogative" and established the new law by the imperial decree of June 16, 1909, the last paragraph of which reads:

All these changes in the method of election cannot be made by the usual method of legislation through that Duma, the composition of which has been judged unsatisfactory by us, as a result of the very method of election of its members. Only that authority which gave the first electoral law, the historic right of the Russian Tsar, has the power to repeal the electoral law and replace it by another.

This action was one of several which supported the characterization of the political regime in Russia during this period as "a constitutional monarchy with an autocratic sovereign." On the basis of such acts the Bolsheviks have insisted that "tsarism prevailed in Russia until December, 1917."

In 1908 and 1909 Pares and I found the third Duma, elected under the new law, less interesting. Measures to insure against a third liberal Duma had been most carefully and ingeniously worked out; and the new law secured to the landlord class the large urban property-owners, and the Russian element in the non-Russian provinces a weighted representation. In this Duma there were 76 extreme rightists, 40 rightists, 155 Octobrists (rightists favoring a constitutional form of government), 52 progressivists, 46 Constitutional Democrats, 35 leftists (including the national groups), and 28 extreme leftists and socialists. Thus the opposition now had only a third of the total number of its members, whereas in the first Duma there had been but 38 Octobrists, only an unorganized group of rightists, practically no extreme rightists, and the rest of the membership had belonged to the opposition under the leadership of the Constitutional Democrats, with 184 members.

These years, 1907–9, brought certain progress to Russian life. Although reactionary tendencies in the government were growing stronger, the Duma as an institution survived and was useful educationally. The crisis of 1905–6 had aroused the country, and the partial success of the revolution had made it possible for new social forces to work in the economic field. There was also a succession of good harvests, and the peasants became engrossed in the new agrarian program being forced upon them.

Among the intellectuals, however—particularly those of the younger generation—these years were definitely a period of decadence. Disappointment, disillusionment, and "Tsaninism" (named for the writer Tsanin), or intellectual hooliganism, prevailed. The writings of the extreme revolutionaries who had escaped arrest and emigrated abroad pictured the revolution as a complete failure. These "professional revolutionaries," among whom the outstanding figures were Lenin and Trotsky, spent their time in polemics and disputes over the causes of the failure. Such writings blinded many to the very real progress which was going on in Russia.

The remnants of the revolutionary organization of 1905 within Russia took two main lines, as they had when earlier revolutionary efforts had failed. One group tried to revive and extend terrorism. It was discredited when a former chief of police revealed from the Duma tribune that Azev, the head of the terrorist organization, was, and had been for many years, in the pay of the police and was therefore a "provocatory agent." I had on one occasion in Paris met this famous Azev, whose treason the real revolutionaries found it hard to believe. The other and larger group of the revolutionaries who remained in Russia went into the co-operative movement—as a matter of principle and also as a useful cover. The "professional revolutionaries" in the exile centers of Switzerland and France, to which they had returned, inveighed against this backsliding, but to little avail, for political reaction was strong in the public as well as in the government.

As part of my purely academic studies in Russia during this period, I did considerable work on the matter of "exceptional measures," a procedure introduced as provisional in 1881 after the assassination of the Emperor Alexander II and continued thereafter. Under this procedure both the political police and ordinary administrative authorities were given the widest discretion for the preservation of "public peace and order." It was under these measures, for example, that Russians were sent into exile without a trial and that newspapers were fined without a hearing. In pursuance of the topic I came to know Vladimir Deryuzhinsky, professor of administrative law at the University of St. Petersburg, who was also editor of the *Journal* of the Ministry of Justice. Under his wing I gained access to higher official circles and became particularly well acquainted with the Saburov family. Alexander Saburov was a senator and also a member of the Imperial Council. During a period of liberalism at the beginning of the eighties he had been minister of education. Mme Saburov was on the board of directors of the Imperial Conservatory of Music.

Every Sunday night the Saburovs were at home to their friends; and in their enormous apartment overlooking the Neva, groups of forty or fifty guests would gather after eleven o'clock, many coming from the Sunday-night ballet, which was one of the social functions of the capital. These "evenings," like most Russian "evenings," lasted far into the morning. The Saburovs' salon was probably one of the most interesting and politically important in St. Petersburg. The tone, if not the actual tendency, of those who gathered there was definitely liberal. Many of the guests held high official positions, and it was from association with them that I came to realize that not all bureaucrats were utter obscurantists. This group was comparatively small, however, and its influence was growing weaker with the advance of reaction. Under the aegis of those adventurers and charlatans to whom the unhappy Russian sovereigns were already turning in their developing mysticism, the worst elements of bureaucracy were gradually gaining control of the government.

On one occasion I was able to feel for a short time this court atmosphere against which not only my liberal but also my conservative friends were struggling. The Grand Duchess Marie, favorite niece of the Emperor, was to marry the Swedish Crown Prince. As there were few American newspapermen at the time in St. Petersburg, the Associated Press representative, Beach Conger, persuaded me to use my newspaper credentials to apply for admission; he didn't want to go alone. This entailed wearing evening dress at eight in the morning again and a trip to the Summer Palace of Peterhof. The group of correspondents, Russian and foreign, were shown through the palace and then lined up in one of the many reception rooms through which the wedding party was to pass. We had orders to stand at attention, with our white gloved hands close to our sides. Twice the procession passed in front of us at a distance of only a few feet. I tried to get a direct look into the furtive eyes of the Emperor of all the Russias, and succeeded for only a second. The cold beauty of the Empress was impressive but bore witness to the stories current about her unhappy and unfortunate attitude toward her adopted country. All the court dignitaries passed before us; and from their faces I got full confirmation of the view prevalent in Duma circles, that one of the chief aims of the public leaders must be to break down the walls that surrounded the sovereign and to work against the influence of his immediate entourage.

We observers were given a good luncheon and sent home in imperial carriages and railway cars. When Conger and I got out of our dress clothes, we felt much relieved but also much concerned over what we had seen and felt. As Conger succinctly put it: "They were a terrible bunch of morons." To justify using my press card, I sent out a newsletter, which fortunately was not printed. Many years later, when I was presented to the Grand Duchess Marie here in America, I expressed frankly my impression of the people at her wedding. She not only confirmed my judgment of the old imperial court but related many incidents which made the picture even darker.

In this period, 1906–9, Pares and I spent the second half of our visits in travel. Every year we went regularly, as guests, to the Petrunkevitch estate of Mashuk, some fifteen miles from Torzhok. Torzhok, the district center of the province of Tver, was a place of considerable historical interest. It had been on the St. Petersburg-Moscow stagecoach route until the railway connecting the two capitals displaced the stagecoach. This railway did not pass through Torzhok because it was not on the straight line which Nicholas I had drawn by ruler to settle the discussion as to the route of the first railway. The tavern of Torzhok was famous for some of the national Russian dishes. This district had been the center of liberalism for several generations. Many Decembrists had their estates there. The Bakunin family, long noted for liberalism, hailed from Torzhok. And the recognized leader of the contemporary period of Russian liberalism, Ivan Petrunkevitch, had come to this district because of its liberal traditions.

Ivan Petrunkevitch had been chosen to make the first speech in Russia's first parliament because of his great contributions to the cause of Russian liberalism. During the sessions of the first Duma, Pares and I had come to know him: and he had invited us to visit his estate. His son Michael, who was living there, was president of the zemstvo of Tver, one of the most progressive Russian district assemblies, not only politically, but also in the fields of public health and education.

It was shortly after the dissolution of the first Duma that Pares and I made our first expedition to Torzhok. From the Petrunkevitch estate we journeyed down to the surrounding villages, where we interviewed every type, from landowner to priest, and studied the work of the district zemstvo. Life with the Petrunkevitches was delightful, and the work of the zemstvo was heartening; but living conditions among the village peasants were primitive indeed. It was my first experience with rural Russia and, following immediately on the intense disappointment of the Duma dissolution, left me considerably depressed. I wrote to my brother from one of these villages:

Dear Paul:

Here I am in the country. It's a change, but I am feeling pretty blue today. Am glad I have come, for it has opened my eyes to much in this godforsaken Russia. We are being well received by everybody so far. Visited the hospital where a nephew of Schlippenbach's is head doctor. Saw victims of disorders which took place last week. The hooligans are at work here. I dare write you this because I shall be out of it in a week. But we have concluded we must be most careful while here. With the government on top now, the police and hooligans are starting in with their dirty work. The streets are full of drunken beggars, who, we are told, are men who have been released from prison and sent home from Moscow. They certainly are a mean-looking lot.

It is very late, but I am afraid to go to bed. I have found three varieties of insects on me this evening—two bedbugs, three fleas, and one of a brand unknown to me but extremely annoying. There is a continual rattling outside. Every house has a watchman, who must rattle the kind of instrument we use at football games, only with a doleful sound, every ten minutes, to show that he is awake.

Although Petrunkevitch was devoting his life to improving the material and cultural conditions of the peasants, the latter always saw in him the landlord. In 1907, after the dissolution of the second Duma, the neighboring peasants tried to burn out the Petrunkevitch buildings, with the idea that then his land would come to them. On that occasion I had to aid my host in the protection of his property, which ruined my standing with the peasants. These same peasants, however, came to the aid of the Petrunkevitches in 1917, and, when finally forced by the Bolshevik agitators to take over the estate, helped them escape. In my later trips, even as late as 1936, I was always able to see members of this family and to get from them a useful interpretation of the events of the Soviet period usually given in terms of the pre-Soviet times. From my talks with them I have come to know the pre-Soviet period in the fullest detail.

On an early journey we stopped over for a day at the estate of Tolstoy. Both of us had expected much of this visit; but it was, in fact, a disappointment. William Jennings Bryan had preceded us by a few weeks, and he and Tolstoy had discussed the single-tax theory of Henry George. With us, too, Tolstoy insisted on discussing this subject, and also Bryan's chances in the coming presidential election, at the same time expressing rather open contempt for the political institutions of the West which were being introduced into his country. On the subject of the Russian peasant, to which our questions were directed, Tolstoy would not talk.

In our broader travels Pares and I went down the Volga by boat, starting from its very headwaters at Tver. At Kazan we took a trip eastward, through Vyatka and Perm, covering many miles of these predominantly peasant provinces of the northeast on horseback. Another year we started at Samara and went the rest of the way down the Volga, working westward across the Ukraine, through Voronezh and Kharkov to Kiev. On a third trip we made a circle to the southeast of Moscow and traveled westward and back to Moscow along the old trade route of the earliest period of Russian history. Those of us who have "done" rural Russia have always had to face the problem of picking up something. Bedbugs and fleas were a commonplace experience. Often we cut our tours short as a protection against lice. Pares and I had traveled the areas where mild cholera was present. Precautions against skin diseases and syphilis were not always effective and were a nuisance. I always carried my own sheets and towels, a folding rubber bathtub, and a first-aid kit. The danger of infection and the menace of the omnipresent bedbug in this country of wooden structures was what made traveling in Russia heroic. Otherwise, in country, as in city, one was reasonably safe, except, of course, in the periods of peasant rioting and actual civil war. One avoided traveling at night over desolate country roads. I generally carried a revolver when roaming around the country, but only once did I have to draw it. Pares and I had lured a peasant to ferry us across a mile-wide lake. He had asked for an advance on the price to get a bit to eat; but what he got was vodka, as we discovered when he wanted to take a swim in the middle of the lake. The point of the revolver had a sobering effect; and he was most contrite when we reached the shore, and literally embraced us when he saw that we were not going to turn him over to the police.

In our trips through Russia in those years Pares and I constantly studied the working-out of Stolypin's agrarian reforms of 1906. Both of us were then inclined to see in the active promotion of private property among the peasants a sign of progress, political as well as economic. The old Russian communal system of land tenure had interested us, as it had earlier students, as something peculiar and novel. But both of us had been brought up in individualistic systems, and, of course, believed in their principles, as did all Russian liberals. We were, nevertheless, concerned to see the extent of governmental pressure behind the new land policy, and the disruption and demoralization which it was producing in many communities which we visited. Our concern was somewhat lessened by the fact that an apparently genuine co-operative movement was spreading rapidly among the peasants, supported by the government as well as by the radicals. The government promoted it to facilitate the breaking-up of the communes. The radicals used it to keep alive the peasants' socialist views through the period of reaction.

In these years I rarely visited the American embassy. When I did drop in for mail, I found that the staff was little interested in the internal situation and that our diplomatic relations were rather meager. But naturally I sought friends in the American colony, as a relief from too much Russian; and here I found not only congenial playmates but people from whom I could learn much about Russian ways and methods. The American colony in St. Petersburg was comparatively small, and its dean was W. E. Smith, of the Westinghouse Company. Mr. Smith, from long residence in Russia, was more Russian than American, and he tended to keep other Americans at a distance. The Westinghouse Company had received a contract to electrify the streetcar network of both St. Petersburg and Moscow; and its chief engineer, Harvey E. Molé, most often represented the company in the social life of the capital. Perhaps the real leader of the American group was Frederick M. Corse, of the New York Life Insurance Company, whose place became my St. Petersburg home.

These Americans did not associate very much with the British or German groups, although there were two places of common interest to the Americans and the British: the English church and the golf club at Murino, a small Finnish village about twenty miles north of the center of St. Petersburg. Not knowing how long they would be stationed in Russia, and recognizing the difficulties of the Russian language, few of these Americans ever tried to learn it. This made them dependent for information on interpreters and on those Russians who spoke English, and tended to isolate them from things Russian. Most of them used Finnish servants, because these were cleaner and could speak a little German. Quite naturally they often developed an anti-Russian complex, which handicapped them in business—a situation which has continued even into the Soviet period.

From these Americans I heard much of the intricacies of Russian bureaucratic administration with which their firms constantly had to struggle. I also learned something from them about the industrial-workman class, the group in Russia with which I found it most difficult to have direct contact. The workmen, like the students, were particularly suspect as to political trustworthiness and were carefully watched by the police. The American employers tried to create somewhat better wage and working conditions in their factories than prevailed in Russia generally, although their efforts were constantly hindered by police regulations. Their estimate of the abilities of the Russian workman was high. They found that the young peasant from the village soon learned to handle machinery and to adapt himself to factory conditions. But these American businessmen had to reconcile themselves to a much lower standard of productivity than they could get in America. I often found consolation over the small amount of work that I accomplished, in the generally accepted view that in Russia one was lucky to have done a half days's work in a day.

Among my American friends in St. Petersburg, there were few who ever ventured farther beyond the large cities than the golf course in the

Finnish village. I therefore felt I should do missionary work for the two families, the Corses and Molés, who were my closest friends; and I invited them to visit some peasant villages with me in the informal fashion which Pares and I had adopted. Our first night was spent at old and famous Novgorod, at that time one of the more backward provincial centers. The limited quarters in the tavern and the noise and dirt rising from the courtyard, where some thirty peasant carts stopped for the same night, put my friends in a bad state of mind that first morning. The drive through the Russian countryside, where no fences interrupted the long view of rolling plains, and our brief stops at picturesque spots along the way made things look somewhat brighter by late afternoon. But toward evening, according to my usual custom, I sought lodgings in the nearest village and gave my city friends their first experience in peasant huts. The next morning I found them fully ready to take the earliest train back to St. Petersburg and bathtubs. Later these friends thanked me for introducing them to the real Russia, for they had been seeing only those centers which, as one friend put it, were the rosebuds fertilized by the rest of the country.

♻ ♻ ♻

CHAPTER VIII

I TRAIN MYSELF IN POLITICAL SCIENCE
COLUMBIA UNIVERSITY

AT THE END OF THE ACADEMIC YEAR 1908–9 I GAVE UP MY POSITION AT the University of Chicago and accepted a university fellowship at Columbia, in the Faculty of Political Science. Because of political developments in Russia, I was being drawn, as already noted, to the study of contemporary politics. My graduate work had been largely philological, and I felt that my Russian studies lacked precision because of my insufficient training in the disciplines of the social sciences. I have sometimes reflected that I might have had a more sedate academic life had I remained in the field of linguistics. The Bolshevik revolution of November, 1917, for example, which created so many problems for the student of social science, concerned the linguist only in so far as the new government passed an edict simplifying Russian spelling.

Another motive for going to Columbia was to equip myself for teaching European history or political science, for I doubted if enough interest in the Russian field would develop to justify complete concentration on it. In subsequent years I have always advised graduate students to consider Russian studies as something of a luxury, which they might work in on the side while teaching modern history or international relations.

My course of study at Columbia included European history, under James Harvey Robinson and James Shotwell; American history, under Robinson and Charles Beard; and public law and politics, under Munro Smith, Frank Goodnow, and again Beard. I also took courses with Seligman, Simkhovich, and Giddings. In all these courses I naturally related my studies to the contemporary Russian field in which I had been working in a practical way. Knowing of this special interest, my teachers were constantly calling for illustrations from Russian history and politics, and my papers were almost always in some way related to Russia.

As a fellow, I was given the privileges of the Faculty Club, and here I came to know younger men in other departments as well as my own. It was in that old building on the corner of One Hundred and Sixteenth Street and Amsterdam Avenue, reputedly a former insane asylum, that I acquired much of what I learned during my two years at Columbia. Among my friends there were Walter Pitkin, Carl Van Doren, Richard Montague, and Fred Keppel, then secretary to President Butler; and among the graduate students, Thomas Reed Powell, Ted Sait, Carleton Hayes, William Ogburn, and Gelhke. I also became a member of the "F.H.G.," an informal group which gathered twice a week at the home of Professor Franklin H. Giddings to discuss specific problems and drink beer. Many of Giddings' former students continued to come to these gatherings, including the Kellogg brothers, who were later to organize the *Survey*. Like the long discussions during and after dinner at the Faculty Club, these evenings in the home of Professor Giddings provided excellent practical training in the social sciences. At no other academic institution have I ever found so many opportunities for real discussion as at Columbia in those years.

My continued interest in Russian developments led me to get in touch with some of the many radical groups in New York City; and I went first to the group which Emma Goldman, anarchist and revolutionary, had gathered around her publication *Mother Earth*. I was already acquainted with Emma Goldman. In 1907 a Russian dramatic troupe, headed by Orlenev and Nazimova, had come to Chicago. Both these artists had been trained in the Moscow Art Theatre, and their repertory included the works of Chekhov, Gorky, and such. They also played Ibsen's masterpieces. Although their playing was in Russian, their acting was of such excellence that it delighted many Americans who could not understand the dialogue. The secretary and general manager of this group was a Miss Emma Smith, who was of Russian origin and clearly had a thorough knowledge of Russian literature. She always accompanied Orlenev and Nazimova as interpreter when they were entertained socially; and in this way I met her at many homes, including that of the Russian consul general, Baron Schlippenbach, a Baltic nobleman who often looked askance at some of my liberal Russian connections.

On the evening before the Russians left Chicago, Miss Smith called me aside and said she felt she must tell me who she really was, lest the fact leak out and be misinterpreted. It was then that she told me she was Emma Goldman. She had offered her services to the Russian artists because of her interest in Russian literature and also because she wanted to protect them from the exploitation to which she saw they were being subjected when they arrived and began the arrangements for their tour. She added that she would never refer, in her political activities, to any of the people whom she had met while acting as interpreter, nor to the views she had heard expressed in these homes of our Gold Coast; and, so far as I know, she adhered strictly to her decision. I believe that, even now, many who entertained Emma Goldman in Chicago are unaware of the fact, although they will undoubtedly recall this very intelligent and gracious person who could talk so well on literary subjects!—particularly on Russian literature.

It was to Emma Goldman, then, that I went in 1909, shortly after taking up residence in New York. Around *Mother Earth* she had gathered quite a number of sympathizers, including Alexander Berkman and Hippolyte Havel. At their general gatherings, particularly at the "international" dances organized under the auspices of *Mother Earth*, one met all sorts of people. The most interesting were the "wrecks" whom Emma Goldman was trying to save. At the more informal meetings I was often greeted as the "bourgeois friend," to which I once retorted by calling attention to the fact that I smoked a cheaper grade of cigarette than did these revolutionary leaders. The intellectual snobbishness which these "leaders" often showed—Emma Goldman less than some of the others—was rather disturbing. Unconsciously I must have acquired a touch of it myself, for one morning at the Faculty Club, in describing a gathering of the evening before, I allowed myself to say that I had sat at the table where were gathered "those of brains and standing." For many months I had to hear this phrase flung back at me unmercifully by my friends.

There were other centers, chiefly modest restaurants, which these radicals frequented, where I would often drop in late in the evening to pick up news on "the progress of the Revolution." The conversation was much like that I had heard among the Russian refugees in Paris, who had, in fact, achieved their revolution of 1905. The young American revolutionaries were just as assured as the Russians had been; and much of their discussion was based on the Russian revolution of 1905, its weaknesses and the causes of its failure. Often fellow-students or younger members of the faculty would ask me to take them to these meetings. Sometimes we would take our girls along, too, and I have to admit that even for me there was a certain element of slumming in these expeditions.

From these connections I soon drifted into a more strictly American group of reformers. At the Washington Square apartment of Mary

Heaton Vorse, I met repeatedly such liberals as Arthur Bullard, Sinclair Lewis, Will Irwin, Max Eastman, and Hutchins Hapgood, to discuss the injustices and iniquities of American life. As I was trying to extend my knowledge of social conditions from Russia to my own country, I found these discussions particularly interesting, for I had neglected American problems in my concentration on those of Russia. In the spirit of research rather than that of idle curiosity, we developed the habit of finishing off a night by visiting the night court at Haymarket Square. But it was surely in the spirit of bravado that we organized what we called "a meeting of outcasts." Fortunately, our efforts to publicize this meeting were unsuccessful. It was a dismal little gathering, and we all agreed not to talk much about the discussion or its leading participants.

These excursions into the radical world were part play and part work. The study of contemporary politics certainly required such contacts; and, happily for me, they led to unpleasant consequences only in one instance. A newspaperman covering one of the meetings sponsored by Emma Goldman saw a good story in the fact that the group contained instructors and graduate students from Columbia, and his write-up was fanciful and exaggerated. The next day I received word that President Butler wished to see me. He smiled in referring to the story; asked if we'd really had as good a time as the reporter suggested; and then discussed the possibility of a teaching position for me which had come to his notice. The publicity annoyed me more than it did him, however, for I found myself being rushed by certain members of the faculty and student body who wished to be taken to these exciting gatherings.

To temper the view of American life which I acquired in this leftist company, I sought out my eastern business friends. Because of former ties in Chicago, I saw a great deal of Mr. and Mrs. C. K. G. Billings, who had an enormous estate at the northern tip of Manhattan Island. Their nephew, Albert Ruddock, was studying at Columbia in preparation for entering the diplomatic service, and we were taking several courses together. I think he was sensitive about his wealth, but I did my best to put him at ease by always insisting that we go "dutch." It was very interesting to take him to some of the radical meetings which I have described above. There, of course, he was known only as a student at Columbia and was able to forget his family and his affluence.

I also visited the Molés, who had recently returned to New York from Russia. Having lived abroad for some ten years, they found it difficult to adjust themselves and longed for those very things in Russia which they had always complained of when they were there. In the little American community in St. Petersburg they were important people, while in the machinery of New York they found themselves very small cogs. I was to observe later another example of the problem of readjustment to American ways after long residence abroad, when the Corses returned in 1917. With the advent of Bolshevism the New York Life Insurance Company closed its business in Russia. From watching the experiences of these two families, I realized the wisdom of the rule which I had adopted when I began my foreign studies, to remain abroad not more than twelve months at any single stretch. But the woes of the Molés as they came back into American life helped me to understand the workings of our system, which was one of the objects of my two years' study at Columbia.

During these years Mr. Rockefeller was living in his New York house, just off Fifth Avenue, and I dined with him frequently. He was always very frank in his talks with me. As a boy I had been taken on visits to the Rockefellers at Cleveland and had learned there to play golf, which was then becoming popular in America. I recall one occasion in the late nineties, during a golf game in Cleveland, when he interrupted his drive, took some small change from his pocket, held it out to me, and asked if I thought it was tainted money. I was a polite guest and, boylike, managed to get the handful of coins. In the spring of 1904, when my father and I were at Lakewood, New Jersey, we often went to the Rockefeller place there. One day at lunch, after an introductory chuckle, Mr. Rockefeller got the attention of Madam McCormick—it was necessary for her to turn her ear trumpet toward you—and told her with much glee that his offered gift, refused by a western university, had been in stock of the International Harvester Company.

In 1909 we were reaching the end of a period of Standard Oil muckraking, and Mr. Rockefeller talked in detail about the articles of Ida Tarbell. He said he was convinced of her sincerity, and he admitted that in his early days the rules had been very loose. He was much interested in my Russian studies and also in my excursions into revolutionary circles in New York. With his usual candor he inquired about my radical friends and their views, and often showed a real interest and understanding but—eminently successful man that he was—with a touch of honest regret in his attitude toward those who, in his opinion, had not been able to take advantage of the many opportunities open to them. Mrs. Rockefeller, too, shared this attitude with a charming sincerity which was well illustrated one winter evening. As I started out in the cold to walk to the subway to return to Columbia, I was given an ingenious paper vest. She observed, as she tied the vest on me, that, if they only knew it, the poor could easily keep warm by putting newspapers under their shirts in this fashion.

During a later visit, after Mr. Rockefeller had started his practice of giving away dimes, I asked him what his purpose was. He answered that there were really two ideas in his mind. In the first place, when he gave them to children he wanted to see if they knew how to accept small favors gracefully, if they had been well brought up. The second and main reason was to start conversation. He explained how hard was the isolated life he had to live. While driving, he would stop to ask the way of, say an Italian laborer on the road, be recognized, and break the strain by giving the man a dime. Then by offering dimes to all the members of the man's family, he would get him to talk about his life and work.

In the early years of the Soviet period, I frequently called on Mr. Rockefeller when I came to New York; and in these later visits Mr. Rockefeller's greeting would often go straight to the subject about which I knew there would be questions.

"How are those Bolsheviks getting along without us capitalists?" he would demand. Even after an interval of several years he would throw back at me some statement I had made about the progress of the Soviet experiment. In 1935, during my last visit, his questioning was particularly detailed and sharp. That evening, after dinner, we did not play the usual game of numbers, in which the guests who won were given nickels or dimes by their host. Despite the remonstrance of Mr. Rockefeller's doctor against interrupting the rigid schedule which his patient had been following in hopes of attaining the hundred-year mark, we continued our conversation for a long while, and I was unusually frank in pointing out the trials and tribulations through which the capitalistic system had been passing since 1929.

The next morning Mr. Rockefeller was late for breakfast, and when he finally turned up, he declared that I had given him a bad night; that he was more worried than he had ever been in all his life before; but that he was confident the capitalistic system still contained enough constructive features to guarantee its survival. After breakfast he read a chapter from the Bible and, despite the cloudy day, made an appointment at the first tee for nine-thirty. That morning, at the age of ninety-six, he played his six holes with the lowest score of the summer. For some reason there was no gift of a dime as I said goodbye to catch my train, but because of the golf game I felt I was forgiven for the previous evening.

My friends in New York who saw me jumping from the East Side to Fifth Avenue, sometimes in the course of a single day, and dining first with Emma Goldman and then with the Rockefellers, often accused me of leading a double life. In point of fact, I was continuing in America the technique which I had adopted for the study of Russia. In Russia, class distinctions were, of course, sharper and more formalized, particularly as political crises developed. By observing the extremes in New York and comparing them to the extremes in Russia, I could see and feel that, despite the hopes and prophecies of my revolutionary friends, the social stratification in America was not so definite, and therefore was much less conducive to class struggle. Or as a Moscow Bolshevik put it: "The American bourgeoisie is of proletarian origin, and all your proletarians have bourgeois aspirations."

PART IV

MY ENGLISH-RUSSIAN PERIOD: 1911–13

CHAPTER IX

TEACHING AND LIFE AT THE UNIVERSITY OF LIVERPOOL

THE YEARS FROM 1911 TO 1913 MIGHT BE CALLED MY "ENGLISH PERIOD," since during the greater part of this time the University of Liverpool was the center of my operations. In December, 1910, while I was still at Columbia, Pares had broached the matter of my joining him on the staff of the university's new School of Russian Studies. His initiative and the financial backing of certain British industrialists interested in the Anglo-Russian agreement of 1907 had brought the school into being.

Four university posts for subjects connected with Russia had been established, and prominent English scholars in these fields from other institutions had also been invited to ally themselves with the school under the title of "members." The school therefore represented officially and practically the British center of interest in the general field of Russia. It was to issue a quarterly, the *Russian Review*, designed primarily for government officers, members of Parliament, universities, libraries, and editors of leading periodicals.

Although I would have preferred to be associated with an American institution, the time was not ripe for this, and Liverpool was the logical opportunity for me. Pares, who knew my work intimately, presented a dossier about me to the Council of the university. The professors with whom I had studied rallied nobly in my behalf, and I was recommended by Charles A. Beard, Vladimir Simkhovich, Munro Smith, and James Shotwell of Columbia University; Maxime Kovalevsky and Vladimir Deryuzhinsky of the University of St. Petersburg; Ernst Freund and Ferdinand Schevill of the University of Chicago; Paul Boyer of the Sorbonne; and Paul Milyukov of the University of Moscow. The Council was sufficiently persuaded; and on March 15, 1911, I was invited to accept a lectureship in Russian legal and institutional history for four years, with a salary of £250 a year. Only six months' residence each year was required, leaving me free for six months' work in Russia. I was also to serve as one of the editors of the *Russian Review.*

Thus, after finishing my examinations at Columbia in the spring of 1911, I sailed on the S.S. "Arabic" for Liverpool, expecting to stop there just long enough to be inducted into office and then go on to Russia for the rest of the summer. That was my arrangement with Pares. But, on arrival, I found that Pares himself had left suddenly for Russia, asking me to take his place at the university until he could return. The assassination of the Russian prime minister, Stolypin had prompted his departure, for he expected serious internal changes in Russia which might affect the work of the school. Pares proved to be a very difficult person with whom to co-operate. I am sure he will not resent this statement, since I must supplement it immediately by noting his complete loyalty to co-workers and his extreme devotion to what had become for him a "cause." It was just that his loyalty was sometimes qualified by his sense of mission, in the name of which he would rush ahead, regardless of consequences to others.

My letters to my mother in the summer and fall of 1911 indicate my first impressions of my new post.

LIVERPOOL, ENGLAND
June 11, 1911

DEAR MOTHER:

Things are going very well. It gives me quite a pleasant feeling to be doing administrative work and making decisions. I am head of the department with Pares away—two men under me and a secretary at my beck and call. It is gratifying to be in a responsible position. I am following your advice, perhaps too literally, and leading a saner life. Everything here is conducive to a quieter pace. Those last months at Columbia gave me such an excess of virtue that my conscience never flickers at an evening of light reading or an afternoon walk. But I am working enough to keep out of mischief.

The people here are remarkably cordial—already I must take measures against entertaining. Yesterday I took a long walk with a young lawyer, ending up with tea in his delightful English garden. This morning I loafed around, lunched with the Vice-Chancellor, and then went for tea to Mrs. Paton's, the good woman who gave the money for my chair. She lives outside Liverpool in a small but charming old estate. An older brother was there, a Scotchman and an intimate friend of old Dr. Bruce, whom you will remember. I stayed for supper and have just got home (11 P.M.). So you see, in a day and a half I have got acquainted with three families with invitations to drop in at any time. What an advantage a foreigner has in this place. I must admit it is somewhat of a strain to be meeting so many people, especially as I have a distinct responsibility on my shoulders; but there is a satisfaction in it all that I hardly expected to find. Pares' absence has perhaps been a good thing, for it has put me more on my metal, and it has made people put themselves out more for me, in sympathy for my rather difficult position.

I am in a boarding-house, very comfortable, just a few doors from Pares' home. The people are almost all interesting. My room is small but pleasant. I can see the boats for America lying at the landing stage. The service is excellent. I am spoiled by these English servants.

June 16, 1911

DEAR MOTHER:

This has been a bad week—weather cold—lots of complications in the work. Mrs. Pares is very ill, and Pares is out of communication. This reminds me that we did not arrange telegraphic address. You can reach me "Harper, University of Liverpool," while I am here, and "Harper, American Consulate, St. Petersburg," in Russia. I leave here July 7, by boat, reaching St. Petersburg July 12. I am undecided as to whether I shall go down to London for the coronation.

June 23, 1911

DEAR MOTHER:

The coronation is over. I did not go to London, for several reasons. I did not wish to leave Mrs. Pares still so sick. I also have to be here to-morrow for a faculty meeting. I spent the day alone but pleasantly. I took a walk against a thirty-mile wind along a Roman road to Park-gate. Starting from Birkenhead, I passed the golf course and went so far that I decided to push on for tea at an old inn near Horton Junction, from which I could look out onto the Welsh Hills. At this point I caught a train back to Liverpool. I covered twelve miles in all. It would have been monotonous alone but for the wind, which kept me too busy to think of anything else.

I stopped off at the park. It was a great chance to study the English type. All classes were represented. I saw just one really pretty girl in the entire crowd. I quite miss New York's display of the beautiful feminine.

LONDON
July 7, 1911

MY DEAR MOTHER:

Here I am in London. I came down last evening after having finished everything at Liverpool. Pares came back, and we had two days together. There was no need for my staying on after all, but it was not time wasted. I got acquainted with the men and the work, and I am off until November 1—that is, they give me credit for the month's work I did. This is much better all the way around. The last days at Liverpool were very hard but interesting. They have a system of external examiners—Oxford and Cambridge men who come up to see that high standards are set. My external was the famous Vinogradoff. It was worth while to meet him. On Tuesday night a dinner was given to the five of us by the faculty. I had to make a speech and had great fun with the fact that I was being formally taken in on July 4th. This gave me a good start, and it seems the speech wasn't too bad.

I had a very interesting time the last week, studying the dock strikes in Liverpool. Am writing an article on it for the *Record Herald*. If it is not accepted, try it on Dr. Matthews.

LONDON
July 14, 1911

DEAR MOTHER:

I am off to St. Petersburg in five hours. I did my Russian shopping and spent considerable money. Had to get a hat, rubber bathtub, shoes, shirts, etc.; so I may have to draw on what is left of my Chicago account before I had planned to.

At last I have seen my goddaughter. She has been living with her grandparents during Mrs. Pares' illness. She is a little dear and took to me right away. Had a long letter from Frances McKinney (age eleven) full of neighborhood news. Tell her she promises to be a faithful correspondent and that I shall keep up my end. I see that you are up to your old tricks of opening my letters; but I have no secrets or scandals, so I do not care.

Have started my list of English connections through my old friend Maurice Baring, socialist and newspaperman. Had luncheon at the Reform Club with Hilaire Belloc and Chesterton. Went to Parliament and met Redmond, the Irish leader. I heard Lloyd George debate his insurance bill. The politics here in England promise to be more than interesting.

Throughout my stay in England I followed closely the extensive development of social legislation under Lloyd George. Much of the conversation at luncheons and dinners concerned this social legislation, particularly social insurance. One heard much the same talk in America in those years when Woodrow Wilson was trying to introduce his "humane" reforms. In Berlin, where I always stopped for a few days on my way to and from Russia, I was constantly impressed with the fact that the Germans were considerably ahead of us in these reforms and that they were accepted there with much less opposition and grumbling from businessmen than in the Anglo-Saxon countries.

The six weeks in England had been something of a strain, perhaps less because of the work at the school than because of the formality of British social life, and I was in no mood to plunge immediately into my studies. As my letters show, I was hungry for the free and easy Russian hospitality; and it was not until fall that I finally settled down to study.

DEAR MOTHER:

I came very near to breaking my good record. We had a rough trip on the North Sea, and this little tub rolled and pitched in earnest; but even so it is much better than the train. We have just passed Cuxhaven, where I have disembarked and embarked so many times. I shall mail this from the Kiel Canal, through which we are now passing to the Baltic.

ST. PETERSBURG
July 23, 1911

DEAR MOTHER:

Here I am spending Sunday with the Smiths at Shetna, just outside of St. Petersburg. The rest of the sea trip was pleasant. There was less wind and more sunshine in the Baltic, but we reached St. Petersburg in a driving rain and I had to open my baggage on the deck under an improvised cover which did not cover. It was a dismal return to the land I have adopted. The hotel I went to at Pares' suggestion was, as are all Russian joints, dreary and cold. I telephoned and telephoned, only to find everyone away. At last I got hold of an English correspondent and had supper with him at a restaurant where they played Russian songs on the balalaika. I saw Corse at his office. He was not expecting me, and the fact almost overcame him. He is living at a village twelve miles from St. Petersburg and insisted on my going home with him that night. We drove eight of the twelve miles to the English golf course, a beautiful spot at the foot of some little hills, and got in eight holes before dinner.

Things are in much better shape politically than I had expected to find them, and the agrarian changes under the new law are even more important than the political changes of five years ago. They have not the dramatic character of the latter, however. The epidemics which usually visit Russia at this date have not arrived; but I am being very careful of food, eating at the best restaurants in spite of expense, and eating very little. In fact, I am hungry most of the time, but I have found it's wiser to go easy on food the first weeks here.

On Friday I lunched at the Hotel Europe and ran into Baron Rosen, Russian ambassador to the United States, and went to his apartment for a little visit. I dropped in at the hotel again later and ran into Mrs. Judson. Poor woman, she had arrived just four hours before, could get no guide, and was down and out. I had already bought my railroad ticket and telegraphed the Petrunkevitches to send horses to meet me at Torzhok, so I could not stay over; but I took her and her friends around for several hours and got my train with three minutes to spare.

71

MASHUK
August 1, 1911

DEAR MOTHER:

I sit here and not a sound, for it is past midnight and I am in the country with the Petrunkevitches—fifteen miles from the railway and three miles from anything. As usual, there is a big and joyous crowd here. I have been talking Russian for four days, and it is really hard work to write this English letter. People drop in on us from all sides every day. I am picking up valuable material, though I confess that most of the time is spent loafing, sailing, walking, swimming, and playing rugby and tennis. I planned to leave after a short visit, but they insist that I stay over.

I have just returned from the cliff, where we built a bonfire and sang Russian songs. There are plenty of young girls here in the party.

MASHUK
August 7, 1911

DEAR MOTHER:

I am still at Mashuk with the Petrunkevitches. It's the sensible thing to stay on, for I am having a most glorious time. They are delightful people and have loads of guests, changing from day to day, so that I have a chance to talk to people of all classes. The manager of the estate is half-English and is my chief chum. I move over to his house today, his wife having gone off for a week. He lets me have a horse whenever I want. I tried riding; but my knee gave me trouble, so now I drive one of their best horses. Yesterday I invited a charming young married woman (with her husband's permission) to drive; and, of course, the horse decided to cut up. My poor hands are in bad shape this morning from the reins, but we returned safely. The young woman is making a "Little Russian" shirt for me, a much better style than those we have. I have been the ringleader in all sorts of excursions. Last night we rigged up a floating bonfire on the river and hid a gramophone in the woods. A fellow-conspirator got the crowd on the bluff overlooking the river, and then I started the gramophone and the fire. It was a great success, only I slipped and went head first into the water.

This morning seven of the guests went off for a three-day hunt. I decided not to go, as I can have much more fun here. Every one is tired after last night's excitement.

I do not know how I am going to repay these good people. They were quite touched by the little presents—I brought six pounds of candy from St. Petersburg for the children and a bottle of whiskey for the manager.

MY DEAR MOTHER:

Many happy returns of the day! I am afraid this will reach you after the 31st, but I forgot that it takes two weeks for a letter. I shall cable you.

I am still here with the Petrunkevitches. Until three days ago it was too hot to think of traveling, and now I have only ten days left for "country" work because, on September 1, I begin library work in St. Petersburg. The supper bell has just rung and I hurry to finish. There are twenty of us for supper tonight and after supper we have a bonfire (I chopped up two big trees this morning)on the cliff overlooking the river. At midnight six of the party leave for Moscow. I have had an inside view of Russian life while here which I never saw before. The three weeks have not been lost, and my Russian has become most fluent.

ST. PETERSBURG
September 15, 1911

MY DEAR MOTHER:

At last the weather has changed and I have thrown off my cold. People are beginning to come back. The libraries are open, and my work is going much better, though I must admit I am not accomplishing as much as I had hoped. I still find it very nice to loaf a bit and do not seem to be able to get up full steam.

ST. PETERSBURG
October 15, 1911

MY DEAR MOTHER:

I have been working very hard this last week. It has been intensely interesting, but I am not sure just how much I am really accomplishing. I have decided that one of the reasons I enjoy it here is because I am looked on as somebody. I get invited around, asked for my opinion, have had two write-ups this year in newspapers. I shall be spoiled if I am not careful.

Professor Andrews (American history), formerly of Johns Hopkins, now Yale, was here for two days with a Baron Korf, the professor of constitutional law at Helsingfors. I spent much time with them. Andrews spoke most highly of my work and said I must come back to America soon. He spoke as though I could ask him for help to get a job. I am not worrying over that, however, for really, so long as I cannot be in Chicago, I don't much care whether its England or America.

DEAR MOTHER:

Your letter of November 14 just arrived. That is not so bad. We could do it more quickly if you looked up the sailings of the "Maure-tania" and the "Lusitania" and other fast ships and posted for these. It is a relief to feel that the letters will not take three weeks and then perhaps get lost or destroyed by the censors. I can tell you, now that I am out, that I lost many letters while in Russia. You will be amused to know that our friend Mr. Williams fell under suspicion of being a spy; "awful rot" of course, but they also kept an eye on me this time, as I had dropped in on him very frequently. I had a detective on my tracks for two weeks, and I led him a jolly chase. He must have thought it funny to follow me to the chiefs of the prisons, the head of the police department, and other high officials.

I have glorious quarters. Moved in this afternoon and am living with a delightful colleague, Professor Montgomery of the School of Commerce, whose work is closely related to mine. Montgomery has been particularly kind in helping me adjust to the situation here, although his first and most emphatic advice was a little discouraging, namely, that I try to avoid bringing Russia and the work of the school into all conversations at all times. It seems that Pares, in his enthusiasm, has overdone it, and the faculty is a little tired of hearing about Russia.

We have separate bedrooms, large and excellently furnished, and a sitting-room in common. I wish you could see the sitting-room. It is larger than our library and has a big fireplace and heavy furniture. As good as anything that we have. At one end are the sideboard and dining-room table; at the other are two work tables; on the sideboard are flasks, pitchers, and a tea set; very good pictures on the walls. I have never had such comfortable, luxurious quarters anywhere abroad. The secret is that the good people, my landlords, lost their money some time ago but have the house and furniture, and they rent it out to recommended persons. And what do you think I pay for it? $27\frac{1}{2}$ shillings a week—less than a dollar a day, and this includes light, fire (all day in the sitting-room), telephone, hot water all day, and very good bathroom, and breakfast. For my evening meal I order what I want and pay for the material only. The cooking is done for nothing. So think of me as comfortable and happy.

I have four students in language and do not begin the history course until after Christmas. Am beginning to get invitations to dine out and am very happy and feel at home. I go down to London Saturday to make the arrangements with the publishers for the first number of the *Russian Review*. I go on as editor (one of three), instead of subeditor, as originally planned. Executive Committee of the school meets tomorrow, and my report is just finished. We get lots of politics at the Club, where I lunch every day. An Irishman and I have joined forces and are having great fun with the Englishmen.

The editing of the *Russian Review* was perhaps the most interesting part of my work at the School of Russian Studies. It was my task not only to secure articles but also to translate or "re-English" those submitted by our Russian contributors, and I handled most of the book reviews as well. Generally on the week-end before publication I went to London to confer with John Buchan, then the head of our publishing firm, Nelson and Sons. Buchan was very much interested in the problem of Anglo-Russian relations, and he devoted infinite time and patience to our quarterly.

Miss Lillian Rhodes, our secretary and general factotum in the editing office, did her best to keep the work in line; but with Pares away for irregular periods and with my own extended absences each year, a great many things went wrong. Two hundred copies of the first run of the *Review* sent on to Russia lay cozily in the censorship office there for six weeks, although Pares was in Russia at the time, supposedly in charge of the Russian distribution. When I took over the work in Russia later, someone failed to send the second run of the review to the mailing list I had carefully worked out, so that when I called on editors to suggest a mention of the *Review* in their publications, or called upon contributors to stimulate their interest in distribution to their friends, I found them unsupplied and in ignorance. There seemed to be a lack of realization that, once published, the *Review* must actually be distributed immediately into proper hands in order to make possible any organized campaign to create interest.

The censorship in Russia also became more strict at intervals and upset our plans. I found that there were gaps in our correspondence back and forth. On top of all this, poor Miss Rhodes would write hurried notes to me asking for instructions, failing to keep a copy of the notes, so that, when my brief replies finally arrived, her memory proved insufficient and my instructions were not intelligible. It was ultimately this inability to co-ordinate effort that greatly discouraged me and helped persuade me to leave the University of Liverpool earlier than I had originally planned.

For after a second year at the school, despite the fact that the work had been, on the whole, satisfactory, I decided not to go on with it. In addition to those difficulties noted above, there were other factors determining my decision. For one thing, the work at Liverpool was tending to become somewhat "official," because of the close relationship of the school with the British-Russian agreement. Our reports to the British foreign office, were in the main, the work of Pares, of course; but I had a certain association with them. The Anglo-Russian Committee which Pares organized, and which arranged reciprocal visits of groups of public leaders and businessmen, was a kind of work that did not appeal to me but which seemed to be a major interest of the head of the school. Even the *Russian Review* became somewhat propagandist in character. Later international developments fully justified the direction which Pares gave to the work of the school, but at the time I was not in sympathy with it. Finally, I really did not want to become a permanent exile, for I had seen what happened to Americans who stayed too long abroad.

Adelbert Stewart, one of my closest college friends, was manager of the British office of the American Radiator Company; and he and his wife were a great joy to me during my Liverpool days. She helped me shop in London and took care of me during my one serious illness. It was with them that I saw, on little week-end trips, some of the beautiful English countryside. They were a great comfort to my mother when she visited me at Liverpool. I had several contacts with the family during my Liverpool stay. In May of 1913 I spent an interesting week in London with my brother Paul, who arrived there after a trip around the world from San Francisco with the Wm. Wrigley Jr. family, of chewing-gum fame. My brother had been acting as tutor for Mr. Wrigley's son, Philip. And my mother had come over to visit me at Liverpool in the fall of 1912. She met me in Russia in the summer of 1912, and I showed her off to all my Russian friends. The Petrunkevitches entertained us at Mashuk, and we came back together to Liverpool. Mother stayed with me there from October to December. We had a delightful time, and having her with me for this period established a strong sense of home in my English life.

LIVERPOOL
April 22, 1913

MY DEAR MOTHER: I sit in the same room, at the same table, hugging the same fire, and trying to arrange that same blooming lamp—and only you are missing. It is going to be a little lonely at first not to see you across the room. The plant has increased to double its size; the wallpaper is still pink; but the "Druid's Prayer" has not been played next door this evening as yet.

Our steamer got stuck in the mud as we were docking last night at seven; and after all luggage was on deck, stewards tipped, and goodbyes said, we were told we would not dock until morning. So a crowd of us got up a dance and "raised Ned" all night. I am off to your old bed in a few minutes. Have just told Mrs. Earp not to bother about chocolate tonight. Mrs. Earp, by the way, is well. She sends greetings. We have a nice little maid now—young, but capable I think.

LIVERPOOL
June 25, 1913

MY DEAR MOTHER:

This is a sad life. I sit here in our old room for the last time, for to-morrow I have to clean out (our musician next door has given up "The

76

Rosary" and the "Druid's Prayer," and it is now ragtime). Everything is packed except my pajamas, and after much hurry and scurry I really got most of the things in. Have taken my last look at the corners of the room for any stray bits of my belongings. The paprika stays behind, as do the bottles of ink and paste.

I did not realize I had so much sentiment in me. It really hurts me to give up these quarters with all their association—pleasant and unpleasant. I now must knock around from pillar to post until I settle down in October.

Next morning
Waiting for the Movers

Things look as bare as they did that noon when we gathered ourselves together last December. Have had my last bacon and eggs à la Earp. By the way, Mrs. Earp gave me, for you, a piece of brass and a small bit of pewter. I did not want to take them, but she insisted that she wanted you to have them—she remembered you so kindly. Mrs. Pares looked at them and said they weren't of much value; so I have taken them. Now it is up to you to write Mrs. Earp a letter of thanks.

Later at the University

Was interrupted by my drayman—am moved—you should have seen me going off with two trunks, three suitcases, a hat box, golf sticks, a small grip, and one more package of things that would not go in.

Am at a commercial hotel for a week. It will be an interesting study. If they ask what I represent, I shall say Spearmint Chewing Gum.

🙟 🙟 🙟

CHAPTER X

DEVELOPMENTS AND TRAVELS IN RUSSIA

DURING MY TRIPS TO RUSSIA FROM 1911 TO 1913 I WAS EXPECTED TO DO certain chores for the University of Liverpool, such as collecting promised articles for the *Review*; but the balance of the time was my own for study and research. As usual, I divided it between the Duma and travels in the country. The Duma, conservative though it was, had by this time developed a certain professional pride; and conflicts between it and the bureaucracy became constantly more acute. Premier Stolypin had defended the Duma, although he had used it for his own ends, but his successors adopted a far more reactionary policy. They were definitely controlled by "those dark forces laying rough hands on the machinery of state," to use the circumlocution which all understood to mean Rasputin. Because of the vast influence of this sinister figure, and in line with my intention to study all manifestations of Russian life, I thought at one time of trying to arrange a meeting with "the monk." My Russian friends advised strongly against any such step, however, assuring me that it would tend to discredit me in my work.

After Stolypin's death, his land reforms were continued by the able men whom he had established under him, and this revolution in rural Russia was the most constructive development of these years of reaction. In this period I found it still more difficult to follow at first hand the conditions in the workman class, to which reaction had brought constantly increasing oppression. There seemed to be no corresponding development of opposition among the workers, either individual or organized. The revolutionary elements were still in a state of despair from failure or dissolution from police measures. But in 1912 there occurred the tragedy at the Lena gold fields, where the excessive cruelty of the police aroused a definite protest from the Duma. There were resolutions against the continued use of "exceptional measures," and a demand for the introduction of those civil liberties which had been promised in 1905 but had never been fully granted. Further, the Duma introduced a comparatively liberal social insurance law for employees. And, finally, it introduced a law requiring universal education, to be attained within ten years, with generous appropriations to support the program. This law attempted to reduce considerably the extensive participation in, and control of, primary education by the church. It was thus clear that even the conservatives were beginning to question the wisdom of continued blind reaction without any effort to correct the conditions that had caused the revolution of 1905.

In 1912, on my way from Russia back to Liverpool, I stopped off at Warsaw to meet and help Professor William I. Thomas, of Chicago. Thomas had conceived the idea of studying economic and social conditions among certain peasant groups in Europe from which many of our immigrants had come, to determine the influence of the latter on the former, and vice versa. He decided to begin with a Polish group and asked me to help him establish the necessary connections in Poland. I was able to put him in touch with many friends among the Polish deputies to the Russian Duma; and through them Thomas found, with a minimum of delay, the very man for his purpose, Florian Znaniecki, whom he brought to Chicago and with whom he published his celebrated volumes on the Polish peasant. Knowing of my interest in the Russian peasant, Thomas urged me to keep in mind the possibility of working with him on a similar study of Russian groups.

Therefore, when I decided in September, 1913, not to stay on in Liverpool, I went to Russia to collect material for Thomas' project. At the request of the American consul at St. Petersburg, I had also agreed to spend some time with W. W. Husband, of the United States Department of Labor, who was investigating the problem of Russian immigration to America. As this immigration was largely from peasant communities, this work fitted in very neatly with the study I was undertaking for Thomas.

From the first of September to the middle of October, I made, with Husband, one of my most extensive trips in Russia. Our object was to visit directly those peasant villages and areas from which, according to the reports of Ellis Island, a new wave of immigration seemed to be starting. To expose the secret agents of the German steamship companies, we had to play around with the Russian police at all points. We traveled down the Volga from Saratov to Astrakhan, stopping off in certain areas to drive along the shore through the villages, talking to peasants who had been in America. We sailed across the Caspian in an old schooner with an auxiliary engine, to the shores of the Caucasus. We had one of our most interesting interviews in the bombproof and windowless office of Beletsky, the chief of police of the territory. Suffering from asthma but having to work in this tightly closed room, Beletsky was forced constantly to use an atomizer. Husband's hilarious imitation of this interview became famous in Washington.

We proceeded to Vladikavkaz in the Caucasus Mountains, where my meticulous expense account rendered to the government shows our first "bath—one ruble." A drive of 140 miles (40 hours) on the Georgian Road, changing horses every 10 miles over the mountains, brought us to Tiflis after two nights spent at strange inns at Kazbek and Duchet. Our nourishment was largely bread and wine. As we moved southward to Alexandropol and Agin on the Turkish border to get into Russian Armenia, the authorities insisted on supplying us with a guard of two Cossacks. We were glad to have this protection when we were besieged by some six hundred Armenians who had been refused admission to Ellis Island. They were sure we had been sent by the American government to reimburse them for their losses when they tried to migrate to America.

We returned to Tiflis and went by rail to Batuum, where we missed our boat connections and were delayed over two of the hottest days I have known. We found much material we were looking for here. A very turbulent Black Sea carried us by boat to the beautiful city of Sevastopol. I missed seeing Balaklava.

We went on to Poltava and Kiev by rail. Here we luxuriated in the best rooms, enjoyed the best food, and went to good theaters for five days while investigating Jewish immigration problems. Then we drove partly and went by rail partly, visiting villages and peasant areas, southward toward Odessa, via Belaya Tserkov, Zliashkov, Vapnyarka, and Slobodka. I had not remembered Odessa as such a beautiful city—perhaps three days in the Jewish pale, sleeping in Jewish inns, five to a room, gave me a different perspective. It was a hard trip but most valuable.

By this time Husband has, I hope, forgiven me for the many sleepless nights he had to spend in peasant huts or primitive taverns. From the material we secured on the spot we were able to get action, not only against the agents of German shipping companies but also against certain clerks and interpreters at Ellis Island, who were grafting, without scruple, off the poor immigrants. I believe our investigation contributed to the successful establishment of the American policy that prospective immigrants must be examined before embarking from European, and particularly German, ports.

After completing my work for the Department of Labor, I spent the rest of the winter in the St. Petersburg library collecting material for Professor Thomas. I was glad to have a winter in Russia, for all of my trips, since 1904, had been in the spring or summer. I lived with Rennet, a retired correspondent of the *New York World*.

With the movement toward liberalism in Russia from 1904 on, anti-Semitism had tended to decline. But in the winter of 1913–14 the Beilis trial was one of the manifestations of the increasing governmental reaction. The more decent conservatives in Russia were deeply shocked by this attempt of the government to prove against a whole people the medieval accusation of ritual murder. While in Kiev with Husband, I saw the lawyers for the defense and went over the indictment papers with them. The trial was the outstanding subject of discussion that year, and the chief issue of the political struggle that was once again beginning to assume revolutionary proportions.

In March of 1914, while I was still in Russia, news stories began to hint at the tenseness of political and commercial relations between Russia, on the one hand, and Germany and Austria, on the other. A new Russian nationalism had accompanied the constitutional development; and those Russians working for constitutionalism were at the same time fighting German influence in Russia, which they held responsible for the reactionary court policies. In Berlin, where I stopped on my way home in April, talks with American correspondents there who had previously worked in Russia made me realize clearly the German attitude toward this new spirit in Russia. The possibility of trouble seemed apparent, and, on arriving home, I allowed myself to talk of the imminence of conflict in eastern Europe. I felt that this fact was of general importance and also that it justified the urging of more interest in Russian affairs.

While the Thomas project was of sufficient scope to keep me occupied in the next months, I had to consider seriously the resumption of academic work in America. Having given up the post at Liverpool, I started the usual procedure of calling attention to my availability and qualifications. It looked very much as if I would go to a women's college to teach general European history. But in August came the outbreak of hostilities, first in eastern Europe and then in western Europe. The responsibility of Russia for the war and the question of the effectiveness of her participation were in the foreground. Immediately, interest in the Russian field was kindled. Mr. Crane again came forward with the offer to support resumption of my work at the University of Chicago, and I returned for the opening of the academic year 1914–15.

PART V

THE WAR AND THE REVOLUTIONS: 1914–17

For the convenience of the reader:

1. During the first years of the war, fortunes varied on the Russian front. Inside Russia itself the independent efforts and organization of the people to support the war brought jealousy and even sabotage from the bureaucracy, which caused gradually increasing disorganization. Rasputin's influence on the imperial family also became disturbing. The Duma and its leaders made great efforts to stabilize the internal conflicts and toward the end of 1916 were pressed to strong action.

2. In March came the first revolution of 1917 (sometimes called the "February revolution," because of the thirteen-day difference in the Russian calendar). The Duma and its leaders formed a provisional government under Prince Lvov as premier. The masses were also organized by the socialist groups through Soviets (or Councils) of Workers' and Soldiers' Deputies in Petrograd and other cities, which at the outset were more Menshevik than Bolshevik in their policies. Both Lvov and Milyukov, as leaders of the new provisional government, soon clashed with the Soviets of Workers' and Soldiers' Deputies; and Kerensky, the leading socialist member of the Cabinet, who was relied on to control the Soviets, eventually became premier. This government lasted until November.

3. The November revolution (sometimes called the "October revolution") occurred on November 7, 1917, under the leadership of Lenin, Trotsky, and Stalin. The Red Guard seized control of Petrograd in the early morning and overthrew the provisional government of Kerensky. This was the day set for the meeting of the All-Russian Congress of Soviets. Some of the representatives at the congress withdrew in indignation over the coup just carried off; but the rest approved the decrees presented, calling for immediate peace and relating to land ownership, and established the Council of Peoples Commissars, with Lenin as chairman, Trotsky as minister of foreign affairs, and Stalin as minister of nationalities.

CHAPTER XI

THE FORCES DEVELOPING DURING THE FIRST WAR YEAR

BETWEEN 1914 AND 1918 MANY AMERICANS BEGAN TO REALIZE FOR THE first time that events in faraway Russia concerned them and actually affected their own lives. Public curiosity about this unknown land ebbed and flowed throughout the war years, but it seemed to me that genuine interest among thoughtful people constantly increased. At the University of Chicago my classes grew and attracted eager and capable students. Invitations to discuss Russia with social, civic, and scholarly groups poured in from all over the country; and personal inquiries from manufacturers, publishers, and teachers flooded my mail.

At the outbreak of hostilities there was a general tendency in the United States to blame the Russian mobilization for the spread of the war—for the failure of the British effort to localize the Austro-Serbian conflict. Then immediately the question arose as to how well Russia could fight. Her late submission to Japan was not reassuring; neither did her internal situation promise much stability. There was talk of Russia's withdrawing from the war by agreement with Germany, and at the same time there was talk of a revolutionary outbreak which would make her further participation in the war impossible. The Russian invasion of East Prussia, however, tended to raise the prestige of Russian arms in American opinion. Even at the time, this invasion was recognized as having in large measure saved Paris from the German attack. There was, in fact, as the Russian military disasters in the spring of 1915 clearly showed, an inclination to put too much reliance on the Russian steam roller.

So many questions were raised concerning the position of Russia in the war for democracy that, in an effort to evaluate the rapidly changing conditions there, I made three trips to Russia in the course of this period: the first, in 1915, on my own initiative; the other two in a semiofficial capacity, as adviser to the new American ambassador, Governor Francis of Missouri, in 1916, and as adviser to the Root Commission in 1917. To reach Russia, with the blockades and fighting fronts, it was necessary to take a Scandinavian boat to Norway and proceed by train from there to northern Sweden, within fifteen miles of the Arctic Circle, cross over into Finland, and then journey southward to St. Petersburg, or Petrograd, as it was now called, in defiance of the Germans. In September, 1915, I set out on this route for the first time.

DEAR MOTHER:

Here I am safely on land, and no more water. The trip so far has been uneventful and most pleasant, though the first day was a bit gloomy. I felt that everyone had real business on hand, else he would not have been aboard—none of the tourist, pleasure-seeking crowd. But then, as we had wonderful warm, sunny weather, we got into the ocean-voyage spirit and managed to have a little fun. I played around with the family of the American minister to Norway, Mr. Schmedeman, and a young Norwegian girl. Mrs. Marye, the wife of our ambassador to Russia, was on board, and I saw a bit of her. She was traveling with her husband's somewhat flamboyant personal secretary, Ray Baker. I must admit that I rather like him and his very direct outlook on life.

As we neared the war zone, we got up some little excitement. The captain of our boat was a clever one and managed to dodge the British patrol boats. He hoisted a lookout to the top of his mast in a canvas bag by day and put out all his lights by night. We had a Marconi instrument which registered the distance of any ship sending out messages. So we slipped along and, thanks to the fog, got by the patrol. It was not entirely safe as we did it; but it is done, and all is well. Had we been caught, it would have meant a delay of four or five days at Kirkwall, Orkney Islands. As it was, we came through in eight and a half days. We went mighty far north to get into Norwegian waters as soon as possible, and beat the last patrol by a dozen miles only. We were not sure we were through until eleven o'clock this morning. As we came to the Norwegian three-mile limit, a submarine—German in all probability—passed to our stern. It was laying for our English patrol boats, I suppose.

It's a cold but interesting place here—all the girls have rosy cheeks. I have been promenading with the little Schmedeman girl. Tomorrow I go to Christiania by train. I have dallied here, to get the day trip over the mountains. They say it is wonderful.

MY DEAR MOTHER:

One more stage of our journey is behind me. You have been having Rocky Mountain scenery, but it certainly cannot be much better than what we had yesterday on the trip over the mountains from Bergen. Some westerners on the train admitted that it was almost as good as America! We had a snow fight at each stop in the mountains. It was a long trip, and I really did sleep last night.

I am having a hard time finding out just what has happened in Russia. The German papers speak of an impending general strike. I shall try to get some information from the Russian minister this morning. If a crisis seems to be at hand, I shall cut out Stockholm and go by a more direct but less comfortable route.

It is great fun to be on the road again, and this is all new to me here. I am not sure, though, that I care for the Scandinavians. They appear to be an obstinate, routine lot; but much of what is objectionable may be the result of war conditions. I just drift along doing everything they tell me to do—opening my luggage at every turn, filling out blanks for the police, giving full information about my business, my route, my plans, etc. Of course, all this police supervision gets more strict as one approaches Russia, but I am used to the Russians and can handle that better. It's rather hard not to know the language of the country, and that's my difficulty here.

Am off to see the town, as I have a whole day here before I leave tonight.

HAPARANDA, SWEDEN
October 9, 1915

MY DEAR MOTHER:

Here I am above the 66-degree line, within eleven miles of the Arctic Circle; and it's warm and sunshiny. Cross over to Finland in a few minutes. It has been a wonderful trip. On the train as we left Stockholm I found several friends from England. Some have their uniforms in their suitcases, for they are joining British military units on the eastern front. Others are going to Russia to organize a British propaganda bureau, to consolidate the British-Russian alliance by trying to explain away the obstacles that hinder full co-operation. Among them are Hugh Walpole and Somerset Maugham. They are going to work with Pares and Harold Williams and a new student of Russian affairs, Bruce Lockhart.

PETROGRAD, RUSSIA
October 12, 1915

MY DEAR MOTHER:

I got here Sunday night, just fifteen days on the road; and that allowed me a day in Bergen, another in Christiania, and a third in Stockholm. All went well. I came in without any difficulty, having attached myself to a Mr. Archibald Harte, of Mr. Mott's Y.M.C.A. work, who was bringing a wounded Russian officer back from Germany—an exchange of prisoners. It was worth the trip over to have the three days with Mr. Harte and to learn in detail of his work. Not only is he doing a splendid humanitarian job, but he is also making hundreds of individuals in Russia and Germany think of America in terms of his work. I would like to help him, but I see that I must accomplish all I can on my own project in the two months that I have to spend here.

In the two days since I have arrived I have done enough already to justify the trip. I shall be able to confound the maligners and reassure the doubters without any trouble when I return. The spirit here is most wonderful, and I am only on the fringe of it. I get down to the heart next week. I had guessed right almost every time these last months.

I spent a good part of this day with Baron Rosen, the former Russian ambassador to the United States. He sends greetings, as do the Corses and others. They all ask about you and wish you might have come along.

I have a nice room at the Hotel France. Do you remember the luncheons there, in the garden? My room is a bit dull and mournful; but it is clean and airy, and I have a telephone at my side here, which is a great timesaver. I am waiting for a call now.

I wish you could have seen the Nevsky today in the bright autumn sun. Everyone moves with more speed, except the groups of wounded soldiers one is constantly meeting. And there is clear determination and absolute self-confidence in the faces as in the talk.

PETROGRAD
October 17, 1915

DEAR MOTHER:

All goes very well. I am seeing people most of the day and night. I have run into my friend Ray Baker once or twice and have found him mildly interested in the political problems of Russia at war, which I am trying to understand. But, like his employer, he seems more interested in the social life of the capital, which continues unabated. Already Baker has become one of the features of Petrograd, roaring through its streets in his bright scarlet automobile and flashy clothes. I have learned a great deal about practical politics in my talks with him.

The newly established branch of the National City Bank is represented here by Mr. Meserve, and around him have gathered most of those war-order men who rushed to Europe last year when the war broke out. As the bureaucracy still handles war orders, most of these people, including Meserve, court the higher ministers and the grand dukes. Since I am interested in the new liberal Russia and not the bureaucracy, I do not see much of these representatives of America's war business. But I can't help seeing and being concerned by their methods and manners, which I think they will regret when the liberals gain greater power in Russia.

A few of my friends have moved down to Moscow, and I shall go there next week for a couple of days, stopping off at Mashuk on the way back.

I went to Moscow primarily to learn about the new "people's organizations," for this movement, it seemed to me, promised the emergence of a liberal Russia after the war. Those progressive social forces which had been released from 1904 to 1906 and suppressed from 1906 to 1914 seemed to be reasserting themselves, in the formation of the Union of

Zemstvos, the Union of Municipalities, the War-Industry Committees, and the Co-operative Committees—all people's organizations which were gradually overshadowing the bureaucracy in solving the wartime problem of supply and distribution. Their central offices were in Moscow, and I spent several weeks there studying their work.

I had known Prince Lvov, president of the Zemstvo Union, since the early days of the Duma; and his two executive secretaries, Shchepkin and Alexeyev (borrowed from the Duma chancery), were my intimate friends. From them I learned of the Union's progress and also of its many difficulties. Lvov had to meet constant restrictions from the administration, especially when he tried to associate the co-operative movement with his zemstvo work. From these co-operatives, particularly the rural units, he could get his supplies direct; but the bureaucrats felt that in doing this he increased the prestige and political aspirations of the co-operative leaders, most of whom they considered radicals. Fortunately, however, the Union had the support of the army leaders at the front.

By work in the Zemstvo Union and other such organizations, in the village co-operatives, and at the distributing points just behind the front, thousands of Russian liberals finally found the possibility of public activity. To be sure, many took these positions in order to avoid direct military service; but this practice was no more widespread in Russia than in other countries. The new experience was a rigorous test of those intellectuals who had always criticized the bureaucratic methods of the administration and demanded participation in public affairs. On the whole they seemed to do well, in contrast to the proverbially inefficient bureaucrats. Naturally they injected the element of political struggle into their work. Later many observers were to be disappointed in the capacity of this class for practical politics when it became fully responsible for the administration of the country after the revolution of March, 1917. But at this time most of us were favorably impressed by the way everyday problems of management were met by the intellectuals. One British writer, Professor James Y. Simpson, expressed this view in the title of his book about Russia in 1916: *The Self-discovery of Russia.*

Wanting to see rural Russia in wartime, I made one of my usual visits to the Petrunkevitch estate of Mashuk, spending several days en route at the district center, Torzhok, where Michael Petrunkevitch, as president of the zemstvo, directed the local work of the Zemstvo Union. Here in the lower reaches, also, police restrictions operated to slow up the collecting and dispatching of supplies of food and clothing. The shortage of labor resulting from the mobilization was also apparent in this particular district. The members and guests of the Petrunkevitch family helped in the fields instead of playing tennis and swimming as they had during my earlier visits. In this region the relations between peasants and landlords were comparatively good because of the liberal views of such families as the Petrunkevitches and Bakunins.

In June, 1915, members of the so-called "progressive bloc" of the Duma had tried to bring about certain democratic reforms which would, in their opinion, work for a united front in support of the war. They were, of course, using the war situation to secure more powers over the administration; but as their political aims seemed progressive as well as in the interest of the more effective prosecution of the war, we out-siders felt they were justified. Bureaucracy was also trying to use the war situation to strengthen its position; and the Emperor, under the in-fluence of the Empress, was attempting to re-establish some of his auto-cratic prerogatives. My friends, as well as my sympathies, were in the liberal camp. The newspapermen, like myself, on the basis of the Rus-sian past, naturally kept thinking of the possibility of revolutionary de-velopment, particularly as we saw the internal political struggle that was going on. One evening we pooled our "researches," and new ar-rivals from western Europe shared their views with those who were working in Russia. We all expressed our surprise that there was no evi-dence of a revolutionary movement anywhere in the belligerent coun-tries even after a whole year of war.

The liberal group in Russia was frankly afraid of pushing things to the point of revolution. Wondering if my more radical friends shared this hesitation, I decided to check up on their attitude while I was in Moscow. At my suggestion, one of these friends gathered together about thirty of his comrades for a quiet evening's discussion, and I recognized among them some who belonged to avowed revolutionary groups. Two who were at that meeting were later members of the Soviet government. Since the moderate socialists, within Russia as well as abroad, had come out in support of the war, I probably should not have been surpised that there was no talk of the imminence of revolu-tion from these men whom I had known as revolutionaries in 1905. At the time of this meeting (November, 1915) the appeal issued from Switzerland by Lenin and his extreme left-wing group had not pene-trated to Russia. The conversation that evening was one of the bases for the statements I made on my return to America that there was no "danger" of revolution in Russia.

Despite the rumors of court intrigues and bureaucratic machinations, and the exposure of traitors in high positions, most of us outside stu-dents decided that there was likewise no "danger" of Russia's making a separate and premature peace. The Emperor, who had taken over the Supreme Command, was distrusted as a military leader; but he was not suspected of wanting to deliver the country to the Germans. In conserva-tive as well as liberal and radical circles, one heard frank expressions of contempt for the Emperor; but this was largely because of the continued influence of Rasputin upon the imperial pair. Rasputin was suspected of being a German agent in the literal sense of the word; and it is possible that he sold to German spies military information which he was able to get from the trusting Empress, to whom the Emperor wrote frequently and in detail when he was at general headquarters. Such intrigues appeared trivial enough, however, in the face of the united effort of the Russian people to continue the war; and I concluded that they would come to nothing. It seemed to me that this view was substantially confirmed in June, 1915, when the special treaty was announced in which England, France, and Russia agreed not to make peace separately.

Alexander Guchkov, former president of the Duma, was at this time president of the War Industry Committee; and while I was investigating the work of this public organization in Moscow, I secured from Guchkov a pass to visit the eastern front. He gave it to me with a warning that it might get me into trouble. Evidently he already knew what became generally known with the publication of the Empress' letters, that she considered him the Emperor's chief enemy and a man who ought to be hanged without delay.

After presenting Guchkov's letter directly to General Alexeyev, chief of staff, I was permitted to go to that sector of the front commanded by General Kuropatkin, who had been commander-in-chief of the Russian forces in the Russo-Japanese War. Through the mobilization of reservists, many of the younger officers were from the intelligentsia; and one of these officers was assigned to accompany me. From my long talks with him and others I got firsthand evidence of the close bond between the fighting forces and the people's organizations and of their common grievance against the bureaucracy, which continued inefficient and corrupt, according to the best Russian traditions.

My experience under actual fire was a comparatively short one. I confessed and showed my fear, which was shared by my officer-guide. It was relatively quiet in the heavy, cold November, but shots were being exchanged intermittently as we pushed forward by underground trenches to within a quarter-mile of the German lines. General Kuropatkin accompanied us to this advanced post and insisted that the usual greeting given by soldiers to their officers be in full voice, so that the Germans, as he put it, could hear that Russian generals were not afraid to inspect their front lines.

There were interesting evenings in the officers' quarters, with music by soldier and Cossack choirs. In return for the courtesies being shown me, I gave informal lectures to officers and short speeches to regiments. It was rather difficult to explain America's position with respect to the war; but I solved the problem for myself personally by declaring that, like many other individual Americans, I was not neutral.

Bernard Pares was at the front, studying the morale of the troops and the effectiveness—or rather, the ineffectiveness—of the supply services. Some of us had thought he could be more useful in the rear, trying to convince the British authorities of the growing strength of the people's organizations, as opposed to bureaucratic Russia. But from the stories I heard during my visit to the front, Pares was probably right in his judgment of where he could best serve. There was much joking about this Britisher, who insisted, even under fire, on having his morning cold sponge in his collapsible rubber bathtub. On the other hand, with the traditional Russian suspicion of the British, it was very useful that such an ardent champion of British-Russian co-operation should be working on the main problem to be solved, that of British help in the supply of armament and equipment to the vast Russian army.

Back again in Petrograd, I looked up Philip Sims, who had come to Russia to represent the United Press and establish its permanent office there. Philip Sims represented the progressive character of the United Press, as compared with the Associated Press, which had attracted many of us to its news reports. For a month he and I lived together at the Hotel France, where I lectured to him informally on Russian history and politics and managed to sell him my views regarding the Zemstvo Union, the co-operatives, and the other people's organizations and their future role. In the past, I had always played around a good deal with newspapermen, learning much from them and giving them, in return, something of my disciplined approach. With Sims this type of co-operation was carried on more systematically and, I think I can say, in a way mutually beneficial. Sims was able to develop in me a little of the "news sense," although he frequently showed his impatience with my academic approach and style.

By the middle of December I started home in order to resume teaching at the opening of the winter quarter in January. The return journey through Finland and Sweden was particularly difficult in fifty-below-zero weather and practically twenty-four hours of night. The Swedish authorities subjected all arrivals from Russia to the most careful examination, political as well as sanitary. Again I had to pass through that spy center of Stockholm. From Stockholm I returned to what was then Christiania on the same day that Henry Ford arrived with his peace ship, "to get the boys out of the trenches by Christmas." Coming from a belligerent country and from the front, and from the new awakening Russia, fighting for "internal liberation" from German influence, I resented all peace moves as pro-German. Mr. Schmedeman, our minister to Norway, whom I had met on the trip out, invited me to the tea which he had to give to the Ford delegation; but I stood behind some portieres and studied them from a distance, refusing to come in to meet them. I made no effort to reach Mr. Ford or his main adviser, Rosika Schwimmer. But I was not thus to escape meeting the probably sincere, but certainly very naïve, Mr. Ford.

After a most difficult journey over the Norwegian mountains to Bergen in a driving blizzard, I finally embarked on the "Bergensfiord."

There were not many passengers. For twenty-four hours after our embarkation the ship continued to ride at anchor in the harbor; and we all became somewhat nervous, although the submarine warfare had not developed by that date. But on the second morning we woke to find that we were at sea; and then it began to be whispered around that the boat had been held up, at a cost of some thirty thousand dollars, to wait for Mr. Ford to get across the mountains. For Mr. Ford had become disgusted, if not with his mission, at least with his associates on this mission, and had sneaked away to catch our boat. The officers of the ship, in answer to our question, insisted that Mr. Ford was not aboard; and when the printed passenger list was distributed, his name was not on it. But Richard Washburn Child, a writer for *Collier's Weekly*, who was also returning from a trip to Russia, insisted that a certain rather quiet, timid man, wandering unhappily around with a constant companion, was Ford. In the smoking-room when we saw these two come in, Child and I would discuss Ford in loud voice and not too complimentary terms. Child, in fact, wrote a song which we sang those cold winter nights on the North Atlantic when it was impossible to be out on deck, the chorus of which ended with the line: " 'Twas Henry put the 'I' in Bergensfiord." Then one day Child told me he was wrong and that it was not Ford—but I learned from another source that Child had been to Ford's suite of cabins and had arranged to get an exclusive interview with him.

Because Ford had delayed the boat for over twenty-four hours, we did not arrive in New York on December 31 in time to disembark; so we all gathered in the dining-room to celebrate New Year's Eve in New York Harbor, opposite Coney Island. A group of us introduced the "game" of calling people to join our table. After we had called over the captain, we shouted: "We want Henry Ford." And he came running over with alacrity. In a jocular tone we upbraided him for having prevented us from celebrating New Year's Eve as scheduled, on shore with our respective families. He very promptly admitted the responsibility and generously set up champagne for the whole crowd. The next morning, while we were still in harbor, I noted the pathetic figure of Ford on the piano stool as I passed the music room. His derby hat on the back of his head, he was picking out a tune with one finger. Then the harbor commissioner's tug came up alongside, and Malone himself came aboard. It was clear what was being arranged: Ford was to be taken off in the harbor because the wharf was crowded with newspapermen waiting to interview him about the success of his peace trip. Again under the influence of the war hysteria with which I had become thoroughly imbued in Russia, politeness deserted me. As Ford started toward his disembarking ladder, I stopped him and expressed sorrow that he did not have the courage to face the music.

CHAPTER XII

I BECOME SPECIAL ADVISER TO
GOVERNOR FRANCIS

IN THE SPRING OF 1916 PRESIDENT WILSON ANNOUNCED THAT A NEW ambassador would be sent to Russia. I was not at all sorry to learn of the withdrawal of Marye and was rather interested in the man selected to succeed him, David R. Francis of St. Louis, popularly known as "Governor Francis." Francis was the outstanding Democratic leader of Missouri at this time, although he had retired from active politics as well as from active business. His one apparent qualification for foreign service was the fact that he had been president of the St. Louis International Exposition of 1903. He may have toured in Europe, but he had never had even business connections outside America. President Wilson undoubtedly chose him, among other reasons, for his well-known liberal tendencies.

A few days after the announcement of the appointment, I had a message from Mr. Crane, inquiring if I could arrange my university work so as to leave for Russia toward the end of May instead of in the middle of June, as planned. Then I received an invitation from Governor Francis to spend a week-end with him in St. Louis, to tell him something about the country to which he was shortly to proceed. Another message from the State Department suggested that it would be very useful if I could get the governor to propose that we take the same boat to Petrograd. These two messages were undoubtedly the result of Mr. Crane's activities, for he had decided that it was most important that Francis' mission be a success—from the Russian as well as from the American point of view—and he felt that I might be of some service to this end.

During the week-end visit Governor Francis did express the hope that I might be on his boat, and his approach to his new responsibility and his general outlook on things were such that I decided it would be possible to undertake the rather delicate job which the Department and Mr. Crane had wished on me. Fortunately, I was able to make adequate arrangements for my students; but, even so, I had a little difficulty with the university authorities, who objected to my leaving before the examination period. Vice-President Angell even suggested that I would do well to decide whether I wanted to teach or to go into diplomacy. To this I replied that the international situation was so rapidly affecting our interests that I felt fully justified in leaving.

The passenger list of the "Oscar II," the small Swedish boat which Governor Francis had chosen, was typical of those wartime sailings. There were various businessmen going to Russia for war orders, among them "Captain" Hayden Eames, a former navy man and one of the best-known trouble shooters for large corporations. Several American firms were having difficulties with their contracts to the Russian government for munitions orders. Eames stuck with us right through to Petrograd, in order to cultivate the new ambassador as well as to get across the Russian frontier, where one encountered not only the customs authority but also that of the military censorship. A large, forceful man, quick of temper, Eames often prefaced his outbursts with the phrase: "In the language of a rough sailor, ..." One evening he told us how near he had come to committing violence in his fits of temper, and he expressed the fear that he might get rough with some of the Russians with whom he would have to do business. I saw much of Eames during the next months and learned from him the details of the war-order business. Early one morning, after he had already said goodbye to me, he burst into my room in a great rage because at the last moment he had been unable to get the last of the twenty-one signatures needed to conclude his errand to Russia.

Another group of passengers was composed of Y.M.C.A. workers on their way to Russia to carry on the prison relief which Archibald Harte had been able to arrange in 1915, shortly after the outbreak of the war. By telling the Russians what the Germans let him do for Russian prisoners in Germany, he had got permission to render the same help to German prisoners in Russia. He effected certain exchanges of prisoners, but he did the greater service by supplying captured men with literature and replacing spectacles and other such items lost in battle and by securing lists of those in the prisons. He was meticulously careful not to let his organization be used for personal messages, lest these serve as a cover to transmit military information.

A third group of passengers was distinctly open to the suspicion that its members were doing espionage work, since this was a neutral boat, sailing from a neutral port and proceeding directly to that center of espionage which Stockholm had become practically from the first days of the war. The boat was taken into the Orkney Islands by patrols from the British blockade and held there for five days while its passenger list was thoroughly checked. After we were released, we did not see on deck several formerly familiar faces. One passenger whom I had regarded with some suspicion, however, was allowed to continue the journey with us.

Before Francis and I sailed from New York, a prominent American businessman who had extensive interests in Russia had come to the boat to see the new ambassador off and had pointed out to me a charming woman and warned me to keep the governor out of her clutches. She was a Russian, and I was not sure whether she represented a firm competing with that of my friend or whether he implied that she was in the intelligence service of some country other than her own. She had a German name; but the husband to whom she referred rather casually was, we were told, a Russian officer in service. Of course, many Russians in high military and civil positions, especially those from the Baltic provinces, had German names. The lady was not a good sailor, however, and we saw little of her during the voyage.

While we were on board, Francis had me give him informal talks each day on the situation which he was going to face. He spent much of his time in the smoking-room, playing bridge and talking with all sorts of people. I felt it was not my job to listen in on all these conversations; but I heard enough of them to realize that our new ambassador was a very blunt, outspoken American, who believed in speaking his mind regardless of the rules of diplomacy. While we were interned in the Orkneys, Francis went ashore for a day. He was not supposed to mention to a soul where he had been, but soon the whole boat knew that he had been shown Scapa Flow and the British fleet lying at anchor there.

During the several days of our stopover in Stockholm, I saw the operation of the game of so-called "diplomacy." Representatives of all the belligerent countries called on the governor, and the Germans were particularly active. I kept on the lookout for any contact between them and our charming Russian lady, who stopped, as we did, at the Grand Hotel. Until that time she had done little more than exchange greetings with Francis, to whom she had been introduced by someone in New York. I thought I had handled the situation well, until just before our departure another American who had attached himself to our party told me that at the last minute he had been able to secure accommodations for our Russian lady on the train we were taking. By the time we reached Petrograd, this lady and the governor had become very friendly; and their friendship continued through 1917, causing much anxiety to the staff of the American embassy. Governor Francis knew of this concern, and on several occasions he assured me that my own fears as to her German connections were absolutely groundless.

When we arrived in the Russian capital, the internal situation, after several months of promising developments, was beginning to get worse. The great effort of the people during the winter of 1915–16 had resulted in the successful drive into Galicia. The military victories there had, in turn, heightened public enthusiasm and effort. But this last development had increased the anxieties, and the consequent restrictive measures, of the bureaucracy. The war burdens were becoming severe even for the ordinary civilian population, largely because of the incompetence of the bureaucratic administration and its refusal to allow the people's organizations to extend their work to the rear, the better to organize production and distribution. This political conflict, of which I heard full details from my friends working in the zemstvos and cooperatives, naturally led to increased suspicion of the Emperor and Empress and of the higher bureaucracy. The Emperor augmented this distrust by dismissing ministers who enjoyed the confidence of the Duma and replacing them with men of mediocre ability and questionable pasts.

It was in these summer months of 1916 that the British and French governments, through their representatives, thought to put some pressure on the Emperor to effect a stronger national unity. The memoirs of the British and French ambassadors to Russia show both their timidity and their failure in this delicate task. It is probable that the main aim of Lord Kitchener's mission to Russia was to urge Nicholas II to co-operate, if not with the Duma, at least with his own ministers. Documents, later made public, show clearly that general policy and administrative practices of detail were being determined in those months by the Emperor himself, as a result of the insistent demand of the Empress, who was, in turn, acting directly under the influence of Rasputin.

Ambassador Francis, as I had hoped, immediately interested himself in the work and views of the people's organizations, whose leaders were soon to head the revolution of March, 1917. In his official position he could not, of course, spend too much time with these leaders, but I could and did see them freely and frequently. While they were firm in their opposition to the administration, they still did not wish to force a showdown which would disrupt the country and make its further participation in the war impossible. This became even more evident in the late fall of 1916, after I had left Russia, when in the Duma the conservative as well as the liberal and radical leaders attacked the stupidity and the possible treason of governmental policy and practices. In November, 1916, in an effort to preserve the monarchial principle, a group of extreme conservative Duma leaders, with the help of two members of the imperial family, finally murdered Rasputin. His removal did not, however, put an end to his influence; the Empress continued to rule the country by forcing the Emperor to make decisions in line with messages which she insisted she had received from Rasputin's spirit. My friend Pares has documented this whole Rasputin matter in his book *The Fall of the Russian Monarchy*.

The American embassy had taken over the protection of German interests at the outbreak of the war. This work covered the problem of German prisoners, which was so important that the counsellor of embassy gave a large portion of his time to it. Working with British and French fellow-students and official representatives, I soon learned of their anxiety lest inadvertently the American embassy should be used for sending out military information. Washington authorities were also worried over that section of the embassy. A higher official, one of the inspectors normally sent from place to place, turned up to look into affairs. Without going into further detail, I must admit that I gave him material for his report. I mentioned this fact to the ambassador and urged him to give more time to supervising the activities of the German section of the embassy.

My position at the embassy was a very difficult one. I had no official connection, but I had the confidence of the ambassador. Even the personal secretaries whom ambassadors generally take with them often disrupt the work of an embassy for which the regular staff is responsible, and my status was below that of a personal secretary in the eyes of the staff. To some I was an interloper and a nuisance. It is possible that I was not sufficiently tactful on all occasions. But, after all, I was carrying out an errand for the Department that did not entail any remuneration for me. Although Mr. Crane's office paid my out-of-pocket expenses, I was really no more than a professor on leave-of-absence with a salary from my university.

Returning home by the now familiar northern route, I stopped over for a few days with the Schmedemans at Christiania. I always arrived at a point of embarkation several days in advance, for, despite my many trips, I have always been a hard traveler, constantly worrying about missing boats and trains. Mr. Schmedeman suggested that I meet King Haakon, and of course I jumped at the opportunity. The minister, after his preliminary instructions about the use of titles and a reminder not to smoke until His Majesty had lighted a cigarette, advised me to keep off the topic of revolution. In telling him about developments in Russia, I had painted a picture of impending crisis because of the stubborn stupidity of Nicholas II.

As is well known, Haakon is one of the most democratic of European monarchs, and within a few minutes of my presentation, we were both smoking and I had dropped the formality of "Your Majesty." Almost immediately he brought up the question of the possibility of a revolution in Russia. He did not hesitate to condemn his cousin's policies. The conversation then took a turn to the topic of the war in general; and this democratic king, with a Social Democratic government in power, made a very interesting observation. He noted that in all the belligerent countries it had become necessary to tell the workmen that victory depended on them and on their willingness to increase production as well as to fight. The days when war was the more or less private affair of the sovereign were long since past. All the belligerent countries, therefore, would face a political and social crisis from workers' movements the moment peace was declared. As the ruler of a neutral country, he was experiencing in wartime the political effects of the rising power of the workman class.

CHAPTER XIII

THE MARCH REVOLUTION
WE ENTER THE WAR

ON MY RETURN TO AMERICA AT THE END OF SEPTEMBER, 1916, I FOUND considerable confusion of mind over the war situation, and particularly Russia's role. Although Wilson's campaign was largely based on the slogan "He kept us out of war," the drift toward involvement was clear to many of us. The British blockade was hurting our trade, but already the alignment of "democracy" against "autocracy" was being formed. The German submarine campaign was just beginning. From the military point of view, the Allies were making little progress, particularly on the eastern front, where Russian arms had suffered defeat and the Central powers had pushed into Russian territory. There was also the disaster at Gallipoli, which had contributed to the Russian retreat.

Russia raised doubts, too, with respect to her internal situation. Food shortages in the large cities, shortages of munitions at the front, conflict between government and Duma, and, finally, the murder of Rasputin suggested an internal breakdown. The appointment by the Tsar of Stürmer as premier had aroused open challenges in the Duma and renewed the fears of a separate peace. At the time there was no indication in our press that these events would lead to the emergence of a new and, from the point of view of the Western democracies, a better Russia.

Then came the news of the revolution in the first weeks of March, 1917. Ambassador Francis at Petrograd urged immediate recognition of the provisional government which was set up. The State Department asked me to telegraph in detail my views on the significance of the revolt and the background of the members of this new government. Several of them were men with whom I had been closely associated in all of my work in Russia, particularly in 1915 and 1916. I wired:

CHICAGO, ILLINÓIS
March 15, 1917

Duma leaders last summer said confidently that revolution might become necessary and urged that I explain in such event its political and not social character. They had tried moral pressure for over a year to secure responsible government. Tried to gain ear of sovereign but unsuccessful despite fact that army leaders cooperated here. Nicholas listened to small group of reactionaries, to Empress who generally suspected of pro-Germanism, and to the recently removed Rasputin who was alleged to be in employ of Germany. Emperor retained in office Protopopov who was publicly accused of being in touch with Germany. Demand for responsible government was primarily to eliminate these so-called Germans. At same time reactionary government especially

Minister of Interior Protopopov was definitely attempting to disrupt the public organizations, Zemstvo Union, Union of Municipalities, War-Industry Committees, and peasant cooperative societies, all working to organize resources of country for successful prosecution of war. Finally government took no adequate measures to prevent avoidable food crises in urban centers. Demand for responsible government made by Duma was supported by Imperial Council, both elected members and members appointed by sovereign such as Baron Rosen, late ambassador. United nobility, strong conservative organization also supported, but Emperor appointed reactionary Golitsyn and retained Protopopov. During Duma session in November Minister of War came to Duma and spoke for cooperation between Duma and government. At the time hailed as indicating that Duma supported by army. Therefore clear that Duma supported by army, and by country as represented in public organizations such as Zemstvo Union. In new cabinet, Lvov is president of Zemstvo Union, Guchkov elected member of Imperial Council and president of Central Committee of War-Industry Committees, in which workmen have elected representatives. Manuilov is prominent Moscow public worker, university and newspaper man. Kerensky is radical Duma member, elected by workmen. Shingarev is one of ablest Duma members of Liberal party. Milyukov is leader of Constitutional Democratic party. Nekrasov is vice-president of Duma and active member of Municipality Union. Godnev and Tereshchenko are prominent Duma members. Such men will be able to hold confidence of public and army, are practical leaders of long administrative experience. Their previous efforts to persuade Emperor to trust people, and the appointment of regent after abdication are evidence that revolution not directed against the dynasty. Aim of revolution as has been aim of Duma for last year and also of public organizations, to create conditions that would make it possible for Russia to bring into force all her strength. Means therefore more effective prosecution of war and war until victory.

I followed this by sending to the State Department more complete biographical sketches of the members of the new government, and from time to time thereafter I gave the Department my judgment on current developments. Mr. Crane went to Washington to report personally, for among the members of the provisional government were close friends of his, such as Paul Milyukov. Governor Francis was given the instructions he requested and was always boastful of the fact that through him America was the first country to recognize officially the government of the new Russia.

The Russian communities of all our large cities began to seethe, for they contained many Russian revolutionaries, refugees of the 1905 revolution. In Chicago there was Alexander Gruzenberg, who later became famous, particularly in China, under the name of Borodin. In New

York, Trotsky was living, reportedly running a restaurant. He had managed to get away from Switzerland, where conditions had become increasingly difficult for Russian exiles. American radicals, too, immediately came forward in support of this Russian revolution. During my spring vacation in the last week of March, I went to New York, where the largest colony of Russian exiles was established. Mr. Crane was helping Lincoln Steffens start for Russia to study the revolution, and we went to the pier to see him off. On the boat on which he sailed, Trotsky also sailed, returning to Russia under an amnesty which the Russian revolutionary government had proclaimed as one of its first moral obligations. Trotsky harangued the whole pier from the boat deck as the ship pulled out. The British, who were not so keen about his return, took him off the boat at Halifax and held him there for a month.

By the middle of April we had come into the war, and there is no question that our entry was made easier by the Russian revolution; it would have been difficult to use the slogan "War for democracy" if Russia had still been tsarist. Japan was far enough away so that the anomaly there was less blatant. The Allies, even Russia, had been careful to resist the Japanese efforts to have Japanese military units brought to the European battlefronts.

My interest and usefulness after our entry into the war naturally centered about Russia. As full information reached us, it became more and more certain that Russia under the old regime would soon have been out of the war. The extent to which the bureaucracy had riddled Russian war organizations, and was in turn riddled by German influence, was great. The question in everyone's mind was whether the new provisional government could bring enough order out of chaos to keep Russia effectively in the war. There was much skepticism throughout this country and little understanding of the caliber and experience of the new men in power or the extent to which they were supported by the people's organizations. I made it my job to try to explain Russia to the American public, and this I did on a broad scale. My lectures took me east as well as west; and I became, in fact, a public lecturer.

I believed the new men would accomplish their task. I had absolute faith in their trustworthiness. They had secured the opportunity for which they had been fighting since 1905. They were the best-qualified leaders Russia had. But I recognized that carrying on a revolution, fighting a war, and succeeding to the mess left by the crumbled tsarist regime presented grave problems. The survival of the provisional government was a gamble; but for our interest alone, now that we were in the war, it was most important to give it full support. Thus, I did all I could to combat uninformed skepticism in this country.

As part of our participation in the war, President Wilson decided to send a special mission to Russia, headed by Elihu Root, to work out the details of our co-operation with the new Russian government. To the mission was appointed Cyrus McCormick, of the International Harvester Company, which had extensive business relations and even a plant in Russia. Another member was John R. Mott, of the International Committee of the Y.M.C.A., which was carrying on relief work among prisoners of war in Russia. Mr. Crane, then in China, was to join the mission. The socialist Charles E. Russell and an American Federation of Labor leader, James Duncan, were assigned to the group to give it a less conservative character. It was first proposed that I be made a formal member of the mission; but then it was decided that I could be of more use without official status, for in that way I could see individuals whom it might be embarrassing for the mission to receive officially. As the mission approached Chicago, on its way to the Pacific Coast, I boarded the train at a halfway point and gave these men my interpretation of the revolutionary situation in which they would have to carry on their work.

After finishing my year's teaching at the university I set off for Russia, via my usual Atlantic route, expecting to reach Petrograd almost as soon as the Root mission, which was journeying by way of the Pacific and Siberia. This I would have done, had not the British held my Swedish boat for a week at Halifax to examine its passengers and cargo. On the boat was a group of American socialists, some of Russian origin; and among these the most prominent was Max Goldberg, a member of the famous Lipitz family, which had contributed many workers to the revolution of 1905 and was to contribute more to the later Bolshevik revolution. Goldberg later became well known under the name of Petrovsky and was often called "General" because of the high position which he held under Trotsky in the Red Army.

I knew Goldberg and suspected that he belonged to a delegation going to the socialist congress at Stockholm which the Russian socialists in the new revolutionary Russia, through the Soviets, had proposed. The Allies had refused to allow their socialists to attend this conference because socialist delegations from Germany and Austria were also invited. One of its purposes was to define the war aims and the peace terms of the Allies. After we got through Halifax, I had many long talks with these American socialists, particularly with those of Russian birth who were returning to Russia to help make the revolution a real one.

I rushed through Norway and Sweden and down through Finland as quickly as possible, in order to get to the center of revolution without delay. In Stockholm I picked up boxes for the embassy, which I later learned contained food, the shortage of which in the capital had been one of the causes of the mass uprising that had developed into revolution. I must confess that my enthusiasm was great, for it seemed to me that with the overthrow of tsarism the liberal Russia for which my friends had been working, and for which, in fact, many generations of the best minds in Russia had worked, was now about to materialize.

At one of the last stations in Finland, I found the illustrated supplement of a leading Petrograd newspaper devoted to America and her entry into the war. The frontispiece was a portrait of George Washington; and, thinking to use this as an entering wedge, I approached a group of Russian soldiers on the platform. I began the conversation by calling attention to the fact that Washington was the father of the American Revolution, and I was distinctly embarrassed when one of the soldiers remarked: "Prosperous-looking gentleman." A few weeks later, in the capital, I got from a cabdriver the best definition of the term "bourgeois" as it was being used by the more radical elements in the Russian revolutionary situation. He defined a bourgeois as "one who lived well under the old regime," and I was soon to learn that this definition covered a large percentage of the intelligentsia as well as the landowning and capitalistic classes and the former officialdom. In my first talk with Ambassador Francis he showed that he, too, had sensed the real meaning of the revolution, for he remarked that now one would have to show why one enjoyed the good things of this life. At the outbreak of the revolution Francis had called in the entire embassy staff and announced that he would send home immediately anyone buying up Russian goods, even souvenirs, and thus engaging in what he called "revolution profiteering." But not all the members of the various missions that came to Russia during the next months could resist the temptation of buying cheap the belongings of rich bourgeois who anticipated the extension of the revolution.

My friend Chapin Huntington, our commercial attaché, met me at the Finland station and invited me to share his large apartment. He had this rather large apartment for a reasonable price because its Russian owners thought it would be better protected by American occupancy.

My work during this period was to follow closely political trends, see representatives of various parties, and go in the evening to the Bolshevik headquarters, where Lenin and others spoke, often from a balcony overlooking the street, to large crowds. I usually reported to the ambassador while he breakfasted and then to the members of the Root mission, who were housed in the Winter Palace.

PETROGRAD
August 12, 1917

DEAR PAUL:

The first evening that I have had free for many a day. 'Tis a busy life that I am living, but an interesting one, as you have perhaps guessed. My duties are many and varied, and sometimes I am not quite sure just what I am and what I am supposed to be doing. In the first place, I am chief political adviser to the ambassador, and that takes some time and means considerable responsibility these days. I get the newspapers early in the morning, go through them, make a couple of telephone calls to run down the views of this or that man in whom I have confidence on some point, and then turn up at the embassy at ten o'clock, where I stay from thirty minutes to two hours, according to the importance of the events of the day. I have been able—in fact, that has been the object of the long talks—to contribute to the decisions made. Then I may have to go out as interpreter if the ambassador is to interview one of the ministers, because I seem to be the man the Governor now trusts the most. So I have gone through at first hand all the big events of the last weeks. I have seen a lot of Kerensky, whom I knew quite well before. The changes in the government have not reduced much the number of my friends in the high positions—a great advantage, standing in with all parties.

My other job, which I have had for the last five days, has been that of adviser, guide, and interpreter to Billings, first of all, and then, as far as possible, to the other members of the Red Cross mission. What a fine lot of men they sent over. Post, of course, has taken a lot of my time, but I got a corking Russian to devote himself to him and to Harold Swift and Raymond Robins; and the four of them have just completed a fine report for the meeting of the mission tomorrow. The mission is already a great success, for they did not come with empty hands—they had a million rubles' worth of supplies and the promise of shipments twice a month; and one of the members, Thompson of New York, bought a half-million rubles' worth of Liberty Bonds the other day. Billings is a wonder as an organizer. Also, he has entered into the spirit of the country in an astounding way. You should have heard his speech—translated by your humble servant with all the emphasis and force I could put behind my words in order to render the original properly—to a meeting of soldiers who escaped from German prison camps and are off to the front now to explain the kind of treatment they received at the hands of the Germans.

My third job is that of running, in co-operation with Corse, a publicity bureau, to get out news items to the Russian newspapers, to prepare, print, and distribute pamphlets, etc.—all this in co-operation with the English and French.

And, finally, I have to turn up at the Y.M.C.A. every so often to go over the situation with Harte. We are working now at many barracks and at points along the front. Also, the Y.M.C.A. is starting up tea-rooms here, and the two excellent workers already on the ground come around to get advice.

Don't think me conceited for enumerating all this, but I thought you might be interested to know what I am doing.

Mr. Mott has been better able to seize the human side of this great revolution than the other men of the commission. And I feel that I have done my little part in acting as guide, suggester, and interpreter for him. I took him one day to a congress of the Cossacks. We just dropped in, without invitation or plan. For an hour we talked to a group of a hundred, answering and putting questions back and forth. Then the session opened. They asked Mott to make a speech. We took the platform; and I translated his words, sentence by sentence. I told Mr. Mott that it was hardly the role of the secretary of the Y.M.C.A. We were given an enormous ovation, and the next order of the session was a resolution demanding the offensive immediately, to consolidate the conquests of the revolution.

The following excerpts[1] from my letters and notes written during July and August of 1917 record my current observations and interpretation of developments:

Had there not been a change of government, a revolution of some kind, Russia would have been out of the war and perhaps even on the side of Germany, through the treasonable action of the men kicked out last March. Therefore, the revolution had to come, and the leaders had to make the best of a situation which was forced upon them by the other side, by the complete breakdown of everything under the old regime.

. . . .

A lot of mistakes were made during the first weeks of the revolution. It is always easy to look back and criticize. But the legacy of the old regime was a terrible one, especially in the habits of mind which were developed. I saw the cable Mr. Crane sent you the other day. He used this same phrase, and I had it also from a socialist who wished me to see that one could not change the habits of mind of a vast people, even with revolution, in four short months.

. . . .

Russia has many problems to face. The heritage of the old regime is enormous and seems to penetrate every phase of life. They all want to discuss and think out the right move to make. This is natural. If there were no war, one would express the greatest surprise at the rapid progress of the readjustments. The German intrigue going on, in Petrograd particularly, but also in the country and the army, has blocked progress in one sense but has perhaps hastened the process at the same time.

[1] [The excerpts are taken from the following writings of Samuel N. Harper: memorandum of discussion with Harold Williams and John R. Mott, July 6, 1917; letters to Richard Crane, dated July 8, July 23, and August 18, 1917; to Paul V. Harper, August 12, 1917; to Mr. Prince for communication to our ministers to Sweden and Norway, July 12, 1917; to John R. Mott, August 28, 1917. These excerpts have been inserted editorially in the scheme of the memoirs to give a graphic picture of Harper's current observations and interpretations and must be regarded as not necessarily reflecting his viewpoint at the time of the writing of his memoirs twenty-four years later.—EDITOR.]

For, as one was beginning to see that socialism would not work, one also discovered that the extreme socialist propaganda was supported by German agents and German money. Repressive measures could not be used by the new government. One had to wait for the intrigue to show itself in its true light.

Russia has a problem such as no other nation has ever had to face. She must at one and the same time consolidate the revolution and wage a war. The war was forgotten for a few months because the revolution naturally absorbed the interest of the whole people. The Germans took advantage of the situation and played it for a time to their own ends. Then the change of psychology came, about two weeks ago. Last Sunday was the test day. The extremists organized a protest against the provisional government and the War of Capitalists. I watched the procession of the organized bands. There were many groups of straight anarchists, but always surrounded by a squad of armed soldiers. There were no disorders. But the marchers looked bored and tired. Then on Monday we got word of the offensive begun on that same day, July 1. Also on Monday they arrested a group of the anarchists. By the way, many of these anarchists come from America. Now, after a week, the spirit of the country is one of healthy enthusiasm for the war.

.   .   .   .

In this situation you have conflicting forces released, and workers and owners do not know how to meet the situation. Thus we have a series of anarchic outbursts without reference to each other. To get this in hand before a collapse is the most important thing. You can understand the view of the workmen, who see the vast profits made by owners during the war. The owners have heretofore had the support of the state and have been spoiled by it. Now they are hankering for the old times. They cannot be wakened and gathered into a sensible organization. They are not equal to the situation. The workmen often make unjustifiable demands. To get sufficient organization during the war to tide over the crisis is the main question. Apart from the war it would not be serious, and there would not be much fear for the general future. Since there is a war, there may be awkward facts which will complicate matters.

.   .   .   .

As I wrote you in my other letter, everyone was insistent that there must be a crisis. It was a very useful one. It showed up the extremists. Before, there was doubt as to their sincerity, but still they were considered revolutionaries, and therefore had a hearing. Now they have been proclaimed traitors, and it will be possible at last to suppress them by force. Lvov could not do it; but Kerensky, as a socialist, who is at the same time minister of war, and prime minister, will be better able to do the difficult job. So far, they are living up to their promise to exercise a strong repressive hand, though the process of repression goes somewhat slowly. But I keep urging patience.

.   .   .   .

It is taking some time for Kerensky to resolve to use the full authority which he proclaims he enjoys. At times he seems to go backward a bit, giving way to a demand from the Workmen and Soldiers Council, of which he is supposed to be independent. But, of course, we have to recognize that it is hard for him to break with his own group, especially when the other side will not give him the fullest support. And they, in turn, proclaim that they will support the government, but find it hard to do so when they see Kerensky giving in to the Councils. The nonsocialists groups have at last shown some measure of organization and interco-ordination. No resolutions will be passed at the Advisory National Conference, in Moscow. In fact, Kerensky says that no demands can be addressed to the government, but everyone is expected to express his views and ideas. With this stock of information the government will return to Petrograd tonight and will direct its action, independent of any party, but presumably in conformity with the ideas of the conference. But the ideas of which camp of the conference—that is the question. General Kornilov and Savinkov are for the same extreme measures in the rear as have been accepted for the front. Both are for limiting the powers of the army committee. This was Kornilov's program, given in his speech of yesterday, which he said was accepted in principle by the government. He asked that all support the government. Savinkov resigned three days ago but withdrew his resignation. This would indicate, then, a victory for the government and a declaration of independence by the government with regard to the Councils on this point at least. In any case, the country can be held together until December without any question. I believe we could hold things here on into the spring, but to December we are secure. But we are getting more and more tired.

.   .   .   .

The new spirit has begun to develop. We are beginning to get what they call "revolutionary" dictatorial government and "revolutionary" authority and "revolutionary" order. You see, the very words "dictatorial government," "authority," and "order," standing alone, were so discredited by the old regime that they had to go. Of course, they were needed, and at last they are brought forward again but always preceded by the adjective "revolutionary." Now, no more meetings on the street and no more meetings at the front; German subsidized papers have been closed; the frontiers have been closed for two weeks now and will remain so for another week; military censorship has been re-established.

.   .   .   .

We have entered the third period of the revolution, and the watchword of this period is to drop all party programs and to work to save the country. Before, one was saving the revolution—now one speaks first of the country. Now all realize the seriousness of the situation; there is a general stiffening through all classes.

We are not out of the woods yet, by any means. But the tone is so much stiffer and firmer that we look forward to the inevitable difficulties with less alarm. The attitude taken by the Governor, by the Billings crowd, and by the other Americans here who really count is one of distinct optimism, growing every day. In this way we hope to contribute to the stiffening process, and I believe we are doing this. And if people over there will only have confidence and continue to give moral and material support, we can hold things together. A dollar spent here will save us a hundred, and I do not think it is a gamble.

.   .   .   .

The most serious problem just now is the Finnish. The Finns are proving themselves mighty poor politicians. They were given everything they had a right to expect. They are stabbing the new Russia in the back. Again it is clear that German agents are at work in Finland. I have always worked for the Finnish cause, as any Finns you may see will tell you. But I am now writing to the *Monitor* that Finland, by her present actions, has forfeited the support that America has always given her.

The events in the first weeks of July marked a turning-point in the revolution. The armed demonstrations against the provisional government and the Bolsheviks' attempt to force the Executive Committee of the Workers' and Soldiers' Soviets to take over authority seemed at the time to have failed. As the Root mission departed in the midst of these disorders, it was assured that the suppression of this uprising would mean the complete suppression of the Bolshevik trend in the revolution. In point of fact, these July days proved to be the rehearsal for the Bolshevik seizure of power three months later.

During these critical July days Huntington and I, as the two people at the embassy knowing Russian, were often sent out to see what was happening on the streets. The first outbreak had in fact taken place practically under the windows of our apartment, and we had hurried through dinner to go out and see the show. The next day we tramped from point to point, several times jumping into corridors when there was shooting. One evening we had to drop to the floor of the streetcar as we crossed a bridge near the Bolshevik headquarters, which we thought had been taken over by government troops and was a safe part of town at last. We watched the crowds besiege the headquarters of the Soviet committee and listened to Trotsky haranguing each group as it came up, from his improvised tribune on the eighth rung of a ladder. As usual, it was unclear to which side he was going to jump, one minute protecting the Soviet committee in its decision not to take over authority, and the next apparently joining the crowd in its demand for "full power to the Soviets."

After these July days I went down to Moscow with Drs. Billings and Post and Harold Swift to discuss with the authorities there co-operation in relief work. Mr. Crane went with us to attend the Convention of the Russian Church, the first to be called since the time of Peter the Great. This convention represented an attempt to democratize the church leadership. Mr. Crane was able to reserve a compartment to himself on the train, which was perhaps not so fortunate, because he is a sound sleeper and was not awakened when, at a station, his window was lowered and his coat, with passport and money, was removed. The rest of us slept in one small second-class compartment, and I was rather glad to have my Chicago friends experience some of the primitive roughness of Russian life—increased, of course, by the conditions of revolution. A few days later, for the return trip, we were again able to secure only a single compartment for four, which we found filled with six "comrades" when we tried to enter. Then my friends did show consternation, and I myself was about to throw up the sponge after our hard, uncomfortable days in Moscow, where things seemed even more disorganized than in the main capital. These "comrades" were part of the "self-demobilizing" Russian army returning from the front, and I understood fully their contention that they deserved the soft berths which they had expropriated. But, fortunately, American prestige was still high; and by noting the length of the trip which these Americans had made to help Russia, I was able to clear our compartment and get back our reserved berths.

As it was clear that the Bolsheviks were responsible for the July uprising, the provisional government, now headed by Kerensky, issued orders for the arrest of Lenin and Trotsky. But Lenin managed to escape to Finland; and the Bolshevik newspapers, ordered closed, continued to appear and carry articles signed by him. One day I acted as interpreter between Francis and Savinkov, the former terrorist, and now assistant minister of war under Kerensky. Francis kept insisting on asking why the order for Lenin's arrest had not been carried out. At this moment there was much talk of the discovery of certain documents alleging treasonable relations between the Bolshevik leaders, especially Lenin, and the German general staff. This was based on a premature statement by the minister of justice and probably prevented the securing of more evidence in support of the charge. In discussing this particular incident some years later in Chicago, Kerensky told me that he could not have proved the charge with the material in hand at the time and that the bringing-forward of this charge really helped Lenin instead of hurting his prestige. Because of the common struggle against autocracy, moderate socialists like Kerensky would not use measures of repression against their opponents; but most of us believed the moderates would maintain control in spite of that handicap.

There were many pessimists, however, and well-informed ones. There was Baron Rosen, whom I had first met when he was the Russian ambassador at Washington in 1905. Retired by 1917, Rosen was trying to make available, particularly to us Americans, his thorough knowledge of Russian affairs. His Baltic origin, as well as his deep pessimism, tended to make us all avoid him, and in a way which he was intelligent enough to fully sense. As things turned out, we would have been well advised to have paid more attention to his warnings.

Two other pessimists were Alexander Guchkov and Paul Milyukov. These two prominent leaders of the March revolution had been forced to retire because of their conflict with the Committee of Workmen and Soldiers Soviets over foreign policy and army policy. As it was unwise for the ambassador or for members of the various American missions to see these men too frequently or openly, one of my tasks was to maintain contact with them. But, as in the case of Baron Rosen, we Americans were too prone to brush aside their opinions. Having just come into the war, we expected everybody, including the exhausted Russians, to do more and better fighting.

Through Mr. Crane I saw a great deal of Thomas Masaryk, who had come on from England (to which country he had escaped from Prague) in order to organize the Czech legions from the Czech prisoners of war. These Czech units were to help the new Russia, and from Russia fight for the liberation and re-establishment of the Czech nation. Masaryk and Mr. Crane could not be classed with the complete pessimists, although both were very much concerned by the many evidences of disintegration. As Mr. Crane put it one day: "The cement seems to be running out."

Thinking that American morale would have to be built up with our entry into the war, I even went so far at one time as to complain to the Associated Press of what I considered the cynical bias of their Russian correspondent, Robert C. Long. Long knew Russian thoroughly and was really a publicist rather than a reporter, writing for the more important British journals. He reacted vigorously to my criticism, and perhaps it was well for me that we were in a revolutionary situation, where we were all busy. I found it very uncomfortable, for the first time in my life, to pass without even a nod a man with whom formerly I had been rather friendly. However, in December, 1936, we met again in Berlin; and after listening together to the broadcast of the English king's abdication speech, we laughed at our former misunderstanding.

Long, like the Russian pessimists, saw nothing but gradual disintegration in Russia in 1917. There were many reasons for such a progressive breakdown, and among them was the inadequate experience in matters administrative, not of all, but of the larger part, of the intellectuals who had come into political leadership. The old bureaucracy had been scrapped, and the new men had inherited its difficulties in organizing production and distribution. During my trip to Moscow I had dropped in at a restaurant frequented by university and literary people and had seen in the corner the two prime ministers of this period— Prince Lvov and Kerensky. Kerensky was on the point of leaving to catch a train back to Petrograd. His last word was that he would now organize effectively the administration of which he had become the head. Lvov's remark, after Kerensky left, was: "Always hopeful but utterly hopeless as an administrator, like most of the Russian intellectuals."

The breakdown in production and distribution affected even us foreigners; it became increasingly difficult to secure even moderate amounts of the most basic foodstuffs. Huntington and I often had to withdraw an invitation we had extended to a visiting American to come to luncheon or dinner, because our cook reported that she had been unable to buy any supplies. Using Huntington's diplomatic privilege, we were able to get a stock of vodka, in the small half-pint bottles called by the Russian workman and peasant the "little devil." With her pockets full of this very effective form of currency, our cook was somewhat more successful at the market places. The shortage of fats was a particular worry. One day Huntington discovered a supply of nuts and came home in great joy with a large bag full. Another time we secured a small keg of butter and spent the evening making up small packages which we distributed next day to our friends, some of whom had had no butter for over three weeks. Driving home one evening in a particularly ramshackle cab, Huntington suggested that it was like Russia and would probably collapse at the next corner. But, like Russia, it bent in all directions but did not break.

I returned to America in September and reported first to Washington and then to my "points of contact" in the business and newspaper worlds. I held out the promise that the Kerensky regime would survive until the meeting of the Constituent Assembly soon to be held, which would then consolidate the country. Kerensky's frantic efforts to hold things together were considered by many of us as going successfully. But it is now clear that we Americans were guilty of wishful thinking, grasping at mere details to support our picture of developing co-operation after an inevitable period of disintegration from the revolutionary upset of March. Some years later, in Chicago, I asked Kerensky if the ill-fated Russian offensive of July, 1917, was the result of this hopeful pressure from the Allies, and particularly from America, or whether it was dictated by internal politics—the desire to stop, by military action, the internal disintegration which was progressing rapidly. I have always been comforted by Kerensky's answer: "Both factors."

PART VI
THE END OF THE WAR AND AFTER: 1918–25

For the convenience of the reader:

1. On November 21, 1917, the Bolsheviks, in line with their cardinal policy of "an immediate, general, and democratic peace," proposed the Brest Litovsk armistice negotiations with the Germans and invited the Allies to join. Receiving no response from the Allies, they started negotiations. The German demands were, of course, very stiff and grew worse as the negotiations went on, until the parleys broke down. On February 10, 1918, the Bolsheviks, completely disillusioned about any "democratic peace," refused the German terms of large annexations but themselves declared the war at an end and walked out. The German armies moved, and surrender was the only alternative. Protesting openly that acceptance was made only under compulsion, Lenin, on March 3, signed away, in the Treaty of Brest Litovsk, Erivan, Kars, Batum, the Ukraine, Poland, the Baltic Provinces, and Finland.

2. Meanwhile, the Constituent Assembly, a body of representatives elected to set up a permanent government, which had been called by the provisional government under Kerensky, met on January 18, 1918. It was dominated by non-Bolshevik groups who refused to recognize the legality of the Soviet government and the Council of Peoples Commissars, and the Assembly was dispersed after two days. On February 8 a decree was issued by the Council of Commissars repudiating the debts of all former Russian governments. (It was the overriding of the Constituent Assembly and the renunciation of debts that were held, on the surface at least, most seriously and protractedly against the Bolsheviks by our own and other democratic governments.)

3. There was no recognition of the new government set up by the Bolsheviks, but there was no breach of relations—no immediate withdrawal of the diplomatic corps in any manner. The United States simply overlooked the Brest-Litovsk Treaty and the new government and spoke to the "Russian people" over the heads of the Soviets. It was, after all, a serious war crisis; and, while the United States saved its rights on recognition, the situation called for many exceptions to the rules of international relations. The ambassador, Governor Francis, handled many critical matters informally. After the Bolshevik demand for a general democratic peace in November, 1917, the Allies were somewhat put to it to formulate their own war aims; and on January 8, 1918, Presiddnt Wilson announced his famous Fourteen Points.

4. *Innumerable incidents arose. The Bolsheviks were suspicious of America, and more so of the other Allies. They tried to force our hand for aid in one way or another, with full reservations as to their own independent status and their principles of world socialism and revolution. When there was no response, the Bolsheviks cried, "The Allies are all imperialists," and disclosed the "secret treaties." They threatened a world revolution of all workmen. The United States government, on its side, distrusted the Bolsheviks and did not believe that the Russian people were behind them. That the Germans had allowed the Bolshevik leaders to cross Germany to reach Russia from Switzerland was in itself a ground for suspicion. The so-called "Sisson papers," uncovered and published by Creel's Bureau on Public Information in 1918, purported to show that the Germans had deliberately aided and used Lenin and Trotsky in order to disorganize Russia. Lenin and Trotsky, on the other hand, had undoubtedly used German aid for their own purposes. No one could tell where or when German action left off and Bolshevik action began. Many were convinced that Lenin and Trotsky were simply German agents.*

5. *Raymond Robins, aiding the Red Cross work in Russia, made it his business to keep in close contact with the Bolsheviks in order to carry on his relief work. He became a useful bridge between the Bolshevik leaders in Moscow and Governor Francis, who moved in February, 1918, to Vologda below Archangel, when the German army threatened Petrograd. It was through Robins that Trotsky made the famous inquiry, which was considered by many an offer, as to what the United States would do in aid if the Congress of Soviets disaffirmed the Brest-Litovsk Treaty. This so-called "offer" was transmitted by the ambassador to the State Department with his own expression of lack of confidence. The story of Lenin's postponing the action of the congress to await, up to the last minute, a reply which never came, is a dramatic one.*

6. *On August 3, 1918, President Wilson announced "aid" to Russia and, with Japan, sent troops to Vladivostok. Although expressly intended not to be "intervention," the expedition at Archangel and other developments became so in reality.*

7. *A large part of the diplomatic group and many in the American colony moved to Irkutsk. Our last officials (except those in Siberia and Archangel) moved out about October, 1918.*

8. *On November 11, 1918, the first World War terminated with the Armistice.*

CHAPTER XIV

RUSSIA BECOMES A DIFFICULT PROBLEM

THE PERIOD AFTER THE BOLSHEVIKS TOOK POWER WAS A MOST DIFFICULT one for a so-called "expert" on Russian affairs and Sovietism—for by force of circumstances I had now definitely become a student of revolution. Hostility in America toward the new "Soviet Russia," as it came to be called, and toward the Bolsheviks became sharper, even in liberal groups. On the other hand, radical groups which had accepted our entry into the war with doubts and reservations saw in what was happening in Russia a justification for their views; for one of the most important features of the Bolshevik program was its opposition to the "imperialist war." They became pro-Soviet sympathizers and urged immediate recognition of the new authority as one established by mass revolution. Their position was somewhat weakened when the Soviet leaders dissolved the Constituent Assembly. Its members had been elected on the basis of universal suffrage, but it had contained an overwhelming majority of anti-Bolshevik groups—socialist as well as nonsocialist—which had refused to legalize Sovietism. Other recognitionists insisted that the new Russia could be reincorporated into the war against Germany if properly handled. The "interventionists," on the other hand, insisted that the new regime could not last, was helping Germany—the enemy— and that intervention not only would be in the interest of the Russian people against a group of sheer adventurers but would be a useful war measure by re-establishing the eastern front. Amid all this controversy I devoted myself to a series of activities.

George Creel, director of the United States Bureau of Public Information, was attempting to bring about some integration in the field of propaganda; and I found myself working with this new unit, to which many university men had been officially recruited. Creel had sent Edward Sisson to Russia in the early autumn of 1917, before the Bolshevik seizure of power, to represent the Bureau and to organize there an outlet for his American propaganda. At Petrograd, and later in Moscow, Sisson joined those who decided that no trust could be placed in the Bolsheviks as rulers. He had secured, in co-operation with the British Intelligence Service, certain documents which tended to prove a close relationship between the Bolshevik leaders and the German general staff in connection with the famous passage across Germany of Lenin and other leaders in a sealed car.

Returning to Washington, Sisson prepared a long pamphlet in which facsimiles of these documents appeared, with his interpretation of them. In October, 1918, on the eve of publication of this pamphlet by the Bureau of Public Information, Creel was urged to check up on the material; and I was called to Washington to be one of the small committee of the American Historical Association to do this job. The tests for documentary authenticity applied by historians were about the only check which could be made under the circumstances. Professor J. Franklin Jameson was the chairman of the group, and Professor Archibald Coolidge was also named as a member but did not formally participate in the work. In the end, Professor Jameson and I were the only signers of the statement added to the published pamphlet.

Professor Jameson and I had access to the original documents where Sisson had such. These we subjected to the tests used by students of history, relating them to the known facts of the moment. With respect to those documents which we had in the original, we expressed the view that, as students of history, we would accept them. We refused to express an opinion on those documents for which only translations had been obtained. We found that certain inconsistencies appearing on the face of the documents, which were pointed out by those disputing authenticity, were unfounded, arising because of erroneous early translations, or misconceptions of the differences of dates under the Russian calendar.

We flatly refused to comment on Sisson's conclusions as to what the documents proved, namely, that Lenin not only had had contacts with the German general staff when he journeyed across Germany but had been and still was a German agent. Jameson and I were ready to state that in the given circumstances, by starting a social revolution in Russia, Lenin was objectively aiding the enemy from a military point of view. We were told that such a statement would not help to promote that emotional upsurge necessary for the mobilization of all our resources to be thrown into the struggle. We stood our ground, however, as our statement on the pamphlet will show. But the general view current at this time was that we had declared all the documents genuine beyond any question. In addition, Sisson's conclusions as to what the documents showed were also laid upon our shoulders. This last phase gave me much concern at the time. With his country at war, the academic man, when called upon by his government to use his academic talents for a war purpose, often faces a problem of duty in two directions and finds difficulty in properly protecting himself.

Raymond Robins was a member of the Red Cross mission to Russia; and when our embassy was forced by the German approach to Petrograd to move to Vologda, Robins, remaining in Moscow at his Red Cross work, served as an unofficial bridge between the embassy and Lenin and Trotsky. Robins received directly from Trotsky what purported to be a Bolshevik proposal to refuse to ratify the Brest Litovsk peace and to resume the fighting against Germany, in return for Allied aid. Ambassador Francis forwarded this proposal by cable, and in code, to the State Department; and, as I happened to be in Washington when it was received, I was asked for an opinion. The cable contained three paragraphs, of which the third went over to a second page; and in this third paragraph the ambassador quite properly expressed his own view, which was distinctly skeptical as to any sincere resumption of war against Germany by the Bolsheviks in the light of their doctrinal views and their actions. No reply was made to this proposal.

Later, during the Senate investigations in 1919, when Robins presented this basic document on the subject to the Senate committee, the third paragraph did not appear in what he said was a copy of the cable given him by Francis himself. I tried to determine at the time, and later, whether Francis had suppressed his third paragraph in the copy which he gave to Robins or whether Robins had suppressed it in the copy which he gave to the Senate committee.

When Robins himself first returned from Russia in the late summer of 1918, I found myself following him around from person to person, calling attention to his unfinished sentences and his glossing-over of fully established facts. Robins and I went through a period of avoiding each other. It was a year or so later, while walking down Michigan Boulevard in Chicago with Charles E. Merriam, that I ran into Robins and, mistaking him for another, shook hands with him, as Merriam had done. Robins responded by saying that he would forgive me because I was in such good company. When we started to argue, Merriam saved the day by suggesting sabers at twenty paces.

Before President Wilson formulated and proclaimed his Fourteen Points, any mention of the Russian efforts to have the war and peace aims defined was coldly received. One day I tried to discuss with Theodore Roosevelt and Mark Sullivan the possibility of defining our peace aims in order to counteract the Bolshevik propaganda. Mark Sullivan, whom I had come to know through Mr. Crane, had arranged the meeting at the Harvard Club in New York. From the point of view of my purpose, the luncheon was a complete failure; but it was useful for my orientation in America after living through the revolutionary months of 1917 in Russia. Roosevelt was in one of his most combative periods, for President Wilson had managed to keep him from going abroad with the American Expeditionary Force; and I was given a very emphatic lecture to the effect that in wartime one does not talk of peace; that one does not fight for peace, but to win; and that you can't arouse fighting spirit in young soldiers by talking about the future peace terms.

The invitation of the Bolsheviks to the Allies, on November 21, 1917, to join in negotiations for a "Democratic Peace" at Brest Litovsk again raised the issue of an allied declaration of war aims; and in January, 1918, President Wilson announced his famous Fourteen Points. One of my friends, who was working at the time under Sisson in Petrograd, wrote how the President's pronouncement was received there:

President Wilson's speech of January 8th came in over the wire on January 10th, and I had to put in two of the most strenuous days of my life getting the thing out in the papers here. It caught me before I had the office in any real shape to handle such a big rush job. My force consisted of about six people, and they worked as hard as they could, up to the limit of their knowledge and ability; but to whip out a translation of such a document in short order, get the Russian copies made, and shoot them around to the papers was strenuous. We were all going it, straining every nerve, and by the end of the day had it out.

I believe it is one of the greatest state papers yet produced in America. And you cannot begin to realize what it meant to us in Russia. It came just at the right moment to show that all we had been saying to these people about the attitude of America was not glossing over dollar imperialism. It simply electrified us, and set us at our job with new energy and zest. What we had been looking and hoping for—a definite, high-minded setting forth of the aim of the Allies—was actually here. That cable as it came in over the wires cost $1,200, but it was worth forty times that amount for every word.

It gave us unutterable relief from a situation which had been getting, day by day, into a more intense strain, in which we feared that the dragging-along of the silence from the rest of the world while the Brest Litovsk negotiations were going on would simply spell the irretrievable loss of Allied influence in Russia. The situation seemed all but lost, and here in one big word from America came new strength and life in the struggle. You can't realize it even remotely.

P.S.—If the German army does march into Petrograd, we have arranged that the Nevsky will be literally covered with copies of Wilson's speech. And we've bought up the strongest glue in Russia."

In spite of all the arguments and quarrels over details,[1] American interest in the Russian people ran high through the year 1918. Those who had returned from helping Russia in her first steps as a democracy during the hectic year of 1917, brought with them a real enthusiasm for this rugged, strange people. The desire was to help Russia. There came in reports of horrors which occur in any period of civil strife, but these did not seem to shake public interest. The negotiations and the Treaty of Brest Litovsk were a serious blow to our military position, but interest in helping Russia survived.

How to give aid was the real question. It was a confusing problem. There were military aspects and responsibilities in connection with any plan. Important nonmilitary considerations were puzzling the State Department, which always has to live with any situation after the military phase is over. Any plan was subject to the determination of broad

[1] [The balance of this chapter is an editorial supplement to cover a period meagerly dealt with in the memoirs. It is based upon a careful review of Harper's correspondence covering the period.—Editor.]

Allied policies and to the personal viewpoint of the President himself, who showed a deep and farsighted interest in the Russian people.

Many nonofficial leaders of public thought gave much consideration to the matter. Committees and groups in the East and Middle West developed programs of wide range—envisaging publicity through the movies and the press, the sending-back to Russia of selected Americanized Russians, and the continuance and enlarging of the Red Cross and similar relief services. There were plans to develop economic trading on both immediate and long-time bases with organizations in those parts of Russia not yet deeply touched by the Bolsheviks—this pointed mainly to Siberia. There were even suggestions from conservative people of "making some sort of a deal" with the Bolsheviks on a temporary basis. Representatives of the All Russian Peasant Council (the Moscow Co-operative) and of the All Russian Railway Union appeared in Chicago and New York, bearing gold in their hands to buy engines and supplies; and groups of businessmen were called together to try to work out the means to meet their requirements.

The American League to Aid and Co-operate with Russia was organized to consolidate all the various groups and co-ordinate their interests and efforts in a comprehensive recommendation to the government. Herbert L. Carpenter, chairman of the Executive Committee, did an outstanding job of organization. Actual action, however, was slow—subject, as it necessarily was, to final determination by the government and the President.

There were many delicate and seemingly finespun distinctions which characterized the discussions of this period. These refinements were significant in those days of high feeling and meant success or failure in matters of large importance. There were those who felt that to "aid" or to "co-operate with" Russia meant the recognition of the new regime. A good many people hesitated to work with the league because they felt it was devoted to technical "recognition." There was the notion that we might deal with the Soviets, as distinguished from the Bolsheviks. In the last analysis, the Bolsheviks were, after all, principally the political leaders in the Communist Party, and not the government; in some respects they were like, let us say, Mark Hanna in the days of McKinley. Undoubtedly, many local Soviets were still independent to a marked degree—both in thought and fact. But the two ideas of "Bolsheviks" and "Soviets" had become synonymous in the minds of non-Bolsheviks and of our own public, and the taint had spread from one to the other. It was at the suggestion of Justice Brandeis that, to get around this issue, I cultivated the use of the expression "Aid to the soviets, peasants' co-operative societies, railway unions, and such representative democratic bodies."

The word "intervention" made great trouble. What we had in mind was "aid and assistance"; and yet the word "intervention," with its implications, spread over the country. On June 30, 1918, I wrote to Richard Crane:

On another point there has been much unnecessary confusion because of careless use of words. Many have said "intervention" when they really meant "assistance." Ambassador Bakhmeteff, for example, never uses the word "intervention" in my presence, though the newspaper may quote him as urging this action. Thus, the *New Republic* writes that Konovalov (a prominent Duma leader) is for "intervention"; and he is not, as the *New Republic* understands the word "intervention." I do not recognize that the state of war between Russia and Germany has ceased to exist. The constructive forces in Russia do not recognize the Brest Litovsk peace; so military assistance would not be "intervention."

In addition to these fine points, there was the serious Allied problem of holding Japan back from an "intervention" all her own, which everyone feared would have aggressive and imperialistic designs.

Finally, on August 3, 1918, action was announced. The note issued by the State Department shows what care was exercised in trying to deal with the difficult problem of aid to Russia:

"In the judgment of the Government of the United States . . . . military intervention in Russia would be more likely to add to the present sad confusion there than to cure it and would injure Russia rather than help her out of her distress. . . . .

"As the Government of the United States sees the present circumstances, therefore, military action is admissible in Russia now only to render such protection and help as is possible to the Czecho-Slovacs against the armed Austrian and German prisoners . . . . and to steady any efforts at self-government or self-defense in which the Russians themselves may be willing to accept assistance.

"The Government of the United States has therefore proposed to the Government of Japan that each of the two Governments send a force of a few thousand men to Vladivostok with the purpose of cooperating as a single force . . . . and the Japanese Government has consented. In taking this action, the Government of the United States wishes to announce to the people of Russia in the most public and solemn manner that it contemplates no interference with the political sovereignty of Russia, no intervention in her internal affairs, not even in local affairs . . . . and no impairment of her territorial integrity, either now or hereafter; but that what we are about to do has as its single and only object the rendering of such aid as may be acceptable to the Russian people. . . . . The Japanese Government, it is understood, will issue a similar assurance."

CHAPTER XV

THE SLAVS COME TO WASHINGTON

AFTER THE DECISION FOR INTERVENTION ON AUGUST 3, 1918, I TOOK A short vacation with the family at Onekema, Michigan, to recover from overwork. I had not been there very long when I received a telegram from a very interesting Russian, P. P. Batolin, announcing that he was in Chicago and reminding me that I had promised to help him if he ever came to America.

I had met Batolin, the head of the large semi-co-operative Russian trading firm of Stakheyev, in the summer of 1917. He was of peasant origin and had become a prosperous man with enormous interests, especially in Siberia, and with foreign trade experience through the export of the dairy products which his co-operative organization marketed. He had the usual directness, almost to the point of brutality, of the Russian peasant. His assumed naïveness was a cover for extreme cleverness and even slyness. As I shall note in some of my experiences with Batolin, he had the traditional peasant suspicion of the intellectual as well as of the politician.

On the occasion of our first meeting, Huntington and I had dined with Batolin in Petrograd. As we sat down, he apologized profusely because he had no vodka to offer us. I immediately telephoned our cook to bring over a half-dozen bottles from our supply, secured through diplomatic immunity in spite of the prohibition law in force. Because of the breakdown of the droshky service, the vodka did not arrive until the end of the dinner, when our host, with much gusto, served it to us and his other guests. He then turned to me and asked me to take out my notebook and write down, for future historians to note and use as the basis for generalization, that things were so upset in Russia in the summer of 1917 that the Russians drank their vodka after, instead of before, dinner.

Batolin came to this country with the following letter of introduction to Mr. Samuel McRoberts, of the National City Bank, from John F. Stevens, the head of the American Commission for Railways, who was still working in Russia:

Mr. Batolin comes from the stock which, to my mind, represents the best elements of Russian life, and upon which the world must depend, in the last analysis, for laying a permanent foundation for Russia's future greatness: that is, the peasant class, the only producers, as distinguished from middlemen and idlers, that this present unhappy country has ever had. His career—as you will note, he is still a young man—reads like a romance, and I personally know that his rapid rise in the conduct of large matters has come from his energy, probity, and, above all, from his rare faculty of looking far into the future and realizing the need of laying his plans upon a secure foundation, which will enable that expansion to be made which the enormous capacity of Russia will demand.

I think that his ideas in relation to the co-ordination of legitimate commercial, manufacturing, and transportation interests with those of constructive statesmanship (or politics in its highest meaning) are wise and farsighted. The problem of politics (call it by that name) in Russia is a large one, but the one of economics is vastly larger; and no government can be formed and maintained there which does not rest on a basis of the successful development of her resources.

Mr. Batolin is a man of national ideals, and such men are rare in Russia. He is a man of initiative and constructive ability, in the broadest sense of the term. The enterprises which he represents—and they are many—are going concerns, not paper projects which require careful nursing to become of value.

It seemed to me that this type of Russian could be useful in bringing a little more real understanding of the Russian situation to Washington officialdom. It was clear that he would be, in a sense, a breath of fresh air in that atmosphere overloaded with reports from representatives abroad, from experts offering their services, and from emissaries of the warring groups of the Russian internal situation. He waved aside all the finespun political distinctions with which most Russian minds were full and talked broad statesmanship. And introducing Batolin to Washington seemed a more constructive project for me to undertake than working with the League, which, beautifully organized though it was, did not seem to be accomplishing anything further. I communicated my thoughts to Charles Crane and to Cyrus McCormick, and they felt as I did.

In order to get Batolin to Washington under promising auspices, I decided to take him first to Colonel House, who had gone to his country place near Boston to escape the summer and political heat of Washington. After telling Colonel House that I thought I had something that would help on the Russian situation and describing briefly my "specimen," I was told to bring him on. As we traveled to Boston, Batolin and I carefully reread and discussed the recent note of August 3, laying down the government's policy of aid. Batolin was opposed to intervention unless it was done on a very large scale and accompanied by extensive economic aid to the completely exhausted country which Russia had become after the first months of the second revolution.

Colonel House found in Batolin a new, fresh, and promising approach to the Russian problem and asked me to take him to Washington and chaperon him around to members of the cabinet, with the view of ultimately getting through, at the proper moment, to President Wilson. As Masaryk had just come to Washington from Russia, seeking recognition for his committee as the *de facto* government of the future Czechoslovakia, and as I was to serve as a kind of informal chaperon for him, telling him of the political position and views of the various individuals to whom he was going with his cause, I was glad to undertake Colonel House's program.

So, for a month I acted as adviser and interpreter for Batolin, reporting regularly to Colonel House and receiving from him short general suggestions on our procedure. Although I was supposed to be Batolin's adviser, he, in fact, controlled the order of our visits and, of course, the content of his statements to the various officials whom we met. I prepared him for these interviews by long lectures on the political position, the past activity, and the general character of each man. From the beginning he made it clear that he would not try to reach the President until the situation had developed to a point where he could make a concrete proposal as to how the relations between the American and Russian people could be best promoted. But, knowing his ultimte aim to reach the President, I suggested that we see Justice Brandeis as soon as possible. Batolin already knew that Brandeis, as he put it, "had the left ear of the President," while Colonel House "had the right ear"; and he remarked one day that he believed the President's left ear had the better hearing.

According to plan, we worked our way up, so to speak, seeing Secretaries Houston and Lane first, because Batolin was a businessman. Then we went to Secretary Lansing, and only at the end did we go to Justice Brandeis. In the intervals we saw many leading businessmen, such as Alexander Legge, vice-chairman of the War Industrial Board and general manager of International Harvester, and Wooley of the International Radiator and the War Trade Board. Even John D. Rockefeller, Sr., expressed a desire to see Batolin.

In all of these interviews I insisted that Batolin take with us another American, Mr. Michels, now of our Department of Commerce, whom Batolin employed as interpreter. I was not in Batolin's employ but, as usual, was getting my out-of-pocket expenses from Mr. Crane's office and giving my services to the government as from the university in my vacation period. Batolin told me frankly that he was keeping track of the number of words used by him or the person with whom he was talking and the number which I used in my translations. To protect myself, I always explained, to Lansing or to Brandeis, that I was acting purely mechanically as interpreter; and I did so because this Russian peasant frequently spoke very directly and at times rudely, although in such a way as not to cause resentment. Thus, when we entered Secretary Lansing's office, Batolin asked me if the secretary had read a brief statement which he had sent around three days earlier, when the interview had been set. When Mr. Lansing explained that he had not had time to read it, I had to ask the secretary, from Batolin, please to have it brought in and to read it before the discussion started. With a smile at me, Mr. Lansing agreed to this procedure; and we sat there in silence while he perused the short document which Batolin and I had prepared.

When we finally decided to go to Brandeis, the justice found it possible to give us the whole morning; and from my viewpoint this was one of the best of the interviews. Several times I asked Michels to take over the translating, saying I was tired; but I really wanted to listen and participate. As we left, Justice Brandeis remarked to me that it was one of the most interesting mornings he had had since coming to Washington. Under my agreement with Batolin, which I explained to Brandeis, I had to translate this remark for Batolin, although it was really addressed to me. As we walked home, Batolin kept silent for some ten minutes; that was his custom after one of our interviews. Finally he remarked: "He is not an honest man, and I guess we have failed." This surprising comment he developed with considerable feeling, declaring that the subject of discussion had been the relations between the American and Russian peoples, that the Jewish question had been a disrupting factor in these relations, that Brandeis was a Jew, that it was up to him to bring up the subject, and that he had failed to do so—thus showing that he was neither an honest Jew nor an honest American.

Sometimes Batolin turned his peasant logic directly on me. Learning of the arrival in Washington of my old friend Baron Korff, a Russian professor married to an American, and an active worker in the cause of Russian liberalism, I wanted to bring him and Batolin together. But Batolin told me quite sharply that it was not my business to introduce him to Russians, and to limit myself to introducing him to Americans. Later Batolin met Korff at the Russian embassy; and on his return in the early morning hours, he woke me up and, sitting on the foot of the bed, gave me a long sermon on the subject of professors and politics. Apparently, he was deeply disgusted by the line which Korff was taking, making use of his American connections. He ended the sermon with a moral to the effect that a professor playing politics is the most despicable type.

With the signing of the Armistice on November 11, 1918, came the lessening of war pressure, the increase of political pressure, the preparations for the peace conference, the beginnings of the Senate investigations—and all this changed the course of many plans. Batolin departed for Paris in January without seeing the President. Cyrus McCormick urged him to attend the peace conference, but Batolin felt as I did about attending "unofficially." He likened himself to the government inspector who was authorized to criticize but not to do anything constructive. "My own position would be like the inspector's," he said.

To Russia, the Armistice brought the withdrawal of Germany from her borders and effectively abnegated much of the Brest-Litovsk Treaty. But, aside from futile efforts by Wilson to bring some form of Russian representation into the League of Nations by agreement of utterly irreconcilable Russian groups in Paris (the remains of the ousted provisional government) and in Moscow (the Bolsheviks), she was left to flounder in the immensities of her civil war and general economic distress. And, as if to isolate her entirely from the rest of Europe, there was established a *cordon sanitaire* of small independent states—the Baltic countries, Poland, and Romania.

The void left by Batolin's departure was soon well filled for me by the problems, pressures, and personalities of Czechoslovakia and Poland. With the Fourteen Points now in the stage of actual establishment, leaders of central European peoples became very active in Washington. The national groups already established in our country were stimulated to activity. I was in close touch with these groups through the American Friends of a New Middle Europe, organized by the War Committee of the Union League Club of Chicago. Chicago had a population of Polish origin second only to Warsaw itself, and a Czechoslovak population second only to Prague. Masaryk came to the fore as the great Czech leader. Among the Polish leaders who had hurried to America were Paderewski and Roman Dmowski.

Robert Lord, of Harvard, was in charge of the Polish question for the Mezes Committee; and I was able to put him in touch with these two leaders because I had known Dmowski very intimately since 1905. He was the same person who, called to the rostrum of the Duma on a Polish question of emergency, rattled over the cobblestones in a racing droshky from a very convivial luncheon to open his speech by calling the Russians "Asiatics."

The Polish cause had been supported by American public opinion with almost as much enthusiasm as the cause of the Czechs, even though the Polish question involved the eternal Jewish problem. The British had found it necessary, or expedient, to issue at about this same time the Balfour Declaration, promising the Jews a "national home" in Palestine; and this had greatly increased the legitimate efforts of the Jews to secure, in the future peace settlement, a better status in those countries in which they were subject to legal restrictions, as well as to general anti-Semitic policy. Such a country was Poland, with a very great Jewish population. Now Roman Dmowski had been openly and actively anti-Semitic in his writings and speeches. Knowing him well, I urged on him the need of meeting the situation which he would face in America, where Jewish organizations and their leaders were demanding that any American support of Polish aspirations for independence should be conditional on definite guarantees that the Jewish minority in any future Poland would be fully protected in all rights. Dmowski refused to compromise on a matter on which he had always taken such a definite stand. It was with some difficulty that the Polish leaders managed to carry out their mission successfully in the face of this refusal.

In 1936 in Warsaw, when I saw Dmowski for the last time, shortly before his death, I allowed myself to say that his anti-Semitic views had been, to a large extent, responsible for his failure in politics. For, despite his outstanding ability and his unquestioned devotion to the cause of Polish nationalism, Dmowski had been frequently in the discard in Polish public life, as I found him on this last visit. Dmowski admitted that my statement was probably true, but he insisted that his interpretation of political conditions had dictated his anti-Semitism.

In those last years Dmowski was writing his memoirs and formulating the general philosophy of life which, as one of the leaders of thought in eastern Europe, he had derived from his experiences. The gist of this philosophy, as he talked of his future and last book, seemed to be that Western people had got from Greek thought the principle of the dignity of the individual but had failed to recognize the social obligation of the individual. Two peoples—the Japanese and the Jews—had either never had sufficient contact with, or had failed to accept, the Greek philosophy of individualism. Nevertheless, these peoples took full advantage of the fruits of Western individualism and turned them against us. And then he made the rather startling statement that it was the Jews in Germany who had made the German people accept the principle of authoritarianism, so that the Germans had now become a third menace to Western civilization. The weakness he noted in Western civilization, of the overemphasis on the individual to the exclusion of his social obligations, he considered also responsible for the rise to power of authoritarian and armed groups.

Early in 1919 a few public lectures showed me clearly what the "Russian expert" was going to have to face. The subject of Bolshevism had become increasingly controversial. There seemed to be Bolshevism everywhere in those first few months after the war; and, in fact, Soviet regimes actually were set up in Hungary and Bavaria and several large cities of Germany. Against intervention, Moscow leaders developed their propaganda of "world revolution." Wherever there was trouble, particularly among workmen and demobilized soldiers, there came the cry of "the hand of Moscow."

As a political issue, the question of our continued intervention was constantly being brought up—in Congress as well as in the press. There was also the supplementary question of recognizing one of the warring factions inside Russia as the government of the country. Anti-Soviet regimes set up in Siberia, in Archangel, and in the Ukraine received our de facto recognition, while those in the Baltic states, for some reason, did not. What made the controversy more acute was the fact that one really could not know just what was going on, not only within the area controlled by the Soviets, but also in those areas held by the Whites.

122

In February I went to Washington on the subpoena of a Senate committee which was to investigate what all this Sovietism was about. Senator King of Utah initiated this move to bring our most dignified body into the picture. So far as Senator King had any specific aim, he seemed to want to prevent recognition and, as the logical corollary, to continue the intervention, which, with the conclusion of the Armistice, had developed as its object the suppression of the "menace of Bolshevism." Although subpoenaed as a witness, I was to be useful also, *sub rosa*, in the selection of other witnesses and in the formulation of the procedure of questioning.

When my turn came to face questioning, I found myself giving not only an inadequate but sometimes even an incorrect picture on a particular point, for I had to answer "Yes" or "No" to loosely or stupidly worded questions. For example, I am on record to the effect that all agriculturists—that is, the majority of the population—were disfranchised under the Soviet system. The Senators were attempting to measure Soviet institutions by the one yardstick which they knew—the vote —and the results were often very unsatisfactory.

The testimony of one witness illustrated particularly well how investigations by such august bodies as the Senate give erroneous ideas the authoritative sanction of fact. This witness had been in a small provincial town on the Volga in those first months of the new Soviet regime and had brought out of Russia a document which he insisted proved, beyond any question, that Sovietism was based on the nationalization of women as well as on the nationalization of land and industrial enterprises. This document had been given to him by his Russian interpreter-secretary, as published in a local newspaper. But the witness failed to state that the newspaper was an anarchist sheet and that the alleged decree was planted on the Bolsheviks by the anarchists in a local election campaign. Thus, through the Senate committee, this alleged decree on the nationalization of women was planted on the American public with long-lasting effect.

There were several later Senate investigations of specific aspects of American-Soviet relations. These investigations accomplished one thing, however. If they did not give a clearer picture of the new social order being established or open the way for a constructive Russian policy, they certainly fanned anti-Bolshevik sentiment into a blaze, which, in turn, made possible the continuation of American intervention even after the termination of the war.

CHAPTER XVI

MY WORK IN THE STATE DEPARTMENT

AFTER THE SIGNING OF THE ARMISTICE, I TURNED MY ATTENTION TO the matter of the enormous growth of Bolshevik propaganda in America. The effect of this on the workingman, who was faced with some degree of unemployment now that the war was over, was worrying many leaders—official and unofficial. Ludwig C. A. K. Martens was in this country as representative of the Soviet regime—unrecognized, of course, and in fact already involved with the Department of Justice on the question of deportation proceedings. Russia was offering contracts to the business world through him, on the one hand, and the millennium of Communism to the working classes, on the other. Even an invitation from Mr. Crane in January, 1919, to attend the Peace Conference at Paris, unofficially with him, did not deter me from the task of trying to assemble and give wide circulation to the facts of Bolshevism. I wrote to him:

It was very difficult to resist your generous suggestion. I debated the question with the family and some of my closer friends on the faculty before telegraphing you last evening. I am afraid the sudden departure, leaving my students in the lurch, would have more than irritated the university authorities here; it certainly would have interfered with my attempt to build up the work here. I have run away very frequently these last years.

Also, I believe it is most important that I continue my efforts to counteract Bolshevist propaganda, which is making considerable headway. The best way to counteract it, in my mind, is to give wider publicity to certain indisputable facts with regard to conditions in Russia. One cannot dissuade the confirmed Bolshevik; and one can do little with the "thinkers," like the editors of the *Nation*, who seem to be playing some sort of game. But one can accomplish something among the workmen, especially the foreign born, by getting before them in a convincing manner the facts of hunger, of economic disruption, and so forth, that we have in Russia today.

The efforts in which I am interested are all "citizen" organizations. Also, I am keeping very close to men on our Chicago newspapers, especially the Bohemian and the Polish. The Union League Club War Committee is using a group of us who have at least some information about Russia. Some months ago we also launched here what we call "American Friends of a New Middle Europe." This last organization is limping still, but will be on its feet soon, we trust.

To Mr. E. C. Porter, of the Russian-American Chamber of Commerce, I complained about the lack of current authentic information:

DEAR PORTER:

I hope you saw the last number of the *Dial*, with the quotation from the *New Statesman* of December 21. It will be worth your while to look up the original. The editors make definite statements, on the authority of men whom they claim are competent and trustworthy, that the whole Russian situation has changed since early autumn. Now Huntington, and, in fact, all our men, are competent to make statements on conditions only up to October 1 at the latest. Since that date we have had no firsthand information. All our generalizations are guesswork, on the basis of what we know about conditions up to October 1. Why don't we try to interview Russians or neutrals who have come out of Russia since that time?

In February I asked Richard Crane of the State Department if more information could not be made public:

I hasten to answer your letter, because I was about to write you on several matters when it came this morning. One of my jobs now is to collect from men here in Chicago who were in Russia, statements on the actual practices and fruits of the Bolshevist regime, in order to steady the workmen a bit, in anticipation of the unemployment situation that we are going to have soon. If you people could give out more facts—say, a summary of the facts that came before the conference in Paris—it certainly would help us. As it is, the Albert Rhys Williams crowd, in which I have every reason to believe that Thompson and Robins are also active, have everything their own way, and keep saying that the State Department is suppressing the real facts.

You see the trend of my remarks, perhaps; namely, that those of us who are trying to get a true picture of the Bolshevik regime before the public, and particularly before the workmen, do not get much assistance. As a result, the *Nation* and *Dial* can go on guessing that the Soviet regime has entered on a constructive period, which I do not believe for a moment, but am unable to disprove effectively.

With regard to your father's generous invitation to join him at the Peace Conference, I must tell you frankly that, aside entirely from my work here, I was convinced some time ago that it would become increasingly difficult for me to play the game as I have played it, that is, to be used without having any official status. With the Root mission and at the embassy it went all right because I had friends who understood and protected me. Your father can play the unattached game and pull it off because of his position. It would have been very hard for me to do it even with his help."

And to Huntington, now in Washington, I boiled over about permitting such general ignorance of current facts about Russia:

The whole mess relative to Russia in the recent Senate debates is just what the administration had coming to it because of its failure to take any active steps to pool and co-ordinate the material that has come out of Russia. The best example is the famous offer of the Soviets to co-operate with us against Germany. Now Johnson has published this. Why the dickens didn't the State Department give this out months ago? The text of the proposal itself, if one can call it that, is enough, if one reads it carefully. Most of the newspapers never saw the point, though I got several of ours here to see it and to comment. But the Bolsheviks and their champions have been making capital of this offer for months now; and when at last it comes out, there is no organization to give proper publicity to the real emptiness of the proposal. The State Department simply sits by and does not say a word. Of course the Republicans have pushed the matter to the full extent, for here is the weakest point in Wilson's program, and the Republicans are not fools. But they have been so stupid in their handling of the weapon they had that it would have been easy to show them up. But no, not a move. No encouragement to outside organizations like the former American-Russian League to do anything, or to any of us who have given some time and thought to Russia.

The general feeling of disgust with the Senate is spreading rapidly. The two men whom many of us progressives looked to as constructive, Borah and Johnson, have certainly been guilty of the loosest talk, abusing Russia and showing astonishing ignorance. Where were the administration Senators: muzzled, or simply unable to get information? Hitchcock's answer to Johnson some weeks ago certainly was weak. But perhaps it was not the poor man's fault; perhaps he tried to get a complete picture of the Russian situation and did not have time to make the rounds. For that is what one has to do, as so many people have their fingers in the pie. I don't want to seem in a generally kicking frame of mind tonight, but I have felt sick at heart for some days as I watched the course of events.

At last what I had been praying for actually happened. On March 15 I received a letter from Frank Polk, Acting Secretary of State, appointing me special assistant in the State Department. A special Russian Division had just been established to serve as a kind of embassy-in-exile, collecting, collating, and interpreting information about Russia. Our embassies and legations in other countries, particularly those adjacent to Soviet Russia, were including in their reports whatever information they could pick up across the *cordon sanitaire*. This material had to be interpreted with great care, since several of the countries from which it came formed links in the blockade against Bolshevism, and some were even at war with the Bolsheviks. Much material, allegedly factual, was appearing in periodical publications; and it was thought that

126

this, too, should be studied. Finally, it was hoped that a special division might be able to get actual documentary material from the Soviets and also, by systematic interviews with fresh arrivals—returning Americans or refugee Russians—secure further reliable reports.

My position with the Russian Division was officially that of special attaché. I was to study mainly public documents and was to have access to strictly diplomatic material only when the latter contained information which could be made public. The rule adopted by the regular staff of the Department, at the instance, I believe, of the Secretary himself, was that I should not be given confidential material, which would, as he said, "cramp my academic style." However, as the regular staff came to know me better and to see that I had no intention of getting "scoops" out of official material, as some academic men have tended to do, I had placed on my desk more and more diplomatic dispatches. My job was primarily to collect and translate the most important of the Soviet decrees and laws, and the speeches and writings of Soviet leaders which shed light on the aims and methods of Soviet legislation.

My work for the Department was on a part-time basis, for I gave it my so-called "research time"; during these years I continued to carry a full load of teaching at the university. Because of this arrangement, I had to do most of the work in Chicago; and this procedure was, in fact, suggested by President Wilson himself, who had a hand in my appointment. He felt that in this way I would not get into the bureaucratic atmosphere of the Department or become involved directly in the determination of policy or in administrative work. Each month I went on to Washington for the last week, to develop orally the written reports which I had sent in. These reports were, in the main, interpretations of the documents I had selected to translate. In a sense, I was conducting informal classes for the members of the Russian Division on the subject of Soviet institutions.

I accepted eagerly the offer of this work for the State Department because it was fully in line with my university work, in which I was expected to keep in touch with developments in my field of study. In fact, my position in Washington gave me access to material which otherwise would have been unobtainable, even though it was of a public nature. For it was impossible, in those years, for an individual or even an educational institution to secure copies of official Soviet publications or Soviet newspapers. It was only with the greatest difficulty that the State Department itself was able to get hold of these publications. Our consular representatives on the outskirts of Russia were our main sources of supply. On one occasion I felt that the man on whom we mainly relied—our consul-general at Helsingfors—was not getting as many newspapers as he should, and had a checkup sent to him. His answer was rather disconcerting, for it gave the full story of how hard it was to get the newspapers of Moscow and Petrograd. He stated the number of his messengers, all Russians and volunteers, who had been caught and shot.

One very useful channel through which the Division secured much valuable published material was the censorship authority of this or that small bordering state of the *cordon sanitaire*. As part of their propaganda abroad, the Moscow Bolsheviks sent out much printed material, addressing some of it to individuals in America. These shipments would be intercepted by the authorities of the small state, and the American representative would be informed of the seizure. He would be instructed by Washington to accept the shipment and forward it to the Department. The addressee, on being notified, would then, of course, hesitate to present himself there to claim the shipment. One such addressee did try to claim his shipment, however. He insisted that it contained only one copy of any particular document, and he had probably arranged that the collection be of this kind. But the Bolsheviks had put in quite a number of copies of most of the documents, which made it a shipment of propaganda materials. In this way, I must admit, the files of the Division were greatly enriched.

It was unusual for a Division to have a library of its own, but here was an exceptional situation, and the so-called "Bolshevik room" soon came to contain an extensive collection of public documents. The Librarian of Congress was helpful in making provision for this special library, because the appropriation for it was secured on the understanding that these files would go to the Library of Congress when they were no longer needed by the Department for administrative purposes. Now much of the material is already in the Library of Congress and represents one of the most complete collections of Soviet periodical publications outside the Soviet Union. I have been told that the other, and perhaps even more complete collection, is to be found in the Library of the Vatican. The Library of Congress collection is being kept up to date. When postal communications were interrupted at the beginning of 1940, the only complete file of Moscow newspapers available in America was that of the Department of State, which received its newspapers by diplomatic pouch from Moscow.

The work of collecting, analyzing, translating, and organizing this vast accumulation of material went well and gave me much valuable information for my studies; it was part of my contract that I might keep for my own files copies of all the documents which I used for my reports. By October, 1919, the Russian Division had completed and published a memorandum, based on all the original sources available, which briefly summarized what appeared to be the fundamental Bolshevik principles, methods, and aims—covering the character of their rule, the economic results of Bolshevik control, and the program of world revolution. By March, 1920, another memorandum was issued on the Bolshevik or Communist Party in Russia, its relation to the Russian Soviets and to the Third International. In October, 1920, a third memorandum was published covering the second congress of the Communist International. The State Department was the first to get a full account of this meeting and published it to anticipate and to guard against expurgated versions of the proceedings. In this work I attempted, with the natural approach of the student, to establish, as far as possible, the documentation on Sovietism. Although I have always acknowledged my authorship of these State Department memoranda, I have never been able, of course, to list them among my published works. That is one of the handicaps which the individual must accept who enters governmental employment, particularly in the State Department.

Some objected to this kind of activity by the State Department, and one such objector was Walter Lippmann, then editor of the *New Republic*. His objection, as I remember it, was not to the content of the documents but to the fact that a governmental department was, in a sense, competing with the press. This argument was met by calling attention to the fact that he, as an editor, was not able to obtain the public material because of the conditions prevailing in and around Soviet Russia, and he was told that he should be grateful instead of complaining. There was a general tendency, even in our better newspapers and journals, to water down a document or to weight it in one direction or another according to the prejudice of the particular publication. I was combating the tendency of some to paint the Bolsheviks as pure angels and the tendency of others to picture them as plain devils.

There were many interesting and unusual incidents connected with my work. For example, I was asked to help the Department of Justice collect material on the propaganda activities of Moscow for revolution in this country, and I worked very closely at times with J. Edgar Hoover. Here I found myself constantly obliged to combat conclusions not supported by the documents, based on too general or even careless interpretations of words or phrases. I was careful not to have any connection with the work of detecting alleged underground activities of alleged Moscow agents. In retrospect, I am bound to feel, however, that my hours of work on documents and in conference were of little avail in tempering the Red-baiting campaign of Mitchell Palmer. But I do not recall at that time any such loose procedure as has characterized the work of the recent Dies Committee.

I was also invited to participate in the study of the authenticity of the famous Protocols of the Wise Men of Zion, because this document appeared first in Russian, the product of one of the most militant anti-Semitic movements of the old regime. But the material available for study was either so vague or so questionable in character that I refused to push through with it.

One of my last official talks with a Secretary of State was with Secretary Hughes, for I had carried on into the Republican administration.

While reporting to Hughes, I had shown him a cartoon from a Moscow newspaper, in which he was pictured sitting in bed, all atremble as he studied an example of Moscow propaganda. The Secretary laughed at this portrayal of his state of mind and then, turning serious, remarked that one of the troubles was that Moscow thought we were afraid of its propaganda and did not realize that it was simply a matter of self-respect. We didn't like it, and we weren't going to stand for it.

The last specific study which I made for the Department was in preparation for the Washington Conference on the limitation of armaments in 1921. The Soviet government was not invited to this conference because the United States government had not recognized it. However, it was necessary to define Soviet policy in the Far East and particularly China, and this I worked out, using official Soviet documents, treaties, and speeches of the leaders. In furtherance of Soviet policy, Moscow had found it expedient to set up, or allow to be set up, the so-called Far Eastern Republic, just to the north of Outer Mongolia. The president of this unit, Alexander Krasnoschekov, was an American Russian who had studied at the University of Chicago. Several American newspapermen had visited its capital, Chita, and were inclined to the view that the republic was actually an independent state. Encouraged by their support, this able and energetic president had dispatched to Washington what was called a "trade mission," which, on arrival, asked to be recognized at the Washington Conference as the official representative of the Far Eastern Republic. The head of this trade delegation was Boris Skvirsky, who later was to stay on in Washington as "unrecognized Soviet ambassador," until the formal recognition in November, 1933, when he became the counselor of embassy of the first Soviet embassy.

On this question of the "independence" of the Far Eastern Republic, the Russian Division insisted that the independence was fictitious and that one had in this delegation a maneuver to gain recognition of the whole Soviet government. In accordance with protocol, the formal reception of Skvirsky by a high-ranking officer of the State Department, for example, could have been interpreted as formal recognition of the Soviet government. The Far Eastern Division was inclined to favor the claims of Skvirsky and his delegation that they had nothing to do with Moscow, represented an absolutely independent state, and therefore should be admitted to the Washington Conference. Stanley Hornbeck was at this time attached to the Far Eastern Division as a "specialist" in somewhat the same way in which I was attached to the Russian Division. He also had been greatly assisted in his studies by Mr. Crane. Our discussions over the status of the Far Eastern Republic served as the basis of the first of our many meetings and friendly disputes. When, almost immediately after the Washington Conference, the Far Eastern Republic, on its petition, was admitted into the Soviet Union, the

Soviet Commissar of Foreign Affairs, Chicherin, made a formal statement to the effect that any intelligent person could easily have anticipated this development. I must admit my special joy when I routed a copy of this statement to the Far Eastern Division.

This work for the Department of State secured to me many close and lasting friendships; and through these friendships, as well as because of my former official connection with the Department, I have had all these years very full co-operation in my studies from embassies and from the Department itself. In a very informal way I have continued to do odd jobs for the Department and have always sent on, for whatever they were worth, summaries of my later trips to the Soviet Union, as well as occasional views on current events. This continued relationship has been possible because it was easy to learn, from actual work in the Department, what matters could not be discussed publicly. I believe that the Department has not seen any indiscretion in any of my public statements.

There was no complete abandonment on my part either of public writing or of public lecturing during this period. But the volume of work for the State Department which I crowded into my research time left little or none of it for other activities. Instead of writing or lecturing, I concentrated on that procedure which had always been part of my method of work: trying to reach and report to the so-called "effectives"—in this case, those who were working on the problem of our policy toward the new type of political organization set up by the Bolsheviks in the old Russia. It was during these years that I came to formulate for myself the role of the "expert" in relation to the "politician," the one who determines policy. To my superiors in the policy-determining branches of the State Department, I presented as full and detailed a picture of any given topic as possible. With this I felt that I had performed my duty. I knew that those to whom I reported had to take into consideration many factors outside the topic on which I reported and that such factors might force them to accept only certain features of the field I was presenting. For this reason, I was generally not disturbed by what might often have seemed to be a failure from my particular point of view. Those to whom I reported showed that it was helpful that I did not, so to speak, fight for a specific policy. However, there is no question that my reports tended to support and perhaps even reinforce the policy of our government not to recognize the Soviet government. When in 1930 in Moscow I had the first of my many talks with Litvinov, this fact was brought out in our conversation; and even at that late date, and to him, I stated my view that formal recognition would serve no useful purpose for either side unless it were based on common interests and mutual respect.

The period of my connection with the State Department was one of great ferment. World policy toward Sovietism was being determined,

131

and significant clashes of public opinion concerning Russia were being resolved. Boris Bakhmeteff, the still-recognized ambassador of the fallen Kerensky regime, wrote to me in January of 1920:

Bolshevism should not be fought at the expense of Russia. . . . . Europe, frightened at the impending threat of a Bolshevik invasion, and having lost confidence in any effective action on the part of the Russian national forces puts all her hope of armed resistance on the border states, Poland, Romania, and the Baltic nations; these states receiving a *de facto* mandate to fight Bolshevism with, as a matter of course, prospective reward. . . . . You can easily see what the outcome of such a policy would be. A victory over Russian Bolshevism would mean dismemberment of Russia and degradation of her sovereignty.

From the other side of the Atlantic, Bernard Pares wrote in June:

As to England, I can say shortly as follows: I never expected to find any foreign propaganda so strong here as I did on my return. All the marks of the beast were here, and you could quite clearly distinguish the actual agents from their very stupid English sympathizers. They made a great push in propaganda from December to the end of February. Then they got quite a strong setback, not at all because of any counterorganization—efforts of that kind have so far been pitiful—but because of the stolidity and good sense of our people. The one magnificent thing which has happened since the Armistice was when our trade-unions turned down direct action by a majority of two million—and Clyne's speech beginning "It is wrong" was almost better than the decision itself.

On August 10, 1920, when Poland was overrunning the Ukraine, our attitude toward the Soviets was officially summed up in Secretary of State Colby's note on the Polish situation:

"The United States maintains unimpaired its faith in the Russian people, in their high character and their future. That they will overcome the existing anarchy, suffering, and destitution we do not entertain the slightest doubt. The distressing character of Russia's transition has many historical parallels, and the United States is confident that restored, free, and united Russia will again take a leading place in the world, joining with the other free nations in upholding peace and orderly justice.

"Until that time shall arrive the United States feels that friendship and honor require that Russia's interests must be generously protected, and that, as far as possible, all decisions of vital importance to it . . . . be held in abeyance."

That the Soviet government was not fully representative of the will of the people of Russia, the note continued, was evident from the dissolution of the Constituent Assembly and the fact that, after two and a half years in power, the Bolsheviks had not yet permitted anything in the nature of a popular election. That its leaders were irresponsible was indicated in their refusal to assume Russia's obligations to other nations. And, finally, that these leaders would abuse the privileges of diplomatic agencies by using them as channels for revolutionary propaganda appeared inevitable in view of their avowed support of the Third International. Therefore, the note concluded, "there cannot be any common ground" upon which this government "can stand with a Power whose conceptions of international relations are so entirely alien to its own."

This heralded a period of waiting.

CHAPTER XVII

YEARS OF WAITING

THE YEARS FROM 1921 TO 1925 WERE A PERIOD OF WAITING, IN SEVERAL senses. My double duties, at the university and for the State Department, had entailed overwork, which resulted in a mild breakdown. Dr. Billings, who stood at the foot of my hospital bed while his interns were going over me, suggested that my nervous system was full of short circuits because I had been trying to understand a completely negative thing—Bolshevism. For over a year I had to reduce my pace and become an academic recluse, teaching my classes, keeping up with the literature on my subject, and giving up public lecturing almost entirely.

This last was easily effected because of the decline of public interest in what had now come to be called the "Soviet Union." The abandonment of many Communist practices, with the adoption of the New Economic Policy, was interpreted by many as indicating the complete failure of the Russian experiment in socialism. Thus, those who did not like socialism could rest more easily, while those who thought socialism might be the answer to our problems were discouraged. For this second group, the Moscow policy of not "going the whole hog" on the *Putsch* in Germany in 1923, on the general strike in Great Britain in 1926, and on the Communist-Kuomintang struggle in China from 1925 to 1927 represented a letdown of the world revolution.

The New Economic Policy, established in 1921, was often referred to as the "NEP." It represented certain concessions to principles and doctrines against which the Revolution was aimed—individual control of means of production, individual employment of labor. "Concession-aires" were permitted; many factories were allowed to operate under it. It had the objective of reviving production and trading processes which had practically come to a dead stop at the beginning of 1918. Large-scale industry and foreign trade, however, remained completely nationalized. The two sectors were called the "capitalist" and the "socialist." The former was under careful regulation and control; and when it became advisable, measures of repression were instituted. Those who operated under the "capitalist sector" were called "NEPmen." It was the expressed policy that when the capitalist sector had served its purpose, speaking in economic terms, of re-establishing production, the socialist sector would gradually take over and prevail. This aim was practically achieved in 1927.

My own studies showed clearly that it was wrong to see in the New Economic Policy a complete abandonment of the program of revolution; what one had was simply a tactical retreat. For the student, the hybrid type of social structure in the Russia of these years was not particularly interesting, as it was clear that it was a temporary expedient. For the moment, one might guess what it would develop into, but long-range guessing was difficult.

To the world in general, the Soviet Union was becoming "respectable," and on that basis was recognized *de jure* by Britain and France. Soviet delegations came to the Conference of Genoa. The Soviet Union and Germany signed the Treaty of Rapallo, which was to be the first test of the possibility of normal political and economic relations between a "communist" and a "bourgeois" country. These developments kept alive in America the question of our relations with the Soviet Union. Because of our isolation, we could, for a time, simply avoid formal diplomatic relations. On the other hand, our businessmen found it possible and profitable to do business with the Bolsheviks. One form which these business relations took was the technical-service contract, under which American engineers went to Russia to help in the reconstruction of the country. Many Americans fondly expected these engineers to contribute to the return of Russia to good old capitalistic methods.

It became somewhat easier to follow general trends, however, despite the difficulty of defining their respective strengths, because the Soviet system was no longer a besieged or even a closed fortress. In connection with the work of the American Relief Administration during the famine year of 1921, many Americans traveled all over the country and, because of the character of their work, were able to see and report on conditions in detail. These reports were not given wide publicity, but with the American Relief Administration several American newspaper correspondents were able to enter and establish themselves permanently. Of these correspondents, the outstanding figure was unquestionably Walter Duranty, who represented the *New York Times*.

134

Although in his first writing, from Riga, he interpreted the New Economic Policy as an abandonment of the principles of the Revolution, he soon learned his mistake after arriving in the Soviet Union. This mistake was useful, because it suggested to him that he should study more deeply the peculiar ways of thinking of the revolutionary leaders. He learned the Russian language so that he would be able to talk with those who were determining policy. In his later summary of his work as Moscow correspondent, he admitted frankly that he had decided to hitch his chariot to the Bolshevik star, which he thought would go fast as well as far.

Walter Duranty was much criticized for what people called loosely "pro-Bolshevik sympathies." But, for the student, his dispatches were the most useful, because from them one could get a reflection of the way Soviet leaders were thinking. So many of our correspondents have gone on the assumption that the Bolsheviks ought to follow traditional patterns of thought, and for this reason have had to feed their readers long stories of unexpected, inexplicable decisions and measures.

As I have said, the question of formal recognition of the Soviet regime was not an immediate issue during these years. There were organizations advocating it, although other groups put more emphasis on the policy of "Hands Off Soviet Russia," as one of them was actually called. The antirecognitionists were not very active either, although the red herring was kept handy, to be used whenever some internal problem cropped up. There was, of course, some reason for our counterpropaganda against Bolshevik propaganda. The Communist International was active and vociferous, and exerted considerable influence, despite the conflict within this body between Stalin and Trotsky and between it and the Soviet government. These conflicts became more pronounced with the loss of Lenin—for, although Lenin died in January, 1924, he had already ceased to be active in 1922.

The death of Lenin tended to reduce American interest in the Soviet experiment still further, because everyone prophesied that there would be a ruinous fight over the succession. The peculiar character of the Communist Party kept this fight behind closed doors for three years. It was not to come out in the open until 1926. Fortunately for my studies, this happened during my first trip to the Soviet Union.

During this period of waiting for the trends in Sovietism to define themselves, I spent several vacations in Washington, talking with the men in charge of the divisions in various departments which covered Russia. At the State Department the Russian Division had been expanded into the Eastern European Division, and several of the younger men who had been in the old Russian Division when I was working there had now become chiefs and acting chiefs of the new setup. The modest file of Soviet documents which I had started had grown enormously. The work of translating these documents and making periodic reports on specific topics had been transferred to the American legation at Riga; but these translations and reports were still filed in this special room, where one could find published material on all important aspects of Sovietism. To these very valuable sources I was given free access, as were other bona fide students.

Because of my former connection and my "good behavior," I was also given access to certain diplomatic documents where these would throw light on the public documents. The rule informally adopted was that I could ask for any document without causing offense; but, nevertheless, I was careful never to ask for a document without feeling very sure that it would be opened to me. In a more informal way, and on a much reduced scale, I thus continued what I had done when I was employed by the Department. These discussions with the officials of the Eastern European Division were most useful to me, and, I think I can say, to them.

Part of these years of waiting had to be given to a matter having no connection with my study or my university work. Because of the illness of my youngest brother, the family bought a farm for him in Wisconsin, and it fell to my lot to help him start this enterprise. The project took a certain amount of time, but it gave me back my health. From the very beginning there were innumerable concrete problems to cope with—the seven-acre marsh, which proved to be a trap for the tractor; the old hog run, which had to be cleared of stumps and leveled off to prevent freezing where the drain went through it; the corn crop that we got stuck with. There were fences to be mended, and sheds to be repaired, and weeds to be grappled with—altogether a healthy contrast to the elusive problems of Communist tactics which had been occupying my attention.

I believe, furthermore, that the handling of the farm—and its frequent mishandling—was very useful in another way besides, for here I came into direct contact with the problems of production and distribution. This experience helped me to understand better the new types of agricultural enterprise which I was to find in the Soviet Union. The attitudes and methods which prevailed among my farmer neighbors or among the dealers with whom I had to do business were fresh and new to me, and often more helpful than those I encountered among my academic colleagues. For the study of the Soviet system, the specific questions asked of me were very useful; and it was from these neighbors in Racine County that some of the best questions came. Later I found it most interesting to make the jump from a collectivized farm in the Ukraine, visited at the beginning of a month, to a group of Wisconsin dairy farms—the most individual of individual enterprises—by the end of the same month on my return home.

Perhaps because I was teaching the full academic year instead of running off to Russia for six months of the twelve, my teaching at the university went much better during this period. I had more and better students. If in the general public or among the businessmen whom I met socially, or even among my farmer neighbors, there was not much interest in the Soviet experiment, many of the younger generation did show considerable interest. My classes, particularly in the history of the revolutions in Russia—a course which was announced in the catalogue under the unprovocative title of "Russia since 1900"—generally contained a group of what can be called "Soviet sympathizers" and another group having rather conservative political views. It was a difficult subject to present, and I must admit that it caused me a good deal of worry. The two extreme groups were constantly trying to make me commit myself either for or against, which good pedagogy forbade. But in individual cases with which I became well acquainted, I was interested to note that the course tended to make the radicals more careful and the conservatives readier to admit that another type of social system might succeed. Like all teaching, this course helped me with my own studies, especially in formulating for me the significant questions to which I would seek answers when, or if, it became possible for me to resume my study trips. It was in 1925 that I finally began first to contemplate and then actively to plan my first trip to the Soviet Union which had replaced the Russia of my earlier days.

PART VII

SOVIET RUSSIA EMERGING: 1926–36

CHAPTER XVIII

1926: SOVIET CIVIC TRAINING

Getting into Soviet Russia Again

IN MY STUDIES, MY INTEREST WAS INCREASINGLY DIRECTED TO THE working-out of the new type of state and the new form of government which, now that their permanence was coming to be generally accepted, however unwillingly, were usually characterized as "Soviet." Thus I was being drawn more toward political science, as opposed to history, just as at an earlier period I had extended my work from the fields of linguistics and literature. Professor Charles E. Merriam, one of my colleagues at the University of Chicago and long a close student of politics, who had looked askance at my first efforts at teaching in the social sciences, was now showing an interest in my work. This interest took the concrete form of a request that I assume responsibility for one of the volumes of a series of studies he was organizing on the subject of methods of civic training in various countries. I was asked to cover Soviet methods of civic training.

This subject had already come to the fore in my general studies of the progress and working of the Soviet system. The Soviet leaders, especially Lenin, had from the beginning of the Revolution put emphasis on what they called "the cultural front," which came third in importance in their minds, after the military and economic fronts. In the second period of the Revolution, when there had been a retreat on the economic front, the emphasis on the so-called "cultural revolution" had become particularly marked. Lenin had once observed that if he could determine, through education and other agencies, the attitude of the younger generation in the first period of the Revolution, he would feel absolutely confident of the Revolution's success. So in that NEP period of transition from 1921 to 1928 the Bolsheviks developed a most extensive program of civic training. Merriam's proposal, therefore, offered the incentive for an intensive study of one of the basic

138

features of the Soviet system. This subject was also one of the least delicate to handle, for there could be no secrecy about civic training. The student of a revolutionary system had to recognize certain limitations with respect to the methods and materials available to him, but these limitations seemed less sharply defined for this topic. I therefore accepted the offer, with the understanding that I would try to arrange to investigate the subject on the spot; but if this proved impossible, I would, in any case, make the study from published material available outside the Soviet Union, particularly in the countries immediately bordering on it.

Then I took up the matter of securing a visa to enter the Soviet Union. I knew that, because of my connection with the State Department, with the Sisson documents, and with the leadership of pre-Bolshevik Russia, I was not *persona grata*. I discovered, in fact, that some people in Moscow looked on me as a Kerensky spy because of my activities as scout for the American embassy in those months after the revolution of March, 1917. At other periods I was supposed to be an agent of the old tsarist government, then an agent of the Jews, and in the last years a "Bolshevik agent," as those terms are loosely used even in academic circles. I might point out that, actually, I have always been meticulously careful not to accept special favors from any of the various governments which have prevailed in my area of study.

Knowing the attitude toward me in official Soviet circles, then, I decided to inquire through an intermediary what the decision would be if I were to apply formally for a visa. I felt it would interfere with my studies if I had on my record the refusal of an application to enter my area of study. I also raised the question as to whether it would be expedient for the Soviet government to have on its record a refusal of a visa to me, at a time when it was trying to develop its trade relations with America, to persuade American engineers to come to the Soviet Union on technical service contracts, and to build up its credit standing with American firms. I suggested that, if the Soviet Union had become so strongly established that it felt it could ask for credit, then it should be willing to admit a student despite the fact that he had been openly critical, particularly in the first period, of the new regime. And I added that, since I planned to make this study of civic training whether I gained admission or not, it would be to the advantage of the Soviet government to admit me, in order for the study to be as accurate and comprehensive as possible.

The intermediary who undertook this investigation for me was Mr. Ruthenberg, the general secretary of the American Communist Party, who was making a trip to Moscow in the winter of 1925–26. I used this channel because no other was available; there were no official Soviet representatives in America. Also, I did not want the American Communists knifing me, particularly while I was in the Soviet Union.

Sidney Hillman, an American of Russian origin, had recently organized a Russian-American Trading Corporation to re-establish trade relations between the two countries. He believed that such relations would be mutually advantageous, politically as well as commercially. It is possible that he was also influenced in this effort by pressure from the members of the Amalgamated Clothing Workers Union, of which he was the effective and, I think one can say, beloved leader. Hillman had sent to Moscow as his representative one of the ablest of Amalgamated's organizers, George Wishniak. I knew Hillman, for on several occasions American businessmen who were being approached by him in connection with his American-Russian Trading Corporation had asked me to sit in on the conferences, and I had been much impressed by Hillman's directness and frankness. Accordingly, I put to him my thought that the request for a visa could be considered perfectly proper both by me and by the Soviet authorities. Agreeing with me, Hillman promised to have Wishniak register this view at the proper places in Moscow.

Wishing to take all necessary preliminary steps, I then went to General Graves, who had commanded our intervention forces in Siberia. I knew that he had a rather close personal relationship with Boris Skvirsky, the unofficial Soviet representative in Washington, whose life he had saved during the intervention. This was the same Skvirsky who, representing the Far Eastern Republic, had sought admission to the Washington Conference on the limitation of armaments in 1921; and of course he knew of my connection with the decision against him. When General Graves agreed that I could properly ask for a visa, I suggested that he say as much to Skvirsky. A few days later he sent me a copy of Skvirsky's reply. Skvirsky stated that any professor except myself could obtain a visa without difficulty, and he mentioned several who had been admitted to the Soviet Union. "If I am not mistaken," he continued, "Professor Harper was one of the 'experts' who vouched for the 'authenticity' of the famous, or rather infamous, Sisson documents." And he concluded that the university would be well advised to select another member of its staff to make the Russian study contemplated. I suggested facetiously that the General inquire if a good bacteriologist would do for Mr. Skvirsky, and asked the General to tell Skvirsky that I thought he had made a mistake. His letter made a poor record, implying, as it did, that the Bolsheviks, in welcoming only scholars who knew nothing about Russia, must be trying to conceal their situation.

This was not very encouraging; but, nevertheless, Professor Merriam and I started off for Germany in June, 1926, having made formal application to Moscow for our visas and asking that they be sent to the Soviet embassy in Berlin. Merriam, as editor-in-chief, was supervising the preliminary studies of those whom he had selected to work on his

140

project, and he went abroad with me to help me get under way. He stopped off in France, and I went on to Berlin.

My recent farm experience made the railway journey from the boat to Berlin more interesting to me than it had ever seemed before. The German farms all looked like kitchen gardens, and the farmers were making hay by hand. There were no loaders, only small wagons with puny horses. The cows seemed undernourished, too; and I saw no barns—only sheds. Nor did I see a single automobile on a country road or on the streets of the smaller towns through which we passed. On the other hand, there were bicycles everywhere. The farmer's wife, and even the old mother, rode home from haymaking on "bikes." There were whole strings of these grotesque figures. In Berlin, although I was told that there had been much progress in the last years, I felt at once how Germany was worn down at the heels. The women showed it particularly, and the young girls who had been war children had drawn, pasty faces.

On arrival I immediately looked up an old friend, Edgar Mowrer, representative of the *Chicago Daily News*, and asked him to go with me to the press representative of the Soviet embassy, to be present when I asked officially if the visas for Merriam and myself were on hand. The man to whom we went told me later that my maneuver was clearly understood, and he complimented me on the directness of my procedure, for I had deliberately handled the matter so that the Moscow authorities would have to refuse a visa to Professor Merriam if they refused mine, and would have to do this in front of an American newspaperman, on whom we could rely to make a good story of the refusal.

When, after preliminary general conversation with Mowrer's friend at the embassy, I asked about the visas, it was discovered that there had been some delay; and with the greatest courtesy I was requested to allow them three or four days to check up. Four days later I was told that the visas were there and could be had at any time. I telegraphed Merriam, and he arrived in Berlin without delay. Those last days in Berlin were like the prelude to entering the jungle; and several times, as we later confessed, Merriam and I were a little nervous about our undertaking. Not many had penetrated the Soviet Union at that date, and there were all sorts of stories about the difficulties—material and political—which outside visitors had to meet.

The counselor of the American embassy in Berlin was Dewitt C. Poole, who had been the chief of the Russian Division when I worked there. He was overjoyed at the thought of my trip, for, like me, he was beginning to wonder if the policy of nonrecognition which we had supported had not ceased to be constructive, considering the course of events. He could not, of course, help me officially, because he could have no relations with Krestinsky, the Soviet ambassador in Berlin. Neither could he very well arrange officially for me to use the German embassy in Moscow in case of need. He handled the situation by inviting Merriam and me to a luncheon which he was giving to members of the German foreign office. We were asked to conduct an informal discussion of recent trends in American life. After the luncheon one of the higher German officials told me that he was interested to learn of my proposed trip, and he asked Mr. Poole if it would cause a diplomatic incident if he suspended my German visa when I passed through Berlin on my way home until I came around to talk over my experiences with him. This gave me, without any document, my introduction to the German diplomatic representatives in Moscow, because I could refer to this request.

While waiting for Merriam, I had frequently visited a certain bookstore in Berlin which was the European distributing center for Soviet publications. This was the first such reservoir that I had been able to tap directly, and the Russian in charge of it was one of the first Bolshevik officials with whom I had the opportunity for long, informal talks. I was interested to hear from him the attitude of the Moscow Bolsheviks toward the German Communists: for the Russians, these Berlin revolutionaries thought too much of order and program. He illustrated this German failing with one of the best political anecdotes I had heard on the German Communists. In 1923, he said, a representative from Moscow arrived in Berlin to direct the proposed Communist *Putsch*. At one meeting he explained to the local group leaders their specific assignments in the procedure of forceful seizure of important control points. When the Germans were asked if they had any questions of detail, the leader of the group which was to seize the main railway station arose and asked where his men were to get the platform admission tickets required at all German railway stations.

When Merriam arrived, I introduced him to this Bolshevik friend at the bookstore. Merriam had been a member of a special class in Russian which I had conducted for a small group of colleagues at their request—and not with the greatest success. But he had been practicing his Russian and had learned one phrase which he expected to find useful during our proposed trip. This phrase was the Russian equivalent of "It's a hard life." Wanting to boast a bit, Merriam told my friend that, though he knew only a little Russian, he knew four words well. Before he could give his little formula, the Bolshevik spoke up in eager anticipation. "I know what they must be," he said, repeating in Russian the four-word Russian slogan, "Proletarians of the world, unite!"

As the date for our departure neared, first Merriam would feel unwell and then I would report a slight upset, until finally we both caught on and teased each other, and thus strengthened our courage. Berlin was hot and noisy, and I knew that Moscow would be hotter and noisier still. I thought with considerable nostalgia of my family at the Wisconsin farm; and when I remembered the oats and clover fields there, the

142

tractor, the potatoes, the Fourth of July barn dance, and even the invincible burdock and the troublesome hog run, I was almost ready to turn my back on the enigma of Soviet Russia.

We were not a very cheerful pair when at last, on the afternoon of July 18, 1926, Merriam and I sat on the platform at the station, waiting for the express train which was to take us to Riga. We were to pass through the famous Danzig Corridor in the early morning hours, and we planned to get up to see the performance when the Poles locked us in for the fifty-minute run across their territory into East Prussia. We had not fully decided how to let our friends know if we got into trouble; but I thought perhaps I would select two people, such as Walter Duranty of the *New York Times* and Paul Anderson of the Y.M.C.A., and arrange for them to make inquiries if they did not see me turn up at least once a week. They would be in a position to verify any suspicions and to get word out to Poole.

In Moscow the drive from the station to the hotel—the same drive that I had taken so often before the Revolution—had a discouraging effect on me. The city had been none too cheerful when I left it in 1917, in the third year of the war. But now it showed clearly the dislocations of the years of civil strife. Merriam seemed less disconcerted than I, having evidently expected very little of this eastern European capital. As we drove down the main Tverskaya, we saw red flags with black borders on all the houses and wondered what sort of occasion we had run into. We were to learn shortly that the Revolution had lost another of its outstanding leaders—Dzerzhinsky, the head of the Cheka, which had directed the mass terror of the civil-war period. We were to see, the next day, one of the largest revolutionary funerals of the regime.

After arriving at the Grand Hotel and getting our single room—for safety, as well as for company, we had decided to share a room—we looked up Junius B. Wood, one of the best and keenest of newspapermen, who represented the *Chicago Daily News* in the Soviet Union. His office and living quarters were on our floor. Merriam knew him well.

We were to get access to the materials and institutions we wished to study, and also to the leaders with whom we wished to talk, through an institution called the Society for Cultural Relations (VOKS). The chairman of this official governmental institution was Mme Kameneva, the sister of Trotsky and the wife of Kamenev. After she had received us and we had outlined our general program, she mentioned that, fortunately, Mr. Boris Skvirsky, of Washington, was in Moscow and that she would arrange for him to see us the next morning. When we came out from this interview, Merriam and I simultaneously exclaimed that Skvirsky's presence might be less fortunate than she supposed. In fact, Merriam morbidly suggested that we might as well go back to the hotel and pack up. Instead, we went to Junius Wood and explained the situation in detail. He said he had been wanting to see Skvirsky for several days and would see him that evening.

Late that night Wood came to our room and told us that we could rest peacefully, without worry about the next morning's interview. He added that, if things did not go well at our meeting with Skvirsky, we might ask him if he planned not to return to Washington. But Wood had proved, as we expected, to be a most able diplomat, for Skvirsky was very cordial and offered to be of any service he could in the further-ance of our studies. He had learned, he said, that we were progressing well in establishing contacts. From that time on, my relations with Skvirsky have always been most friendly and useful.

Soviet Russia under the New Economic Policy in 1926

It was shortly after our arrival in Moscow that the fact of the Stalin-Trotsky controversy was made public. The current newspapers printed full texts of the decisions of the Party congress in favor of Stalin. Long extracts from the debates of the congress, always held behind closed doors, became available. I found it very interesting to translate these to Merriam to get his reaction to this important development in the political working of the Soviet system. Merriam, of course, was sure that the two-party system was about to emerge in the Soviet state, for he could not envisage any political system that did not have two or more parties.

The Party discussion and the "new opposition" of Trotsky, Zinoviev, and others were constant topics of conversation among the Russian non-Communists. Individual Communists did not discuss the matter freely, generally referring one to the official statements appearing daily in the newspapers. The first reaction of these non-Communists seemed to be to welcome the fight among the leaders, as promising a weakening of the dictatorship. Soon they realized that the opposition was forcing the majority to take measures and steps to meet its criticisms. A mild but definite Communist reaction was the result. I found myself taking a distinctly subjective attitude on the Party conflict and was guilty of campaigning for Stalin on several occasions. For the non-Communist, Stalin represented a more nationalist tendency. Many assured me that Stalin probably did not believe that the world revolution would come even in "the decade or so," which he gave as the minimum in his pub-lic statements.

My own impression, based on a study of published statements, on informal analyses furnished by non-Communists, and on talks with other outside observers, was that the opposition would fail. It had no constructive program. It did not seem to have any broad following, even among the unemployed workmen of the large industrial centers. The fact that the leaders of the opposition were Jews was very much against

144

them, for anti-Semitism was present in Russia even in Communist ranks. The opposition had the best orators, and they were the old guard of the Revolution. But the younger and more "Russian" Communists were sick and tired of these "heroes" of the Revolution and of their oratory.

It seemed to me that here was an effort on the part of the "constructive workers" of the Party to rid the movement of two distinct elements, both of them in a sense the "heroes" of the earlier years. The old guard, who would seem to be capable only of propaganda—the Trotskys, Zinovievs, and Kamenevs—represented one set of "heroes." The other set was composed of the hooligan, rowdy, element, which did the dirty work of the first years and now insisted on positions of power, at least in their small city or town. It was going to be a hard task to eliminate these elements. Stalin did not attract by his personality, being of a cold and unpleasant manner. Dzerzhinsky, had he not died, would undoubtedly have dared a more aggressive policy with respect to the opposition leaders. Gossip had it that on the occasion of his last speech, when he attacked Trotsky and Kamenev, he pulled his revolver on the latter to make his remarks more forceful.

At the Dzerzhinsky funeral on the Red Square, which Merriam and I watched from the press box, we saw Trotsky, Kamenev, Zinoviev, and Lenin's widow, Krupskaya, as they passed right in front of us to the speaker's stand from a side entrance of the Kremlin. And they stood below the higher rostrum on which the others were stationed—Stalin, Molotov and Rykov. They looked very distressed, particularly during Stalin's speech. This was the first time I had heard or seen Stalin, for he was not an outstanding speaker, as was Trotsky, and had not been one of the orators at the public Bolshevik meetings I had attended during the Kerensky period.

Merriam wanted very much to talk with Trotsky, because he was, after Lenin, the outstanding figure of the Revolution, as portrayed by American correspondents and other writers; and in those early years he merited this position. But his sister, Mme Kameneva, to whom we addressed the request, made it rather clear that her brother was too busy with his new executive position in the Committee on Foreign Concessions to receive us.

For the foreign visitor, living conditions in 1926 seemed quite normal, as compared with western Europe; the prices for room and board were about the same as those prevailing in Berlin, though the quality of both was much inferior. We exchanged our dollars for rubles and paid for our meals as we got them. A sharply graduated tax on all bills made us pay for our rooms each day and for our meals singly when a group dined together. There were two types of stores at which we could buy food to prepare in our room or to take to friends who invited us to supper. The private store charged somewhat more than the government distributing agency, but its service was better and its choice of foods more varied. One of the foreigners found a French bakery which served meals in a small room which could hold about a dozen at a time. Here the dinner was excellent, and this place became a kind of club for the correspondents. I went there several times a week.

The National Hotel, which had been the best hotel in Moscow before the Revolution, was now reserved for members of the Party, a kind of dormitory for the higher officials. I had often stopped there in other years; and as I passed it one day, I recognized several of the old porters. So I suggested to Wood that we try the dining-room of this so-called "Soviet dormitory." Despite Wood's fears, we got past my friendly porters by walking in without hesitation, as though we belonged, for I knew the way to the dining-room. And here we had an excellent meal for about half of what we would have paid in our own Grand Hotel. Several officials of the Commissariat of Foreign Affairs were there; and we greeted them most cordially, paying no attention to their looks of surprise and embarrassment. We repeated the performance several times without difficulty; but we kept the fact to ourselves, so as not to spoil the little racket which we were working on the Soviet people, in company with some of their leaders.

Around the corner from the Grand Hotel, one enterprising NEPman set up a small café, accommodating about twenty people. His coffee was not bad; and Wood and I, who often ate there, taught him to make ham and eggs. From this small restaurant-keeper I learned much of the difficult conditions under which private enterprise had to be conducted in the Soviet Union, even in this period of the New Economic Policy. One evening he greeted me with particular vigor, which I interpreted, from past experience, to mean that he had somehow been able to add some new article of equipment to his modest little place. And this was, indeed, the case, for he said with pride: "Now we have napkins." Above each of his six small tables was pinned a neat package of toilet paper.

For the Russians, housing conditions were hard in Moscow. In Leningrad the housing crisis was less acute. It was almost impossible to secure apartments, since a law passed some six months before forbade "buying into" an apartment by undertaking to make some repairs. There were plenty of restaurants, but the food was generally poor. The best places to eat were the "vegetarian" restaurants, for they were fairly clean.

Transportation in Moscow was excellent; the streetcar service was adequate and was supplemented by a dozen autobus lines. The old cabbies were reduced in number, very expensive, and most disagreeable. They were the bitterest critics of the new order, which had removed their main clientele. There was not a single *private* automobile in Moscow, and only a few public taxis. The streets, however, were full of "official" automobiles, many of them new and expensive cars.

146

The shopwindows were well stocked, but the long lines of people waiting for stores to open would indicate a shortage of supplies on the shelves. Many luxuries were displayed in the windows, and one wondered who could buy them. The "new bourgeoisie" probably supported these luxury stores, being afraid to deposit profits in banks; there were many such economic contradictions. Food prices seemed to be going up somewhat, and several times it was impossible to buy butter. But, on the whole, food prices in Moscow were not much higher than those that prevailed before the war, except for meat and fruit.

I soon found that it was possible for me to look up old friends of pre-revolutionary days. Some of these belonged to what was called "the incompletely slaughtered bourgeoisie." They had fitted into the new order as "specialists." The large size of this particular group produced the current abbreviation for it of *spetsy*. Others were of the new so-called "Soviet bourgeoisie," which was allowed to develop under the New Economic Policy; several were of the constantly abused and harassed class of private traders. With them the basic question of the moment was whether capitalism would be restored or socialism built up from the present two-faced economic structure. My own prophecy, after this first trip, was that the socialistic sector would win out; and this view was based in part on my study of Bolshevik methods of civic training, the main aim of which was to prepare the younger generation for a second drive for socialism.

My friend Petrunkevitch gave me a detailed account of the seizure of his estate, which I had frequently visited during my earlier trips. I spent hours hearing how he and his family had fled from place to place during the civil war, and how several had died in prison while others escaped abroad. I noted, among those who had lived through the civil war, a certain bitterness toward the ones, even of their own family, who had run away. These old bourgeois friends of mine in many instances recognized the inevitableness of the Revolution and foresaw the triumph in Russia of the socialistic system over the capitalistic system to which they had belonged. But they were of the liberal intelligentsia and were quite different from the group of NEPmen—the new bourgeois elements temporarily tolerated under the New Economic Policy. I saw the latter at the gambling casinos, the old restaurants with gipsy choruses, or the semi-illegal drinking holes where Junius Wood and I often went of an evening.

My old friends saw me quite freely; and, although some of them were later difficult to reach, when, with the resumption of the so-called "socialist offensive," a second liquidation process set in, I have always felt, and have been told by the relatives of those that suffered, that their contacts with me had not caused them injury. Several, in fact, were able to tell me how, when questioned by the political police, they were asked about their relations with me. They always defined these relations carefully; and the examining official, referring to a file, indicated by a nod that their stories corresponded to the police records.

The economists among my friends were naturally having the most difficult time. A former landlord could be safely used in a governmental department interested in improving the breed of horses. Dramatic artists could go on with their work without becoming politically involved. But economists were expected to report honestly on the gradual success of the socialistic sector over the capitalistic sector. In the light of later developments, I am afraid that several of these showed their prejudice in favor of the capitalistic sector in their reports. The charge of "sabotage in handling statistics" was brought against them.

Merriam accompanied me when I spent an evening with one of these economists, whose home had been the first which I had entered on my arrival in Moscow in 1904. It was the same apartment; but my friend, his wife, and his aunt had been able to retain only two rooms—the study and the dining-room. Much of their furniture was stacked in the hallway, taken from the rooms which they had been obliged to cede to the new ruling class—the workmen. This university man had always been something of an invalid; but that evening he seemed very close to the end, as he lay on a couch in his crowded and disorderly study. His complaint was not that the Bolsheviks were killing him but that they were killing his name—his reputation, abroad as well as in Russia, as one of the outstanding authorities on public finance. He was working for the Commissariat of Finance in a technical capacity, and the government was using him and his knowledge but suppressing his name. Later he was involved in an alleged conspiracy and given three years in a concentration camp. After that period he was released, his pension was re-established, and he was given a room in the Home for Scientists. But his name is never cited in any of the Soviet economic publications, and his library was seized and turned over to one of the research institutes.

Another friend, also an economist, had a position which carried extensive administrative authority. He was, at the time, a little over fifty; but he said frankly that he realized that his period of continued service was limited. Part of his work, he explained, was to teach young assistants of proletarian origin, who would replace him as soon as he had given them the proper training. This man also went by the board a few years later, when, with the resumption of the socialist offensive under the Five-Year Plans these *spetsy*, trained under the old regime, came to be suspect and, on that basis, no longer desirable in the new order.

It was with my old friends in the theatrical world that I could have the freest and most frequent relations. The fact that I had been of some help to the Moscow Art Theatre when it had toured America had brought me very close to many of those in this important center of artistic life. Stanislavsky gave me some of the most objective accounts

148

of the conditions and methods of that first period of Bolshevism. Many of my questions were directed toward confirming from personal stories the course of the Revolution as I had plotted it from my studies of the written documents. In answer to one of these questions, as to the character and standing of Lenin, Stanislavsky described Lenin's coming to the Moscow Art Theatre on an evening in the first year of the Revolution. Looking through the curtain hole, Stanislavsky had seen him enter and had immediately sent him an invitation to come behind the scenes during the first intermission. Lenin had rather curtly refused the invitation, asking to be left alone and to be allowed to enjoy the play, which was what he had come for.

Some years later, I put the same question about Lenin to Angelica Balabanova, who had worked closely with him in the establishment of the Communist International, of which she was the first executive secretary. To illustrate what kind of person Lenin was, Balabanova recounted the story of the same visit to the Art Theatre which Stanislavsky had mentioned, and the accounts agreed even in the smallest details. For Balabanova had accompanied Lenin to the theater that evening and had heard his answer to Stanislavsky's invitation. Zinoviev had also been one of this party; and Balabanova contrasted him and Lenin, for Zinoviev had wished to make a demonstration of their presence, to get special recognition from the troup of actors as well as from the audience.

Visitors to the Soviet Union were supposed to be followed at all times by representatives of the political police—the famous G.P.U. The extensive and intensive activity of this institution of the Soviet system was undeniable. We foreigners scrupulously abstained from even using its name in public places or when talking over the telephone. Many of the short-term visitors, to the embarrassment of the permanent residents, liked to shout the word around to show that they knew all about the Soviet Union. We had several substitute names, however, such as "the fraternity" and "the unmentionables." After my departure I received a postcard from Junius Wood with a picture of the headquarters of this dread authority and the words, "Our little forget-me-not."

Waiters in hotels, as well as the interpreters assigned to foreigners by the Cultural Relations Society, were said to be agents of the G.P.U.; and most of us went on the assumption that it was best to be suspicious of all of these. The waiter who served the room which Merriam and I occupied was an older man, however, and one who remembered me from my former visits. So one evening after he had brought in our supper, my zeal as a student overcame my caution and I began a conversation with him. This time I was not translating for Merriam; and he was, so to speak, left out. The waiter complained rather bitterly of the conditions which had come with the Revolution; and, fearing that I had started something which might prove embarrassing, I tried to stop him. At this point Merriam decided to join the party and pulled off, with a long face to match that which the waiter had developed, his one Russian phrase, "It's a hard life." This broke down whatever restraint I had been able to re-establish in the poor waiter, and we had a torrent of angry words, with shaking of the fists in the direction of the Kremlin just outside our window. Merriam insists that I turned pale, and I must admit that I showed considerable impatience with him after I had finally shut up the waiter and got him out of the room. We confessed what we had done to our unofficial ambassador, down the hall, Junius Wood; and his advice was not to repeat the performance.

This was not the only difficulty I had with Merriam in Moscow. Because of the help he was giving me, I always translated the conversation for him when we were interviewing some rather highly placed person in connection with our study of civic training. Frequently the procedure was for Merriam himself, who, of course, knew the subject better than I did, and was, in a sense, breaking me in to the job, to conduct the conversation. But several times he asked questions of a digging or even wicked character, which he would not have put if I had not been between him and the man interviewed, acting as interpreter. I found it impossible to translate such questions literally, or even to convey the spirit of them, and suffered considerable embarrassment on this account, to Merriam's undoubted enjoyment.

Study of Civic Training

Finding conditions on this first visit much more favorable than I had anticipated, I made plans to go to the provinces. At first I thought to revisit, for purposes of comparison, the estate of Mashuk, which had belonged to my old friends the Petrunkevitches; but, realizing that I might well be handicapped there as a friend of the former landlord, I decided to go off into an area in which I was not known. I was very fortunate in tying up with Maurice Hindus, who had already made trips to peasant villages, particularly to his old home in a western province.

Hindus and I did not ask permission to make this trip, nor did we even report our plans. We simply selected a group of rural centers, bought our railway tickets, and set forth with a minimum of luggage. Arriving at a provincial town, we played around there for a day and made no effort to conceal our movements. From among the public cabbies on the market square we picked one with a good horse and made our proposition to him. We wanted to drive about twenty-five miles to a certain small administrative center, which we had decided upon after consultation with several former zemstvo "agronoms" whom we had met at the Soviet headquarters of the district.

The peasant cabby whom we selected was, of course, one of the NEPmen; and he drove a hard bargain with us, emphasizing the cost of repairs to carts and of fodder for horses. The next morning he picked us up at our hotel, and we drove to his little hut on the outskirts of town.

150

Here his wife gave us breakfast while he changed the horse from his town carriage to a peasant cart. All that day we journeyed leisurely along the country roads, stopping at small villages and at a former estate which had been converted into a commune. We had clear evidence of the complete failure of the first effort to collectivize agriculture, for this commune was almost in ruins. Toward evening we finally arrived at the district center—simply a larger peasant village—which we had selected for study. The local tavern was full of schoolteachers of the district, who were holding a conference; but we were admitted immediately and joined them at supper and for an amateur performance of a revolutionary play by the local young people. The girl who played the leading role was also in charge of housing the visiting teachers, and she took us to her parents' home for another supper and to spend the night.

Although this house was one of the more prosperous, despite the fact that the father had been in exile for participating in the 1905 peasant disorders, the quarters were crowded. I won the toss of the coin and got the one and only bed. Hindus was actually the lucky one, however, for his pile of fresh straw in the corner was less inhabited than my mattress. We awoke in the morning to find that there were about ten other sleepers in the room.

We spent the next day at the sessions of the teachers' conference, where the discussion was carried on quite freely in our presence; and we were brought into it on several occasions. That evening we accepted the invitation of two teachers, brother and sister, to go to their village for a day. They were the children of a local priest who had left home in order not to interfere with their future. This comparatively small and poor village contained an enormous brick church; and the priest's house at which we stopped was a big one of several rooms, with a large orchard-garden behind it.

At this second village Hindus and I visited another priest, living in a single room in a peasant hut, who explained that the collapse of the Greek Orthodox church in the revolutionary situation was the result of the small spiritual content of its dogma and the meagerness of the social service work which the priests had been allowed to do by their hierarchy. Using our need of cigarettes as an excuse, we visited the local private store and heard the complaints of the trader who ran it. At the co-operative store we saw the scant goods on hand.

As we wandered around the village, we suggested to various peasants that we would like to have a group gathered, so that we could put our questions and answer theirs. With the peasants it was always good technique to promise in advance that they could ask questions about America after we had inquired about their country. Our effort was too successful, for what we got was a whole village meeting, called by the ringing of the church bell by one of the villagers, who had thought to celebrate the arrival of distinguished guests by getting roaringly drunk.

151

He and the village dogs were our only troubles; and both proved to be quite annoying, particularly the overenthusiastic host.

Word of the proposed meeting reached a neighboring village, where one of the few Party members in the community was helping his parents get in the crops. He also came to the meeting, and, in fact, took over its chairmanship. But Hindus and I put our questions without hesitation and in complete frankness. After individual peasants had expressed themselves, the Communist-Party member asked to be allowed to interpolate his views and to interpret the general situation. He was very intelligent and very candid in admitting the mistakes of the past and the unsatisfactory conditions of the present—always, of course, emphasizing the splendid plans for the future. One old peasant in bast shoes, his legs wrapped in dirty rags, put his foot to Hindus' nose and asked if the Americans had ever seen human beings dressed like that. We quite readily admitted that only in eastern Europe and Asia were such sights to be seen.

That evening, at the priest's house, with the help of an old gramophone, Hindus and I gave a little lesson in American dancing, about which Hindus has never ceased to tease me. After a comfortable night in these very good quarters, we set out next morning for another and still smaller village. A soldier who had been a prisoner of war in Germany, where he had picked up considerable German, had heard of the arrival of foreigners and had come over to show off to the other peasants his linguistic accomplishments. He insisted that we visit him; and, once arrived at his hut, we had to accept his hospitality. Watching the preparation of the food which we had to eat upset Hindus' digestion in advance, but I carried on. We were in a straw-thatched hut without a chimney; and the smoke from the stove hung under the ceiling, seeping out through small holes in the side walls. The ordeal of this visit was about the hardest we had to endure, particularly after the room became crowded, to the point of suffocation, with our host's friends. With this group of peasants we discussed the Revolution, the after-life, the role of the Communists, and the feeble educational efforts already begun in this backward area.

While there was some complaint about the absence of work, we found, particularly among the young people, the hope of more opportunity in the new order. Two young men on leave from the Red Army had brought back a football and organized a soccer game, to replace the intervillage fights which had been the main sport of rural Russia. Many of the young people had gone off to work in the slowly reviving manufacturing enterprises of neighboring towns. Some were leaving soon for near-by wheat fields. Thus, already, there was evidence of the quickening of economic life, although the general picture was still one of extreme backwardness and poverty.

From this village we had to drive back some twenty miles to the railway. We hired a local kulak, or rich peasant, who, alone in the village, had a cart with springs and a good pair of horses. Heavy rains had brought a so-called "roadless" period, and for a while we thought we might have to stay on a week. The kulak got us through, however, after a day of hard driving, during which we had to listen to a violent attack on the Soviets and the Bolsheviks. Our driver boasted of the way he had outwitted the local commissars as well as those sent down from the town to carry out the first liquidation of the kulaks in 1917–21. But he himself was undoubtedly liquidated three years later, in the second drive for collectivization.

When, on our return to Moscow, Hindus and I mentioned to our Soviet friends the rural area which we had visited, they expressed concern and even reproach that we had gone to such a backward group of villages. But we had, of course, deliberately selected such a region, thinking to be better able to determine the force of the Revolution by examining its effects in the kind of villages we had studied. And, indeed, as we frankly admitted, the results were all in favor of the Bolsheviks.

One of my chief aims during this 1926 trip was to get acquainted with some of the younger men and women in Soviet institutions who were being trained by older bourgeois specialists. My study of civic training gave me an excuse for working my way into all types of institutions. These young people, mostly members of the Communist Party or of the Komsomol, were very co-operative, perhaps because I scrupulously refrained from trying to get too friendly on a personal basis. I ruined one connection which might have proved very useful by suggesting an evening at one of the restaurants having a gipsy chorus. The Communist said sharply that such places were for "you bourgeois elements," and after that our discussions were much less fruitful. On the other hand, another worker in the Komsomol, a very ardent young Communist, seemed to find me "an honest bourgeois" because of certain admissions I had made regarding the capitalist system and its methods. This young man would go with me to the theater or come to my room for supper.

My study of Soviet methods in civic training—"political grammar," they called it—took me to the headquarters of the Komsomol, to schools, newspaper offices, clubs of all kinds, and also to theaters and movies. At the public institutions I gained admission without difficulty by presenting a general letter of recommendation from the Commissariat of Education. In the schools I was admitted to classrooms and was allowed to sit in the corner while the teaching continued.

There was one institution, however, which I was not able to study as closely as I had hoped, namely, the Party. The conflict within the Party which had just come to a head made it difficult to gain admission to headquarters or even to the Party groups in the institutions which I did visit. In 1930 it was possible for me, for the first time, to enter and work in the headquarters of the Party's Central Committee, and this I was able to do only with great difficulty and considerable formality. My passport had to be left with the commandant of the building before I could enter; and, of course, I had to reclaim it when I left, thus being temporarily under police surveillance. My failure in 1926 to cover adequately the Party institutions and functions constituted a weakness in my work, because the Party headed up and controlled the civic training which I was studying. On this aspect, I had to be satisfied with the published documents; but these, fortunately, were very comprehensive because of the type of Party activity involved. For my book I decided to designate the Party member as the "citizen with special responsibility," but I was not able at the time to get a full picture of the instructions which Party members received from the higher Party authorities. Later these were published in a series of annual volumes entitled *Guide Book for Party Workers*.

I hesitated even to try to study the Red Army, although I knew that the civic-training work was best organized among its young recruits, especially those from among the peasantry. But Mme Kameneva smiled down my hesitation about having any contact with military organizations; and I was allowed to visit barracks, talk extensively with political workers of the Red Army, and attend lectures and discussions on domestic and foreign political topics conducted among the Redarmyists. (The word "soldier" had been eliminated from the Soviet vocabulary.) I spent several hours in the editorial office of the official daily newspaper of the Red Army, and here I secured a textbook used in the courses on political grammar in the barracks schools. This textbook was well arranged from the point of view of propaganda, for at the end of each chapter the conclusions to which the discussions should lead were given in detail and with precision. The textbooks used in the ordinary schools, and particularly on subjects related to civic training, could be ordered without difficulty; and I was able to send out a very complete collection.

In my study of the schools I was helped by several older teachers whom I had known before, and particularly by a Russian girl who had just returned from three years' study at Teachers College, Columbia, full of the ideas of Dewey, Counts, and Kilpatrick. She admitted that she still had "a bourgeois soul," though she kept pointing out the fact that she was adapting herself to the material conditions of a Soviet worker. Some ten years later I was to find this same girl in a high position in the Soviet educational setup, living most comfortably but insisting, in response to my remark about her material well-being, that she had developed "a proletarian soul."

CHAPTER XIX

1927–29: WHAT OTHERS THOUGHT ABOUT SOVIET RUSSIA

ON COMING OUT OF THE SOVIET UNION AT THE END OF OCTOBER, 1926, I settled down in Berlin for six weeks, to work over the printed material I had secured and to record and organize the oral material, much of which I had hesitated to put down in notes so long as I was in the Soviet Union. At this time the scrutiny at the frontier was very thorough for all outgoing travelers. In Berlin, moreover, I could order recent Moscow publications through the official bookstore. Perhaps even more useful was the presence there of a great many German university men who were studying Russian developments. There had always been a larger number of such students in Germany than in England or France, and the close co-operation of this period between Russia and Germany had not only brought them to the fore but had also developed a new generation of German students of Russian affairs. These people proved to be excellent consultants as I worked over the material which I had gathered.

There were many Russian émigrés in Berlin, but I did not find it either politically expedient or academically helpful to seek them out. In Prague, however, where I went before returning home, there was a group of Russian specialists in education and economics who had not emigrated in 1918 but had been exiled in 1921. The difference in psychology between the emigrant and the exile was very marked, and with the latter I found it possible and fruitful to discuss my observations and to compare my findings with theirs. My trip to Prague had the very definite additional aim of reporting, in a sense, to my old professor, now president, Masaryk. Through him I had access to Czechoslovak sources of information, and Czechoslovak representatives aided me in many ways.

Masaryk himself, of course, had given much attention to Russian affairs in his academic work as well as in his later political activity. He did not like Bolshevism and had been skeptical of its potentiality for solving internal, much less international, problems. He and his group had tied their newly re-established state to the League of Nations, with which the Soviet Union was at times in very active competition. But by 1926, although formal Russian diplomatic relations had not yet been established, he and the other Czech leaders were beginning to see the possibility of *rapprochement*. It was not a question of the revival of Pan-Slavism, but rather the fact that this small Slav state, thrust westward between Germans, tended naturally to look for economic and political support to the large unit in the east. In Prague, then, at the time, I found a hopeful attitude toward Sovietism and a verification of those constructive features which I had noted for my study of civic training.

When I returned to the United States in December, 1926, the family farm again demanded my attention; and I devoted a considerable amount of time to it during the next years, despite Merriam's impatience at the slowness with which I completed my book. But it required a good deal of weighing and thinking to decide just what I had discovered and was willing to put down in black and white about the Soviet government. The subject of civic training was, as I have explained, a very comprehensive one and had taken me into a large number of fields. While mending fences or digging tile or riding the tractor, I thought out the outlines of most of my chapters. At the time I was not able to convince Merriam that this was what I was doing, but I believe that the final results did eventually persuade him that I was not simply lazy. On the subject of Sovietism one could easily write whole volumes, because in almost any aspect of it there are novel and even thrilling things that could be described. I had seen many writers caught in the toils of undigested impressions which they had allowed themselves to publish, and I wished to avoid this myself. Furthermore, the time I gave to the farm brought me still closer to the small practical problems of production and distribution to which the Soviet leaders claimed in 1928 to have found the answers.

When the book was finally completed and published in the fall of 1929, I sent a number of copies to the institutions and individuals who had aided me in gathering my material. The review in the official *Isvestia* pronounced the work a fair and accurate analysis of Soviet methods of civic training, though it characterized some of my conclusions as "typically bourgeois." This particular review proved to be of considerable use to me. Several old friends that I had either not ventured to look up or had lacked time to see when I was in Russia wrote to me, inclosing the review for the censor's benefit as well as mine. On my next trip to the Soviet Union, I used this *Isvestia* review as a kind of general pass to get to people or into institutions without the formality of specific introductions from the Cultural Relations Society or the Commissariat of Education.

Meanwhile my university work went on in a very satisfactory manner. My classes were growing, and I had the further pleasure of having several graduate students doing specialized work on Russia either in Berlin or in the Soviet Union. I was also asked by the university to give a course on contemporary Russian history in the Home-Study Department, and thus was enabled to reach a wider group of students. For scholars and teachers in this country, I served as a sort of travel agent, supplying them with information on the best way to get to Russia and on what to look for when they got there.

In 1927 my colleague Paul Douglas was a member of a "labor delegation" to the Soviet Union. The members of this group made a serious study of the various aspects of Sovietism. They were received by Stalin, who answered in detail the questions they had prepared in advance. Their findings were later published as a volume of essays by the individual members of the group. Douglas came back very enthusiastic, particularly because at that time he thought to see the gradual rise of the trade-union as the basic political factor which would supersede the Party. His particular field of study was precisely that of labor and wages. Douglas wished to organize a group, with the university as the center, to make a thorough study of the Soviet system. Such a project would, of course, have included me; and presumably I would have had a kind of directing role in it. But there were many obstacles to such a group effort. For one thing, the number of those adequately equipped to make such a study was limited, for a specialist in a particular field would not know the Russian language, and one knowing Russian would have no special qualification for this work. Finally, the long discussions about the project convinced me once more that the subject would have to be handled by individuals, each assuming full responsibility for his own work without sharing that responsibility with others.

During the years from 1927 to 1929 I attended the Christmas meetings of the American Historical Association and the American Political Science Association, alternating between the two fields in which I had come to work. One year I read a paper, or took part in a panel discussion, at the historical meetings; the next year, at the political meetings. At these meetings I carried on what some of my friends designated as my "propaganda." Here, of course, I was doing professional work; but even in these groups I encountered prejudices, loose thinking, and "counterpropaganda."

At the beginning of 1927, shortly after my return from Russia, I again entered actively on a program of public lecturing. I had seen Sovietism in action and therefore felt that I could speak with more authority than I had been able to when my information had come only from long-distance study of documents. I inaugurated my return to public lecturing by giving a kind of report to the Chicago Council on Foreign Relations, which I had helped to organize and which was, perhaps, the most appropriate forum for reaching the Chicago community.

This report was covered by a couple of semiofficial representatives from Moscow, both of whom I recognized in the audience. The presence of one of these—Anna Louise Strong—was of particular interest to me. I had tended to avoid her in Moscow because I had found her writings more Bolshevik than the Bolsheviks'. The other, more official, spotter came up to me after the lecture and complimented me on the fairness and focus of my exposition of the basic facts, but added that, of course, he could not agree with my conclusions, some of which he frankly characterized as typically bourgeois or even naïve.

The attitude of my American audience at this lecture, as at subsequent ones, was a disappointment to me. Some openly criticized me because I did not say that the Soviet system was either a complete failure or an unqualified success. Some thought that I had turned pro-Bolshevik because I was not censorious enough for them, and they were seriously worried that one who had had a record of being strongly anti-Bolshevik and antirecognitionist had, as they supposed, changed his views. Others felt that my story of what I had seen was colored by the fear that if I spoke unfavorably the Soviet authorities would not allow me to return. One of my friends even interpreted my effort to be objective as a deliberate attempt to improve my standing with the Soviet authorities. He knew me better than that and later reduced his charge—at least to the point of saying that such an effort was perhaps subconscious.

As a matter of fact, I really could not tell with any degree of certainty what statements might offend Soviet leaders, because, despite my careful study and my long talks with them, I still did not fully understand the peculiar psychology of these professional revolutionaries. One thing I knew well, however, was that any facetiousness or flippancy in my interpretation would incense them. I collected many of the political anecdotes that all revolutionary movements produce, for they represent the one open form of expressing opposition in the tight political atmosphere of a revolutionary movement. It has always been a temptation to use these anecdotes in my public lectures. I have refrained from doing so, however, because it would give a flippant tone to my discussion. The repeating of such anecdotes would make the Moscow leaders feel that I was laughing at them or that I took the anecdotes seriously. I was both frank and serious in my discussions withBolshevik leaders, explaining to them that my study of their system was a purely professional and serious study. Their Bolshevism had come to a country which I had chosen to study. In a word, I would put it: "I came to Russia before you did; and since you have come, I have had to study you."

I had one unhappy experience with Professor S. N. Prokopovich and his wife, Guskova, who had been exiled in 1923 and were living in Prague. On one of my returns from Russia I stopped over there; and, after we had finished a long and serious discussion with interchange of facts and interpretations, I relaxed and relayed to them, with a light touch, various political anecdotes current in Moscow. Guskova wrote an article outlining some of the anecdotes and, without mentioning my name, expressed deep and apparently sincere grief and dismay that any student would collect such ridiculous stories, not able to appreciate, perhaps because of the seriousness of her life, the humorous side of either the anecdotes or of my repeating them. Sometimes my old pre-Bolshevik friends in Russia would ask me if I were going to tell the whole truth. "Better not if you want to come back, and we do want to see you again," they would comment. I argued that they were wrong; that so long as I kept what I said in proper focus, I could describe, for example, both the G.P.U. and the position of Stalin. I admitted that a book on the G.P.U. with little reference to any other institution would probably close the doors to me. In the *Izvestia* review of my book on civic training one of the favorable comments was that my viewpoint was not malicious. I did avoid consciously the tendency, which I noted in so many writers on Soviet Russia, to put in at regular intervals the "pin pricks" which would protect the author among those readers who were always looking for "Soviet sympathizers."

My failure to condemn, out of hand, everything that the Bolsheviks had done or had tried to do led many to protest against my lectures. On one occasion I spoke at a Saturday afternoon meeting of the University Club of Chicago. Here it was possible to have a long period of discussion after the more formal lecture. It was a bad winter day; and, perhaps because of that, the crowd stayed on into the late afternoon. Next day the president's office, I was told, had several telephone messages from irate alumni, and even from members of the board of trustees; and I have never received another invitation to speak to my fellow-members.

On the other hand, in smaller places in the Middle West where I was asked to lecture, either in an educational institution or on some public forum, I found much less prejudice on the question of Bolshevism. In the same audience there were employees as well as employers, instead of a predominant number of one or the other, such as characterizes the audiences of our big metropolitan centers. So I did not have to meet the strongly felt views of a particular economic or social group; also, in the smaller communities I found, not only more information on important matters, but an encouraging evidence of the basic common sense of the ordinary American, albeit he is considered less educated or "cultured" than the facile large-city intellectual.

It became my practice during this period of rather extensive public lecturing to insist on the setting in which I would speak. Thus I refused to give the hurried after-luncheon talks because I found it difficult to cover the controversial subject of Sovietism in forty minutes. My rule was that there should be provision for a question period after the more formal lecture or talk of an hour. In this way, members of the audience could bring up points which they thought important but which I had omitted because of the greater importance, in my opinion, of other aspects. Very frequently, one of the questions from the audience would be on the "nationalization of women," and I would have to spend five minutes explaining how this misconception of Bolshevik doctrine and practice had developed.

Also, I refused to speak at meetings where it was proposed that "both sides" be presented. Often an invitation to speak at a meeting of this kind inquired which side I took and asked for my recommendation of a speaker to take the other side. My usual answer to such queries was that my approach was that of the student and not of the partisan. I always added that I would be glad to debate the question of whether the Soviet system had accomplished this or that specific objective, with anyone who had studied the question and under the strict rules of formal debate. This made it impossible for me to appear at any of the many branches of the Foreign Policy Association of New York City or at the meetings of its important central forum. In general, however, and particularly on my topic, I believe such attempts were not particularly useful, for it seemed to me that they often degenerated into a kind of bullfight, where everyone picked on a particular speaker, perhaps selected in advance because his viewpoint would not be popular with a particular audience. My judgment may have been wrong, but I had no desire to become the bull in one of these thrill performances.

One of our forums prepared an extensive list of potential speakers on the Russian question, some pro-Soviet and some anti-Soviet, with a description of each speaker and brief notes on his qualifications. On this list my name appeared among the antis and was followed by the bald observation that I was "not a very good speaker." I was amused, but took to heart this comment and made considerable effort to improve my delivery and to let it be known that I would welcome criticism from members of my audiences. Some of the comments I received were highly amusing; others were instrumental, I believe, in correcting some of my major faults. It appeared that most of the women liked my delivery and, as one of them put it, my manner of treating what might have been treated by some as melodrama; but, most of all, they liked my smile. An anonymous critic hoped that I would learn not to drop my voice at the end of a sentence and would in the future try to avoid swinging myself back and forth as much as I did on the occasion when he was in the audience.

There was one other group of people with whom I frequently discussed my 1926 findings in Russia which I do not wish to overlook. Various commercial organizations that had been doing business with Russia asked me to discuss the entire Russian problem with their executives. I also had much correspondence and a good many conferences with American engineers who were accepting employment from the Soviet government. I always explained to the engineers that they would find working in Soviet Russia an entirely different matter from working in the United States and that, to get any satisfaction from it, they should have an adventurous spirit and a desire for new experiences.

In the years from 1927 to 1929, little of importance happened in American-Russian diplomatic relations, and therefore I made fewer trips to Washington. Organizations such as the Friends of the Soviet Union were still active in urging American recognition of the Soviet government, but they were not sufficiently influential to bring about a

160

large-scale movement in favor of recognition. American-Soviet trade relations developed, however, and the businessmen at Moscow or the engineers who went to work in the various centers of industrial expansion did not seem to suffer greatly from the absence of an American embassy. These business interests, operating through an American-Russian Chamber of Commerce, of course kept the State Department informed of what they were doing. Thus, by their trade relations, individual Americans and individual American firms were recognizing the existence of the Soviet Union, though organized business was still strongly against any formal recognition. In 1927 the United States Chamber of Commerce issued a rather indignant refusal in response to a suggestion from Ivy Lee that it open an office in Russia; and in 1928 Matthew Woll, representing the National Civic Federation, sent a circular statement opposing recognition to many American leaders, asking their approval of it.

In contrast to this, those in other countries who were doing business with the Soviets worked actively for recognition. In 1927 I was informed that one of the main reasons for Czechoslovakia's recognition of the Soviets was Masaryk's feeling that Czechoslovakia was suffering from the competition of business done in Russia by other national groups. In November, 1929, my friend Pares wrote me that in England there was no enthusiasm for recognition except among conservative traders. Some thought that the Russian note of 1928 expressing adherence to the Kellogg Pact would raise the issue of recognition in the United States also, but nothing came of it.

Only one diplomatic incident occurred during these years. It resulted from the Soviet incursion into Manchuria with Red Army units to settle a dispute with the Chinese government over the Chinese Eastern Railway, of which the Soviet and Chinese governments were joint owners. As both these governments were signatories of the Kellogg-Briand pact, Secretary Stimson felt that the situation called for action on his part. The timing and wording of his note were unfortunate. It reached Moscow indirectly, because of the absence of diplomatic channels, after the withdrawal of the Red Army from Manchuria. This gave the Bolsheviks an opportunity to be sarcastic in their reply—an opportunity which they were not slow to take advantage of. It was also possible for them to point out that the State Department might have been better informed on the actual facts of the situation if normal diplomatic relations had existed between the two governments. This proved to be an unimportant misunderstanding, but it pointed to the possibility that the impasse in relations between the United States and the Soviet Union might eventually be cleared away in connection with events in the Far East.

During my trips to Washington, I spent hours arguing our policy with my friends in the State Department and exchanging with them documents which we had found in our respective studies of the question.

As was natural, the Department realized the many ramifications of recognition which individual groups did not take into consideration and still held to its position of refusing to see a basis for mutual trust so long as the Moscow leaders continued to support the Communist International and refused to recognize the debts of the previous Russian government or to compensate American nationals whose property had been nationalized. Whatever pressure there was for recognition dwindled with the resumption in 1928 of the socialist offensive and the inauguration of the Five-Year Plan.

During this period Stalin rose to supremacy. With the death of Lenin in 1924, his immediate lieutenants carried on as a unit under the influence of his ideas and precepts. But after a few years, controversies developed. There were differences of temperament which led to personal rivalries. I had noted the first open antagonism in 1926. The main basis of the disputes that arose was the proper interpretation of the writings and speeches of Lenin, of which, by the way, there were over thirty large printed volumes.

Of Lenin's closest co-workers in the first years of the Revolution, the four most prominent were Trotsky, Dzerzhinsky, Bukharin, and Stalin. Trotsky was the orator of the Revolution, who harangued the governments of other countries, inspired the Red Army, and wrote the histories of the Revolution. Dzerzhinsky was the "watchdog" of the Revolution, the chief of its police, repressing ruthlessly all opposition to the Revolution. Bukharin was the theoretician of the Revolution, interpreting its doctrine, giving the theoretical basis for the policies and measures of the Revolutionary authority. Finally, Stalin was the field organizer of those selected groups that were carrying out the principles of the Revolution. He was the general secretary of the party which had led the Revolution and which occupied a "ruling position" in the government set up by the Revolution. Stalin was something like a party-boss; but the party of which he was the boss was a strictly disciplined, highly centralized, political organization of carefully limited membership, and this organization based its authority on the principles and rules of a revolution. A country in revolution is in some respects like a country at war; in any case, it is quite different from a country in normal evolution. The party of a revolution is therefore a powerful organization—powerful with respect to its own members as well as with respect to the country as a whole. The man responsible for the functioning of this organization is powerful with respect to all rivals.

Dzerzhinsky died in 1926. So only three were left, each with his following—Trotsky, Bukharin, and Stalin. Trotsky was always a good deal of a prima donna, an individualist despite his acceptance of Communism. He was always wanting to give expression to his interpretation of Leninism—often, it seemed to the outsider, simply for the pleasure of discussion. Moreover, he accused Stalin of backsliding from the prin-

162

ciples of the Revolution. Trotsky's ideas and mottoes sounded radical enough; but, even if there existed a basis for criticizing the Party authorities, it was felt that he should have accepted the discipline required of a party actually carrying on a revolutionary program. So Stalin found it necessary in the winter of 1927–28, in the interests of unity and discipline, to expel Trotsky, first from the Party, then from the capital, and finally from the country itself. Bukharin's end came shortly after.

In 1928, simultaneously with the elimination of Trotsky, Stalin initiated a sharp change of policy. There was only an indirect relation between Trotsky's fall and the new policy, although it is often alleged that the new policy was precisely what Trotsky had advocated. This is a question of Communist polemics, which cannot be discussed here. In any case, Stalin claimed the credit for the new policy, basing it on Leninism and insisting that it was the only correct interpretation of the doctrine and tactics of revolution as evolved by Lenin. The new policy called for militant methods of revolution—at least on the home front—after a period of respite and rest. It was the resumption of the so-called "socialist offensive" after a forced retreat during the period of the New Economic Policy. It was explained that in its first effort the Revolution had simply cut off the head of capitalism and then had set to work to cultivate and develop the new social order. But the roots of capitalism, during the period of the New Economic Policy gave forth new shoots, which were impeding the growth of the new order. Therefore, it became necessary to make a more thorough job of it and, to quote the current slogan, "pull out the very roots of capitalism."

It is this policy that gave birth to the famous Five-Year Plan of economic expansion, which practically eliminated private enterprise in industry. This Five-Year Plan called for the gradual suppression of private trade; and—more important still—it provided for the collectivization of agriculture, not completely, but to a point where individual peasant enterprises would be subordinate to state grain factories and large collectivist agricultural enterprises.

It was to a Russia geared to a high revolutionary pitch at the end of the second year of the Five-Year Plan that I made plans to return in 1930. Because this new policy involved such revolutionary economic principles for the study of which I considered my training not fully adequate, I looked about for a good practical economist to accompany me on this trip; and I was fortunate in finding Walter Lichtenstein, secretary of the First National Bank of Chicago, who was well grounded academically in economics and had, in addition, a broad practical background in banking and foreign exchange. He was also a stimulating traveling companion.

CHAPTER XX

1930: MAKING BOLSHEVIKS: THE
FIRST FIVE-YEAR PLAN

HAVING COMPLETED MY ACADEMIC WORK IN APRIL, 1930, I SET OFF IM-
mediately for Berlin, to wait there until the middle of July, when
Walter Lichtenstein could join me. My frequent stopovers in Berlin on
my way to Russia had definite aims. Germany was, after all, the great
European nation nearest to Russia. What was done in Berlin had a far
more direct influence on Moscow than what was done in Washington.
Also, Berlin watched Russia very closely. In Berlin I could explore a
wealth of currently published materials about Soviet Russia—in 1930,
particularly about the new Five-Year Plan—and could interview German business and university men who had kept abreast of Soviet developments. With this background I was always better able to formulate the significant questions to be investigated on Soviet soil. I must
admit, too, that the transition from the comforts of America to the hard-
ships of Soviet Russia was simplified by this intermission in a country
which had something of both.

Before leaving the United States, I made my usual round of visits to
friends in Washington and found that they were a little jealous that I
could get into Russia while they, being officially connected with the
government, could not. I also saw Paul Scheffer, the German correspondent recently expelled from Moscow. He was very anti-Soviet, and
I had a feeling that he exhibited a bit of resentment at the lively development of trade relations between America and Soviet Russia. In New
York I saw Bakhmeteff, the Russian ambassador under the Kerensky
regime, who had now given up hope and left Washington. He, too, was
regretful that he could not go back to see what Russia was doing.

I sailed on the S.S. "Dresden" and arrived in Berlin on the fifteenth
of April. This time I found it possible to establish direct relations with
the German foreign office. The German ambassador to Moscow, von
Dirksen, happened to be in Berlin; and I met him through friends in the
American embassy, where Poole was still counselor. I attended regularly a weekly luncheon of students of Soviet affairs. Because my conversational German was not so good as my Russian and these Germans knew
as little English as I did German, the discussions at these luncheons were
often carried on in Russian. One day a member of the Soviet embassy,
lunching at the same restaurant, noted, as he passed our table, that we
were speaking Russian, and remarked with a smile that he was glad to
see that Russian was gradually becoming the international language.

My life in Berlin, waiting for Walter Lichtenstein, was intensely
strenuous and interesting. I outlined it in my letters.

DEAR MOTHER:

I have spent most of the day with Mowrer of the *News*. As usual, he was most cordial and helpful; he brought me up to date on the question of Russian-German relations and took me around to the Soviet embassy, where I was most cordially received. Letters of recommendation are to be written to Moscow. This is the first personal contact that I have had with the Soviet foreign office. I did not ask for the special recommendation—it was offered in a very gracious manner and will prove most useful. I reported fully what I plan to do in the way of study and travel in the U.S.S.R. I explained that I did not wish to go in for four or five weeks, because of some preliminary study and writing, and got permission to use some of the files of the Soviet embassy. Lichtenstein was not mentioned by me—I shall leave that to the next visit. I was told that my visa was on hand and that I could have it any time. All of which means that I am waiting over for Walter. The four or five weeks will become five or six weeks.

Now for a little bite of supper—I had a big luncheon—and then I am going to my old favorite haunt, the vaudeville of the Winter Garten, all by myself, because I am talked out and have a hard day tomorrow, doing our own embassy in the morning; the commercial attaché, who is an old friend, in the afternoon; and a dinner with the Mowrers and other American newspaper friends in the evening. Then on Thursday I do the German foreign office and the German university people, and the preliminaries are off my hands—that is, the formal calls. If Friday is good weather, I shall hit out into the suburbs, for Easter is the big holiday here and everything will be closed.

BERLIN, April 17, 1930

DEAR WALTER:

There is deep skepticism here, among the Americans as well as the Germans, about the Soviet Five-Year Plan. The formula generally accepted is something like this: the present policy will bring a crash in a year or so; there is no possibility of back-pedaling—another New Economic Policy simply would not work, as nobody would trust it. Moscow papers, which I receive within thirty-six hours, admit a serious situation in the matter of the spring sowing on the individual farms, which represent about 50% of the area sown to grain in spring. When I press people here about the positive features to be noted, I find distinct fear lest the Soviets do succeed in pulling through the next difficult year. We are certainly going to be there at a most interesting moment, but it will be a hard life.

BERLIN, April 20, 1930
Easter Sunday evening

DEAR MOTHER:

Well, to start with today and work backward, as usual my lucky star shone on the holiday. Do you recall that nice lawyer, Heinrich Freund, expert on Soviet law? I had dinner with him and his wife last evening, and then we danced to the gramophone. Coming home for a short night of six hours, I turned up again at his house at 8:00 A.M., helped the children (aged 4 and 7) find their Easter eggs, and then we started off in a Ford for a small summer place he has about forty miles south of Berlin. It was a beautiful day—the first one in a week. Lovely country. At this small town, like Libertyville, we played around with local friends—the postmaster, banker, etc. They reminded me of our Wisconsin small-town folk, so different from the big-city breed. At 2:30 we had a Russian Easter dinner (his wife is German-Russian). I got home at five o'clock and slept two hours. Now for a little work before I go to bed.

Freund was in Moscow for two weeks a month ago. From him I am getting a great deal of material; he is, in fact, one of my best sources of information. I shall be seeing him often. He and his wife like to dance, and there is a sister-in-law. We are going to do some of the middle-class dance places one of these evenings.

It is well that I decided to stay over in Berlin, for all the American newspapermen in Moscow started off this morning on a four-week trip to Siberia to inspect the new railway connecting Siberia with Central Asia. It would have been difficult and dull without them. The wives of two of them are here. I lunch with them tomorrow.

Wow! how expensive living is in Berlin—about 25% higher than it was in 1926. The "reparations," the Germans answer when I complain. I am getting along with one good meal and a snack for the other, and only rolls and coffee for breakfast. When the maid brought my laundry bill for over two weeks, I almost fainted. So now I shall wear a collar for two days—other details I shall not explain.

BERLIN, April 25, 1930

DEAR MOTHER:

At 1:20 I turned up at the Kaiserhof, where Kroll (former German vice-consul in Chicago) gave me a luncheon. Three heads of departments in the German foreign office were there and Professor Palyi, the Hungarian economist who was at Chicago two years ago (had a Russian wife, you will remember). This lunch lasted till 4:00 P.M. I was, by force of circumstances, the chief speaker, but I picked up a little good information. Palyi took me to tea at the Deutsche Bank, where I met Bonn, the expert on Russian credits. I am going to have a long talk with him soon.

Sandomirsky (International Harvester representative) called for me and drove me out to their beautiful apartment—gorgeous, in fact—in a new suburb of Berlin. Here were the department heads of the German branch of the Harvester, plus a Russian Easter celebration—vodka, caviar, pigeon, cakes, etc., etc. It was 1:00 A.M. when we broke up and (I will be honest) I had a terrible stomach-ache the next morning, which has stayed with me for two days.

Wednesday I worked till 11:00 A.M. and then had a session with the commercial attaché of the German foreign office, an expert on Russia, just back from Moscow. It was in German, difficult also as to content, for he was cussing Americans for doing business with Moscow—the Germans want it all. I was so disturbed over some of the things he said that I called up Wily, our first secretary of embassy, in charge of Russian information, and we lunched together to talk it over.

Yesterday was another hectic day. I studied from 8:00 till 11:00; then drove to the International Harvester and studied some reports on Russia from 11:00 till 1:00. From there I went to a special society for the study of Russia here, attached to the university, and talked with Dr. Jonas, editor of their monthly *Ost Europa*, which you probably see lying around the house. They have an excellent library. From 3:00 to 4:30 I was at the embassy for a long talk with Wiley. He sees all Americans going in and out of Russia, and his summary of their reports was most valuable. He also gave me a clear picture of the international line-up with respect to Moscow.

From 5:00 to 6:30 I had tea with the staff of the *Christian Science Monitor*, and at 7:00 I had dinner with Mrs. Chamberlin. I went afterward to the radical workmen's theater where the famous revolutionary troupe of Meyerhold (Moscow) were giving in Russian the best propaganda play of the Revolution, *Groan* (under the heel of imperialists) *poor China*. The audience was composed largely of German and Russian Communists. They sang the "Internationale" and shouted "Hoch Lenin!" The play was marvelous.

BERLIN, May 2, 1930

DEAR PAUL:

I wrote mother Tuesday noon. Tuesday night I went to the Philharmonic, guest of a Berlin lady. We dined at Wertheim, a "Theatre Gedeck." She tried their "Bowle." It cost me only 50 pf. It must have been straight alcohol, for it went to her head. But we made the concert and enjoyed it. Howard Goodman was there, just out of Russia, installing some of the Goodman machinery.

Wednesday I ran down my old friend Knickerbocker, for three years a Hearst man in Moscow, and now Berlin, *New York Evening Post*—a redheaded Texan, keen and fearless, with a good mind. He introduced me to a new restaurant—the whole German foreign office seemed to be there—and a new drink which I shall not try to describe.

167

Knickerbocker is involved in a libel suit against the best criminal lawyer in Berlin, who called him a G.P.U. provocatory agent because he encouraged a group of forgers of anti-Bolshevik documents a year ago when the latter were trying to prove that Moscow had bribed Senator Borah. The famous Zinoviev letter is supposed to be the handiwork of this group, of which the head is a famous spy of tsarist times, a worthy hero for Oppenheim. All the newspapermen are behind Knickerbocker, as the question of newspaper ethics is involved. I am interested because the Sisson documents may be mentioned. Don't worry, I am not going to be a witness.

On Wednesday, Howard Goodman and I dined. After two and a half months in Russia, he had taken three baths and was ready for a good meal. As he had not had any vodka or good Russian cooking in Russia, I took him to Förster, where the famous cook of former Petersburg fame is the chef, and the best gipsy violinist of old Russia is in charge of the music. As Howard's company was paying the bill, we had the best the house could give. Howard likes vodka. So, after the first glass, in good Russian style, we said, "One must stand on two feet." Then, "God loves the Trinity." This was followed by "But a table has four corners." Then you need no more excuses. Howard gave me the whole story of his Russian experience. Like all the reports I get, it was so mixed with light and dark that one hates to say what is going to come of it all.

The reports reaching Berlin from Moscow of the difficulties, even for foreigners, of obtaining board and lodging under the conditions of militant socialism were a little disconcerting. Jim Mills, of the Associated Press, turned up soon after Lichtenstein arrived; and his account delayed our departure for the U.S.S.R. by several days, which we spent buying food in concentrated form and making arrangements to have food packages sent in to us through the German embassy. This time our preparations did indeed resemble those that are made for a trip into the jungle. When Lichtenstein and I finally set off, at least half of our luggage consisted of canned goods, chocolates, cheese, sausages, and bread. Recognizing the shortages that had developed, the customs authorities at the Soviet frontier made no difficulty over our food supply when they examined our luggage.

Although I had warned Lichtenstein that it would be a hard trip, he looked discouraged as we drove from the station in Moscow to the Grand Hotel, and more so when we were told at the hotel that there were no rooms and that we would have to wait until midnight to have our reservations filled. But we spent the day pleasantly, according to my usual custom on returning to a city where I had lived before, walking around from place to place, visiting my former haunts, in order to recover the atmosphere. During our walk we also looked up friends, who promised to take us in if the hotel failed us; however, our quarters were ready at midnight, as promised. We were both assigned to one enormous room filled with elaborate but not very artistic paintings and vases, some of the latter standing six feet high. It had been one of the old private dining-rooms. Here we lived for some three weeks without any serious quarrel; and to make up for the lack of privacy, we set periods each day when first one and then the other of us could have uninterrupted use of our room.

Lichtenstein had even better standing with the German embassy in Moscow than I had; and when my friend, Professor Hoetzsch of the University of Berlin, turned up, he brought us still closer. We used its chancellery for handling money matters and getting railway tickets, for example; and the ambassador invited us to receptions, of which he gave many. At one of these receptions I met Litvinov for the first time and was asked by him to call formally at the Commissariat. He was to become in the next weeks the People's Commissar, succeeding Chicherin. On this same evening a group of us got Karl Radek, also a guest, in a corner and, after plying him with German beer, started him talking about his attempt in 1923 to engineer a Communist coup d'état in Berlin, to the consternation of Soviet foreign-office officials, who kept trying to persuade him to go home.

At this reception I noted the distinctly military bearing of several of the German commercial attachés. Later I was to run into Red Army men in Moscow, looking very German and talking German, buying Berlin papers at the International Bookstore, to which I went to buy my English papers. Furthermore, during a walking trip outside Moscow, I came upon one of the aviation training camps before I realized what it was, and scurried away, but not before I had observed more of these Germans in Soviet uniforms. At the time it was generally believed among newspapermen that there was a definite tie-up between the German *Reichswehr* and the Red Army.

Besides the various commercial attachés at the German embassy, there were also an agricultural attaché and several attachés for so-called "cultural" relations. All of these men had had thorough training in Russian history and language. Every summer the embassy brought on one of the teachers of Russian at the University of Berlin to help them improve their knowledge of the language. Several of these men were of Russian-German families—sons of German merchants or manufacturers in Moscow or the old St. Petersburg, who had married Russian women. This large corps of specially trained men at the German embassy presented a marked contrast to the modest staff at the British or French embassy. It all made me ponder, but it was a great advantage to me to be able to talk to so many experts in my field.

The economic and political conditions which Lichtenstein and I found prevailing in Moscow immediately suggested those of a country at war.

The shortage of food, housing, and consumers' goods, the frequency of arrests, the strictness of censorship, the state of high tension and nervous strain which we encountered everywhere, reminded us of wartime as forcefully as did the red bunting and patriotic slogans which were lavishly displayed. The economic dislocations were largely due to the cost of the expansion program, which mobilized most of the national income for new capital construction. This expansion program required short rations at home to allow export abroad, in order to purchase the equipment necessary to carry out the Five-Year Plan. The people were called on to accept these present sacrifices for the benefits of the future. In five, or even four years, the U.S.S.R. was to be transformed from a backward agricultural country to a great industrial nation. Any man who doubted the possibility of this achievement was a "damage-worker" and was dealt with as a traitor is dealt with in wartime. Thus the class struggle was intensified by the new economic goals, as Lichtenstein and I were not long in discovering.

I took Lichtenstein to see many of my old friends in Moscow, generally arranging the interviews in a formal manner through the Cultural Relations Society. As I had anticipated, Lichtenstein served his purpose well. Because of his economic training and his interest in problems of public finance, he was able to put significant questions to Soviet economists of the research type as well as to those with administrative duties. One man whom we saw very frequently was Kondratiev, an outstanding economist; specializing in matters agricultural, he was at the head of the Soviet Institute of Statistics. He had visited America and apparently was in good standing with the Party, despite the fact that, as he was of peasant origin, he had been a member of the Socialist Revolutionary party. But in our very first talk he told us frankly that he anticipated arrest. He had stood out against the policy of forcible collectivization of agriculture which had been put through the previous winter with some disastrous consequences. Kondratiev assured us that our calls could not make his position any worse, and might even stave off the disaster he was expecting. He had been offered the choice of discontinuing all studies or of arrest. He had agreed not to write; but, as he said frankly, he would rather sit in prison than go to a small provincial town without his books or access to books. Our discussions centered around the country's situation in the midst of the first Soviet Five-Year Plan.

One evening, by appointment, we turned up for another session of discussion with him, and our ring was answered by G.P.U. officials and a rather hysterical wife. Kondratiev had finally been arrested. After showing our passports, which we always carried with us, we were allowed to leave. Lichtenstein was quite naturally upset. He remarked that he had never entirely believed me when I had described the methods of suppression and terror of the Revolution. I immediately went to

170

the Cultural Relations Society, under whose auspices the meetings with Kondratiev had been arranged, while Lichtenstein rushed to the German embassy to report on the incident. For there was the possibility that our involvement in the Kondratiev case would lead to an invitation to leave the country without delay.

Another friend with whom I had many discussions was the student who had been my first tutor in 1904. Full professor at the University of Moscow by 1917, he had found it expedient in the first years of the Revolution to accept a transfer, first to the University of Kazan and then to that of Tashkent. In 1930, he was the legal adviser of the Soviet publishing trust and was writing extensively on Soviet law, although his field had been Roman and administrative law. He would not come to my hotel room, but urged me to come freely to his apartment. Because he spoke only Russian fluently, and also for reasons of safety, I did not take Lichtenstein along. Charges of sabotage were being made against many of these experts from the old regime. One never knew to what extent we foreigners were followed. When making these calls, therefore, usually of an evening after dark, I wore a cap and an old suit of clothes. In this proletarian outfit I could be less easily spotted as a foreigner, and my friends were not anxious that other people living in the apartment house should see a foreign visitor.

I had agreed to take Lichtenstein on a trip to smaller towns and to peasant districts. Afterward Lichtenstein admitted that he had not taken me literally enough when I warned that it would be a hard journey. And I did not realize how hard it was going to be. We lived and traveled in what was left of the capitalistic sector of the New Economic Policy, and there was precious little left of it in this third year of the socialist offensive. We paid our way in rubles, whose purchasing value at the official rate of exchange was about on a par with the currencies of western Europe. Our trip was not planned, even by ourselves, except in a very general way. But we were armed with letters of introduction from the Commissariats of Agriculture and Industry and from the Cultural Relations Society, and we carried a large quantity of food in a duffle bag and a knapsack, taking turns wearing the latter. When we got back to Moscow after four weeks' absence, Lichtenstein, who went directly to the German embassy, was refused admission because he had lost so much weight and looked so dirty that the porter did not recognize him. As for me, I had scraped my knuckles working my way into a crowded train, and the story went around that I had been in a real fight.

In our travels we covered Ivanovo-Vosnesensk, Nizhny-Novgorod, Kazan, Samara, Stalingrad, Rostov, Kharkov, and back to Moscow. Part of the time we traveled "hard," that is, in compartments for six. We had our pockets picked while trying to board a train. Some of the rooms in which we stayed were dirty beyond description. Certain laps of our journey entailed twenty-four hours in slow-moving local trains.

Several nights we had to wait at stations for delayed trains. In three places the temperature was well over a hundred; and, as I recall, we found usable bathrooms only three times. There was one somewhat easier stage, when we floated down the Volga for three days, from Nizhny-Novgorod to Stalingrad. To a considerable extent we lived on the food which we took along, although we found we could buy bread, butter, and eggs along the route. We tried the meals on the boat and in hotels, but we always suffered from them even when we were able to stomach them.

The difficult traveling, and particularly the long train trips, were not without their usefulness. We talked at length with fellow-passengers, and many of these conversations were more significant than those formally arranged.

We visited several of the large new industrial plants, including a textile plant at Ivanovo—our first stop—and a tractor plant at Stalingrad, where we hoped to meet the American engineers and technicians who were aiding in its construction. The factory authorities evidently suspected that this was our aim, for they put every difficulty in our way, refusing to send a car to the city to take us out to the plant—a distance of more than five miles. We made the trip with a peasant driver, to whom we had to pay rubles which cost us some fifteen dollars. This driver was one of the last kulaks, or NEPmen; and he squeezed us because he was being squeezed out of existence.

We were much discouraged by the state of the new construction which we visited. The American engineers and technicians filled us full of stories of miscalculations, excessive costs, and constant delays in this enormous program of building. They were not afraid to talk, and our supply of American cigarettes won their immediate appreciation. That new construction was going on everywhere was so evident that we decided the slogan of this third year of the Five-Year Plan should be: "Build until it hurts."

From Rostov we went out to the largest of the state "grain factories," as they were called; it was, in fact, "giant number one," an enterprise covering 250,000 acres. Our welcome at 3:00 A.M. was far from cordial; and after the manager had given us our quarters in a room with five others, the guard told us what a poor manager he was. An American technician, servicing the caterpillar tractors being used there, whom we recognized and accosted, told us more of the inadequate management. We had asked him for another talk; but he came around later and said he had been ordered not to talk to us, although we got in a few more words in the confusion of a fire which broke out in one of the buildings of the administrative center. By good luck, at least for us, an American expert on large-scale farming had just arrived at this farm. He seemed very glad to see us, although it was a little embarrassing, because Lichtenstein knew of the complete financial failure of his grandiose schemes for large-scale farming in America. We sat in on several of his conferences with the management, and I found it difficult not to interrupt when the official translator kept making mistakes. This translator later admitted to me that he had taken the job in the hope that practice in the language would help him learn it.

We inspected a few of the institutions of the enterprise and saw the careless character of the work and the abusive handling of the machinery. The manager himself drove his Ford so thoughtlessly and hard that it was difficult to ride with him without protest. Lichtenstein and I found a phrase to summarize our impressions of "giant number one": "Children playing with big and expensive toys."

One of the most interesting places which we visited was a completely collectivized commune, which had been formed by a group of American Finns who had migrated to the "Soviet paradise" because of their political leanings. They had brought their machinery with them and had set up a commune in the full sense of the word. Here we found all the families eating in a common dining-room and sending their children to the central children's home. No house was more than five minutes' walk from the children's home, and the parents saw the children several times a day and even brought them to their own quarters for short periods. This was the most progressive and the most efficiently operated agricultural enterprise that I have ever seen. I heard later that it declined both in prosperity and in organization when it was absorbed into the bureaucratic machinery eventually set up to run collectivized agriculture. Many of these Finns had married local Russian girls, for a large percentage of the original group had been young bachelors. A considerable Russian element had thus been brought in.

On this trip I acquired a fuller picture of the procedure of liquidation of the so-called "rich peasant," which was still going on but which had been almost completed during the previous winter. We passed one train transporting these recalcitrants to the lumber camps of the north. Porters on trains with whom I started conversations as we stood along in the corridor described these "shipments" as they had seen them some months earlier. The peasant who drove us to the Finnish commune had taken an active part in handling the rich peasants in his district, and he had no compunction over the methods which he described, for he had been fully convinced of the complete wickedness of this social group from the point of view of the mass of the peasantry; also, he admitted frankly that he had profited personally from the confiscation of the property of his richer neighbors.

As we were waiting for the train at one station, a man in peasant garb sat down beside me and quietly and somewhat nervously started to talk; he had heard me speaking Russian with the stationmaster and our porter. He said he was a kulak, but from his speech and his face I guessed that he had really been a landlord and had escaped liquidation earlier by be-

173

coming a kulak. But now, he explained, he had been completely eliminated, economically and socially, from the new order; and his main complaint was over the lot of his twelve-year-old son, who sat silently beside him. This boy, under the regulations then in force, could not be admitted to the higher classes of the elementary school because of his "kulak" origin.

This incident, like that of the arrest of our economist friend in Moscow, made a very deep impression on Lichtenstein. Perhaps it was because I had to maintain the professional attitude if I was going to continue to study the Soviet system that I found myself less moved by such occurrences. Studying the Bolshevik statements of what they felt they had to do, and taking these statements literally, I had evidently come to the conclusion that I would run into such instances at every turn, and on that basis had, to a certain extent, steeled myself against them. In talking with the old friends whom I have already mentioned, I always emphasized that my questions on details of the Revolution were dictated by my professional interest, not by morbid curiosity; and these friends in almost every instance understood the situation and never showed any resentment.

In my lectures on "The Soviet Five-Year Plan" after my return, I always emphasized the liquidation of the last capitalistic group—the rich peasants who represented about one million households, or about five million "souls." My audiences reacted to this particular topic in different ways. The conservatives saw in this Soviet policy only destruction, while the liberals were inclined to want one to pass over this disagreeable aspect of the subject. It was interesting to note how the active Soviet sympathizers were particularly concerned when I brought up the subject of the place of liquidation procedure in the Soviet economic planning. When some of these suggested to me that I soften down somewhat my statements respecting the "sharpening of the class struggle" in my lectures, I disconcerted them by asking if they thought the Moscow leaders would like to have me do this when addressing workmen audiences or only when addressing more conservative groups.

Lichtenstein and I returned pretty well battered from our four weeks of travel but, in a sense, heroes. At the Grand Hotel, where we tried to secure rooms, we learned with considerable dismay that the capitalistic sector had been liquidated during our absence, with respect to rooming facilities; and one could now rent a room only on an order from some Soviet institution. Here we encountered Maurice Hindus, about to set off on a trip to the countryside with a small "open-road" group. In his party was my colleague Ernest Burgess and his sister, and Julian Bryan. We gave such a terrifying picture of the food difficulties that poor Hindus spent the afternoon collecting supplies for his party. Later he upbraided me, for in the villages he visited he found plenty of food of the best quality. In these particular villages, I might add, we had found no shortage either.

The Grand Hotel, we found, had been taken over by the Soviet travel agency, Intourist. A large group of American tourists from a North Cape tour had been brought to Moscow for a two-day visit. The dining-room was reserved for them; and I was refused admission, although the head waiter knew me. Hungry, as well as tired and dirty, I stood out-side waiting until the tourists had finished their dinner. When I saw one of these Americans come out with a satisfied look after the good meal served to these special guests, I lost my temper. I went up to him and, calling myself a "proletarian," which I certainly looked in my wrinkled traveling clothes, suggested that on his return to America he should not report that everybody got as good dinners as those served to him. The poor man on whom my wrath had fallen looked quite distressed and a little frightened, and with mumbling excuses got free of me as soon as possible.

That night Jim Mills, of the Associated Press, let me use a couch in his dining-room. The next day, very fortunately for me, he went off to Petrograd, and I got his bedroom as well as his cook. Then I went to the Cultural Relations Society and told them that, if they did not secure a room for me by the end of the week, I would have to pack up and go home. Meanwhile, Lichtenstein was sleeping on a couch in the small apartment of one of the younger secretaries in the German embassy.

About this time I was invited to one of the periodic receptions given by the press section of the Commissariat of Foreign Affairs. It was on this occasion that Litvinov announced his appointment as full commis-sar, which, I might add, brought much relief to the foreign diplomats, who had feared that Chicherin's successor would be Kirov of Leningrad, already then considered the second man after Stalin and one of the rougher of the "Stalin boys." I put my problem of quarters to Litvinov. I remarked that it was useful for my understanding to be having this ex-perience in the Soviet system as a "bourgeois element"—a status which by this date had come to be called officially "the deprived ones," be-cause they had been deprived of practically all rights. Litvinov took up my cause, and I was assigned to one of the Soviet dormitories used by the clerical staff of the Kremlin. In fact, I had the room of the secretary of one of the commissars.

My room was one of four on the same corridor, whose occupants shared a common bath, although there was running water and a gas stove in the corner of each room. I was told that I would be adopted into full membership in the group, which meant that I had to clean up the corridors and the bathroom every fourth day. I got Mills's cook to sub-stitute for me, I might add. In the adjoining room, which was about 12 by 20 feet, there were three secretaries. When I asked them if they were not a little crowded, they answered that there was a free fourth side to the table around which the three couches were placed.

My room had the usual supply of animals, but I had long since become immune to these as the result of a severe poisoning in my early travels. For three weeks I lived like a Soviet citizen, although I must admit that I accepted invitations to meals from friends, had Mills's cook shop for me, and enjoyed gifts of food from the embassy. One advantage of living this way, rather than in one of the hotels, was that my Russian friends could now come around to see me very freely. These were the hardest but probably the most interesting weeks that I had in Moscow on this or other trips. For I always realized that the actual conditions of living could not be seen from hotel windows or fully comprehended in short visits, for an evening or afternoon, with Russian friends in their crowded apartments.

Lichtenstein and I did not hesitate to describe the conditions which we had found in some of the enterprises we had visited, particularly in the tractor plant at Stalingrad and at the "giant" state farm. We talked to everyone, including Soviet officials. Later, when I read in the Soviet newspapers that a special investigating commission had been sent to Stalingrad, I felt that we had had some little part in exposing the situation which prevailed there, which was fully described in the published report of the commission as a lesson to other enterprises. We had been particularly outspoken in what we said about the manager of the state farm, who had become so displeased with us that he would not supply us with transportation to the railway station. We had been forced, in consequence, to walk the two miles, carrying our luggage, in a driving rain. I must admit that I was rather pleased to read later in the Soviet press that he also had been "exposed" and severely penalized.

Lichtenstein left Russia before I did. He decided to fly to Berlin in order to get back to the comforts of the Hotel Esplanade as quickly as possible. When I came on, several weeks later, we went around together to see several German friends, reporting, from our different angles of approach, our experiences. Lichtenstein would tell of the hard use which the new industrial machinery was getting, and I would then call attention to the fact that this new machinery was being used not only to produce goods but also to produce a new type of citizen—the Bolshevik. Lichtenstein would tell of the squalor and backwardness of some of the provincial towns which we had visited, and I would qualify his statements by describing the Park of Culture and Recreation where we had spent the evening. This Soviet institution, which we found in practically every city and smaller town, was often rather crude in its equipment and entertainment; but in the old Russia there had been nothing like this.

Both of us emphasized the enormous amount of new construction which we had seen, which in the next years was to change the whole face of the country. The question of costs was one which we had tried to discuss in detail with Soviet officials and Communists, but we had soon found that it was a social experiment and not a business enterprise that was being conducted. As to what would eventually come out of this grandiose program of high-speed industrialization in a woefully backward country, neither of us, of course, ventured to say. We had been impressed by the enthusiasm of some of the leaders with whom we talked, but also sobered by the more realistic approach which we noted in other Soviet officials. We had to weigh the overoptimistic statements of the Louis Fischers and the Anna Louise Strongs against the very pessimistic accounts of some of the American correspondents. Our most valuble sources of information had been the engineers and technicians— German as well as American. Most of these had signed contracts with the Soviet economic organizations not entirely because of the profitable nature of the contracts; in many instances they had been attracted by the ideas, economic and political, of the new order.

Outside interest in the Soviet industrialization program was enhanced by developments in the Far East—Japan's incursion into Manchuria. There was difference of opinion among the so-called "experts" as to whether the Five-Year Plan had, as its first aim, military preparedness or the raising of the standards of living. Although Stalin had, as early as 1929, warned of the dangers of another intervention, the Soviet citizenry expected fruits by the end of the Plan—that is, in 1932—from the effort to which they were being driven. The American authorities, as I learned from talks in Washington, were looking particularly to the military-preparedness aspect of the industrialization and its relation to the Far East. On this basis the question of the recognition of the Soviet government came up in a more definite form. The point on which there was variance of views was whether American recognition would deter the Japanese from further aggression, beyond Manchuria, or incite them to even more aggressive action. Secretary Stimson's policy to take a firmer stand would have seemed to lead to the recognition of the Soviet government. As one looks back, one can raise the question as to whether John Simon's action in opposing the Stimson policy with respect to Japan was the cause for the further postponement in the resumption of normal relations between Washington and Moscow. For we know that Simon's argument in 1931, opposing any stand against Japanese expansion in Manchuria, was that Japan had to have more room somewhere and that its action in Manchuria might bring it into conflict with the Soviet Union. This was the beginning of the policy of that group of British statesmen who not only hoped that Japan would go against the Soviet Union—and later that Germany would go against the Soviet Union—but tried to further their hopes by diplomatic and other manipulations.

Despite the many examples of waste, inefficiency, and human misery which we had encountered, I was inclined to feel that the first Five-Year

Plan would be by no means a failure. Perhaps the positive factor which impressed me most strongly in 1930 was the great enthusiasm of the Young Communists, who were the products of that civic training which I had studied with such interest in 1926. Here, in the younger generation now coming into productive life, one found the results of the twelve years of Communist training through the Soviet schools, the Komsomol, and the whole propaganda side of the Revolution. Not, of course, that the period of propaganda was over. There was more propaganda now than there had been four years earlier, but now it was more closely tied up with workaday and immediate tasks. Each group had its assignment of work "to complete the Five-Year Plan in four years" and "to catch up with and outstrip America." The speakers now were the economic leaders instead of orators of the type of Trotsky and Zinoviev. Because it was more concrete and practical, the new propaganda impressed me as more effective, and the young people seemed to react to it with interest and vigor.

The whole people fairly worshiped the new machinery and were having a glorious time with it. It was the lack of sufficient skill in its use which made them handle it roughly. Interested particularly in the cultural side of the Five-Year Plan, I noted how the new plants and new machinery served as instruments for retraining the people. The utilization of machinery for educative, as well as productive, purposes struck me as a significant political fact which many had failed to take into account.

The cleansing of the Soviet apparatus of "harmful" and "hostile" elements, as the sharpening of the class struggle was called, had also delighted the young people, even though it brought confusion and inefficiency into the important field of management. Among the new young leaders I met able and conscientious workers, but I also found wholly incompetent ones. In fact, I found more "class struggle" than my study of the newspapers had prepared me for. The kulaks had been liquidated as a class, and the position of the technical experts and the intelligentsia had become very hard indeed. The constant search for "damage-workers" was one of the worst aspects of the period, particularly as there seemed to be no clear definition of just what constituted "damage-working." In many cases it served as a convenient alibi, and several friends remarked to me that perhaps, when the Russian *spetsy* were exhausted, it would then be the turn of the foreign *spetsy*. Some of the foreign *spetsy* seemed to have got into the state of mind of their Communist bosses and were beginning to suggest "dirty work at the crossroads" when their own work did not go smoothly.

The class-struggle side of the Five-Year Plan was constantly emphasized, for this plan was not simply one of economic expansion. It was primarily a political plan, a program of class struggle. The *spetsy*-baiting on the basis of the class struggle was depriving the country of the knowledge and experience of many of its well-trained economic

178

workers, technical experts, and managers, even though it was recognized that the biggest task of the Five-Year Plan was precisely to find adequate and proper experts in management. If one did not accept the principle of class struggle as a constructive force, the subordination of all policy to this principle would seem most shortsighted.

Stalin was the undisputed leader of Soviet Russia; and the single leader was evidently necessary to enforce the principle, first of a single party in the Soviet system, and then of absolute unity within that party. However, there was no question that personal rivalries existed within the ranks of the Party. The Party-cleansing in many instances had amounted to little more than a climbing-up over the back of somebody else. The remarkable comradely attitude that had prevailed under Lenin's leadership was no longer present, and it had been one of the sources of Party power. Stalin seemed hard and ruthless, but he also struck me as an able and resourceful revolutionary strategist and machine boss. The evaluation of his abilities given by Trotsky seemed to me wholly incorrect.

That the situation was very tight, politically and economically, was clear. The tempo of the Five-Year Plan was responsible for the food and goods shortage and also for the rigidity of political control. This tempo could not be reduced, it was claimed, because of the danger of foreign intervention and also because the whole plan was a unit and must be put through as such. Another reason often advanced by the Communists for the speed of the industrialization program was that psychologically there must be this driving, in order to stir up an apathetic people and break down their traditional habits of mind and ways of doing things. When, in talking with Communists, I used the expression "terrible tempo," I was always corrected; I should have said "wonderful tempo" or, even better, "Bolshevik tempo."

This term "Bolshevik," after the first few years of the Revolution, had been pushed aside in favor of "Communist" and "Soviet." But on the resumption of the socialist offensive in 1928, with its militant policies and methods suggestive of the earlier period, the word "Bolshevik" again became current as the symbol of all-out action. The Communist referred to himself as a Bolshevik. The masses were urged to work "Bolshevik fashion," to meet obstacles "as Bolsheviks would meet them." The sowing of wheat on the collectivist farms was called "Bolshevik sowing." Frequently an institution or a policy was described as aiming to "make a Bolshevik." *Making Bolsheviks* was therefore the title I chose for the book which I wrote in the winter of 1930 after my return from Russia, to describe the various highly developed products of the Soviet civic training I had studied in 1926. In this book I analyzed the six cadres, or groups, which bore the chief responsibility for carrying out the Five-Year Plan: the Communist Party workers, the Young Communists, the shock-brigade workmen, the collectivist-peasants, the Soviet cultural-workers, and the Redarmyists.

CHAPTER XXI

1932: THE BOLSHEVIKS TIGHTEN THEIR BELTS

IN JUNE, 1932, I TOOK ADVANTAGE OF THE DEPRESSION PRICE-CUTS TO book passage on the "Bremen," first class. The minimum was $203 for a small single cabin. To quiet my conscience, I reflected that it would be enlightening to talk with the people who would make up the passenger list of a luxury liner on a June sailing date. And my decision was, in fact, fully justified by several long talks such as one can have on a leisurely ocean voyage.

Some young married people from the Chicago Gold Coast took me on for the more frivolous evenings of dancing and drinking. They needed an extra man for a "countess," returning to her husband in Italy. The depression did not seem to bother these heirs to the fortunes of Chicago pioneers, who were off to the Riviera, after some golf in Scotland, to be followed by big-game hunting in Africa. Of course, they didn't like socialism and were sure it would not work; but they kept questioning the "professor," and I gave them quite a number of informal lectures, which were probably only half-understood.

Maurice Hindus was on board, doing the same thing that I was, getting a taste of the "higher life" at a relatively low cost. He and a buyer for Macy's and I observed and commented upon our fellow-passengers from our more common ground. Hindus also took me with him to visit some friends in the fourth class, up in the very prow of the giant ship. These were Soviet sympathizers on special tour, and we put the brakes on their enthusiastic anticipations.

Of the "Bremen" passengers, it was the bankers whom I sought out particularly. One banker to whom I was introduced vaguely recalled having met me before; and I told him that I had been quoting him for several years without giving his name because I had, indeed, forgotten it. He retorted that, if I had been quoting him correctly, he would buy me a dinner at the Ritz Café on the upper deck. The comment of his that I had frequently used to illustrate our loan policy to Germany in 1926, I had heard at a dinner given in Berlin. He had turned to me with the remark: "Well, Professor, you are supposed to know this Europe. Do you know of any other countries that want to borrow money?" That evening we had the Ritz party, and he began an explanation of the wild gambling of the twenties. "We behaved like drunken sailors," he said, "and now what headaches we are having!"

Charles E. Merriam met me in Berlin, where he was writing his book on *Sources of Political Power*. He was on the platform when the boat train pulled in at Friedrichsstrasse, and he told me that he had engaged a room for me adjoining his own at the Bristol. After leaving my luggage

180

at the hotel, he rushed me to an evening conference, with Frederick Kuh, the foreign correspondent, and Harold Lasswell, our colleague from the University of Chicago. That conference, like the political posters and speeches of the election campaign which was going on, revealed the utter hodgepodge into which German politics had drifted. Communists were defending the parliamentary system, socialists were conservatives, and the Nazis were the direct-actionists. None of us appreciated the strength of the Nazi movement, although after a few days in Berlin I became aware of some of its potentialities. I was much impressed by many talks with young Germans, who admitted that the Nazi program lacked logic but excused their acceptance of it because "it promised to solace the hurt German soul."

Merriam and I attended several election meetings. One, where Bruening spoke, struck us as distressingly academic in the current atmosphere of political tension. The Hitler meeting, on the other hand, was really alarming. Ivy Lee sat just behind us; and he and Merriam, both of whom had attended Moscow Red Square celebrations, suggested to me that the Communists had been outstripped as technicians of propaganda by the Nazis. The enormous stadium crowd was gradually prepared for the speakers by marching athletes, torchbearing youths, and the simple, repetitious, martial music of bugles and drums. In front of us, attended by nurses, were several groups of bandaged young men, who, we were told, were the victims of attacks by the Reds. At last Hitler drove in, with Goebbels. At that moment Goebbels was Berlin's favorite. Hitler gauged his words to allow the echo to pass, so that his speech was a series of explosive sounds. As we left, Merriam characterized the meeting as a combination of Ku Klux Klan, Negro revival meeting, and Billy Sunday harangue.

It was of this period that many have said that the Communists and Nazis co-operated, in effect, against the middle-of-the-road socialists and liberals. By staging their constant street fights they were both—perhaps as a deliberate policy—discrediting and disorganizing the regime in power. On several occasions the Communists voted with the Nazis, thus giving a majority to the opposition. Moscow-Comintern policy, at this time, was directed toward discrediting the social democratic leadership in workman masses, and Moscow had forced in the German Communist Party a leadership which was intellectually mediocre and often politically inept. Critics of Moscow will say that this was the inevitable result of the kind of leadership that had come into power at the center of Bolshevism, where Stalin had triumphed not only over Trotsky, Zinoviev, and Kamenev but also over the Soviet trade-union leaders.

The trend of German politics at this moment was well illustrated by the way in which the Prussian government was overthrown when it was merged into the Reich. We witnessed the performance from our hotel window, opposite the Prussian Ministry of Interior, where a few dozen men effected the coup d'état. It had been agreed in advance that there would be no resistance if force were used. A hand was laid on the shoulder of the minister, and he "yielded to superior force." Merriam seemed very depressed a few hours later, when we started off to a supper party; and when I inquired if he were feeling ill, he answered: "Yes, for we have just seen the democratic system murdered in one of the larger states of Europe."

Our supper was a gathering of German professors for a visiting American colleague. It was a hot July night; and after the beer and sandwiches we went from the close, smoke-filled dining-room into the cooler front parlors. One of the guests turned to Merriam and remarked on the breath of fresh air that drifted into the room, adding, "Like the political fresh air that came this afternoon." I was afraid that Merriam, who had done his graduate work in political science in Berlin, was going to faint; but he merely uttered an inarticulate sound which the German could interpret as he wished.

An amusing letter from my friend Sonya, the wife of William H. Chamberlin, who had long lived in Moscow, where he represented the *Christian Science Monitor*, brought me up to date on the commodity situation to be expected in Moscow: Food was no problem, she said; but such items as soap, toilet paper, quinine tablets, and tooth brushes were impossible to come by. And would I please bring some dark lisle socks, size 11, for William Henry!

Making my final preparations to proceed to Moscow, I found that it would be possible to go on the same train with Dr. Otto Hoetzsch, professor of Russian history at the University of Berlin, an old pre-war friend of whom I had seen much in Moscow as well as in Berlin in 1930. Hoetzsch was one of the most intelligent leaders of the German Nationalist party and one of its more active spokesmen in the Reichstag. Because of his professional interest, he was for closer Soviet-German relations. He had founded the monthly publication *Ost Europa*, which gave the bulk of its space to the Soviet Union. Consequently, he was, at the present time, *persona gratissima* with the Soviet leaders; he was co-editor of the valuable series of diplomatic documents being released by the Soviet authorities from the old files and archives. The Soviet ambassador in Berlin gave me a *laissez passer* for the Soviet frontier because Hoetzsch enjoyed this privilege.

On this visit to Moscow I was again impressed by the dominance of Germans, and not only among foreign officials, but now among foreign visitors as well. Through Hoetzsch I saw the German embassy more intimately than I ever had before. The German visitors I met at their embassy, where there were frequent gatherings, always with Russians; and all spoke Russian. French, British, or Americans seldom came to these gatherings, because they seldom knew Russian. Indeed, the Americans, who had no embassy to integrate them, could usually be found only at the American Bar in the Hotel National.

I was invited to a German embassy reception within a few days after my arrival in Moscow. This was a gathering of diplomats, and not of Germans and Russians. The major domo informed me that I was to come to the ambassador's table for supper; and I found that it was set for four, the other two being the Italian and Japanese ambassadors. The latter, Hirota, was particularly friendly and also very fond of my Chesterfields, of which I still had a supply. I kept feeding Hirota so many cigarettes that one of the younger men of the German embassy staff, assigned to stand near us in case an errand had to be run, asked me if they were poisoned. The conversation centered on the trials and tribulations of the capitalistic system, and I found myself associated with the German in insisting on the considerable strength still manifesting itself in private enterprise in our respective economic structures.

During this 1932 visit I saw Hirota often. One evening I ran into him in the lobby of the Hotel Savoy, and we exchanged our usual cordial greetings. After he had left, the hotel manager, a simple but interesting proletarian, came from behind his desk, where he had evidently been watching the chatting between Hirota and me, and said quite earnestly: "Professor, they are a wily people, we must be very careful." This had been the attitude of the Russian man in the street when I first had occasion to mingle with him—the day after the Japanese attack on Port Arthur in 1904.

It was in 1932 that Moscow and Tokyo came to a tentative agreement on the Chinese Eastern Railway situation and also on the eternal question of fishery rights for the Japanese in Soviet waters. It was clear that the Soviet government could insist on its rights in the Chinese Eastern only if it wished to use these rights as a *casus belli*. Secretary Stimson's notes had remained purely academic, as had the resolutions of the League of Nations. Therefore, it seemed to some of us that it was perfectly logical for the Soviets to effect some sort of an accommodation with Japan. With America and Britain apparently hostile to Japan, the Soviet Union must have decided that it should make as good a settlement with its eastern neighbor as possible. I have always thought that this was the beginning of the interplay of America and Great Britain, on one side, and the Soviet Union, on the other, with respect to Japan, which has continued to this date of writing.

In many ways this 1932 visit to Russia was unsatisfactory. Living conditions for the foreigner were easier than in 1930, but for the Russians life was particularly strained. Even the secretaries of the various leading men I wanted to interview, usually very efficient, were edgy, seemed worn out, and were often almost impolite. Everyone was busy. I got tired of spending whole mornings calling at offices, only to be told to come around a few days later. The Cultural Relations Society did not handle my schedules of interviews well. I attributed all this to the fact that everyone was exhausted and impatient under the long-continued pressure. I also began to suspect that my close relationship with the German embassy on this trip may have had a bearing on the matter. There was some compensation in this situation, however. Unable to get through to official Bolsheviks, I had time to see friends, wander into institutions, walk the streets, do the theaters, and, in general, get the feel of life in the proletarian capital.

The four-year drive of the Five-Year Plan had proved an even greater drain on the resources of the country and the nerves of the people than might have been anticipated. The people looked tired. The falling-off of the productivity of labor was the best evidence that the country was revolution-weary. Some of my friends, whom I could study closely, were not getting enough of the right kind of food to work effectively either at the desk or at the lathe. Three hours' standing in line to secure food or wearing apparel was harder on the nerves than six hours of work.

The cost of four years of capital construction, industrialization, and collectivization of agriculture at the Bolshevik tempo was clearly visible. Standards of living had gone down, despite official figures on increased wages, increased earnings of collectivized peasants, and increased production. But even non-Communists were inclined to accept the cost as justified, in view of what had been accomplished to make the country more economically independent of the Western world and also more prepared for national defense. The question of preparedness for defense was strikingly prominent. The military defense feature of the Five-Year Plan had always been present and visible; but that first place was given to military and political considerations, as opposed to economic, had not been previously so clear, at least to me. Perhaps it was because of this emphasis on political and military considerations that the question of dollar and cents cost did not enter, or at least did not have primary importance. This fact led me to the conclusion that, to date, there had not been any really scientific economic planning.

In the case of collectivization of agriculture, there had been established in May, and continued through July, something in the nature of a "peasant NEP"; and some of us were looking for a general extension of this method of letting up on the pressure. The decision of the Party given out the first days of October, however, showed the contrast between "bourgeois" and "Bolshevik" logic. To the outside observer, the obvious exhaustion suggested concessions and a breathing spell; but to the Bolshevik, they dictated a more daring and more positive assertion of the principles of the Revolution. The pressure was kept on. Instead of being opportunistic, a drive against all deviations from the program was inaugurated to discipline any fainthearted leaders. More discipline and severer conditions were required throughout education and training;

184

and in the schools and institutions there developed a better spirit of work among the teachers and the serious students and consternation among the slackers.

I visited three important examples of the new industrial giants—Dneprostroy, the Kharkov Tractor Works, and the Amo Motor Truck factory. I had, in each instance, the advantage of the company of a foreign engineering expert in the particular line—in two instances not associated with the particular enterprise in Soviet Russia or with business in Soviet Russia. It was difficult to gain entry, as visitors interfered with production; also, defense equipment was being produced in at least one of the three. My impression from these visits was that there had been some progress in management and in organization and discipline of labor. The inadequate supervision of the superfluous number of workmen was the most striking feature. On one occasion I saw a sturdy girl, bearing the red kerchief of the shock-brigade, drive a quarter-inch bolt into place with a huge wrench and then fumble to fit the nut on the smashed threads; and there was no one to tell her to stop her too enthusiastic whacking. The fluidity of labor and the jerky supply of raw materials had led to overstaffing of the plants. The aim to train skilled workmen added to this difficulty. The large staffs gave rise to "gossip" that there was a plan to re-establish an unemployed group in order to reduce costs and to promote labor discipline.

These new giants of industry were perhaps at this point very inefficiently run, their failure to produce according to plan being blazoned daily in the press; but, nevertheless, they were a source of pride and of hope that in time—and soon—they would bring about easier conditions of life. They created what may perhaps be termed an "economic patriotism." I sometimes felt that what had been going on under Sovietism was simply the Industrial Revolution coming to this backward country under the discipline of Communism.

The question constantly arose in my mind: "How have they kept the people going so long at such a pace and with such enthusiasm?" One would think that the bag of tricks in the technique of propaganda would have been exhausted after fifteen years of revolution. But, as I studied the matter, I was impressed by the effectiveness of the many means used to stimulate individual effort. An integral part of the program was competition between individual factories to meet the quota of the Five-Year Plan. In some plants the workmen gained special recognition by increasing the quotas fixed originally by the central planning authorities. Piecework wages and bonuses were used. Public recognition was given to successful competition between shock-brigades. "Heroes of labor" received the Order of Lenin. In the newspapers one found pictures of factory workers who had met their quota of production rather than the faces of the Capones or the members of the Hollywood community. Promotions to positions of power also served to keep up enthusiasm.

185

The force of public opinion, brought to a high level, acted as a stimulating standard. The general psychology was whipped up to a pitch kindred to that of war. There were "mobilizations" of specific groups of qualified workers. There was "labor discipline," promoted by education and propaganda. A definite concept grew up of "labor desertion." There were drives for the accomplishment of a particular result that were similar to our war-loan drives. The control figures for each period, made up by quarter-years to permit more frequent inventories, were used—and most effectively—to stimulate and exploit, if you will, the human material as well as to check the natural resources. These measures formed the basis for the sweeping charge that the labor was really forced labor, but in Russia it was called "self-discipline"—"Bolshevik self-discipline."

A former foreign concessionaire visited the plant which he had built and which had been taken over by the Bolsheviks during the new socialist offensive. He expressed to me the wish that he might have dared to drive his workmen as they were being driven in the national enterprise. A Communist who overheard the remark was pleased and boastful; but he changed the wording of the comment, of course, insisting that the new manager "got the workmen to work better" and did not "drive them to work more."

Despite the food shortage, goods deficit, inefficient management in the new giants of industry, abuse of machinery, impoliteness of secretaries (which was my particular personal grievance), and other evidences of difficult and costly wastage, my feeling that distinct progress had been made during the two years between my visits of 1930 and 1932 was not shaken.

🙶 🙶 🙶

CHAPTER XXII

1932: THROUGH THE SPECTACLES OF THE NEAR EAST

RETURNING "TO EUROPE" AT THE END OF SEPTEMBER, I DID NOT STOP over in Poland, as I often did; there seemed to be no new or interesting developments there. The phrase put above in quotation marks was a customary one, not only among us foreign visitors, but also among the Russians before 1917. And foreign students of the Soviet experiment were seeing, already in 1932, much of the old Russia and much of the "Asiatic" in this Russia. On the train from Moscow to Berlin was a German embassy courier, an elderly retired army officer from East Prussia. When going through the Polish customs—with some difficulty because my notes and papers were considered propaganda, although I was going straight through without stopover—I joined my German colonel and remarked: "Well, here we are in Europe." But he demurred with the remark, "Not yet"; and the strenuous half-hour fight over my notes with the Polish authorities tended to make me agree with him. When, twelve hours later, I was passed by the German frontier authorities with a friendly salute—thanks probably to a word from the German colonel—the latter came rushing up to me with the cheerful greeting: "Now, you see, we are in Europe."

Like the Russians, the Germans have been sensitive about this question of being in Europe. And one wonders if much of the present trouble has not come from the snobbish attitude of the British, French, and ourselves, about our so-called "Western civilization." In this connection the Poles should be noted. For they, with some foundation, claim to have taken over more of the "Western civilization" than the Russians or even the Germans. This claim has not been given the recognition it deserves because of the customary arrogance with which the Poles have made it. For in this Eastern situation the contemptuous arrogance of the Poles —this "gentleman" race—has been one of the factors making for trouble. I have never been able to decide whether the Pole's contempt for the Russian was a more active one than the German's contempt for the Pole. On one occasion in 1932, when talking with a high Polish official in Berlin, I had to interrupt in order to determine if we were making the same assumption, for we were getting more divergent in our views the more we talked. So I asked my Polish friend the simple question: "Do you recognize those things that walk around on two legs in the country to the east of Poland as human beings?" And he answered, and, not entirely facetiously: "The question is relevant and well worded and I probably don't." Russians and Germans have the same attitude toward the Poles. To draw both the Russians and the Germans out in conversation, I used to repeat what Kuno Meyer, a colleague in Celtic literature, once said at Liverpool in a public lecture, causing, of course, quite a scandal. His statement, as I remember, was that the Irish, like the Poles, were capable only of poetry, romance, and intrigue.

The constant distinction between "East" and "West" had been one of the points of attention in my Russian studies. I had never been in the "East," properly speaking; and, in order to get another perspective on Russia, I had decided to spend the autumn of 1932 in the Near East. Mr. Crane was giving me the trip, because he wanted his representative in the Arab world, George Antonius, to get from me a firsthand and full account of Sovietism. I also wanted to see what the Near East was thinking about the Soviets. So, after hanging around Berlin for a week, recovering from laryngitis and writing up my "report," I started off for Jerusalem, via Trieste and by boat to Jaffa.

I used the trip to meet new types of people, as I have always done on my travels. My compartment companion on the train from Berlin via Munich was a Hollander headed for Teheran, to help the Persian government work out its tariff policy in a new law on customs duties. This able Dutchman gave me an insight into the politics of tariffs in Europe which made me feel less discouraged over our American tariff policy. A lively, ruddy-cheeked, young German Jewess was soon talking to all of us; she had just finished her preliminary training in a Zionist school and was going to one of the colonies. Later I met her of a Saturday night at Tel Aviv, at a dance hall, where she introduced me to a large group of the Jewish youth who had come in from a near-by colony for the week-end. Another passenger on the train was a true "Aryan-blond" type of German, who responded coldly when we held a door open for her as we worked our way to the dining-car. Later, in Trieste, seeing her on the street, I ventured to address her, and then looked for a hole into which to crawl when she slapped me down with the coldest of stares. It was amusing revenge not to speak to her when we found ourselves again fellow-passengers on the small Italian liner, or when we passed in the Hotel David in Jerusalem or in the British tearoom at Haifa. She was, it turned out, a governess-companion in a British family, and I took pleasure in being the snob.

On the boat was a professor of mathematics at the Hebrew University at Jerusalem, with a charming daughter. I learned as much from the girl as from the father about the university, where I was later to meet Judah Magnus and others, missing, however, Hans Kohn, whom I had met in Russia. As on transatlantic liners, we danced every night, and the professor's daughter was one of my steady partners. She liked Americans, it seemed—even older ones—who were good dancers. She had met another good dancer on her trip out to Europe from Palestine, she said, and coyly remarked that she had a snapshot of him. So, of course, I asked to see it; and I was amused to recognize my good and handsome friend, Max Eastman. Another fellow-passenger was a practicing woman physician from Tel Aviv. She told me a lot about the new Jewish settlement. Something, perhaps the hot climate, was having a somewhat loosening effect on the habits of the young people from colder climes, which was causing concern among the Zionist leaders. When, later, I asked the grand mufti of Jerusalem if he would not recognize that the Jews had brought certain cultural values, he caustically asked if I had in mind the public necking which one had to see in Tel Aviv—particularly on Zion Square, the movie and restaurant center in Jerusalem.

I was met at the pier, where the little dory landed me, by George Antonius. Though we had heard much of each other from our mutual friend, Mr. Crane, and had corresponded, we had never met. We agreed to be quite frank with each other, for Antonius was in the midst of gathering some of the material used in his later book on the Arab awakening, and he hoped I would not require too much toting about. I assured him that I knew the game of traveling and that I did not like too much chaperonage. Later, I believe, Antonius became disturbed at my independence, for the British queried him about my being seen with Communists, the official Zionist leaders warned him that I had been seen with "revisionists," and his Arab friends told him of my being seen at a public hall, dancing with Jewish girls. The one thing about me which I believe really disturbed Antonius was that I always forgot his last injunction and crossed my legs during our talks with highly placed orthodox Arabs.

For the Near Eastern situation I could not have had a better person to introduce and vouch for me than Antonius. He had the position of the student and was respected as such by all the three parties in Palestine—British, Arabs, and Jews. We went to Beirut and then on to Damascus, where I had access, through him, to the Syrian leaders. He arranged for my reception by King Faisal in Bagdad. And in our hours together he gave me freely of his studies and firsthand experiences, in return for my lectures and conversations on Sovietism, either with him alone, or in a group now of British, now of Jews, now of Arabs, which he had arranged for me.

The problem of settlement by the Jews in the country of the Arabs, stimulated by the Balfour Declaration and by the cry of the revisionists for a Jewish state; the volcano of protest against the French maladministration in Syria under the mandate; the history of the establishment by the British of Iraq as a model Arab state—these not only were in each case interesting problems in themselves but were matters which one needed to know about to get any understanding of the Near East situation.

My "passports" to these groups were either "friend of Mr. Crane, with greetings from him," or "I have just come from Moscow, are you interested in this Soviet experiment?" In Syria I had to whisper Mr. Crane's name, for a French court had passed formal sentence on him for allegedly stirring up Arab rioting. Also I had to whisper, "I've just come from Moscow," in some quarters, because of the British or French police commissioners. Frankly, I was interested in finding out to what extent either Jews or Arabs were looking to, or in any case at, Sovietism. In talking with a group of schoolteachers in Bagdad, the capital of Iraq, after they had questioned me for an hour about the Soviet system, I asked if their interest were purely intellectual or whether they had been attracted by the Soviet republics of the Caucasus or of Central Asia, set up as show windows by the Moscow leaders, precisely for the benefit of the peoples of the East. The answer, given with a smile by one of the group, was: "But don't you know that we are Britain's show window?" There was not the same smile on the face of the British commissioner when I told him of this answer a few days later.

When King Faisal received me, he had several of his ministers present. He questioned me in detail on the actual functioning of the Soviet system. Then the conversation was directed, by the King of course, to the depression in the capitalistic world. It was at this conversation that I worked out, as a kind of formula to meet the situation in which I found myself, the following: "Sovietism is having much trouble getting production, while capitalism does not seem to be able to handle the problem of distribution. So 'Will Sovietism learn to produce before capitalism learns to distribute?' is the basic question."

The interest in what I had to say about my studies of the Soviet Union was, in the main, purely intellectual, as my question to the group of schoolteachers in Bagdad suggested. People liked to hear about the experiment, but that was about all. I can gauge the reaction of a group by the kind of questions they ask. Some, like King Faisal, seemed to be comparing the competing systems of capitalism and communism, and also the other system developing in Italy under the name of fascism. Naziism was not considered of great import at that time, although I kept bringing Hitler up, having been impressed by the strength I thought to see in him as revealed by the July, 1932, campaign and election.

In Syria one had, it seemed to me, a most clear instance of the application, by the French, of the principle of "divide and rule." There was a cynical reliance on that French logic which has contributed so much to the present catastrophe. When Syrians seemed to recall, with pleasure, the old Turkish rule, one had the measure of the French colonial methods as used in Syria. Even the French archeologists in Damascus irritated me.

The trip from Bagdad to Istanbul was over the finished section of the famous Berlin-Bagdad railway, of which there was so much talk in the 1914 period, in connection with the "world domination" aims of the Germany of Kaiser Wilhelm. It showed the usual efficiency of the German and was a historically interesting and aesthetically pleasant journey. There were only two of us in the International *wagon-lit* car, my fellow-traveler being a League of Nations medical serviceman returning from Persia. Through him I learned that the Soviets had a stronger position, politically and economically, in Persia, than I had noted in the other Near Eastern countries I had visited. I should have included Persia in my trip, but time did not permit.

The days in Constantinople were difficult because of indisposition— the well-known "Bagdad tummy"—too much heat plus too much sand on the desert crossings. Howland Shaw, our embassy counselor and the State Department's authority on the Near and Middle East, was at Ankara; but I could not accept his invitation to come to the new capitol because of my illness. Miss Anne Morgan was most kind in making me use her car, to do sightseeing in the old city, with Paul Munroe's daughter. Professor Munroe, temporarily president of Roberts College, proved an old friend from earlier Chicago days. At Roberts College, from members of its faculty, I learned of Mustapha's *Primer on Civics*, which he had helped the favorite "adopted niece" of the moment compose. The re-writing of Turkish history under her leadership and guidance suggested what I had found in the Soviet Union, though in Turkey I found extreme nationalism as the underlying motif, as opposed to Russian dialectic materialism and Marxian internationalism. History-teaching in Roberts College itself had been officially eliminated, for only a Turk could properly teach the right kind of history. "Civics" also had become a state monopoly in Turkey. Soviet educational methods—or, rather, perhaps one should say "propaganda methods"—were being consciously copied. In their program of civic training the Turks, while anticlerical, were not antireligious. They seemed to be weighing the relative points of strength and weakness of private capitalism, Italian fascism, and Sovietism, trying to take from each what was considered more positive and adaptable to Turkish problems. The policy of industrialization was to be based on an *étatisme modéré* (moderate form of state enterprise and control), I was told by one prominent Turkish economist.

The college for women at Constantinople was trying an experiment the week I was there. They had invited the parents of the girls to come to a reception, at which the girls would give exhibition dancing. There was a question in the minds of the school authorities whether many parents would show up, though none had objected to the participation of their daughters. As a "visiting fireman," I was asked to stand in the reception line. The parents came, and I made a large number of appointments with fathers for the next days. The party ended in social dancing, and I found partners among the young Turkish girls. It was a successful experiment, and indicative of the extent of the emancipation which the Young Turk movement had brought.

Although my days in the new Turkey had been less than a dozen, I decided that, though small, this country, being situated at one of the great crossroads of the world, presented a fascinating field of study. It was apparently looking into the various social economic systems of its neighbors and seeking to build up its own new Turkey. There was good material on which to build, since the Anatolian peasants and their leaders had good military discipline. The intellectuals had been consigned to a less prominent place—for some this meant exile. To satisfy the yearning for debate, an attempt was made to have more than the one governmental or governing party; but it had failed because it was a promoted thing. The one party was led by a military man, who had suffered at the hands of the old vested interests, in army, church, and government; and he was ruthless in chasing these out. The abolition of the fez and the caliphate had been effected with a minimum of disruption; and in 1932 Mustapha was "modernizing" in a constructive way, in the economic field and in education. Here was an example, it seemed to me, of statesmanship capable of directing the economic and other forces that had been released by way of revolution. I came away an admirer of this Kemal, as one of the real statesmen of our period. I forgot the reports of his drunken brawls or his severe treatment of individual opponents—in the light of the positive aspects of his leadership. The Young Turk movement, which had been encouraged by the 1905 revolution in Russia, was progressing also partly under the protection and influence of Sovietism but without Communists.

When I returned home, Walter Rogers, the head of the Institute of Current World Affairs, thought I was showing laziness when I kept holding up a report of my Near East trip to be sent out to a limited number of individuals in government, academic, journalism, and business groups. Finally I sent in a mere list of questions, raised in my mind by my talks and discussions—questions which I would study if I had time to get a background and more material for judgment.

Working my way home from Constantinople, I stopped over a few days in Prague. Behind schedule, I could not do the same at Sofia and Belgrade, as originally planned. I had no particular interest in even a superficial glance at either Romania or Hungary. The trip to Prague was, in fact, in order to talk with Masaryk and to see S. N. Prokopovich. Prokopovich was an old friend, as was his wife, Guskova. I had seen them in 1926 and again in 1930. They were not *émigrés;* that is, they had not run away, but they were "exiled" in the technical sense in 1923. Prokopovich, as well as several other outstanding Russian scholars, had been ordered to pack up and clear out because, as Lenin himself explained to one of them, it was feared that they would become the nucleus of an opposition when, under the New Economic Policy, the pressure was somewhat reduced. Prokopovich, an outstanding economist, published at Prague an economic bulletin, which has been most useful to the students of the Soviet experiment.

My talk with Masaryk lasted a whole evening. He was much disturbed by the method, rather than by the fact, of the policy to collectivize agriculture; and he anticipated peasant resistance, even to the point of sabotage. And he was justified in his concern, although collectivized agriculture in its later development would probably have been accepted by him. For he saw the many positive features in the policy as related to Russian past and conditions. But he was more pessimistic about the Soviet experiment than he had been before, and more so than I was. I gave to Masaryk my impressions of the growing strength of Hitler as I had noted it in July and have here recorded. Masaryk was also disturbed by the feeling that Hitler was getting stronger and stronger and also by the fact that so many of his advisers just wouldn't see it. He saw, as did so many of us, the hodgepodge of the Nazi program, as well as its immorality; and also how it was appealing to so many Germans and, as Masaryk put it, "to so educated a people as the Germans." But he paused and said: "No, that is not the word, and that is why we don't see more clearly, for the Germans are not an educated people but a trained and drilled people."

While not very sympathetic toward Hungary, I recognized, nevertheless, that the country still nursed many raw spots from the treatment it had received in the so-called peace settlement of 1920. I ventured the thought that Czechoslovakia would strengthen its own position by showing a little generosity toward Hungary. I knew that Masaryk had urged on his colleagues such a policy. Perhaps it was his experience of failure in this effort that was responsible for the statement, made in Masaryk's customary friendly manner: "Young man, you cannot expect states to act like gentlemen."

I came away from the few days in Prague rather discouraged, both by the views on the Soviet situation expressed by my Prague friends and by their views on the situation of Czechoslovakia.

Because Paris was en route, I squeezed in twenty-five hours there. I had not been there since 1913. A Communist friend I had met in Jerusalem had returned to her position with the Pathé Cinema, and she met my train, to act as guide in the city I had previously known so well as a student. The weather was of the worst, a melting, slushy snowstorm. But with taxis I managed to take a quick look at some of the places where I had lived—in Montmartre, back of the Panthéon, at No. 5 Rue de l'Odéon, and especially the old "hotel," still set in a small court with garden, off Rue du Bac, at an address I always enjoyed giving: "Impasse de la Visitation." Then I had lunch at the Café du Panthéon, where there had been an "American table" in my student days. I avoided advertising the return of an old American client because at the moment a student parade of indignation over America's demand for the payment of war debts was marching down the Boule Miche.

I spent the afternoon with my old professor of Russian, Paul Boyer. We had not seen each other for years, although we were constantly exchanging letters. Except for a few "friends of Russia" the feeling of the French toward the Russians, as well as the Bolsheviks, was bitter. For the *sacrés* Russians had repudiated their debts to the French people. Boyer, like a few other Frenchmen, was much upset by the popular demand to default the December 15 interest payment on the American debt; but, as he explained, they had been unable to make any impression on the "politicians." And part of the attitude was the feeling that we, by our participation in the depression and contributing to it, were letting down the capitalistic system.

My one evening in Paris was spent at a Russian restaurant, with one of the best of the Russian gipsy orchestras and cuisine. It was in these *émigré* Russian restaurants all over Europe that I had my feasts of Russian food rather than at the Metropole or Savoy in Moscow. Always I managed to reveal my association with Russia; and almost always I found these Russian *émigrés* anxious to hear all about my travels and impressions, for they were very homesick for their country. I missed the old *cochers* and the horse-drawn omnibuses. And the girls who were on the watch for me as I came back to the hotel were no longer "street-walkers," for it was from behind the wheel of an automobile that they suggested a little drive. I decided I had "done" my old Paris rather well when I caught the "Golden Arrow" express for London.

⇔ ⇔ ⇔

CHAPTER XXIII

1932: LONDON

IN THE CASUAL CONFUSION OF A BRITISH RAILWAY STATION I COULD NOT find the person who had promised to meet the train, but she also finally gave up the search and came to the hotel. She was the Luba (Moura's friend) of Bruce Lockhart's *British Agent*, whom I knew in Moscow and had run into again in Berlin; she had now married a British friend, a former colleague during my years at the University of Liverpool. She and Moura were to give me the low-down, first, on British-Soviet relations and the standing of Soviet Russia in British circles and, secondly, on the various Russian *émigrés* in England. I was also to see much of my old chief, Bernard Pares, now of the School of Slavonic Studies at the University of London. Through his daughter, for whom I had stood as godfather, I had the entree to an interesting group of young Britishers in their early twenties.

The formal excuse for my stopover in London was an invitation from the Royal Academy of International Affairs to lecture and lead the discussion on the "Role of the Communist Party in the Soviet Union," a topic which had become my special research subject after I finished *Civic Training in Soviet Russia*. Finally, my most helpful chaperon in London was James Somerville, of our Department of Commerce, one of whose tasks was to study British-Soviet trade relations. He seemed to know everybody—in business as well as official circles—who was interested in the matter, and he tore around with me from place to place. His wife was a Russian, whom he had met when he was with the American Relief Administration during the 1922 famine in Soviet Russia. Every day of my stay was to be a full day.

The evening at Chatham House, as the Royal Institute is generally called, went fairly well. London fog and perhaps the many parties given for me had roughed my voice, but I managed to get my lecture across. My interpretations and conclusions went over also, although through a barrage of hostility and suspicion, for the audience included many Russian *émigrés*. Among these was an old friend who had been most hos-

194

pitable to me for many years in Russia, where she had been an active social and political worker. She had hesitated about coming to my lecture; but there she sat, clearly ready to jump on me. Her one comment was a statement of further detail on a point I had made, which I accepted as simply reinforcing my interpretation. After the lecture she asked me to come to her home for an evening, adding that she had waited to ask me until she had heard my lecture. This institution at which I spoke had many interesting and typically British rules. One was not supposed to quote publicly what was said there. Also, there could be no guests, not even out-of-town guests. Later, in 1939, I asked to be allowed to hear a report on Russia by a British official who had just returned. The correspondence in connection with the refusal was very amusing, particularly as it included an invitation to speak if I returned from Moscow by way of London. Presumably a rather closed "British" forum, there were, nevertheless, many foreigners—wives of members or naturalized Britishers—in the membership.

The question of resuming more extensive trade relations with the Soviet Union was to the fore in England. The scare over the 1926 general strike had worn off. It was seen that private concerns could do business with the state monopoly of foreign trade of the Soviet system. A parliamentary committee was working on the problem and had arranged a dinner at which several large industrialists were to be present. I was invited, as the one outsider, by several members of Parliament whom I had recently met in Moscow. The general approach of the group was realistic; there was a basis for mutually beneficial trade. It was interesting to me, as an American who had heard many stories of keen British trading methods, to hear these Britishers express the need to keep close watch on the Bolshevik methods. The Bolsheviks, it seemed, were beginning to follow Lenin's precept to them ten years earlier, "Be good traders." I told the group that several Bolsheviks had spoken to me quite seriously of the difficulties they were having in their efforts to develop commercial relations with the outside world. As they put it, the "capitalist world," with its depressions, drops in prices, and methods of competition within national units and between units, was so uncertain. Nevertheless, the Bolsheviks took full advantage of these features, playing off one group against another. In this game they did not always adhere strictly to the truth in citing to one prospective customer the price offered by another, but I have always understood that this is a general business practice which is not considered too sharp.

It was necessary, though a little difficult, to talk with Bernard Pares. He had failed to get into Russia in 1926 because he tried to do so in an indirect way. He had been outspokenly anti-Soviet, outraged particularly by the Moscow part in the 1926 general strike in Britain. The "Moscow hand" in this situation has always seemed to me to be the last, and decisive, manifestation of Trotskyism. I have seen and talked with the man who, in my belief, was the person sent on to London to direct the strike. Although he was purged in 1937, I still hesitate to name him. With this background I expected a difficult evening with Pares. There was another problem that I had to face: I had seen many of our former mutual close friends; but I had decided not to mention them or, in any case, quote them, for I feared that Pares, in his active anti-Sovietism might publicly repeat their statements, and in a way that might identify them through me.

I dined with Pares at a small Italian restaurant where he was a regular boarder. We stayed on and on, talking away; and evidently I warmed up to the subject of what I had seen of Sovietism, to meet his constant doubts and general skepticism. And, in warming up, I must have raised my voice, for the waiter brought me a note, signed by one of the outstanding labor leaders of England, who was dining with his wife at a near-by table. In the note this neighbor admitted to having heard some of my statements, described them as the most sensible he had heard on the Soviet situation for some time, and asked if I could give him a couple of hours of talk on the same subject the next day. Pares knew the man and invited him to join us immediately. It was interesting to sit between rather conservative Pares and this somewhat leftist labor leader. It was clear from the latter's remarks that Sovietism was making a strong appeal in certain groups of British labor. But the British conservative was afraid of Russia as well as of Bolshevism; and, despite his devotion to his field of study, Pares revealed this attitude at many points.

One man I wished particularly to see in London was Michael Farbman, who had written the short but useful study of the Five-Year Plan under the title of the Russian abbreviation, *Piatiletka*. Our talks in Moscow had shown that he had got below the surface; his book developed a more serious attitude toward the Soviet experiment among those who read it. But I soon learned that he was in a hospital, dying from a skin infection which he had contracted in a Russian village he had visited while he was studying collective farms. This trip to the collective farm was illustrative of his efforts to see how the Soviet system was actually functioning.

Through my friends in Parliament I asked for a ticket to the gallery for a session. Half-facetiously, I remarked that, after studying Sovietism in Russia and seeing fascism in Italy, Kemalism in Turkey, and the rapid growth of naziism in Germany, I felt I needed to renew my faith in the Western representative form of government by visiting the Mother of Parliaments. This remark was repeated in the eight quarters and secured me the special privilege of being the "guest of the speaker," in the little alcove on the main floor, separated from the members by a low railing. As special guest, I had at my right the procedure expert of the House of Commons, to explain to me the way things were done. The day was the important one, when it was voted not to pay the interest on the debt to

America. When Churchill rose, he was not ten feet from me. Two points made by him stick in my memory, on which I rely in summarizing what he said. He expressed regret that the prime minister was absent and unwell, suggesting that he was naturally worn out by rushing from country to country, looking at himself in the broken mirrors of Continental Europe. To a suggestion that the debt be handled by ceding to the United States some of the Western Hemisphere possessions, Churchill came out, with emphasis, against giving up a "single jewel of the imperial crown." In the light of the events of 1939–41 these two statements—the only ones I recalled vividly—are of special interest.

Lloyd George also spoke, and for payment of the debt, for it was under his prime ministership that it had been contracted. Bonar Law also spoke, and some of the lesser fry. But the decision to repudiate the debt and the whacks at us did not disturb me, for I was by then a strong "internationalist"; and the parliamentary style of expression used softened the sharpness of the decision, although its tendency toward equivocation by double negatives and other stylist tricks left me unconvinced, even if unprovoked. I could, and did, enjoy the tea my friends gave me in the members' room, although under the rules we could sit there only fifteen minutes because I was an "outsider."

☙ ☙ ☙

CHAPTER XXIV

1933: RECOGNITION

It was a strange America to which I returned in 1933, for the "panic" was in full swing at the turn of the year. I found that Roosevelt had become the Santa Claus for Americans, just as I had noted people looking to him in England and the Near East. It appeared that I was going to have my innings again, the interest in some plan, even a Soviet plan, having become very active. I had plenty of invitations to lecture at councils on foreign relations, Rotarian meetings, Kiwanis Clubs, and women's clubs, as well as at universities.

I was also asked to take part in a session of the New York Academy of Political Science. The other papers were to be from economists, and I hesitated to venture into that company. My paper was written, as announced, from the point of view of a student of government; and I tried to show that, under the Soviet system, politics and economics could not be separated, political considerations being made to prevail over economic, the classical economic laws to the contrary notwithstanding. A colleague economist, Harry Gideonse, read my paper beforehand; and his comment was not devastating, although not very enthusiastic. I ventured to proceed with it, and felt rather uncomfortable both during and after the performance, for clearly I failed to get my thesis across. The comment on the paper was made, by arrangement, by Paul Scheffer, the Berlin correspondent, who had had some seven years of assignments in Moscow. He implied that I had swallowed the Soviet propaganda, although in response I pointed out that part of my subject was precisely the technique of the propaganda of a system which was trying to change economic and social relationships within a community.

Another, more important, appearance was at an institute on the international situation held at Williamsburg. Again I felt out of place, because the subject assigned me was "The Russian Peasant and the Bolshevik Revolution." This subject had an international bearing, of course, although I doubt if I was able to convince my audience that the Soviet solution of the problem of agriculture would affect developments in the East. The policy of collectivization of agriculture, I pointed out, was certainly the most revolutionary feature of the entire Bolshevik program and would perhaps be the most revolutionizing in the world in general. The paucity of the questions put to me after I had presented my paper testified to the fact that people were desperately clinging to established methods, even in that year of trial and tribulation of 1933.

Later I tried this same paper on neighbor dairy farmers of Racine County, Wisconsin, gathered one evening in the play-yard of the rural school a mile from the family farm at Kansasville, Wisconsin. There the questions were far more searching, and I had a really interesting session. At the end of the discussion one farmer asked me if I thought the system would work in America. In answer, I reminded him of the difficulty we were having organizing a small co-operative to dispose of our milk at prices that would pay for the cost of production, and gave him a vigorous "No," adding immediately: "But if we have twenty-five more years of depression and of the conditions we are 'enjoying' these days, we may be ready for some kind of collectivism, and our co-operative may function effectively."

When I was lecturing in the East, I usually stopped over in Washington for a few days. In 1933 the subject that interested me in Washington was: "When will Roosevelt recognize the Soviet government?" From his campaign speeches it seemed clear that he intended doing so. Recognition of the Soviet government would be consonant with the New Dealism of the first period. Already in 1926 I had begun to feel that our policy of nonrecognition was ceasing to be constructive. As late as 1930, however, I had argued with Litvinov and other Soviet leaders in Moscow that it was still too soon to expect recognition; for I still felt that resumption of diplomatic relations would be meaningless unless they were based on mutual understanding and some common aim. In that conversation with Litvinov I had suggested that the situation in the Far East might provide the common aim and break the deadlock that had developed in Soviet-American relations. But in 1931–32 this deadlock seemed to have become more definite—largely, I believed, because of Stimson's too legalistic approach to the problems of international relations, despite the idealistic basis which seemed to underlie his policy and action in the Far East. In 1932 those prevailed who feared that any step such as recognition of the Soviets would still further "infuriate the mad dog that had broken loose in the Far East," as Japan was described. Others, like me, who recognized that Japan was shielding her aggression behind a slogan of anti-Communism, argued that she was mad anyway and might be sobered and restrained by some positive action on our part. It seemed to me that, in the interest of maintenance of peace in the Far East, both Washington and Moscow would now forget some of the principles which had led to the deadlock in their relations. "For a higher principle—peace—one can forget certain other less important points," I had argued. It seemed to me that peace in the Far East was definitely menaced by the continuing Japanese aggression. In my view, we needed peace in the Far East as much as did the Soviet Union, so that a basis now did exist for mutual, full reciprocal accommodation.

So in my trips to Washington I argued, when occasion offered, for recognition. It seemed to me that there was a growing public demand for the normalizing of our relations. I was not of the group that thought and said that recognition would bring tens, if not hundreds of millions of dollars of purchases of American goods, though I knew, from conditions I saw in the Soviet Union, that there was a real, almost desperate, lack of consumers' goods and even of food. And we certainly needed to sell our surpluses to stimulate our own flagging economy and meet the increasing problem of unemployment.

As I dropped in to see old friends in the State Department, it was suggested several times that I should see Bullitt, who had been introduced there by Roosevelt as part of the New Deal. I had heard that the State Department was to be one of the first to be "purged," although at that time this word was not current. Bullitt, I surmised, was to conduct the cleansing process. But I declined the offers to introduce me to this new man in the Department, remarking that I believed in integrity and loyalty and had never forgiven Bullitt for what I considered his inexcusable breach of trust in talking too openly about his acting as President Wilson's personal and confidential emissary to Moscow to sound out the possibilities of a settlement in connection with the Versailles Treaty. When I expressed this attitude regarding him, I had no evidence that he was still interested in the Soviet experiment or in our relations with the Soviet government. I had not heard of his talks with Litvinov at the London Economic Conference, which served, apparently, as the first step in the resumption of diplomatic relations between Moscow and Washington.

On the other hand, I did know that Morgenthau, then in the Agricultural Adjustment Administration, was handling a cotton deal with the Soviets, the Reconstruction Finance Corporation also being in the picture. This was public knowledge; so on my trip to Washington in June I decided to try to see Morgenthau. This was arranged by my old friend and former colleague, Harold G. Moulton; and to my surprise and pleasure, on entering Morgenthau's office I found another friend and former colleague, Herman Oliphant, as his immediate adviser. These friends served as a liaison for me, for I rather dreaded the first talk with any man, which I always considered exploratory and designed to establish mutual confidence.

Morgenthau went immediately to the meat of the subject interesting both of us and asked me relevant and searching questions about the Soviet economic structure and its functioning. I was then passed on to George Peek, of the Agricultural Adjustment Administration, in whose office I again found someone I knew, Wayne Chatfield Taylor. Peek's views with regard to foreign trade, as later expressed in his pronunciamentos, were somewhat opposed to my own. He argued them with vigor and conviction; but, in any case, he wanted to learn about the aims and methods of the Bolsheviks. The net result was that I was informed of the plan to put American-Russian trade relations under the direction of a new and noninvolved person—a hardheaded businessman with experience in the field of international trade, who had no sentimental or promotional tie-up with the Soviet Union. With the broad hints one had that trade relations were going to be promoted, accompanied by the re-establishment of diplomatic relations, all those who had been for recognition of the Soviet government, or who were trying to get orders or technical service contracts in the Soviet Union, began to pull wires, as well as make speeches, to get in on the inside track. It was interesting to note how many hoped to be ambassador, and for some reason I was credited with having this ambition also.

Later, on October 23, I again happened to be in Washington and dropped into the Eastern European Division in the afternoon, asking what the developments were with respect to recognition. I put the question thus bluntly because I knew that the State Department people were not very enthusiastic about extending recognition. My friends looked at me in an odd way and asked what I knew and what I was doing in Washington. I could not understand why they adopted the tone they did, and continued to tease them in a semifacetious way. Finally, losing patience, the chief of the Division, Robert Kelley, asked me if I could possibly sit quietly, with my mouth shut, for fifteen minutes. He seemed serious, as well as much excited; so I acquiesced. At the end of fifteen minutes he handed me the press release—Roosevelt's message to Kalinin—suggesting that the Soviet government send someone to Washington to talk with him, not with the State Department, about normalizing relations between the two countries. I felt sure that the division heads of the Department, even those connected with areas covered by the Soviet Union, had not known of this step by the President many hours before the public was informed.

There was no one in this country who had studied Soviet legislation and literature more thoroughly than had Kelley. He knew Russian well. We differed considerably in our interpretations of Sovietism. He was often too legalistic; and he thought me often too idealistic, because I felt the Soviet experiment could not be understood without a little warmth of soul. The assistant chief of the Eastern European Division, Earl Packer, seemed to me to have a somewhat more human approach to the subject than had Kelley. I had known Packer when he was a telegraph clerk in the Petrograd embassy, and by work and ability he had entered and risen rapidly in the formal foreign service. He also was the student type and had a thorough command of Russian.

That night Kelley, Packer, and I were to dine together. I took them to my room at the Cosmos Club to have a drink of the synthetic vodka I had brought from Chicago. Louis Brownlow, the head of the Public Administration Clearing House, joined us. I wanted to know who had arranged the Roosevelt communication outside of, and perhaps above, the Department. They could not tell me, for it was still a secret; so I said that I would not ask them but would guess. I spoke one word—"Bullitt"—and the very effort of my friends to look frigid convinced me that my guess was right. We went to a Russian restaurant for dinner; and as we ate Russian dishes, I suggested that they give their Russian souls a little chance to function, and break through the rigidity of department protocol. It was a good dinner, but it did not have the effect I had hoped it would.

Before I came to Washington, I had written Boris Skvirsky, the unrecognized Soviet ambassador, as some called him, for an appointment, which he made for Saturday morning, October 24, at 9.30. I called up to ask if he still wished to see me as arranged, in view of the big news; and he answered: "I want to see you more than ever." He was, of course, very happy over what had happened, for he had worked for recognition since 1922 and his position had been none too easy in Washington. He was happy also because there had been no premature leak at his end. Because of the difference in time, the newspapermen in Moscow always got a scoop; and this tended to make the Washington authorities believe that Moscow would not observe strictly the agreement that announcements were to be made in Moscow and Washington at exactly the same moment, not hour, of the day. When I asked him who had arranged the parley on our side, he named Bullitt, as the newspapers were already printing.

It seemed to me that the situation justified my asking if Secretary Hull could spare me a few minutes. Our talk was mainly on the general trend within Sovietism. Was it developing genuine cultural values, and could its announced peace policy be considered as sincere and consistent with internal needs as well as with Soviet dogma? Then I had a longer talk with William Phillips, through whom I had established my first really close relations with the State Department in 1915. He asked me nine practical questions about preparation for the reception of Litvinov, whom Kalinin had announced would leave for Washington without delay. I urged that he be met with all formality and also that the President receive and talk with him in a formal manner, for I had found that any attempt at familiarity with a real Bolshevik made him suspicious. I urged that the President have a man like Kelley, who knew all the dots and commas of Bolshevik documents of the past, at his side, as the President could not be expected to know the details of previous Soviet policy and practice. I also told him that, in Litvinov, the President would find a man of keen intelligence and marked directness of manner and speech, which required similar qualities in one who wished to thrash out with him the questions which required settlement before we could extend recognition.

In the meantime it had been suggested to me again that I should meet Bullitt. I postponed response to the suggestion until I had seen the Secretary and Mr. Phillips. I walked twice around the third floor of the State and War Department Building before I finally decided. Then I returned to my friend in the Department who wished to introduce me to Bullitt, and he took me down. Bullitt was most cordial; impressed me as keen, as well as enthusiastic; and within a few minutes had me talking away as fast as his rapid fire of very relevant questions would allow. On the difficult question of how to make the Soviet government responsible for the actions of the Third International, I gave him the formula I had worked out for my own public statements; and this must have impressed him, for he wrote it down. It was: "The American government takes cognizance of the fact that the Communist International is an integral part either of Bolshevism or of the Soviet system." I suggested that an attempt should be made to get Litvinov to accept the second of these alternatives, if possible, but that, if he refused, he must be persuaded to accept the first at least. I argued that it would be futile to try to get him to accept the position that the Communist International was an integral part of the Soviet government, or vice versa.

Bullitt asked me to prepare memoranda for him on six points, this to be absolutely confidential between us. I told him I would have to tell Kelley that I was doing this, disclosing to him the topics on which I was going to give my views, without, however, sending him copies of these documents. I also said that on one topic Kelley was much better informed than I. So, after reporting back to Kelley, as agreed, I went home to meet my classes on Tuesday and wrote the five short memoranda, for which Bullitt sent me a very gratifying letter of thanks.

When Litvinov arrived, I went down to Washington, admittedly to sit on the side lines. This was a somewhat unusual move, for I was not invited or called on by either side, and I did not try to see either Bullitt or Litvinov. I never tried to see Roosevelt. Hull once suggested to me that the President should hear my interpretation of the Soviets. There were many friends, including Mr. Crane, who could have presented me. But I have always preferred to see and work with, or on, the official expert in the field to which I had a relation. I have hesitated to see the "highest" up. Not wanting any job in Washington, I did not care to play politics; and seeing the President seemed to me to be the latter.

Nevertheless, I was anxious about the conversations the President was going to have with Litvinov. Having often acted as moderator, or at least interpreter, in the field of American-Soviet relations, I thought I might do so again. That was the justification in my own mind for hanging around Washington during the first days when, behind closed doors, Roosevelt and Litvinov were having their talks.

I dined with the State Department Soviet experts, Kelley and Packer, again going to the provocative Russian restaurant, in hopes that this would awaken their Russian souls or any souls they might have. But again my efforts were fruitless. The State Department men were putting emphasis on the question of propaganda from Moscow—that is, on the Communist International. Correctly they took the view that the Soviet government could not be considered a national government with which another national government could have useful diplomatic relations if it were, in fact, an agent of an organ of international revolution. For the internal political situation our government had to get some sort of guaranty that the Soviet government would not support, directly or indirectly, an organization which aimed to overthrow our form of government by force and violence.

So the State Department experts got out all the Soviet commitments to other governments on this point, used the Soviet treaty with Afghanistan as the basis, and, by scissor-clipping from other treaties made by the Soviets, got quite a comprehensive statement on the point. Litvinov was expected to recognize in this statement his own commitments, and thus to accept it. The varying circumstances behind the other Soviet commitments were not taken into account. The Communist International was not specifically mentioned when the respective commitments of Roosevelt and Litvinov were made public in the form of letters exchanged between them. I felt that the language of the letters on this point was so broad that it was apt to lead to future misunderstanding.

Another point in the talks with Litvinov, which created, I believe, much misunderstanding, was religious freedom. It seemed to me futile to try to get the Soviets to accept religious freedom, as we understand it. I had to smile when I read that our embassy staff in Moscow must have the opportunity of religious teaching for their children, for my observations led me to doubt if they would be much concerned over this right.

203

The third moot point in American-Soviet relations was that of debts and future loans. I do not know whether Morgenthau, already, by November, Secretary of the Treasury, sat in with the President and Bullitt when this problem was discussed and settled. In any case, the eternal questions of Soviet repudiation of debts of former Russian governments and of compensation to American nationals for property seized under the Soviet policy of nationalization of industry were not satisfactorily thrashed out. The Export-Import Bank set up—called, in Washington slang, "Bill Bullitt's Bank"—did not ever assume real functions; and it took cover under the Johnson Act, by which credit could be extended only to those nations paying their war debts, and claimed that this law excluded credit to the Soviets, perhaps in order to have an excuse for its failure with respect to its original purpose.

Although the resumption of official relations between America and the Soviet Union did, as the President publicly stated, "strengthen the structure of peace" in the Far East, it did not rest on mutual confidence, as I had hoped that it would. Both the President and Litvinov, I believe, felt that, on one score or another, the other had tried to deceive him. Some insisted that the President put the recognition of the Soviets across with the American public, and especially the Catholics, with his usual political skill, to which I replied that the indirection led to later misunderstanding between Moscow and Washington, which was not conducive to mutual trust or to world peace, as evidenced by events in 1939 and 1940.

Bullitt was, as I expected, the first ambassador. I had urged publicly that the ambassador be a career-diplomat who would observe protocol meticulously, or else a hardheaded businessman who could promote mutually beneficial trade—but not, in any case, one who had taken a somewhat sentimental attitude toward the Soviet experiment. And, when asked where I put Bullitt in my classification, I had designated the sentimental category, adding that many put me, also, in that category. Bullitt wanted the position; and he was, in a sense, the logical man, for he had conducted the preliminary negotiations with Litvinov and had been at the President's side during the Roosevelt-Litvinov conversations in Washington. Bullitt made much of the fact that in 1918 he had talked with Lenin and had urged recognition of the Soviet government at that time. He played this card not only with Roosevelt but also with the Moscow people. The latter, therefore, were "for Bullitt." I continued to ruin any political ambitions I might have had, by opposing, to the last moment, the selection of Bullitt. When he was appointed, I almost hoped the Senate would at least delay in its confirmation. Finally, after confirmation, I wrote to Bullitt the difficult letter I felt I had to write. I received a very cordial answer and an invitation to use the embassy freely when I returned to Russia upon my projected study trip in 1939. Bullitt had a real flair for handling people and a charming manner, resembling in this, as in other respects, his chief and friend, Roosevelt.

While the purpose of my trips to Washington was always to get information in my field, and also to impart it when I found anyone wanting to listen to me, in 1933 I could not fail to be interested in the first stages of the New Deal. Of course, there was the question of whether it had an element of "Sovietism" in it, as its more violent opponents charged. I knew several of those connected with the National Reconstruction Administration—Donald Richberg, Dudley Cates, and, later, Sidney Hillman. I used to drop in at the headquarters in the Department of Commerce Building and wander about the corridor. I once remarked that I could have entered any of the open doors and dictated a letter to any stenographer without troubling to identify myself, as she would have thought that I was a new worker who had just turned up. The effort to organize and plan production à la America furnished an interesting contrast to the Soviet planning system.

Catching the Capital Limited at South Chicago, I was asked by a fellow-traveler if I were going to Washington to work on an N.R.A. code. Though I denied the allegation, he insisted on telling me about his troubles, and I was glad to listen. He had been secretary of an organization of several thousand units in a particular field, and so was called to Washington to help draw up the code. To this end he had sent out a questionnaire, more detailed than any he had previously sent; and he had received only about a 50 per cent response. He admitted that some of the questions could not be answered because of the inadequacy of the accounting methods of many of the units of his group. But he added that some just would not answer, and told the much repeated anecdote of the period to illustrate the point. It was the story of the two businessmen who were buying tickets for a trip to Springfield. When the ticket agent asked whether their destination was Springfield, Illinois, or Springfield, Massachusetts, one businessman said to his companion: "Bill, don't tell him, it's none of his damn business."

One evening, at the Brookings Institute, I heard John Dickman describe the aim of the N.R.A. program: to supply a gangplank by which management and labor could come to the government and get the latter's assistance in settling their business problems. He implied that the friendly bosom of the government would give warmth and comfort to both parties. After the lecture I asked Dickman if some help—perhaps even a little forceful push—would not make the using of the offered plank a little more effective. To this he answered quite shortly: "You darn Bolshevik!"

The planning in Washington struck me as much less scientific than that which I had studied in Moscow, though political considerations were prevailing over purely economic ones in both capitols, it seemed to me. As a political scientist, I had here a basis to tease my economic friends. As a citizen, I wondered how much it was going to cost us consumers, for I had seen in the Soviet Union the terrific cost of the mistakes when planning was being applied on such a vast scale.

To Mr. Legge of the International Harvester Company, on my return to Chicago, I gave my impression of the New Deal in Washington in 1933 in the same words I had used to describe Moscow in 1930: "Children playing with big and expensive toys."

☗ ☗ ☗

CHAPTER XXV

1934: LIFE IN RUSSIA HAS BECOME MORE JOYOUS

RESUMPTION OF NORMAL DIPLOMATIC RELATIONS BETWEEN AMERICA AND the Soviet Union meant more "business" for me. People wanted to hear about Sovietism. Some used the recognition as a basis to attack Roosevelt and the New Deal, which to them suggested Sovietism. The latter term came to be used to designate anything anybody did not like, as the word "Bolshevism" had been used in the earlier period of the Revolution in Russia. Those who were for some planning in our capitalistic system looked for suggestions to the Soviet experiment, and such people tended to give an expurgated version of Sovietism. The Bolshevik writer Karl Radek—one of the sharpest, if not always the most scrupulous of the Moscow journalists—commented on this tendency of foreigners to present Soviet planning as a rather mild, gentle process. He compared its popularity with that of Russian dishes served in the bourgeois restaurants of western Europe. These Russian dishes were served, said he, without the good strong sauce of the original and genuine Moscow cuisine. Of course, he added, this sauce was pretty strong for the bourgeois stomach, for it was composed of three ingredients without which it was not the real dish—social revolution, dictatorship of the proletariat, and a ruling Communist Party. I used this statement of Radek's in all my public lectures on the Soviet planned economy, feeling that he had ably exposed, as I was trying to do, the fraud of those who picked from Sovietism the features that would fit into their program of propaganda for Americans, leaving out all the unpleasant or disturbing features of Sovietism.

I was called on to give many lectures; and for budgetary reasons I accepted many invitations, making it a rule, however, to give about as many free talks as I did paid ones. I did not wish to lay myself open to the charge of profiteering on my field of study.

Sovietism had now become so thoroughly respectable that I was asked to give a series of public lectures for the students of the Social Science Division at the university. The series involved ten lectures, and even my colleagues attended them. I tried to present the subject of "How do you get social revolution, and what is it when you get it?" putting it colloquially. I traced Russian history from 1900 on, in terms of the background and course of the three revolutions of a single generation—those of 1905, of March, 1917, and of October–November, 1917. In this series I concluded with a rather homely comparison, suggesting that social revolution is the cathartic which the doctor advises you not to let your system get to the point of needing.

Our recognition of the Soviet government brought a regular Soviet ambassador and staff to Washington and the opening of the old Russian embassy, the mansion built originally by Pullman and used by Senator Lowden during his term of office. Moscow showed very good judgment in the selection of the representatives sent over. Alexander Troyanovsky was a very happy choice. He was a former Menshevik, but fully loyal to the Bolshevik leadership; son of a former army man, he had been trained as an engineer abroad when, after 1915, he had to go into exile to escape arrest by the tsarist police. Among the members of his staff were two younger men, Nieman and Romm, of unusual intellectual ability and social charm. They were to suffer in the 1937 "purge," although I have never been able to understand why, because during the many hours I talked with them, or sat in while they talked with others, I never detected the slightest indication of disloyalty to the regime they represented. They, like Troyanovsky, were guests at my mother's house on several occasions, or at my brother's place in the country, or up at the family farm in Wisconsin.

The Soviet embassy had a grand formal opening. It was a sumptuous affair; and Washington turned out en masse because it was an "experience," and, also, it was expected that there would be champagne. Champagne was indeed provided, and vodka as well. There were many "casualties" at the reception, limited exclusively to the American side of the fights over the caviar bowls and the champagne bottles. Not a single Russian was guilty, for they had been told that any overindulgence would mean being sent home. Troyanovsky never served vodka to Americans again at any large reception. As he remarked to me, "Americans do not know how to drink."

After a hard academic year of teaching, extra lectures on the campus, and lectures at other institutions, I took two months off to go to the farm in Wisconsin. We had made new arrangements there, having been pretty well bled white by our attempt to run it on a wage basis. So I sold a half-interest in machinery and livestock to the son of a farmer neighbor. This neighbor—a grand man, originally from Denmark—had helped my brother start the farm and then had helped me when this younger brother could not stand the mental strain of the inevitable deficits that all farming had to face in those years. I ran the farm on shares with my new partner. He was an expert mechanic. When his father had given up farming, I had helped the boy to get a job with International Harvester, introducing him personally to Alexander Legge. He could tell Legge's engineers just how the machine did or did not stand up in the field, and why. He was such a good practical tractor-driver that he demonstrated the corn-cultivator of the International "Farmall" at the Century of Progress Exposition.

But he did not like factory work; nor did he enjoy the uncertainty of employment, for, as one of the younger men, he had been employed only a few days a week. He wanted to raise a family and did not want to double up in living quarters with another brother. As he put it to me, he thought he would like to return to farming, going temporarily, so to speak, into cold storage until the depression was over. So I spent July and August helping him clear up buildings, machinery, and fences, which the man who had worked on a wage basis had allowed to break down and go to pieces.

The two months spent on the farm were aimed also to prepare me, physically and mentally, for another study trip to the Soviet Union. This time I decided on a new route via England and by boat from London to Leningrad. In this way, as a Soviet consular official suggested, I would already be in the Soviet system at London Bridge, from which the Soviet liner, the "Sibir," sailed. I bought a ticket from Chicago to Leningrad from the United States Lines and took the first lap on the "Manhattan."

William Phillips was on board, returning to his embassy post in Rome. In our discussion of Professor Dodd's work at the Berlin embassy we analyzed frankly the qualifications of the academic man in foreign office work and concluded that he is, perhaps, the least qualified of all men to serve in a diplomatic post, as the game of diplomacy has come to be played. I believe the subsequent publication of W. E. Dodd's *Diary* supports fully this view, because of the content of this book as well as the very fact of its publication. In all my contacts with the State Department and individual foreign servicemen—our own and those of other countries—I have always refused confidences, lest they "cramp my academic style," to use the phrase current about my position when I was formally connected with the Department. We teachers must talk; it is our stock in trade; and the diplomat just cannot, except with strict observance of the rules of protocol. On one occasion a businessman whom I urged to attend a discussion group at the university remarked, in explaining his refusal to come: "You professors have to talk, a banker sometimes talks, but we manufacturers never talk any more than is absolutely necessary to make a contract and carry it out."

Much of my limited stopover in London was wasted over details of travel, for I had two accidents which were unusual for me. As a hard traveler, I always planned every detail in advance and watched the ball all the time. My family and friends often said that with all my traveling I should have learned to take it more easily. But this time I lost my luggage at Victoria Station and spent a whole day running it down with the help of an embassy courier. It was found in the ladies' restroom, which got around and gave my London friends a grand laugh. More serious was the failure of the London office of the United States Lines to get me the cabin ordered several months before, on the London-Leningrad boat. Almost literally, the steamship agents did what they had told me they would have to do to get me on the boat—namely, murder someone.

The life on board the "Sibir" was, of course, very different from that on an Atlantic liner. Pearl Binder was there, the leftist cartoonist for whom the *Standard* of London some way or other found space on its pages; and Blanche Gurko, with six college girls she was instructing. Then there was Myrtle, an English girl giving private lessons in Moscow, there because of leftist tendencies. Finally, there were several Americans of Russian-Jewish origin who had finally got permission to enter the former "fatherland" as tourists. This six-day trip on the "Sibir" was one of the most interesting of my boat experiences. With Russian vodka and food, and the Lenin Corner for the crew, one was in the spirit both of the old Russia and the new Sovietism. We danced on the deck every night to a gramophone. My stewardess would not dance with me, however, for she explained that she was on probation as a candidate for Party membership and had to be careful with whom she associated, particularly when they were bourgeois.

The three days in Leningrad I spent, in the main, as an out-and-out tourist, going on the conducted trips to museums, factories, hospitals, and schools. I did not advertise my knowledge of Russian, and suppressed a smile when the interpreter would water down the translation of the mottoes or banners dealing with world revolution or with atheism, which appeared everywhere. Many of my former favorite hotels and restaurants were now rather dowdy eating places "for comrades." In the evening, using Blanche Gurko as my excuse, I got her and several of her girls into the State Theatre on the old Nevsky. We walked the Nevsky, and on that first summer night in Leningrad I could see more clearly than in Moscow how the Revolution had brought the proletarians onto the boulevards, where formerly the walkers were the military and the bourgeois. It was interesting, although also a little depressing, to see how the "democratization" had made other centers of former tsarist splendor rather seedy-looking.

On the other hand, on the annual Youth Day, when the young athletes gathered and then marched to the Winter Palace Square and demonstrated their physical prowess, I got the impression of a stronger and healthier younger generation. It was a cold day, and the athletes wore rather scanty shorts and skirts. I managed to get into conversation with several groups as they formed on the side streets leading into the large square. The scene was in sharp contrast to the tragic one I had witnessed on my first visit to old St. Petersburg, when I had seen the massacre of workmen on this same Winter Palace Square on Bloody Sunday of 1905.

At the hotel that evening there was dancing, which was again permitted. In addition to our foreign group, there were many Russians—young and old—engaging in what had formerly been considered a demoralizing bourgeois practice. I realized that there was real meaning in Stalin's recent declaration that "life has become more joyous" in the Soviet Union, remembering 1932, when I had left it facing a hard winter of reduced rations and, in some areas, of famine.

In Moscow there was, at last, an American embassy to which to go for mail and to register my passport against possible loss, for it had been a serious matter to lose one's passport before the re-establishment of diplomatic relations. Bullitt himself was just leaving on a vacation, and I had only a short forty-minute talk with him. But one of the older men in foreign service was at the embassy; we had often talked over the problem of Sovietism in Washington when he had been attached to the Russian Division after field service in the Baltic States. I brought myself up to date with him.

The embassy was lodged in a large new apartment house, overlooking the Kremlin. In addition, there was the ambassador's home, a large "palace" of a former rich merchant, situated in the Arbat quarter, where the intelligentsia of old days had also tended to concentrate. Several older men from the Far East had been brought into the staff, and quite a number of young men; also a marine and a medical attaché, in addition to a military attaché. It was a large and pretentious setup—too much so in the opinion of some of us, who thought it would have been better to take our place in the proletarian capital in a somewhat quieter and more modest way. Plans for a big embassy building on the outskirts of the city were being worked over, and these represented an even more pretentious physical plant.

From the start, I was a bit concerned over the spirit I found. Except with my old friend, I seldom talked shop—that is, about the functioning of the Soviet system—with people at the embassy; they were uninformed and therefore not particularly interested. Perhaps I bored them, for they certainly bored me; and I found that I was doing what I did before we had an embassy, going to the Germans or British or Poles to get the point of view of those responsible for official relations with the Soviets. It seemed to me that the tone of the American group, as set by its leader, was too frivolous and even flippant, in view of the special and difficult conditions under which, at long last, from the Moscow viewpoint, we had returned. Of course, it was a difficult job to get settled and establish contacts—living conditions were hard and Soviet officials not always too courteous. My viewpoint about our embassy may have been too austere, for, after all, Russia was cheering up.

Later I made the mistake of giving to a high official of the State Department my impressions of the American embassy at Moscow, which cost me several acquaintances and an exchange of nasty letters with Bullitt himself. Perhaps I should be glad that there have been so few such instances in my long relations with the Department of State. The role of a friendly adviser is a thankless and a dangerous one, but I have been induced to continue my efforts to play it properly because of the sincere thanks which I have had from time to time for having contributed to a somewhat better understanding or for having helped in ironing out a particularly troublesome wrinkle in the development of American and Russian relations.

This trip I stayed on for the biggest holidays of the revolutionary calendar—the anniversary of the Revolution—lasting from the sixth of November to the eighth. There was a gala performance at the opera. Then, on November 7, the military and the civilians paraded on the Red Square, reviewed by all the leaders from the rostrum of Lenin's Tomb. It was a well organized and impressive show. Journalists and students like myself were assigned to a section of the reviewing stands provided for the diplomatic corps. An old and also new figure in the group of journalists was Hubert Knickerbocker. I had met him for the first time in Moscow in 1926. He had been back in 1931 and had come on for another survey. As we watched the Soviet leaders at the Lenin Tomb, he remarked that they certainly looked like an ordinary bunch. Irritated by the tone as well as the content of his remark, I retorted that he should study their faces, not their caps and simple dress, and compare the faces with those we saw under silk hats on similar occasions in the West. Knickerbocker had become eminently successful and was less interested in the man in the street or the youth than he was when I saw him studying the Nazi youth in Berlin two years earlier. He had a key question on this trip which he put to all of us. It ran: "Are the workmen here as well off as they are in America?" I told him I thought that it was a rather meaningless question and that in each country or in each of the systems crystallizing in the world, including American New Deal capitalism, the question should be whether the workmen of any given country or system were better or worse off than they were before the "experiment" being tried on them.

Life was, in reality, more joyous that autumn. There were many parties in Moscow—some quite gay. The biggest party was the one given at the Kremlin on the night of the anniversary of the Revolution. It was in the famous St. George Hall, one of the largest ballrooms in Europe. We were told to come in business clothes, and only the Japanese wore dinner coats. In addition to diplomats, journalists, and a few students, leading artists of drama and music were there. Most of the Soviet leaders, except Stalin, came, some staying on until daylight. We danced and ate and drank. After dancing with wives of diplomats and correspondents, I went for the Russian artists, and even had a dance with the most famous ballerina of the moment, Semenova. A group of us decided to concentrate on Kalinin and Budenny, who were the most social and human of the Soviet leaders—at least toward us bourgeois. But it is a task, as I had often noted, to keep up with a Russian in drinking and eating; and several of our group were in worse condition than the convivial Russians when the party finally broke up.

The sunrise over the Kremlin was a marvelous sight as we drove home. This was the first party of the kind given in revolutionary Moscow. The following year the sheep were divided from the goats: the diplomats were entertained one evening, and the journalists the next. Some of the newspapermen refused to go when it was the "second table" for them. The Soviet protocol chief expressed surprise that people asked for invitations to parties in which they were not included; and this made the group of newspapermen, the "special correspondents," even angrier.

I was pleased one day to run into Vincent Bendix, whom I had met socially one evening at a North Side party in Chicago and to whom I had taken a liking. For he was, as I have told him, such a direct and blunt person, making no bones about his forceful actions. That he had come to America as an immigrant with socialist views and affiliations seemed hard to believe when he explained in utter frankness how he handled this or that problem of management. He was in Moscow to sell more of his valuable automotive equipment to the Soviets, and the Russians wanted to buy. Bendix did things on a grand scale; he used good American salesmanship methods, despite my efforts to keep him a little modest; and, like the new American embassy, he was ostentatious. He bought old tsarist plate and silver and church robings by the hundreds of dollars—perhaps thousands, for I lost track as I helped him make the selections. Part of his technique was to give a grand dinner to commissars, engineers, and high officers in the armed forces (officially, the titles "marshalls" and "generals" had not been reintroduced at that date). At the dinner I sat between two army men, who were subsequently shot, and opposite two "economic workers," who were also caught in the purge three years later. I had warned Bendix against serving French champagne; but it flowed like water, and until five in the morning. There were gipsy singers, and later dancing partners. In a word, it was like the old carousals of the Moscow merchants, in some of which I had participated.

Often in my free time I attended the theater to get some literary, as opposed to political, Russian language. At one theater young actors and actresses from the provinces, and even from collective farms, were being trained by leading Moscow artists. I got interesting side lights on provincial and village conditions as I lunched with them. Quite a number came to my room for supper occasionally and stayed on for long general gossipy talks. I must admit that these evenings often turned out to be boresome, for it did not take long to cover the horizon of these first products of the rather artificial Communist training of the Soviet schools of the first years. In the early period propaganda reigned supreme on these occasions. My wardrobe had to be carefully guarded, for, in line with the more cheerful life that Stalin had announced, some of the young men wanted to buy my neckties or my hat. A young agricultural expert looked at himself in my mirror with my hat on for a long time.

My trip to the country in 1934 was a short but interesting one. I could no longer start off on my own and drift along; it was impossible to get railway tickets except through the Intourist, and at the small towns where I used to leave the train I could not find that relic of the old order in the person of kulak cabdriver, with whom I could arrange to drive out to villages. In the villages there were no kulaks who would drive me to the next village. To go on an escorted tour did not appeal to me. Instead, I accepted the proposal to see me through that came from the son of an old friend—in fact, the son of the tutor who had given me Russian lessons in Moscow in 1904.

Igor, who thus came to my rescue, was a man of thirty-five, an engineer, on leave from a responsible position in an industry in Central Asia, with loads of rubles on his hands from a prize earned by the invention of a special process for rope manufacturing. Igor was the type of Russian that prevails in novels: reckless, imaginative, honest, and fascinating. His father told me that he had always been that kind—with a "Russian soul" in the full sense of the word. Because of his recklessness in general, I had no compunctions about letting him run the risk which his proposal entailed. He used a newspaper card which he had (for he also wrote—excellent fiction as well as reports) to get our tickets and hotel rooms, and his charm to get a horse to drive us out from the small town to which we went. He sat in on my interviews, keeping silent for the most part. He also picked up chance acquaintances and then brought them to his "American comrade." We went to a small town I had visited in 1926 with Maurice Hindus, and slipped out to the countryside without delay, remaining for a day.

Returning to the town, we found the "authorities" looking for us to give the visiting American proper courtesies and attention. We called immediately on the highest authority, the secretary of the Communist Party committee, who proved to be a real person. I told him frankly that I wanted to go on my own, with my friend, without official chaperonage; and he thought it was a good idea. From this man I had the clearest statement of the role of the Party and of his own role as the local Party secretary, with no concealment of the positive leadership which the Party assumed. Later my friend Igor expressed the wish that the

213

Party leaders under whom he had worked as a "specialist" had been as intelligent and informed as this particular member. Without official document we went into schools, banks, and stores, Igor introducing me always as a "well-known American professor, whose books on Sovietism have been reviewed in *Izvestia*"; that was our formula, and it worked beautifully.

The lodging and food in this small provincial town were pretty bad: plenty of bedbugs and the meat distinctly putrid. But the town was big enough to have a *torgsin* store, where one could get good food for gold or foreign exchange; and we stocked up and had pickup meals in our room with the samovar which was always available. On the return train trip we organized a regular picnic in the car and made many friends among the passengers.

The villages we visited were not well run. The Party secretary upbraided us for having gone to these particular ones, for, he explained, he could have taken us to some which were infinitely better organized and run. The peasants here were accepting collectivized agriculture as inevitable. We saw several "individual peasants" still holding out against the collectives (kolkhoz); and their stories served to convince me that this group would not survive long, that collectivized agriculture would ultimately and soon engulf them. For, hard as was the lot of the peasant in the poorly managed kolkhoz, the lot of the "individual peasant" was even harder—deliberately made so by legislation and administrative practices. From many others—the old servants of old friends and dramatic artists who had been down in the country on vacation—I got the same spotted picture, of bad as well as good kolkhoz.

One small town that I revisited after some eight years showed comparatively slight progress. Some Moscow leaders who scolded me for going to such a backward place insisted it was exceptionally slow in getting into the new order because it was primarily a trade center in the past, with no important industry and therefore no proletariat to supply leadership. The policy of promoting local industry more actively by using local raw materials had not moved very far from a "paper" project. The school and its work were not bad. A local church was still functioning. The old earth wall, built against the Tatar invasion, was covered with children at play in the late afternoon as we also climbed it, to get the view and the breeze. The stores were not so well stocked as the Moscow stores, and in 1934 that meant they were pretty poorly stocked. There was no "Park of Culture and Rest," for the town was too small and backward for this new institution. As in 1926, I left the dreary place without much regret.

I was impressed by the current attitude of my old pre-Bolshevik friends. One of my closest friends, who had suffered in every way, including a term of prison and of exile to Siberia, kept complaining that he and his co-workers could have accomplished so much more than they did under their liberal program if they had only had such an awakened peasantry with which to deal. One day he suggested that I compare the corner policeman, called "workman-peasant militiaman," with the óld *gorodovoy* and note the cultural advance. I did this, pretending to have lost my way, and had a long and interesting conversation. I followed this suggestion up by dropping in at a police or militia station, knocking first at a door marked "Party Committee." This was, as I knew, the right procedure; and with the Party supervisor I went over the station, into the cells, and sat at the "sergeant's desk" while cases were brought in. This Party leader gave me a very clear idea of the role of the Party in a very homely and forceful phrase. I had been questioning him on the subject in a rather indirect way, and he showed a little impatience that I was not fully aware of the position of the Party, even in a militia station. His phrase was: "Why there is the odor of the Party everywhere and in everything." The Russian word "odor" can mean a pleasant or an unpleasant one, and was well chosen, for the supporter or the critic could use the same word to represent his view.

My emphasis on the role of the Party in all conversations aimed to get a more human approach to the subject on which I was working—the position of the Party in the Soviet system. This topic had to run through an analysis of the Soviet government which I had contracted to write as one of a series on European governments. My old friends asked me whether I was going to describe the G.P.U. And then our discussion turned to the question of how much weight, how many pages, should be given to this tried institution of the secret, political police. Such discussions on a generalized basis with former bourgeois who knew the G.P.U. from personal experience were more illuminating than the discussions with diplomats or newspapermen who had collected and kept repeating all the stories they had heard about specific cases of arrest, treatment, forced confession, and such practices.

There was one Bolshevik family in Moscow which I visited very often. The father was an "economic worker" and a trouble shooter for the Party. The wife taught in the Moscow University. The young daughter of twelve, Sonya, was an ardent member of the Pioneers, the children's organization of the Party. One evening, while we were discussing Soviet-American trade relations, the young girl spoke up and asked her father why they had any dealings with the "bourgeois." Later on, the father was questioning me about the family farm in Wisconsin; and, to give him a full picture, I told of the number of cows, horses, hogs, and so forth on this 160-acre dairy enterprise. Sonya was listening in and kept rather quiet, I observed. The next morning the father telephoned me that I had ruined myself with the girl, for at breakfast she had remarked: "I cannot like that American uncle any more, for he is a kulak." At a later supper she had relented, gave me a little hog, cut from Ural stone, and said: "This is for your collective farm in America."

Shortly before my departure, a cable from the Harris Institute of the University of Chicago informed me that the subject for the 1935 institute was to be "The Soviet Union and World Affairs." I was authorized to arrange for several guest lecturers to come on from Moscow. The Soviet ambassador at Washington, Troyanovsky, was in Moscow on vacation and also on an official errand, and he agreed to help me. The invitations were to be given through the Society of Cultural Relations, but the problem was to decide to whom the invitation should go. I refused to give a blanket invitation, leaving it to Moscow to select the persons to be sent. Of possible lecturers and also worth while ones from our viewpoint, I thought of Karl Radek. First I had to get assurance that the State Department would let the embassy give him the visa, for he had been on an executive committee of the Communist International. All such officials, as a matter of policy, were refused a visa to enter the United States before resumption of formal relations.

☭ ☭ ☭

CHAPTER XXVI

1935: DIPLOMATIC INCIDENTS IN A UNIVERSITY

By 1935 THE SOVIET GOVERNMENT HAD BEEN RECOGNIZED BY THE United States government, invited and welcomed into the League of Nations, and supported by France in its effort to bring about an "Eastern Locarno." The selection of Soviet relations to world affairs as the topic for the 1935 session of the Harris Institute of the University of Chicago was a natural one. As soon as I returned to Chicago from Moscow, I set about to work out the arrangements. The chairman of the committee, Quincy Wright, had always handled the annual sessions; but I decided that I had to be acting chairman, and after several amusing incidents I convinced him that my election to that position really meant that I was in charge of it.

Knowing that, in all probability, Moscow could not come across with any definite list of guest speakers available on our invitation, I arranged with the Soviet ambassador for him and his staff to carry the load if necessary. Anyone coming from Moscow would be official; and, as Troyanovsky had just returned from Moscow, he was therefore practically the same as an *ad hoc* lecturer. I set a date at which I would call on Troyanovsky to come through with his guaranty if Moscow did not answer in a positive sense. I sent a cable of inquiry to Moscow every few weeks, but just before the dead line an "incident" occurred which forced an immediate decision in the matter.

The incident had several aspects. A student organization arranging a series of lectures on public affairs had gone to my younger colleague, Frederick L. Schuman, for suggestions. Schuman had written his Doctor's dissertation on American-Soviet relations, publishing it with the International Publishers. The Hearst papers had been riding Schuman very hard for some of his public statements, probably misquoting, or at least misinterpreting, his remarks.

Now Schuman, with these interests and tendencies, recommended to the student organization that it ask Troyanovsky to lecture on Soviet foreign policy. Schuman, as a member of the Harris Institute, knew that this was to be the subject of the coming session in the early summer and also that it was for May that the lecture organized by the student body was set. Troyanovsky agreed to give this lecture. It was not, I believe, a deliberate effort on Schuman's part to sabotage the Institute; he simply did not think of the Institute, but only of his own work. This absence of any real sense of co-operation with colleagues has unfortunately become very widespread in academic circles. The tendency to work one's own little racket has spread even among the so-called "communities of scholars."

The conflict between the student organization and the Harris Institute to be held a few months later was not very serious. But another kind of conflict soon developed with respect to this lecture, produced by the "Walgreen Incident" over alleged teaching of Communism at the University. Mr. Walgreen was president of the chain drugstore company bearing his name and had a niece attending lectures at Chicago. As a result of newspaper publicity over his protest, a formal investigation of the University was undertaken by the state legislature. I believe that Walgreen quickly realized that he had been made use of by "Colonel" Watson, the publisher of Chicago's Hearst paper. The Chicago newspaper world was graced with three "Colonels"—McCormick, Knox, and Watson—and at this time Watson was perhaps the most militant of them all. So here were the students arranging a Troyanovsky lecture on the campus just when the investigation by the state senators was going on Down Town! It was suggested to me that I rush to Washington and diplomatically arrange for Troyanovsky to find some excuse—sore throat or pressing engagement—for withdrawing his acceptance. This I refused to do, for, as I explained, it involved a stultification of the University to which I could not be a party.

However, within a few hours after I refused to listen to the above suggestion, I submitted a telegram, signed by me, as acting chairman of the Harris Institute, to be sent to Troyanovsky. In view of the fact that no positive answer had come from Moscow concerning a guest lecturer for the Harris Institute, the message ran, the Institute wished to invite

Troyanovsky to be the principal speaker, the student organization having generously agreed to release him from his earlier commitment in order to allow for this arrangement. The University authorities complimented me, as a real diplomat as well as a student of diplomacy, and the investigation was not given what might have been a rather embarrassing turn by the appearance of an out-and-out Bolshevik on a university platform right in the middle of its progress.

The senators gave the university a clean bill of health. Walgreen accepted the situation in a most generous way—by a large gift of money for the establishment of the Walgreen Foundation for the Study of American Institutions.

I had some fear that "Colonel" Watson would break forth again when the Harris Institute meetings opened at the end of July. We had invited quite a number of Down Town men, as was the usual procedure; but everybody seemed to be leaving town that Monday evening, including President Hutchins. Several businessmen told me they were afraid of what the Hearst papers would say about their attending a dinner for a Moscow Bolshevik. Even the donors of the Harris family had to be out of town that day. And some of my colleagues, as, for example, Charles E. Merriam, found they could not come, although I frankly asked them if they wouldn't be ashamed to look at themselves in the mirror the next morning.

In order to soften, if possible, the blow that I felt Colonel Watson was poised to deliver, I put pressure on Vincent Bendix to be at the Englewood Station to greet the Soviet ambassador on his arrival. The real pressure to which Bendix responded came no doubt from the very large orders which the Soviet purchasing agencies were giving him. The photographers from the Hearst papers snapped Troyanovsky standing with Bendix. Bendix was a close friend of Watson's and apparently was not afraid of him or of any "personal" items the Hearst papers might run.

The rest of that first morning the ambassador and I went over his speech, which he was to give for the opening of the Institute that evening. We argued over only one point of detail. He used the phrase "our democracy" and did not wish to qualify it more specifically as "our Soviet form of democracy." The speech advocated that "good-neighborliness" was the basis of the Soviet policy.

The Institute session passed off well. There was real discussion by the experts assembled, including several White Russians. The Soviet representatives were most communicative, excellent debaters, and fully co-operative. As I later went over the stenographic report of the discussion, I was impressed by the fact that the Russian Marxists and the American engineers were much more concrete than the American "intellectuals" who had made up the majority of the group. There was one "Soviet product"—an economist from the Amtorg (the Soviet semi-official purchasing agency in America). A bit uncouth but very keen intellectually, this young man gave to the proceedings a touch of the basic, mass character of the Soviet system. Limited to some two hundred persons, these discussions were, I believe, of considerable value, for they showed to what extent there could be co-operation, or in any case co-ordination of parallel action, between the Soviet sixth of the world and the other "bourgeois" five-sixths. Fundamental features of Sovietism as a form of government were made to stand out clearly in the give-and-take of real discussion.

It took me most of the summer to prepare the lectures of the Institute for publication, to get out the stenographic report of the round-table discussions, and to recover from the strain of trying to organize a serious study of "Sovietism in World Affairs" in an atmosphere of suspicion and basic antagonism toward all things Soviet. The signing of an American-Soviet trade pact in August tended to rehabilitate Sovietism in the minds of many, for it would seem that mutually beneficial trade relations, at least, could be had with these Bolsheviks, who, by the way, proved to be very able and keen traders.

There had really been a "diplomatic revolution" during the period 1933–35, with American recognition of the Soviet government, Soviet entry into the League of Nations, and pacts of mutual assistance between the Soviets and France and Czechoslovakia. What amounted to loans were being extended to the Soviet government—guaranties of credit by Germany, Britain, and other countries. The able Soviet Commissar of Foreign Affairs, Litvinov, was attending conferences, his speeches always getting attention, largely because he had something to say and said it in a forthright and forceful manner. Communists were working within popular-front movements, in France and Spain, giving strength to these forms of European "new dealism."

Then came the Congress of the Communist International in August, 1935, with its official adoption of the changed policy in favor of supporting popular-front movements and programs of collective security. American Communists were present and spoke. Our government saw in the very calling of the congress a violation of the agreement reached between the President and Litvinov and made most formal protest. European governments gave little attention to the congress, and those which felt that some protest was called for, for the record, protested very informally. We shook our fists, as one writer put it, and then our little finger, for we apparently realized that our first reaction had been a bit premature, and certainly immature.

The incident did not lead to any permanent breach, but it added to the mutual distrust that had been developing between Washington and Moscow. The really serious result was the strengthening of those conservative and reactionary elements in Europe which were fighting not only popular-front movements, as was to be expected, but also collective-security programs. For me personally, the incident meant trouble, for again, as so often before, I had to hear how unreliable and untrust-worthy were the Bolsheviks. My attitude at the time did not make my position any easier, for I seemed to be siding with the Bolsheviks against my own government. As so often in the course of my Russian studies, I had to withdraw into my academic shell for a while. That Christmas of 1935 I did not even attend the meetings of the Historical or of the Political Science Associations.

⚓ ⚓ ⚓

CHAPTER XXVII

1936: THE YEAR OF THE CONSTITUTION

THE EXCITEMENT OVER THE CONGRESS OF THE COMMUNIST INTERNA-tional gradually died down. The fuss raised by Bullitt and the President did its bit to help on the general anti-Soviet crusade of the next years. On the other hand, with the increasing tension in Europe over Italy's war with Ethiopia and in the Far East over Japanese aggression, the positive and constructive role for peace of the Soviet Union was grad-ually being recognized, especially in Great Britain. In France and Po-land internal politics prevented clearness of vision respecting the strength of the Soviet Union and the part it could play against aggres-sors. To emphasize its constructive role, though this was not its primary purpose, came the announcement in June, 1936, of a new Soviet con-stitution. More than a year earlier there had been the promise of a more democratic system of elections; but what was decided on was even more extensive in scope—the new constitution. This document reg-istered the achievements of the Revolution as claimed by the Bolshevik leaders, and furnished a somewhat modified framework within which the Revolution was to work toward its ultimate goal of Communism. The leaders announced that socialism had been "in the main" estab-lished. In the outside world, the new constitution was expected to make the Soviet Union a more acceptable partner in the program of collec-tive security which many were trying to save from the machinations of the Chamberlains, Halifaxes, and Hoares in England and of the Lavals, Daladiers, and Bonnets in France.

This project of a new constitution did contribute to the general standing of the Soviets. It also meant for me that the time had come at last to finish the textbook on the Soviet government for which I had signed a contract. I decided to hold up the publication of this textbook until after the formal adoption of the new constitution by the Soviet Constitutional Convention, to attend which I arranged my 1936 study trip; but I prepared the material for the Source Book, to accompany the text. The first document I gave was the "Program of the Communist Party of 1918," and one of the last was to be the new constitution; thus we could, by comparison, determine the extent to which the constitution did, in fact, register the carrying-out of the program of the Revolution. The proofs for the Source Book were to be sent to me, for correction, in Moscow. I arranged to have them sent through the Soviet embassy in Washington, as well as through the open mail, to insure their arrival. It was also a "political" move on my part to have the material seen in advance by the Soviet censorship.

The effect of the new constitution on opinion abroad was, as I have noted, very much to the advantage of the Soviets. At the Harris Institute meeting in 1936, devoted to discussing "neutrality," the members from abroad questioned me eagerly as to the significance of the move.

It was at this meeting that one of the guests from Geneva gave me a very interesting estimate of the role of the Soviet Union delegation to the League of Nations. Because of the trend to suspect the Bolsheviks, I asked Sir Alfred Zimmern, the Oxford authority on the League, if they had behaved well. After a moment's thought, the answer came: "Yes, like the new member of a club, asking always about the rules of the club, when some of the older members were wanting to forget the rules they themselves had made." Unfortunately, the supporters of the League were toadying to the politicians, who, in turn, were deliberately undermining the League. They would not rally to the Soviet stand; and the Soviets time and time again stood up for the League as "a block in the road to war," as Stalin phrased it in his interview with Walter Duranty in 1934. The League went into compromise after compromise. Hoare's speech in September, 1935, promising full and wholehearted support from England to the steadying influence of the League, deceived all of us. That it was intended to deceive is indicated by Hoare's miserable deal with the French shortly after to appease Italy with a part of Ethiopia— so miserable, in fact, that British public opinion boiled up and Hoare lost his portfolio.

The stand taken by the Soviets at Geneva rapidly gave concrete content to the Soviet claim that its system provided the best protection to small states. For the latter clearly were looking to Moscow for leadership in the program of collective security, if not in their internal social-economic structure. So evident was this that, when the British government decided to appease Mussolini by ejecting Ethiopia from the League, Litvinov was asked by the British delegates to take the initiative in the move—in the interests of peace, of course. It is probable that Litvinov's refusal was couched in even more caustic terms than were his public speeches from the tribune of the League. One may well ask whether the Soviet policy might not have been more effective had Litvinov let pass the opportunities offered to show up the British and

French policies. He would not compromise, however, even in respect to language; and by his directness he irritated the protocol-bound British or French politician without effectively exposing the devious methods and subterfuges to which those "democratic" representatives constantly resorted. In the eyes of many he made these politicians "martyrs" for the cause of peace.

After the rise of Soviet stock with the publication of the constitutional project, there came a sharp decline, when in August the first of the Moscow treason trials took place. Those directly involved were the two former leaders, Zinoviev and Kamenev; and Trotsky was indirectly brought in under the charges made against the accused. Trotsky I have already characterized as the "prima donna" of the Revolution. Zinoviev's character was expressed in his very words—for he did the mud-slinging with the vocabulary of the gutter. Kamenev had impressed me as really not a "revolutionary," being too timid and formulative. He was a "liberal" or "radical" rather than a "revolutionary," as Lenin or Trotsky understood and used the term. Trotsky, Zinoviev, and Kamenev were the three leaders for whom I had not been able to eliminate a personal feeling of resentment and even hatred. Lenin and Stalin had never aroused in my "bourgeois soul" the bitter anger that these three did, and I found that many of my old Russian friends who had really suffered at the hands of the Bolsheviks felt very much as I did.

In my travels to Russia in the fall of 1936 I found in Berlin that everything was "anti-Communist." Hitler in his annual speech to the 1936 Nazi conference had suggested that the possession of the Ukraine and the Urals would guarantee a happy and prosperous life for Nazidom. Moscow was restrained but bitter in its comments. Soviet newspapers were no longer allowed to come into Germany. None of my friends among the experts on Soviet affairs dared to call his soul his own. I was relieved to get out of the place.

It was in a rather worried state of mind that I journeyed on to Moscow. The battle of words between naziism and Sovietism was in full swing; and, although it seemed clear that it was still only a "verbal" conflict, the atmosphere was threatening. The stopover in Berlin had made me "more interesting" to people in Moscow, as Troyanovsky had suggested; and I did not hesitate to give expression to my concern over the developments I had found in Hitlerism, since I had lived under it for a while in 1934. With my German friends in Moscow I felt a certain restraint. The welcome at the German embassy was markedly less cordial than before. The older friends there tipped me off with respect to the new men—Nazi chaperons or spies—who had been planted on them. I went to a lunch at the German embassy but left with a secretary of the American embassy in order not to be there alone with only Germans. At official receptions I tended to avoid the Germans, even before

222

the announcement of the Anti-Communist Pact in November, which proved to be a first step to the axis that Hitler later maneuvered.

I went to the United States embassy often on this trip, to talk things over with the chargé d'affaires and other secretaries. With the former I had been more or less in agreement in the interpretation of the Soviet system in Washington before the "recognition." Preparations for the arrival of a new ambassador, Mr. Davies, were going on. A summary of the three years of American-Soviet relations was being prepared for him, to give him a full background for his new responsibilities. I was interested in this and was allowed to suggest points to be emphasized. As was the rule, such a document as the one being prepared was not shown to me, because of its confidential, diplomatic character. On the other hand, reports on features of the Soviet system, economic or political, consisting in the bringing-together and interpreting of published facts, were given to me to read and even to make notes on; and this was of real service in our discussions, for the man on the spot would have a somewhat different focus from that which my studies in Chicago had brought out. It was such constructive discussions with local Americans that I played for, rather than the complaining sessions into which social evenings in the foreign colony usually degenerated.

With the picture of well-drilled Germany in mind, the still slovenly appearance of a Russian-Soviet street crowd impressed me strongly as I wandered about Moscow. The bad early autumn weather contributed to this appearance. Under the influence of the talk in western Europe, I kept wondering how these people would stand up in the event of a drive against them by their two very efficient neighbors to the west and to the east.

In my first talks with Soviet officials I became aware of their concern over policy, or rather lack of policy, in London at the Committee on Nonintervention. Their disappointment in the British and French leadership with respect to the Spanish situation was frankly expressed. Moscow regarded the concrete activity of both Germany and Italy in Spain as just one more aggressive seizure, this time of a European country, by naziism and fascism. Moscow felt forced to counter it. The blindness of the British and French to the real aims of Hitler, the spread of aggression, and the sacrifice of imperial interests to narrow class interests on the part of the British statesmen were the points emphasized. A sincere desire to co-operate with others for the preservation of peace was clearly present in the minds of all the Soviet leaders with whom I talked. There was no suggestion of the possibilities of revolution of a Bolshevik type in any part of the world—and silence on this point in the Soviet press was noteworthy, confirming the dominance of the peace note in the Soviet foreign policy.

The Soviet policy had a solid basis in the need of peace to round out the new social structure which was believed to have been at long last established. While boasting that they had "in the main" attained social-ism, the Soviet leaders recognized that much effort was still necessary to make the system function really effectively and produce the promised abundance, thus giving finally the fruits of social revolution.

The continued mobilization of national income for industrial expan-sion, and at the same time the continued marked shortage of consum-ers' goods—despite a very considerable increase in the production of these—have to be related to the programs of armament and reserve war stocks. For in their usual realistic way the Bolsheviks increased the size and equipment of their army, first, to meet the corresponding program of neighbors and, secondly, to make up for the weakness of the pro-grams of collective security and of the League of Nations. While still adhering to these latter programs, often more positively and consistently than the Western democracies, the Soviet Union was relying for its de-fense mainly on its own resources.

Although confessedly not an expert on military affairs, when I re-turned to America I expressed my layman's judgment that the Soviet army was technically well equipped; on the question of its morale, which falls within the scope of my field, I had no hesitancy in characterizing it as unusually good. The army was the favorite but not the spoiled child of authorities and people, and it naturally stood out in the setting of the new Soviet patriotism that had been promoted and, it would seem, se-cured.

If one means by "nationalism" "love of country and an active pa-triotism," then one had it developing in the Soviet Union in a constantly stronger and broader sense. The term also had an economic content in line with the revolutionary doctrine—it was love of the giants of indus-try that had been built at such terrific cost, supplementing those seized from the capitalists, or love of the collective farms which held the land in perpetuity and for toiling peasants. To strengthen this, two changes in policy in the cultural front were made. The first was an emphasis on the Russian people, and their contributions to culture through leaders like Pushkin, Tchaikovsky, Menshnikov, and Lenin. The second was further emphasis on the cultural life and achievements of the national minorities, expressing itself, for example, in the Olympiad of "home talent" in art, especially in music and dancing. There was thus recog-nition of the position of the national minorities in the Union by the Russian majority, and concessions to the former, as, for example, the amendment to the proposed constitution by which the Council of Na-tionalities was to be elected directly by the national units, with a dispro-portionate representation of the minority nationalities.

Soviet patriotism had, and may still have, in it an element of the de-sire eventually to carry the blessings of socialism to other peoples. The status of equality given to the national minorities has a propaganda value abroad as well as at home; and if ever the competition between the

Soviet and non-Soviet worlds becomes active, this factor will be of great importance. For the moment, however, this feature of Sovietism was in the background. Sovietism was preoccupied with the big task it had on hand of cultivating properly its own very large garden. It was interesting, even if there was the deliberate propaganda aim in mind, that the first speech at the Constitutional Congress, after Stalin's report on the new constitution, was by the head of the Ukranian Soviets. Reviewing the history of the Ukraine under the tsars, Kerensky, the temporary German occupation in 1918, and the Soviets, he outlined what the Soviets had given to the workmen and peasants of the Ukraine, and answered Hitler's constant reference to the Ukraine by quoting the current Ukrainian saying: "As a pig never sees the sky, so Hitler will never see our garden."

An economic analysis of the Soviet organization of production had begun to be possible at last. While such a study revealed many shortcomings—perhaps more than the Soviet leaders themselves advertised in their constant efforts to overcome them—it did show marked progress. The Soviet leaders emphasized that their labor productivity was still much lower than that prevailing in Western countries and that management was still very bureaucratic and inefficient, in that quality was often sacrificed in the drive for volume records. Campaign methods were still used to secure production, but they were increasingly more economic and less political in character.

The year 1936 was officially named the "Stakhanov Year." I suppose the Stakhanov movement was nothing more than what we know as the piecework system of pay, personalized strongly by Stakhanov, the worker who "made the record," who set the pace. It certainly had some spontaneous character which showed the development of the new attitude toward work on which the Soviet system had counted to bring its productivity to higher and higher levels. It represented a real advance in attitude toward work over that of the old Russia. In looking back over the years of 1930, 1932, and 1934 it occurs to me that the Stakhanov movement was a good example of the Soviet technique of using education and training of the people, coupled with, first, compulsion, then persuasion, and achieving, finally, individual adoption.

This year showed marked advance in the operation of collective agriculture. The management was better because a considerable degree of self-government had developed within the framework of the collectivization imposed from above; real co-operation appeared. The organization within the unit by brigades eliminated the "depersonalization" of work. The introduction of a piecework system of payment proved an effective incentive to work. The granting of a limited amount of personal property rights to the individual households within the collectivized farm unit was another device for promoting individual interest, in conjunction always with the social interest of the larger group. An improvement of methods in agriculture had been effected, and a marked cultural advance had also come—both made possible by the new collectivized organization of the peasantry.

The school reforms, started in 1931 and extended in 1933, had entered organically into the structure and curricula of educational institutions. More discipline of a constructive character, more emphasis on individual work and attainment, better grounding in the basic subjects of general education, a more reasonable approach to political training for children and young people, "Communist training" with less sheer indoctrination—these were the current outstanding features of the Soviet schools as compared with the period of experimentation during the first years of the Revolution.

The Pioneer movement, the Communist movement among children, had been subordinated to the educational authorities and at the same time made more educational. I visited pioneer homes in several places. In a very constructive and efficient way these pioneer homes helped the more active and bright children develop their individual tastes and talents. The laboratories for physics, chemistry, and botany, or the studies for art and literature available in these pioneer homes, supplied equipment which the individual schools could not afford.

The Soviet stage was now "educational," in a real sense, being considerably less propagandist. The same was true of the movies and the radio. The newspapers and journals now supplied more interesting reading, in the pictures of everyday life—even of individuals—to which more and more space was being given. Science continued to be, in a sense, worshiped and to be actively encouraged and promoted in every possible way. The simple laboratories found on all the larger and better collective farms had contributed to the rise in agrotechny.

While freedom of criticism had increased with the development of discussion in all fields, discussion was required to keep within the established framework of the new socialist order. In the fields of the social sciences, the tenets of Marxism, as officially interpreted, ruled. In the writing of history, more freedom in the presentation of facts had come; and the positive contributions of the great leaders of the past, apart from revolutionary activity, were being recognized. In the fields of literature, the narrow approach of previous years had been abandoned.

The pronouncement of Stalin, "Life has become easier and more cheerful," was one of the slogans of the year. It was related to the rise in the supply of the cultural, as well as material, services and was particularly true of the cultural. If in the lines that still formed at streetcar stops or at shops this slogan was repeated with a note of irony, it nevertheless was, in the main, true. The comparative was used, it should be noted; and life was much easier, if not yet easy, and for many it had a larger element of cheer than it had two years or four years before, at the

226

end of the first Five-Year Plan, with its terrific driving and constant pressure. And even those who never were and never will be reconciled to the Soviet system—many among the intellectuals, the older peasants, and even some in the workman class, representing then perhaps 10 per cent of the population—would admit the material progress for larger and larger groups and the cultural progress in, and cultural opportunities for, all groups.

On my return through Warsaw, I found that my academic friends were buckling under Colonel Beck's regime, in part to hold their jobs, their explanation being that national security required it. Apparently, those who had been urging reforms had abandoned their efforts, in the interest of national unity. They admitted the gross mishandling of an incipient peasant political awakening; the President, unprepared for a demand from the peasants for real elections, ran away from a meeting. But, again, "national unity" was the important thing, for they saw clearly the threat of Hitler's policy, as it was developing. But all seemed to be more afraid of Sovietism than of naziism, and I gave up trying to present my view of the progress being made by the Russians under the Soviet system. Poles always resented anybody's pretending to know anything about Russia, for they wanted the world to accept their Polish interpretation of Russia as well as of Bolshevism. The prevalence of fear of the Soviet Union, rather than of Germany, was indicated by the recently signed Polish-Romanian mutual-assistance pact, which was specifically directed against the Soviet Union.

Talks with Polish officials, particularly of the foreign office, had to be less frank than those with university men, although it was with officials handling relations with the Soviet Union that I talked. They let me give my views, looked at me with a mixture of pity and contempt, put in a few demurrers to my interpretations, and we passed to another topic. I have understood the reasons for the arrogance of so many Poles; it was developed to maintain Polish nationalism during the century or more of "foreign domination." But this arrogance often irritated me and also seemed to me politically inexpedient in view of Poland's position, despite its re-established independence.

In Prague, my friends S. N. Prokopovich and his wife Guskova were now ready to admit the progress of the Soviet's planned economy. Were these *spetsy* of the first planning commission removed as "unconscious *saboteurs*" because of insistence on theories and dogmas of bureaucratic control, while Stalin saw that the need was to get production? Prokopovich himself made this suggestion to me. Paul Milyukov happened to be in Prague, and we sent word to him to join us. These three Russians were not so sure as I was that the new constitution had the promise of less political rigidity in the Soviet system; and they were more right than I, I must admit, though perhaps they would lean toward my more optimistic view in the light of what actually came when the country became involved in total war and the Soviet system helped to make it a successful "people's war." Nor would these Russians go as far as I did in seeing actual conspiracy in the first of the treason trials of the purge— that of August, 1936, of Zinoviev and Kamenev. Perhaps, again, they would now see conspiracy and treason in the activities of the "oppositionary elements" in the light of developments since 1936.

My old friend and teacher, President Masaryk, had died. It was, therefore, to the new president, Beneš, that I went, although I had never previously met him. I forgot to arrange it through John Crane. This time I arranged the matter through the personal secretary of the President, somewhat to the displeasure of our minister. I had forgotten about our minister, Mr. Wright, at Prague, or I could have written him, for we were old friends from Petrograd 1917 days. I was in his office when the word came of the time Beneš could receive me. Wright thought me pretty radical and was not very enthusiastic over the good things I reported on developments in the Soviet Union. He knew and liked the old Russia and was unhappy even under the Lvov-Kerensky regime, I fear.

In preparation for the talk with Beneš, I asked my Russian friends living in Prague to suggest some questions to put to him; I always prepared for interviews of this kind. What seemed the best suggestion was that I ask him for the basis of his continued optimism—Beneš had always taken an optimistic view—and I hoped he would get the note of skepticism which the question was supposed to imply. The answer, however, was full of enthusiasm, as well as definite—the complete agreement between Britain and France, which he believed he had helped to bring about, was, he explained, the main basis for his optimism. A few years later he was to be faced with the question of undoing what he felt was a big part of his whole public effort, when he was told that, if he did not submit to the British-French plan which was to ruin his country, he would be responsible for provoking friction between Britain and France.

It was more unpleasant than usual to get out of Germany one Sunday afternoon, before Christmas—the stores were open and I could spend all my marks; it was hard to know just how many one would need. And a new law made it a crime, punishable by death, to try to smuggle out German legal tender. I purchased knives and little table trinkets to get rid of marks and also to bring home some simple souvenirs.

What I was really concerned over in connection with the baggage inspection—and possibly a thorough search of the person—were some Bolshevik newspapers which the Soviet ambassador had given me. These covered the last days of the Congress of Soviets and gave the text of the new constitution as finally adopted. I had these dozen copies of *Izvestia* and *Pravda* between shirts; but the examination of my lug-

228

gage was not so careful as I had feared it might be—my subversive literature was not found.

It was a rather uninteresting passenger list, and one of the stormiest crossings I had ever had. An American engineer and his Russian wife were my main talking companions. The latter helped me complete my translation of the new Soviet constitution by incorporating in the translation I had already made of the constitution published in June the few amendments adopted. My table group consisted, in the main, of traveling men; and evidently business was not so good, for they were all very grumpy. I played a good deal of bridge, and my frequent partner was a New York clothing merchant with whom I discussed in detail the "Jewish question." He left asking: "What are you going to do with the fifteen million of us? And we are increasing rapidly and causing more and more problems."

THE PRESS

PART VIII

THE PRESS

CHAPTER XXVIII

THE PRESS

THE PRESS AND ITS FOREIGN CORRESPONDENTS HAVE PLAYED A LARGE part in my life. We were working, to some extent, with the same materials and, in a way, trying to do the same kind of thing—find out and let people know. Our viewpoints were different, of course. Mine was academic, the so-called "search after the truth"; theirs was tempered by a race against time and a strong business purpose. From my earliest days in Russia I worked closely with them. I used their position by accepting various press credentials for the entree this gave me to current situations. Although I often wrote for newspapers and periodical publications to eke out a student's expenses or a professor's salary, I covered "spot" news by wire only occasionally, generally to take care of an assignment for some correspondent who was sick or away.

I saw much of these men in Russia and got much help from them. I could sometimes reciprocate by giving them the perspective which many did not have, having just arrived, or could not develop because their job was to report spot news from day to day. There were many outstanding men in the corps. Two must be mentioned particularly, and in a certain sense together—namely, Walter Duranty and Paul Scheffer. Though he came to Russia to represent the *New York Times*, Duranty was an Englishman and quite frequently spoke from a British point of view. Paul Scheffer represented the Berlin *Tageblatt* and, like many German foreign correspondents, had a broad historical training and a rather definite philosophy. This can be said also of Duranty, who had formerly been a schoolteacher. Scheffer had married a Russian and was able to read Russian. Duranty rapidly picked up the language. From these two men I received possibly the best interpretations of general Soviet policy, and I have learned more from them than from the seasoned American correspondents like Wood and Mills or from the younger men like Chamberlin and Knickerbocker, who got into the game later.

Duranty and I never got along together very well, though I found him the best equipped and the keenest of all the correspondents. At parties given by Russians he was often the only outsider present in addition to me, for he knew Russian and could and did participate in discussions. He tried to study and follow the somewhat odd—in any case different from ours—mental processes of the Bolsheviks; and, as a result, he had the hunches more than any of the others, many of whom tended always to apply our yardstick to the new Soviet system. In time Duranty came to feel that he was the dean of the group of correspondents, and to a certain extent America's representative, because he wrote for the *New York Times* and was allowed by this newspaper to send out the largest volume of reports. On occasions I was a little irritated by the condescending and superior tone which Duranty adopted toward me, and answered in kind, so that sometimes I missed my usual long talks with him, which was probably a real loss to me, for Duranty continued to be the best informed of the foreign correspondents and the one who could interpret Soviet policy more truly than any of the others.

A somewhat antagonistic attitude developed at times toward Duranty and his methods among his colleagues in Moscow. In the later years he did not join in their sessions, where most of the conversation was on the difficulties and problems of getting rooms, theater tickets, food, and so forth. It was at these "bull sessions" that the attitudes of many of the foreign correspondents and diplomats seemed to be formed. The attitude toward Duranty was illustrated at a luncheon in 1926, given to the group by a visiting newspaperman, H. V. Kaltenborn. Like many of the fresh arrivals, Kaltenborn was full of enthusiasm, carried away by the novelty of what he saw. This was the line he took as host to a group of us at this luncheon at the Savoy. He told us of his talks with the higher Soviet officials, in which he said he had assured them that there were good possibilities of a rather immediate American recognition of the Soviet regime. Duranty interrupted Kaltenborn at this statement, saying he felt it was perhaps a courteous thing to say but not a very accurate statement and adding that he would not have made such a statement although he went very far in "cultivating" the Bolsheviks. The other men at the luncheon—Junius B. Wood, James Mills, and Hubert Knickerbocker—in turn interrupted Duranty and, in chorus and with vigor, almost shouted at him: "You certainly do cultivate them!"

Another group of newspapermen who served their time in Moscow included William H. Stoneman, of the *Chicago Daily News;* Ralph Barnes, of the *New York Herald-Tribune;* and Edward Denis, of the International News Service. These were definitely the spot-news men, scurrying for scoops on one another, forced to do this by the checkup cables of their home editors. Of the representatives of this type of foreign correspondent that I met in my study trips, these men impressed me as the most competent. Perhaps only the better men would accept the very difficult Moscow post. They studied, as well as chased down handouts. In their rush to break in on an item of news, they were often left out on a limb, not having had time to check up fully. Then I would allow myself to return the "ribbing" they often felt called on to give the "naïve professor," as they sometimes called me. For I took occasion often to criticize them—to their faces, of course—feeling free to do so because of our intimate friendly relationship. Once, in connection with some diplomatic negotiations in progress, they thought I knew the precise content of the proposals of one party, and wanted me to tip them off. So I asked them if diplomatic negotiations were conducted to try to prevent a troubled world from getting into more trouble or to provide them with scoop material to make the front page and get a raise in salary. They might have slapped me down, and perhaps wanted to; but I was sure they wouldn't, because I said it with a smile. They had some basis for their argument that it was their "duty" to the American public to try to find out what our State Department was doing or planning to do.

Another "impudence" I allowed myself with those of the correspondents with whom I had been able to establish a basis of mutual trust had to do with their interpretation of the Bolshevik Revolution and the Soviet system from their own personal viewpoint. I was driving home from one of the "complaint sessions," where they had spent the evening telling of the inefficiencies, stupidities, and so forth of the Moscow leaders. My bathtub, also, had no stopper, and my sheet was too short, and the omelette tasted just like the fruit compote at breakfast; but I was irritated by this group of correspondents stewing in its own juice. To the three with whom I was going home I suggested that the Revolution had not been initiated and carried on for their particular comfort, or for us intellectuals in general, but for the workmen and peasants. This thought, apparently, had not occurred to them.

Lest I be accused of picking out petty points, let me say here that many of the correspondents must be praised for the way they stood the hard living conditions of Moscow, the handicaps of a strange language, the peculiar psychology both of Bolshevik leaders and Russian masses and got down to many of the basic facts of a very complicated situation. In their files in Moscow I found copies of the serious studies of this or that political or economic aspect which had gone by mail to the editor, only to be filed away for reference and not "found available" for publication—not enough "human interest" element of mystery or scandal.

In Soviet Russia the foreign correspondents had to work, of course, under a special type of censorship, which presented many difficulties. One day while I was talking to Duranty, for example, the censor called him to say that he could not pass one phrase in the cable which Duranty had just filed. The offending expression was the statement that, with Stalin's victory over Trotsky, "Lenin's mantle had fallen on Stalin's shoulders." This phrase had to be eliminated, which killed the point of

Duranty's paragraph. I insisted that Duranty should have realized that Stalin had not grown godlike enough at the time to wear the Lenin mantle.

American editors often used reports from outside the Soviet Union—particularly from anti-Soviet Riga and Stockholm—and then sent to their correspondents checkup cables of fantastic alleged happenings. One morning in 1926, Junius Wood received such a cable, to the effect that there were reports that Trotsky had started a revolt and was actually attacking the Kremlin with armed forces. Wood casually asked me to step to the window of his room, which overlooked the Kremlin, to see if perhaps we had been asleep on the job.

The worst offender in the matter of sending unverified stories from outside on what was actually going on inside Russia was Donald Day of the *Chicago Tribune*. The newspapermen in Moscow were naturally rather bitter against Day, because his stories often put them in an awkward situation and in a bad light with their own editors. At an informal gathering of the newspapermen on the eve of my departure for home in 1926 I was dared to play a trick on Day. I was told that Day would be after me within a half-hour of my arrival in Riga, because of arrangements he had with the porter of the hotel where I would have to stop. The suggestion was that I should give him an absolutely wild story, so wild that because of its utter outlandishness it would really discredit him. The story suggested was that the Soviet authorities had finally decided to handle the really acute problem of the thousands of wandering waifs in their large cities by mowing them down with machine guns and that, as I drove to the station, I had seen the motor lorries gathering up the bodies. I declined to be a party to this scheme because I did not feel sure that such a story would discredit Day in the eyes of the American reading public, which seemed only too ready to believe the most impossible tales about happenings and conditions in Bolshevik Russia.

However, I did play another trick on Day, for which later I asked and received credit and praise from the Moscow-American colony. Because at this time a trip to Soviet Russia was considered a real feat, involving some danger, I naturally wished to report to the family that I had come out safe and sound. On my arrival at Riga, before going to my room, I therefore went to the telegraph office to send such a message to my brother; and in my cable I asked him to telephone the *Tribune* editor that I had not given any interview to Donald Day. Returning to the hotel, I found, as expected, Day on hand; and when he asked for an interview, I showed him a copy of the cable. He was a good sport and paid for my breakfast.

Of the newspapermen stationed in Moscow in 1926, I played around particularly with Junius B. Wood, of the *Chicago Daily News;* James Mills, of the Associated Press; and William Henry Chamberlin, of the *Christian Science Monitor*. Wood and Mills were older and more experienced newspapermen than most of the others, and they were covering the Soviet Union as old hands at the game. It was useful to have them as a check, for I will admit that my approach on my first visit in 1926 was a somewhat overenthusiastic search for those constructive features which I had not at first seen in Bolshevism but which I felt must be there, to account for its continued hold on the politics of the country and, apparently, on the mass thinking of the people.

Chamberlin was more the student than the spot-news reporter, being able to take this approach because of the policy of his paper, which preferred that its correspondents be a day or so behind others in their reports so that these reports could be more carefully thought out and balanced. Chamberlin's wife, Sonya, was of Russian origin and of the same general socialistic tendencies as Chamberlin himself. She knew Russian; and "William Henry," as everybody soon came to call him, was plugging away to learn the language as quickly as possible.

Another interesting couple in the small group of American correspondents were the Knickerbockers—Laura and Hubert. I have put Laura first because she was then a more experienced correspondent than her husband. In 1923 he had joined the group in Germany under Dorothy Thompson and was now covering Moscow as his first independent assignment. These two were the most active of our group; and I came to appreciate Knickerbocker's intellectual keenness, although I sometimes had to suffer from his slightly irresponsible boldness on festive occasions. One night, at a dinner given by Kroll, a Czech newspaperman, he might have made me much trouble, although I am sure that this was not his intention. The host, like many European newspapermen, was half correspondent and half foreign-office representative, the latter capacity being evidenced by residence at the official Czech trade-mission headquarters, since the Czechoslovakian government had not extended diplomatic recognition to the Soviet government at this stage. There were Soviet officials present at this dinner, and toward the end of the evening Knickerbocker was asking them if they realized that I was really working as a kind of agent for my State Department. I got Knickerbocker home that night only after he had insisted on arguing something out with our cabman and a policeman on duty.

On another occasion, however, I was delighted with Knickerbocker's highhandedness. During my first visit to Soviet Russia, Sherwood Eddy arrived in Moscow with one of his study groups. The delegation, as he called it, took a trip to the rural district; but its secretary, Jerome Davis, remained in Moscow. While the Eddy group was traveling, Davis was received by Stalin, and he published in the Hearst papers an account of his interview with him. The fact of this interview became known in newspaper circles; and one evening, when Junius Wood and I were playing bridge with the Knickerbockers, Laura Knickerbocker calmly informed us that she had known all along that Davis was representing the Hearst papers. She and her husband were the official representatives of the International News Service, and Davis had come to her to inquire about the procedure for sending out mail stories. That very evening, she said, the Eddy group was giving a party for the Cultural Relations Society to which the newspapermen and students had not been invited.

When Knickerbocker learned from his wife of Davis' newspaper connections, he called up the place where this party was being held, got the assistant chairman on the phone, and asked if other newspapermen could not come, since Davis was, in fact, a newspaperman. The answer he received was rather equivocal and started Knickerbocker on one of his rampages. He called up the press bureau and asked the censor if he knew that Davis was a newspaperman, and also suggested to the censor that he might be interested in knowing just what Davis' other and permanent position was—namely, professor of practical philanthropy in the Divinity School of Yale. It was with incision that Knickerbocker spoke these words "practical philanthropy" and "Divinity School," knowing the Bolshevik attitude toward the institutions they designated.

By 1932 two of the younger men, William H. Chamberlin and Eugene Lyons, who had been rather enthusiastic about the Soviet experiment, were beginning to go sour. They began to ride me for what they considered my continued optimism. Chamberlin was getting more pontifical in manner; and one of the sights of Moscow was an evening at his home, where he would sit in state, lecturing to a group of visiting Americans. He had planned to leave Russia in 1932 but hated to give up the rather permanent place he had made for himself in Moscow. It is too bad he did not leave then, or else stay on beyond 1933, for he left at the moment of one of the low points in the zigzag of the Soviet experiment— the semifamine situation, particularly acute in the Ukraine, in 1933.

Eugene Lyons was getting cynical. He was going out of his way to tell the most caustic of the current political anecdotes to those of the Communists with whom he had developed rather close personal relations. One got a little tired of his constant reference to his hurt Communist soul and a little doubtful of the sincerity of his claim to such. These two were good examples of people who had come over full of enthusiasm, with a set pattern in mind, and who subsequently became the most severe critics—and not always, as previously, the most correct in their criticism.

Of the other foreign correspondents, I saw much of both the British and German. The Germans were better equipped, by knowledge of language and from graduate university work in Russian history and economics. But they were always in line with the politics of their particular paper or even of the German foreign office. The group of correspondents was enriched in later years by a representative of the London

Daily Telegraph, Cholerton, a British correspondent of the type that has played so important a role in European affairs during the last decade. With a broad historical and economic training as a background, he was an interpreter rather than a reporter of spot-news items. He had definitely socialistic views. He had married a Russian and, through his wife and his own knowledge of Russian, was able to reach into the Soviet community. Like their German colleagues, these British correspondents were used by their embassies, which did not have to fear that advantage would be taken of them for a "scoop," as was so frequently the experience of the American embassy.

The Poles had several correspondents in Moscow; but I did not find it particularly useful to talk with them, for they always revealed the special bias against all things Russian, so long engendered and deeply rooted in them. The Czechs, on the other hand, had the best information and the best judgment of any foreign group. The citizens of small neutral states have, in general, seen more clearly the trend of events, though their governments have not always been able to react adequately to their clearly visible course.

Among Washington correspondents, too, I had many friends. In 1933, after the Litvinov conversations in the White House had been going on for several days with no "leak" as to the progress being made, the newspapermen began to show a little impatience. It was on a Friday that I went to the Department pressroom and, learning that there would be nothing for the press, suggested that the President might announce the result in a fireside chat Saturday or Sunday evening. And did my journalist friends jump on me! According to them, the President had to make his announcements through the newspapers, as that was what they were there for. My response was a question I often put to these Washington correspondents: "Have you a governmental function, and from whom have you your mandate?" This phase of the institutional setup in Washington frequently caused me concern. The established position and attitude of the press in this country was making it difficult for the President and his chief aides to speak directly to the people. The development of radio talks was much resented by the press.

The press, it always appeared to me, was itself an indirect medium—a medium which, consciously or unconsciously, was bound to pick up, by its very use, the bias of the individual reporter or the policy of his editor. On one occasion some years earlier an announcement through the press conference of a statement allegedly made by the then Secretary of State Stimson disturbed me because of its indirect "slaps" at the Soviets. I suspected that the statement reflected the individual bias of the reporter as well as the policy of his editor; so I asked to be allowed to see the stenographic report of the conference. I had several division chiefs call up the Press Division to ask if I could see the stenogram; and the answer was a refusal, the rule being that only accredited correspondents could check on their memory by seeing the verbatim record. I therefore went to one of the older and most trusted newspapermen, Roy Vernon, and asked him to call up McDermott, the chief of the Press Division. Mac, whom I knew, first asked, in answer to Vernon's query, if "that Sam Harper" was back of the request. But he let me see the report under the guaranty of Roy Vernon. I could not copy it; I could only read it, but I got what I wanted, for I could find no deliberate pinpricks aimed at the Soviets in what the Secretary had said. I had been right in my guess that a couple of individuals had read into the Secretary's statement the "sting" that appeared in their accounts.

I often felt that the press was not qualified to claim for itself exclusive institutional rights in so important a function as communication between the rulers and the ruled.

PART IX

THE NEXT FIVE YEARS: 1937—JUNE 22, 1941

For the convenience of the reader:

TIMETABLE OF VARIOUS IMPORTANT EVENTS

Standing alone, this list of events traces the spread of aggression which led to the second World War. It makes more understandable the Soviet foreign policy of this period, which was based upon the doctrine that aggression and war are "indivisible" and which urged effective steps toward collective security. The constant recurrence of the treason trials, on the other hand, makes a strong argument for timidity on the part of the rest of Europe to depend too heavily upon Russia. If looked at in the light of later developments of German technique, however, these trials would suggest that "cleaning house" for the inevitable conflict perhaps showed straighter thinking on the part of Russia than was apparent in the rest of Europe.

1931	September	Japanese invasion of Manchuria
1933	January	Adolph Hitler became chancellor of Germany
	November	Recognition of Soviet Union by the United States
1934	September	Soviet Union became a member of the League of Nations
	December	First clash of Italian and Ethiopian forces
		Serge Kirov, associate of Stalin, assassinated
1935	March	German repudiation of Versailles disarmament clauses
	May	Ethiopia protested, to the League of Nations, Italy's obvious intention of making the clash a casus belli
		Alliance between Soviet Union and France
	August	Seventh World Congress of the Third International held at Moscow
	October	Italian invasion of Ethiopia
	November	Economic sanctions of the League of Nations went into effect to last until July 15, 1936
1936	March	German militarization of the Rhineland
	May	Mussolini announced that Ethiopian war was over and that Abyssinia was annexed
	June	Léon Blum became the first Socialist premier of France
		Civil war in Spain
	August	The treason trials of Zinoviev, Kamenev, and others

[Death came to Samuel N. Harper, suddenly and unexpectedly, in the early morning of January 18, 1943.]

	November	Anti-Comintern pacts between Germany, Italy, and Japan
	December	The Stalin constitution was adopted by Soviet Union
		King Edward VIII abdicated
		General Chiang K'ai-shek was kidnapped at Si-an and forced to agree on national unity in opposition to Japan
1937	January	The treason trials of Radek and others
		Hitler repudiated admission of responsibility by Germany in the Versailles Treaty
	March	English, French, Italian, and German navies, under the 27-government pact (the Spanish Non-intervention Agreement), police the shores of Spain
	June	Treason trials of Marshal Tukhachevsky and seven Soviet generals
	July	Japanese invasion of China
1938	January	The Supreme Soviet, under the new Soviet constitution, held its first assembly
	February	Anthony Eden retired as foreign minister. King Carol of Romania abolished the existing parliament and established the corporative chamber and senate
	March	Hitler marched on Vienna. Unification of Germany and Austria decreed
		Treason trials of Bukharin, Rykov, and others
	August	Border clash between the Soviet Union and Japan
	September	The Munich Conference
	October	Occupation of Sudetenland by Germany
		Japanese seizure of Canton
	November	Partial partition of Czechoslovakia by Poland and Hungary confirmed by von Ribbentrop
1939	January	End of Spanish civil war
	March	German invasion of Czechoslovakia
		Hitler annexed Memel
		Communist Party congress held in Moscow
	April	Invasion of Albania by Italy
	May	Molotov replaced Litvinov as Foreign Commissar
	August	New border clash between Japan and Soviet Union
		Trade agreement between Germany and Soviet Union
		Nonaggression pact between Germany and Soviet Union
	September	German invasion of Poland and Soviet occupation of eastern Poland
	November	Beginning of Soviet-Finnish war
	December	Soviet Union expelled from League of Nations
1940	March	Soviet-Finnish war terminated
	April	German invasion of Denmark and Norway
	May	German invasion of Netherlands, Belgium, and France
	June	Occupation of Baltic States by Soviet Union

		Occupation of Bessarabia and Bukhovina by Soviet Union
	October	Italian invasion of Greece
1941	April	German invasion of Yugoslavia and Greece
		Nonaggression pact between Japan and Soviet Union
	May	Stalin takes title of "premier"
	June	German invasion of Soviet Union

Then came the stand at Moscow, and the strength of Soviet Russia and the development of the Russian people began to be recognized.

Then came Pearl Harbor, and once again the United States and Russia were fighting a common enemy.

Then came Stalingrad, and the greatness of Soviet Russia and the Russian people was accepted by the world.

☙ ☙ ☙

CHAPTER XXIX

SOME SUMMARIES OF RUSSIAN PROBLEMS

Soviet Democratism

WHEN MY BOOK ON "THE GOVERNMENT OF THE SOVIET UNION" WAS AT last about to be published, on November 17, 1938, I had occasion to send the following telegram to my publishers: "Suggest you look up original contract for believe I shall have ground for legal action and if so shall act to limit if you publish my book under another title namely quote European dictatorships unquote." The cause of this outburst was a proposal, later withdrawn, to combine my study of the Soviet Union with two other studies of Germany and Italy as a single work on "European Dictatorships," this work to be paralleled by a companion volume on "European Democracies." There had taken root the unfortunate implication that the international struggle developing in the world was one between "dictatorship" and "democracy"; and this, too easy, classification of the matter continued, despite the protests of many of us, right up to 1941, when the Nazi attack on the Soviet Union finally showed the superficiality of this oversimplification. The particular problem of my book was soon satisfactorily disposed of, but it served to focus attention very sharply on a problem which has been fundamental in all my studies of the Soviet Union—namely, the relation of the Soviet system to democracy.

In their general statements the Soviet leaders describe their new constitution and its attendant elections as the "world's most democratic."

The terminology used in specialized writings, however, is more precise; and it is "Soviet democratism" that is contrasted with so-called "bourgeois democracy." In the Soviet Union particular stress is given to the question of effective mass participation in public activity, such participation tracing its origins to the slogan, formulated at the very beginning by Lenin, that under the Soviets "the housewife will learn to run the state"; and the carrying-out of this slogan is what the Soviets mean by their term "democratism." For "democratism," it should be noted, is claimed by the Soviets more for the result of their program, the achievement of mass participation in the activities of the social state, than for the methods used in reaching the result.

The Soviet system is based on the one-party principle; the revolutionists offer the masses leadership in the form of the Communist Party. Oppositional rights receive no real protection. These facts definitely differentiate the Soviet pattern from our own. But it does not follow that one should dismiss the Soviet elections as meaningless just because there were no contests, or the opening sessions of the Supreme Soviet as equally meaningless because no bills were voted on by roll call. The Soviet pattern, to be sure, has been characterized by a continued avoidance of the full formalism of the Western parliamentary system. Nevertheless, in the evolution of that pattern there has been a clearly observable tendency toward more formality both in elections and in legislative procedure.

The Party normally uses a combination of educative and compulsive measures in the furtherance of its program, with the promise that persuasion will gradually replace force and violence as the program is carried out. The election campaigns of 1937–39 were examples of the "educational" approach, and each in practice represented a two-month mass discussion period. The Soviet system, in current terminology, is a "Party" state; the elections aimed, therefore, to tie the Party up more closely with the masses. Education for the masses and critical checkup for the leaders were regarded as the proper functions of an election campaign.

In the original proposals the element of contest between candidates had been promised for the elections, but in practice all candidates but one usually withdrew from the race well in advance of the election date. The critical political situation, both internal and external, was suggested as the reason for the nonfulfilment of the promised contests. Nonparty people were, in fact, eligible under official practice as candidates even for membership in the Supreme Soviet, to the extent of a significant minority. Nonparty candidates and party candidates on a given ticket were officially referred to as a coalition group or a "block" of "Party and nonparty Bolsheviks."

The whole election picture of Soviet practices is difficult to measure by our own American yardstick. Also, it must always be remembered, as the police commissioner told me when I was looking over his headquarters in 1934, "there is the odor of the Party in everything, everywhere"—even in elections. In the case of the Soviets, the campaign is directed more to the critical selection of candidates with its "educational features," and the balloting tends to be mainly confirmatory. However, even without the promised contests, the Soviet interpretation was that the elections did demonstrate the moral and political unity of the people. And the reality of this interpretation must be judged by the economic and cultural development of the period, as well as by the national defense of the Soviet fatherland when the supreme test took place.

As for legislative procedure under the Soviet system in 1938, Molotov, as chairman of the Council of People's Commissars, resigned his post and then presented his own candidacy and that of his fellow-commissars to the new Supreme Soviet for reconsideration. The practice of discussing the qualifications of candidates for the various commissariats was an innovation and, despite indications of prearrangement, suggested the beginning of the institution of ministerial responsibility. Questions of policy, as well as of personality, came up in this discussion, particularly in the case of Litvinov. There was thus a development from the "mass-meeting" procedure which had previously characterized the Soviet congresses.

More important than the commissars in this period, however, was the position of Stalin, a position which has led to the current practice of designating him as a "dictator." There is no question of his dominant leadership; he is usually called "teacher," as well as "leader," and placed on the same plane as the other prophets of Bolshevism—Marx, Engels, and Lenin. The expression "Stalin constitution," which at first was merely a popular title, has now become the official terminology. It has been politically expedient to use the Stalin personality to symbolize even "Leninism," the "Party leadership," or the "dictatorship of the proletariat." Such a technique is part of all patterns of government, even the most democratic. In the Soviet pattern the resort to this technique is intensified by the doctrine of the single political leadership and the single-class policy. Stalin himself relates his position always to the Party—and through the Party to the Revolution. This is exemplified particularly when he sometimes joins in the applause which always comes at the mention of his name, or in a speech himself will make reference to "Comrade Stalin" as a sort of symbol. By thus coming out openly in speaking of "Comrade Stalin" at congresses, conferences, and general gatherings, the "teacher" by his very manner has striven, apparently deliberately, to avoid a purely individual interpretation of his position. Like Lenin before him, he rarely uses the personal pronoun "I," in this respect differing markedly from his main rival for the Lenin succession—Trotsky.

It was Troyanovsky who best summed up Stalin's role for me. Stalin, unlike some of his colleagues, studied his charges and saw the trends of thought in the young generation—what they, at last aroused and given the opportunity to secure it, wanted to have in the way of life. Stalin therefore fitted into the trend and was able to guide it. This was true Marxism. The new society was never rigidly outlined in detailed blue-print. The Revolution was intended, above all, to release new forces; and then, from experiments (costly) and experience (often bitter) and mistakes (many of them), these new forces were themselves to give the shape to things to come.

The Moscow Trials

In 1937 I had just started to lecture on the new "Stalin constitution," describing it as an encouraging indication of Soviet trends, when along came the period of the purge and my troubles began. The biggest problem was to determine whether these two phenomena—constitution and purge—were supplementary or contradictory. The official interpretation, of course, was that they were supplementary. The constitution, it was held, registered the achievement, or carrying-out, of the program of revolution, while the purge, for its part, represented the protection of these achievements—the defense of the Revolution. The thesis of all Soviet speeches at this time was a statement by Lenin to the effect that "revolutions have been lost because they did not know how to protect themselves." And the unsheathed, punishing sword of the Soviet revolution was the G.P.U.

The policy of initiating such a purge was very much in conformity with the traditions and practice of the Bolshevik Party. And without reviewing the record in detail it may be said that from these former purges the Party did, apparently, emerge more united and with better morale and therefore better able to supply positive leadership to the rest of the country. So, also, in my opinion, the 1937 purge started out as a protective and constructive measure directed against political conspiracy within the Party and against treasonable relations between certain Red Army leaders and the German *Reichswehr*.

On my 1936 trip I had found that Trotsky's outspoken opposition to the Stalin regime was having an embarrassing effect on his former associates within the Soviet Union. Among my friends, many seemed to be striving with particular zeal at their jobs in order to prove their loyalty. And well they might, for with war a real menace in that winter of 1936–37, hostile preparations were being pushed not only through increased armaments but also through espionage activity. And espionage activity always rests on bribing the nationals of a given country or catching them in a net because of their political or moral instability.

But, while the purge started constructively, it unquestionably became destructive later on, when it got out of hand. One of the most prominent

243

of the Bolshevik leaders, Zhdanov, for example, gave a summary in March, 1939, of the overreaching of the purge, with details on specific instances, which reads like a nightmare—though the frank admission of mistakes and the attempt to repair the damage did bring a certain relief. The purge, it seems, went through four distinct stages. First it involved the out-and-out conspirators and saboteurs; next it affected ordinary, nonpolitical racketeers and chiselers; then it overreached and intimidated many innocent bystanders; and, finally, it reversed itself and carried through a purging of the purgers. In the course of it, a couple of thousand people were executed and thousands more were arrested. It was, indeed, a "purge"—a blood purge that reached into the innermost circles of Soviet society.

Methods such as those used in these purges are, of course, not easily controllable. But what chiefly distinguishes the 1937 purge from its predecessors is of a twofold character. For one thing, the 1937 purge was of larger scope, was freer in meting out the death penalty, and reached a larger proportion of the higher-ups than did any other. For another thing, the charges levied against those reached were not, as previously, for violation of Party discipline or "passiveness" in Party work —this time the charges were for *treason*.

Now, some of those involved in the new purge were themselves revolutionaries trying to save the Revolution—as they understood it— from Stalin and his group, who, they thought, had turned traitor. And some were survivals of classes ruthlessly suppressed by the Revolution and out for revenge on the basis of what they had suffered. The leftists charged betrayal of the Revolution at home and abroad; the rightists saw the defects of the state-controlled economy and wanted another New Economic Policy. And among these groups many had got a strangle hold, through the Party, on positions with political power and so could be pried loose only by extreme political methods.

What was charged by Stalin as a program to "restore capitalism" was spoken of by the accused themselves as one to "save the Revolution." Talking about the Revolution was a principal stock-in-trade of the "old Bolsheviks" among the accused anyway. These men would have found a talk with Trotsky on the theory of revolution, at any rate, a stimulating experience; but when they did have a talk with Stalin, they had to confine themselves to production figures and tons of cement. Both groups claimed to be marching under the banner of Marxism; but for one side the road seemed to lead to "world revolution," whereas for the other it meant "socialism in one country."

It must be remembered, in this connection, that practically all the accused were members of that peculiar organization which we call the Party—that they had accepted the iron discipline of this revolutionary order and were fully aware that any organized opposition within its ranks was impossible. If they did try to organize an opposition, it became, by force of circumstances, a conspiracy. If they said, "Stalin must be removed," they had to mean "by assassination." If they said, "This isn't socialism," they were guilty of saying, "Let's overthrow it."

And when this internal situation is related to the external, the picture begins to be completed. For the Anti-Comintern agreement of November, 1936, put those who had started purely local conspiracies in a very difficult position; some, without any question, had fallen into the trap of German intrigue and preparations. Objectively, if not subjectively, the "old Bolsheviks," because of their adventuristic doctrinairism, were becoming instruments making for war. Or, as one Soviet spokesman put it when asked about the alleged Trotsky-Gestapo tie-up, the working principle seemed to be that "the enemy of my enemy is my friend."

In all the charges brought against Trotsky at the trials, the one that seemed to Westerners the most dubious was precisely this one of having a working arrangement with the Nazis and Japanese military to sell out the Soviet fatherland. But Trotsky did not recognize "fatherlands"— considered it a betrayal of the Revolution to do so—and attacked Stalin precisely for having exalted the Soviet fatherland at the expense of the world revolution. In fact, what Trotsky was accused of in this instance was much the same as what the Sisson documents had accused both Lenin and Trotsky of doing in 1917. In both instances Germany was a direct military menace to the Revolution and in both instances a policy of appeasement directed toward Germany may have seemed a necessary means to power. If Trotsky did make a deal with Hitler, he might only have been repeating in 1937, with respect to Stalin, the role which he played in 1917, with respect to Kerensky.

Meanwhile, a flood of revelations was pouring out from the Soviet side, so much so, that one of the principal problems for Western students of the trials became the authenticity of the famous "confessions" on the part of the accused. To some, these self-accusations and breast-beatings seemed the result of prearrangement, a sort of play-acting in the interest of whipping up Soviet morale. To others the G.P.U. seemed the all-sinister cause, which in this case was operating through some new and character-destroying "confession drug." But perhaps the simplest way of handling the confessions would be to take them more at their face value as acts of repentance by men who had started out in the ranks of the extreme left but who had wound up dangerously close to the extreme right. For as revolutionaries against revolution, they had, as some of them said, been turned into their own opposite—namely, counter-revolutionaries.

Whatever the real basis for these confessions, there is no question but that Stalin was systematically smashing much of the old Party leadership. He eliminated those old leaders who were constantly saying, "When I talked with Lenin," or "Lenin would have done it this way." He was getting rid of what were termed in Lenin's time the "patent-leather comrades." These so-called "old Bolsheviks," he said, weren't true Leninists in the first place, especially in view of Lenin's own warning in 1917 against clinging to outmoded slogans because of their glorious revolutionary past. Also, many of these men were inefficient—the sort who would not learn and were resting on their laurels. In several instances the replacement of former political leaders was a good move from all points of view—production, conduct of foreign relations, and teaching of the young generation.

As for Trotsky, who, of course, was out of Stalin's reach, he set to work soon after the trials to establish a Fourth International in competition with Stalin's Third. The first important document to issue from this new body was dated September 15, 1939, and was drawn up at a meeting somewhere in Switzerland. Trotsky's hand was clearly visible in this document, for, while written in the best terminology of Marxian doctrine, its logic was very finespun and it seemed far removed from the realities of the moment. A second manifesto, issued in June, 1940, resembled at many points the 1919 documents of the old Third International, and critics suggested that it was an effort to repeat the policy of world revolution of that earlier year, regardless of its failure. It was a definite appeal for world revolution to be led by Communist (Trotskyist) parties in each country. It was also an appeal to the Communists of the Soviet Union, calling on them to overthrow the "Stalin bureaucracy" and re-establish the Leninism of the first period of the Revolution.

Despite this latter appeal, Trotskyism, in my opinion, was dead in Soviet Russia. Trotsky's last books showed him to be completely out of touch with Soviet actualities. But, while the trials did undoubtedly discredit Trotsky inside the Soviet Union, they seem to have made a martyr of him *outside*—seem, in other words, to have enhanced his position beyond its real value—to all of which, of course, Trotsky himself contributed by his pathological egoism. In Europe, however, in the spring of 1939, I failed to find any evidences of a strong Trotsky following; and there were, in fact, several instances where former Trotskyists were critical of what they considered an attempt to repeat the mistakes of 1918–21. Perhaps it will turn out that Trotskyism has become mainly an American phenomenon—a New York phenomenon—which, if true, is a good thing for the peace of the world.

The years 1937 and 1938 were somber ones for a Russian specialist—a sort of foretaste of the still more somber period that was to follow. Little news was to be had from the Soviet Union, and that little was none too good. Foreign newspapermen were reduced both in number and in their freedom to travel; Soviet newspapers became dull and ranted against Trotskyites, etc. No real statistics were available. Whether the system was facing a crisis economically as well as politically, it was difficult to tell. American and British scholars working in

246

Russia were obliged to leave because of the antiforeign attitude. New students were not permitted to go to Russia. And for myself I decided there was no use in my going over either, for I could not have got the answers to any of the questions I was formulating.

Staying at home was none too satisfactory either, for the more trials there were in Moscow, the more trials there were for me. As a rule I tried to meet the question "Why the confessions?" by the fact of the Oriental in the Russians—"We Westerners can't understand." One Oriental student of mine, however, chimed in by saying he couldn't understand either. Equally disconcerting was a response to a remark of mine that in a collectivist state, where all responsible positions are public offices, those who fail to live up to the trust involved cannot be eased off into private business, because there is no private business. It was thereupon suggested to me that this certainly left the Soviets in a quandary and that they evidently had decided that, for the nonconformist, one wall was better than four walls.

This whole controversy was the more difficult for me because it was during this very period that I was engaged in completing my textbook on *The Government of the Soviet Union*. Since the text was to be one of a series, the necessary space limitations and scope requirements were themselves a circumscribing factor. But when, in addition, I had to draw conclusions on a highly controversial subject at a time when everybody else was guessing, the difficulties proved tremendous. I had constantly in mind the interrelation between the two principal phenomena of Soviet internal affairs at this time—the constitution and the purge—and every new election or trial that came along obliged me to take time off and reconsider the situation. To some of my close friends[1] I let off steam:

As you may have guessed, those damn trials in Moscow have had a devastating effect on the attitude of our public toward the Soviet system. The news tonight of the new trial in the offing (Radek-Pyatakov) started one of my colleagues after me with the statement that, though of the "leftist" wing, he is now able to understand the policy of London conservatives and even, as he expressed it, of "people to the west of France." This man is essentially conservative, I admit, and also given to emotionalism; but, nevertheless, he represents a current of thought which I am encountering at every turn. I expect to have quite a hell of a time when I expose myself to the graduate students of the social sciences next week.

And I had sympathy for some of the purging:

[1] [Excerpts from letters written Harper to Van Nostrand & Co., February 13, 1917; to John N. Hazard, January 21, 1917; to Loy Henderson, May 28, 1937; to Harriet L. Moore, March 3, 1938; and to a member of the diplomatic staff at Ankara.]

Your figure of speech about the purges—the "trimming of the old tree"—is most apt, and I am going to lift it from you. Wish I could give you proper credit. From here it looks as if some good wood were being included in the pruning, but I have enjoyed the removal of certain branches and have interpreted these instances as constructive.

I had more or less successfully explained away the 1937 purge when, bang!—the charge against the doctors, against Rykov and Bukharin, the charge that Trotsky was practicing treason way back from the beginning (which very interestingly brings up my old friends the Sisson documents). Some of my articles now read a bit silly, I'm afraid. I had convinced myself, and perhaps many others, that the purge, up to the elections of 1937, was supplementary and not contradictory to the so-called "constitutional" development. Now I shall have to reconsider the whole matter in the light of this new trial and the continuation of the purge which it represents. This will take some time, of course.

The Bolsheviks were moving too fast for me:

"I really almost envy you your detachment from things Russian, for one can get fed up with this darn Bolshevism. If I did not have the farm to which I can go every now and then and fight the weeds, I would find it difficult to keep the balance and at the same time recognize what has been accomplished. When I get my political textbook done, I shall be tempted to go back to history—and way back to the earlier periods, about which it is easier to come to conclusions."

In connection with my trips east in this period, I found that the Soviet chargé d'affaires, Oumansky, was in even greater difficulties than I was. But Charles A. Beard, whom I ran into at an American Historical Association convention, did cheer me up somewhat with his advice: "Don't weaken in defending your Bolshevik friends, for we may need them yet." However, it was Charles R. Crane, my lifelong friend and benefactor, who really put me on my feet again.

Mr. Crane, it seems, when I visited him where he was convalescing at Wood's Hole on Cape Cod, had at last reconciled himself, to a large extent, to the Soviet setup in Russia. "There is much of what old Russia was striving for in this new constitution," he told me. "The Russian people have secured the most promising channels of self-expression and self-assertion I have yet known them to have in all the thirty years I have studied them. And don't get too discouraged," he added. "The Russian people are coming through and on top. The Russians, I believe, are going to contribute very considerably—perhaps even more considerably than any other nation—to the whole solution of our common internal and international problems." These proved to be virtually the last words that Mr. Crane ever said to me, because by the time I was free to visit him again, Mr. Crane had passed away.

The Isolation of Russia; Munich

In a talk during my 1936 trip to Russia with one of my close friends in the Soviet foreign office, I had asked him what he would wish American policy to be, from the viewpoint of his own country, of course. With little hesitation he answered under two headings: (1) close relations and, if possible, co-operation with Britain and France; and (2) a strong stand for freedom of the seas. After thus formulating the answer he asked to be allowed to change the order of the two points, so that America's first interest should be the maintenance of the freedom of the seas. It was logical, he held, that the great continental state on the Eurasian side of the planet should have a community of interest with the American continental state on the other side.

My friend knew better than to suggest American-Soviet "co-operation"; for he was fully aware of the strength of American isolationism—which I often tended to forget during the months I was abroad, perhaps because I wanted my country to appear more of a force in world affairs than it was, even if only to enhance my own personal standing. Presumably this Soviet expert wished American provincialism to be moderated by functioning through Britain, if or when America woke up to its place in the world or decided to do some missionary work. But the weight of America, even if exerted through England and France, was desired by the Soviet leaders. This weight, it was believed, would strengthen these two empires which in 1936–38 the Soviet Union clearly wanted to have strong as counterweights to aggressive Germany and Japan.

Not all Bolsheviks were always so realistic as this when discussing American policies, however; and, oddly enough, one such was Litvinov himself. For I brought the subject up with him, too, in that November of 1936 and got as an answer a laudation of a speech President Roosevelt had just made in South America—a laudation which implied that the Soviet commissar was expecting another and more positive statement, covering the whole world, and that almost immediately. I felt called upon to suggest that he was a bit too enthusiastic and going a little too fast. With his usual frankness he admitted this, adding a remark which I believe I am quoting practically verbatim because it impressed me as such a wise and useful one: "Yes," he said, "we are always expecting more than we should from America, forgetting that for a variety of reasons, some of a constitutional nature, America is really incapable of drawing the proper organizational conclusions from its words." That last phrase in the quotation was a current Bolshevik slogan—to do something about whatever you are proposing, and at least start an organization, rather than just make your proposal and let it go at that. "Orgvyvod," the Russian abbreviation of "organizational conclusion (from your words)" was one of the many current gems of Soviet slang.

If I ever thought, along with Litvinov, that American isolation had been very much weakened by the President's speeches, I was soon set right after a few talks with more realistic Americans back home, who, most helpfully, threw cold water on my optimism.

I had noted that the German-Japanese Anti-Comintern Pact of November, 1936, had originally been interpreted by both the London *Times* and the *New York Times* as really affecting Britain and America, and particularly the Dutch East Indies. And I had not expected that this first—and correct—interpretation would so soon give way to the pressure of the anti-Soviet campaign which many found it expedient to foster for their own special vested interests—in most cases unaware that they were fitting into a deliberate Nazi-Japanese propaganda scheme. For very rapidly it was assumed that the Axis was just an anti-Communist pact and that Japanese and Nazi aggression would really be directed only, or at least primarily, against Russia.

More and more, American isolationism took the form of hoping that somebody else would do our job for us. This attitude often found expression in the question: "Why don't the Soviets attack Japan to help China?" It was assumed by those who put this question that war between Japan and Soviet Russia was "inevitable anyway." I met this latter assumption so frequently right up to December, 1941, that I placed several bets with my friends that Japan would go for and get the Dutch East Indies before she went for and got Vladivostok. This was the sister-bet to the one for the European sphere, of which I placed more than a dozen between 1936 and 1940, that Hitler would go for and get Alsace-Lorraine before he went for and got the Ukraine. It was Troyanovsky, in Moscow in December, 1936, who had first worded these bets and dared me to take them on.

It was also Troyanovsky who gave me the best answer to the question about the Soviets attacking Japan in 1937. I had told him how frequently the question was put to me, and asked him what he thought about it. And his comment was: "Suppose the Soviet government should decide on such a policy and, after announcing that it would turn Manchuria over to China, should cross the Amur frontier. Then, how long do you think it would be before powerful forces in London, Paris, and even Washington would begin to shout 'Soviet imperialism' and start measures to prevent the 'Reds' from driving the Japanese into the sea?" This was not the only reason for the Soviets' purely defensive policy, of course; but it was undoubtedly a factor which the Moscow leaders found it expedient to consider. When a serious frontier dispute did take place at Lake Hassan in 1938, the anti-Soviet habit did, in fact, lead to a general consensus that the Soviets were to blame; and it took some months for the American public really to see that Japan had been the aggressor and had also been slapped down on rather sharply.

Relations between the Soviet Union and the Western powers during this period became still more tense over Spain as the Soviet government continued to be the only major power giving aid to the loyalist side. A Soviet delegation also continued to sit in on the Plymouth Commission on Nonintervention, though, as Litvinov put it, the object of the commission seemed to be not to intervene with respect to the intervention. The Soviet role in Spain was widely condemned—by conservatives as the spreading of Bolshevism, by liberals as the usual disruptive machinations of Moscow, and by socialists as another episode in Stalin's personal feud with Trotsky. Few, at that time, would accept the explanation that the real Soviet interest was to try to help stop aggression because "aggression is indivisible" and, if not stopped, might also reach the Soviet Union.

Many were taking the view that it was the Soviet Union that had let the Western democracies and the collective security system down by weakening itself with its purges. A further view was that the Soviet Union was working for war—to sow the seeds of revolution in the confusion that would follow—and that Chamberlain and Daladier were the champions of peace. Soviet application of the oil sanctions against Italy, Soviet opposition to nonintervention in Spain, and Soviet insistence on identifying the so-called "pirate" submarines in the Mediterranean as Italian—all were interpreted as warmongering by the supporters of appeasement. Our conservatives were saying: "A day more of peace, if only a day, is at least a day gained." War for them was something to be avoided, not alone because of the terrible cost, but lest it mean the overthrow of Hitler and Mussolini and the rise of Bolshevism in their stead.

The net result of the triumph of fascism in Spain, the weakening of the security of France, and the abandonment of the program of collective security was the four-power conference at Munich. In August, 1938, at the moment of Munich, the Soviet government, by all the best evidence, stood ready to give aid to Czechoslovakia—if aid had been possible. But the then French foreign minister, Bonnet, seems deliberately to have misreported the Soviet official position, not only to the world at large, but also to his own cabinet. Even the Soviet answer to President Roosevelt regarding the latter's second message to Hitler was not published by our own American State Department; in fact, no one in the Russian section seemed to have a copy when I was in Washington a few months later. My own copy I had taken from *Izvestia*. What Moscow proposed in this note was a general conference on neutral ground, with America and the Soviet Union both participating. Instead of this, Chamberlain and Daladier met Hitler and Mussolini *à quatre* in Hitler's own workshop—"two gangsters and two undertakers," as one man characterized it.

The conclusion from all this was that the Soviet Union had become isolated, that isolation had been forced upon it, and that it had been left out at Munich in an attempt to turn Germany eastward. As a result, the Soviet Union withdrew into itself—in a sense pouted—and developed a spy mania and a distrust of all foreigners. The Soviet leaders continued to insist that they could be counted on for a program of collective security because collective security gave more security and was cheaper. But, at the same time, they warned that, if such a program were not forthcoming when the lessons of appeasement had become fully clear, then the Soviet Union would make its own arrangements for its own security.

⇔ ⇔ ⇔

CHAPTER XXX

LAST LOOK AT EUROPE

Some Slavic Diplomatic Portraits

AFTER THE FINAL RAPE OF PRAGUE IN MARCH OF 1939 AND SHORTLY before my departure for another visit to Soviet Russia, the university decided to invite former President Beneš to become a member of its faculty. He accepted our invitation, in preference to others, because Chicago was the largest Czechoslovak center in America and because President Masaryk had been visiting lecturer at the university as early as 1903, one of the first of the Slav scholars under the auspices of Charles R. Crane.

On his arrival Beneš showed a certain reserve in his remarks about Chamberlain and Daladier, as his country was still dependent on the good will—or was it the worst of bad will—of Great Britain and France. At a luncheon a group of us got Beneš to review the European situation, but even behind closed doors he continued to go easy on the two "undertakers" of Munich. In answer to questions, however, Beneš made two remarks which impressed me, perhaps because on these points I had addressed the query. I asked if the German businessmen of the Sudetenland did not realize that they were better off in the Czechoslovak economic setup than in that of Nazi Germany, as the latter had developed even by that date. He replied that this was a proper question, though he was surprised that I had put it, considering my studies of eastern Europe. Other Americans might well puzzle over it, he added with a little stab at me, from lack of realization of the extent to which intense national feelings and political frontiers play a role in Europe.

My other question was whether he and others like him, representing eastern Europe at the Versailles Peace Conference in 1919, had had constantly in mind the terms Germany had forced on Russia—and eastern Europe in general—at Brest Litovsk. In answer he said that they had in mind even more specifically the detailed blueprint, drawn up at Salzburg about the same time by German and Austrian representatives, for the territorial settlement to follow a German victory. This document, copies of which they all had, contained an even more positive program for German domination in central and eastern Europe than had the treaty of Brest Litovsk. None of us at the luncheon recalled this Salzburg "program," as we had to admit, which was just another illustration of American ignorance, even among specialists, of the European situation.

Before I left for Washington, I had a long talk with Beneš, a summary of which he suggested that I could give as a kind of message from him to Secretary Hull, whom I hoped to see before sailing. The substance of the talk was the quandary in which the smaller states found themselves. What Nazi Germany offered—that is, threatened—was a perfectly clear thing. Also, the proffered Soviet pattern was clear and was preferable to the Nazi pattern. But the pattern of behavior toward smaller states of the so-called "democratic" powers was not only unclear, it was ambiguous; and because of its ambiguity, it seemed at times even worse in its consequences than the Nazi pattern. The rape of Prague, it was admitted, was in line with the constant Soviet warning that such would be one, and one of the first, results of the Munich "appeasement."

In preparation for a proposed stopover in Poland I secured an invitation to lunch with the Polish ambassador, Count Potocki, when I passed through Washington in April. I also saw to it that there should be other academic men present, in order to make this re-establishment of official Polish contact somewhat less official and more personal. The day set was precisely that April 6 when Colonel Beck finally put through his pact of mutual assistance with the British government. That very morning I has seen Potocki in the State Department lobbies, bustling around in considerable frenzy. We therefore suggested to the ambassador that he might wish to cancel the luncheon in view of the pressure of work, but he insisted that we go through with the program. On the way to the luncheon I stopped in at the Soviet embassy for another talk with Oumansky; and when I mentioned, as I did deliberately, where I was lunching, the look and remark were what I had expected—they suggested I was wasting my time and that one could not believe anything Poles told you anyway. Arrived at the Potockis', I settled down on a sofa with an older man whom I had not clearly identified—too much Polish brandy perhaps—although I assumed he was on the embassy staff. He asked me what I thought of the pact just signed; and I remarked—again perhaps because of this Polish brandy—that, were I a Pole, I would feel more comfortable if Chamberlain's signature to the pact were countersigned by Churchill and Eden. This remark was to be thrown up at me by Poles in London a few weeks later, having been passed on. For it was to Alfred Potocki, the ambassador's older brother, that I had made it.

In this same talk, and before I had clearly identified the very gracious man with whom I was gossiping, the question of whither the world was bound came up, in the free and easy way Slavs have of raising and discussing subjects. I gave my views in two capacities, I explained. As the owner of a 160-acre dairy farm in Wisconsin, I was a strong individualist; but as a social scientist, I had found that I had to face the fact of a strong collectivist tendency, and that not only in my field of study —the Soviet Union. Potocki looked a little surprised and asked me if I knew who he was; and when I admitted that I was not sure, he told me that he owned 200,000 acres—as opposed to my 160—the famous Polish estate of Lancut, and that he was in full agreement with me as to the trend of things being definitely toward collectivism. And he invited me to visit him at his estate when I reached Poland, suggesting that it would be valuable for me, as a guest at Lancut, to spend a couple of days "in the eighteenth century." He added that at a later date the estate might not be there—which wasn't a bad prophecy for a Polish landowner from the Lvov area to make in the year 1939.

Before leaving Washington I arranged a luncheon of my own between Oumansky, the Soviet ambassador, and Loy Henderson, the then Russian expert in the State Department. Both welcomed the opportunity. No sooner had we taken our seats than Oumansky suggested to Henderson that the two of them take advantage of the presence of an outspoken professor, take off their diplomatic coats, and put to each other direct questions as they were used to having them put to them "by this professor here." Henderson readily agreed, and I started the show by one of my more outspoken suggestions—as I recall, it was why the Soviet Union was not admitting freely the Jews of eastern and central Europe who were being so violently persecuted by the Nazis. After this start, things went well, and I sat back and listened to the questions the two put to each other. I cannot, of course, repeat them here. As we started to break up, Henderson asked if I would object to leaving him for a moment alone with Oumansky, to mention a matter which could not be discussed in front of me.

As we later, after a few minutes, walked over to the Department, Henderson thanked me for staging by my presence a most useful exchange of views. Here I had done, more directly, what I had developed as a general practice—acting as a channel between diplomats, putting questions they could not put to each other, and on occasion, at my discretion, when I thought it would help mutual understanding, repeating to the other party the answers I had been given. Such a game had its dangers, for the aim had to be constructive, and one had to be very accurate in transmitting the question put and the answer received.

This was, perhaps, a good example of my "organized indiscretions," the using of which was a characteristic attributed to me by some of my friends. It started in Moscow in 1932, when a counselor of a foreign embassy asked me to dinner to help him entertain—with a little instruction on things Russian and Soviet slipped in—some important men of his country. Introducing me, with a statement on my long period of study of Russia, before and after the advent of Bolshevism in 1917, he told them not to be frightened by my rather direct manner in both question and answer. As he explained it, he had discovered my technique, which he called "organized indiscretion." I considered this a real compliment to a talkative professor from a diplomat and, without becoming self-conscious as a result of having my method labeled, continued with this encouragement to carry on indiscreetly. I always emphasized that my "indiscretions" were "organized" to an end, and, I hoped, a useful one.

London in 1939—April

Reversal of my original order of travel—Poland, Russia, England—brought me first to London. London at that moment was the center of indecision crossed by eleventh-hour and contradictory currents; and arrival there on April 13, when Chamberlain announced formally the guaranty to Poland and the proposal for a pact with the Soviet Union, proved very opportune for the student of eastern Europe.

I found many, like myself, as my change of itinerary suggests, using the phrase "Adolf willing" when speaking of plans; and always one had a certain sense of shame that things had been allowed to come to such a pass that so much depended on this irrational individual. Bankers in the Hotel Carlton and the clients of the more modest pubs of London were heard to remark that such a situation could not go on much longer, as it was too demoralizing. While much time was spent, perhaps quite futilely, trying in conversations with others to find the reasons for Chamberlain's "inconsistencies" and to decide whether he had been "naïve but not a knave," as one English friend expressed it, the general tendency was to refrain from wasting time trying to guess what Hitler might logically do next.

One very important factor in bringing a more friendly attitude toward the Soviets was the increased difficulty which businessmen were encountering in trying to do business in Nazi Germany. It was rather interesting to hear the remark that it was easier to do business with the Soviet system than with that of the Nazis. The extension of fascist aggression (Spain, China, Austria, Czechoslovakia), was seen to be restricting, at a rapid rate, the area open to normal international trade. Thus the "Toto-intern" as I had been calling it, had replaced the Comintern as the more direct and immediate threat to peace and order and the capitalist system.

In his speech in Parliament on April 14, however, Chamberlain had not intended even to mention Russia, and did so only when it was demanded from the floor. Relations with the Soviet Union were thus affected by the peculiar political situation. The predominant view, even in the Eden group of conservatives, and also in business groups, was that the Soviet Union would have to be accepted as a reliable and respectable partner in the new program of collective security if the latter was to mean anything. The record of the Soviets before and after Munich, especially in the light of the now accepted "lessons of Munich," had at last brought this attitude into clearer outline. But Chamberlain, it would seem, while now very much afraid of Hitler, was still, as always, very much afraid of Stalin; and also, apparently, of "the red man in the white house," as he was reputed to have remarked.

And not only were Chamberlain and his group afraid of Bolshevism; but some of their supporters still gave the impression that they would rather like to see naziism satisfy its appetite at the expense of Soviet Russia—"let them eat bear," as the British remarked about the Germans during the first World War. Lack of confidence in the acumen of this "man in blinkers," as Chamberlain was described to me on my first day in London, seemed to be universal. His failure to put Churchill into the Ministry of Supplies was spoken of as an insult to the country. Chamberlain's own followers in Parliament turned their heads in shame when he named another man. That he was very stubborn, petty in his personal dislikes and jealousies, and something of a "Tammany chief" as a party leader was constantly emphasized. Skepticism was widely expressed in speeches and writings but did not seem able to register politically—that is, bring change in or even influence the government. Many, indeed, urged me to note that for the moment the democratic controls were not fully functioning in this first home of the parliamentary system.

My three weeks in England were the most strenuous I can remember, and before they were over I had begun to feel the weight of my fifty-seven years. For, along with a constant round of social engagements, I was running the gamut of political opinion from extreme left to extreme right—as the following excerpts from letters to the family will show:

Sunday morning I jumped on a bus and drove twenty miles west to see my "adopted niece," Pearl Binder, the caricaturist—and Communist. She has married a Labor party leader, Elwyn Jones, writer on international affairs. Little Josephone (14 months old) took a fancy to me, and I acquired another "niece"—grandniece, shall we say?

Then Cafe Royal with some Socialist party and trade-union people —on the conscription law. What a bunch of futile word-slingers! I got mad when they attacked the Soviet government, and suggested they read a few documents.

256

Later in the week I went to a lunch given by Ramsay Muir of the executive committee of the Liberal party. Sinclair, the leader of the latter, and I were, so to speak, the guests of honor. After a lengthy discussion we "liberals" decided that if we are to survive in this wretched world we must "think tougher and act rougher." I got back in time for dinner at the Cambridge and Oxford Club with the writer E. H. Carr —a rather destructive mind but a relief, with his sheer realism, after the somewhat musky idealism at lunchtime.

Next day I went to Harold MacMillan, member of Parliament as well as head of the English branch of the big publishing firm. He has taken the lead on the floor for the Eden group since the latter's resignation. How he criticized the present leadership! He wants me to give my views on Soviet strength, etc., to a half-dozen of his group in the Conservative party at a luncheon one of these days. This should be one of the most important lunch meetings I shall have.

Rested all afternoon for evening affair.   It was a dinner at the Carlton, arranged for me by the G. M. P. Murphy Company as a chance to talk to some twenty British bankers. Sir Arthur Salter, whom I rode hard, was also there. A sumptuous dinner and a lively debate—poor me the goat. Have had six telephone calls thanking me. Admit I was at my best. It lasted till 2.30 A.M.

Wednesday at 10 P.M. I went to a private house to meet two representatives of what they call the "Empire Group" in the Conservative party. Not of the "ruling class." Typically middle class with social inferiority complexes—but good brains. Gave me their "Scuttle and prepare for later effort" program—defeatism. Won't have a thing to do with atheistic Soviets; if British Empire must collapse unless it asks for or takes Soviet help, better that it collapse. This is the most "immoral" group I have met. Worse than Chamberlain.

Looked up an old friend today—Jan Masaryk.   Poor man is terribly worried. He confirmed all my doubts, even filling in several blanks in my picture. Urged me to keep on doing what I am doing—that is, frankly expressing my fears and suspicions.

Then I jumped to Bernard Pares again for dinner and went with him while he did an Empire broadcast on "Security and Russia." I had helped him prepare the script, and he acknowledged it. His statement was almost the same as my "Soviet Union and Munich" last winter. He has really been magnificent, most thoughtful, clearer in his thinking. He seemed touched by our being together at work again, as in those prewar years. He can't have much longer to go—he is 72. I shall always remember this last co-operation with him.

Tomorrow is my last fling.   It will be lunch with the Russian experts at the Foreign Office—when I shall learn all about the negotiations with Moscow. Then 15 minutes with Maisky at the Soviet embassy—tea with some nice lady friends and Bruce Lockhart—dinner with Pares and his two girls—and curtain, on three most interesting weeks.

The European mess looks black for the future but not for the immediate present. All agree that any sheer adventure on Hitler's part should have come before May 1st and that now we may be able to count on 3 or 4 months of this qualified peace. So I go ahead with my plans—leaving Wednesday for Stockholm by boat—then by airplane to Riga (my first air trip!)—and finally by train to Moscow. This way I skirt the German-Polish danger area. Being on the fringe of things is very helpful for a better understanding of what it all means anyway. And trust me to move north if the fringe moves northward too!

P.S.—I probably won't be writing any more frank letters like this until I get back to Warsaw.

Moscow in 1939—May

In the Soviet Union, after a first ten days in Moscow, I repeated a trip of three years before—to Kiev and Kharkov in the Ukraine. It was possible to get away from Intourist's fixed route and run up for a long day, with two nights of travel, to the textile center of Ivanovo, previously visited in 1930. The remaining ten days were spent in Moscow again, where the Supreme Soviet was holding its third session. At that session the budget for the year was adopted; and, what was more important, at that session, also, the new Soviet foreign minister, Molotov, who had just replaced Litvinov, reported on Soviet foreign policy in general and on the British-Soviet negotiations in particular. My thirty days in the Soviet Union were therefore very fruitful. On this trip—thanks to the events of the last few years and months, both internal and external—the questions uppermost in mind were very specific. For, aside from watching the progress of the British-Soviet negotiations, what one wanted to know was whether the crisis which called forth the purge, and the methods of the purge, had in fact weakened the Soviet system politically and economically. And as the foreign policy of the Soviet Union was closely related to political and economic factors, the answer to this first question would also give the background for that other burning question of the day, as to the role which the Soviet Union might play in any program of collective security.

It was frequently pointed out that production had been "falling off" in 1937 and 1938, or, more exactly, that the curves of increase of production were flattening out. One alleged reason for this slowing-down —along with deliberate sabotage and petty racketeering—was the incompetence of the old leader personnel. Many had been given positions in economic enterprises as rewards for their political services in establishing the new regime. The red director of a factory might have been a very able revolutionary liquidator of bourgeois elements in the first years of the Revolution but he was not well adapted, by training or temperament, to the task of getting smooth and good production out of an economic enterprise. Many of those incompetents, it appeared, had been removed by the purge—not executed, of course, but demoted—and, if they had grafted too extensively, sent to work building the railway across northern Siberia.

At the Party congress in March of 1939 Stalin had spoken in his report of five thousand new local leaders, who had risen to responsible positions. And in those Soviet institutions which I studied, I could note these younger elements which formed the new Soviet generation, trained in the years of revolution. They were, in some respects, more rough and ready, but often technically better equipped, than were the old Bolsheviks who had passed, or had been pushed, out of the picture. The foreign colony in Moscow referred to them as "Stalin's boys," and under their leadership the economic enterprises seemed to be working better. Official statistics, at any rate, showed a general rise again in the production curves.

One of the most popular current political plays on the Soviet stage during my stay in Moscow was on the topic of the overreaching of the purge. As I saw the portrayal of the stupid, treasonable activities of local Bolshevik leaders purging honest, loyal Party workers, I felt at first uncomfortable; but when the audience applauded the exposure by the central leadership of those abusing their positions of power, I understood why the play was given. The central leaders had come to the rescue; had, as on other occasions, saved the people from dishonest elements in the Party. That what had happened reflected on the whole system was likely to be the conclusion of the outside student of government. The Soviet citizen, on the other hand, generally took the view that the central leaders were their saviors, guarding against such mistakes and ready to correct them when they occurred.

On this subject of the purge, I should like to quote the remark of one of the older workers who had very narrowly escaped from the destructive overreaching. After telling me of this terrible aspect of the purge, this old friend remarked: "But in view of what we now see that Hitler and the Japanese were able to do in Austria, Spain, Czechoslovakia, and China, I realize that Stalin was right and wise." Let me add a similar statement, from an old friend from China whom I met in Moscow, to the effect that, had the Chinese authorities dealt with treason and intrigue as Stalin had done, so much of his country would not now be in the hands of the Japanese military invaders. And the case of France offers further parallels.

For all her five-year plans, Soviet Russia was still backward economically. One of the most interesting discussions that I attended was at the Marx-Engels-Lenin Institute, where one of the leading Soviet economists, Varga, spoke on "How can we overtake and outstrip America?" We often heard Bolsheviks use the slogan "Outstrip America." That was a slogan to stir up this backward people. I am afraid too many people went to Moscow expecting to find that it was already done. I should like to note again the danger in comparing Russia with America, of applying our yardstick to the conditions in that country, which has had a hard history and, as a result, is still backward in economic and cultural standards. I had a dispute with another student of Soviet affairs on the subject of how soon the amalgam of Europe and Asia in the Russian would produce a people as systematic and technically efficient as the British or German worker. He thought it would take one hundred years. I expressed the view that it could be done in considerably less time, judging from what had been accomplished in the last twenty years.

With regard to general cultural development, outwardly the progress had been very definite. An experiment of helping a backward people of the Asiatic part of the Union to use the opera as a channel of self-expression was politically interesting, although artistically it was not wholly successful. Also interesting was a session of the historical section of the Academy of Sciences to which I was invited. The old professors of history were helping younger colleagues from the trans-Caucasian republic of Azerbaidzhan to prepare a textbook on the history of their people. Marxian doctrine and approach were being carefully followed, of course. For the contemporary period the role of Stalin, as well as that of Lenin, was given great prominence. And Trotsky's "treasonable" activities were duly noted. I spent much time with teachers of history and the editors of the new textbooks on history. On one occasion I sat in on the oral examinations of fourteen-year-old boys and girls on Russian literature, and it was a very creditable performance on both sides of the table.

To summarize my impressions of internal conditions on the eve of the second World War: I found the situation better than I had expected to find it—less tense politically and less tight economically. Others studying on the spot agreed with me that the Soviet system was strong internally—just how strong one could not say at the time, but certainly stronger than a year before, strengthened in many respects by the purge, while in other respects temporarily somewhat weakened.

Warsaw in 1939—June

I wrote[1] soon after my arrival in Warsaw:

These 48 hours of bourgeois luxury have been pleasant—for the body and stomach at least—but in mind I feel already bored. Fact is I'm homesick for the more real life of Sovietism.

"Still backward culturally and economically," the Soviet leaders

[1] [Excerpts from letters written by Harper to his mother, June 8, 1939; and to Sir Bernard Pares, June 9, 1939.]

260

keep admonishing as they press and drive for their Communist goal. And as I compare my environment here, and at the Cafe Europe across the street, with what I had three days ago in Moscow, I see that backwardness very clearly. But, on the other hand, I did not see a single tractor or motor truck between Brest Litovsk and Warsaw; and everywhere I saw the old strip-system of farming.

Yesterday was a Polish religious holiday, and I walked in the riverside parks and through the Jewish quarter and wondered what real progress had been made here the last twenty years. The faces of the old people and children in the religious procession did not have the vigor and forward look which I saw two weeks ago in another procession on the Red Square.

Those last days in Moscow were hectic ones. Hope you didn't get a shock by the news item U.P. sent out on my introducing the Lambeth Walk with Jean Denny [*New York Times* correspondent's wife]. I was sober, but the U.P. man evidently was not.

And what about Warsaw? The latest political gossip is that Hitler expects to be here, where I am sitting in the Hotel Bristol, in his carpet slippers (not his war boots) by August 20. I shall be safely on my Kansasville farm by then, I hope.

I spent two weeks in Poland, first traveling to Warsaw, where I spent most of my time, and then taking a two-day trip to the famous estate and palace of the Potockis' at Lancut, near Lvov. In addition to official connections from former trips, I looked up old friends, some dating back a third of a century, to 1906, when I studied the effects of the first Russian revolution on the then "Polish provinces" of the Empire. Thus I saw socialists, as well as members of the government; businessmen, both Polish and Jewish; landlords and peasants; and Ukrainian leaders.

From all quarters there had been criticism of Polish foreign policy and its leading exponent, Colonel Beck. At one moment, in March, demonstrators were even shouting that "von Beck" be put in a concentration camp, my Polish friends told me. But in June, when I was in Warsaw, it looked for one brief moment as though Poland had learned the lessons of Munich. It was after the seizure of Prague, and Beck had been forced to a more positive stand, which was hopefully regarded as having at last broken the vicious circle in which Hitler had had the whole world milling about. In fact, I opened a talk, which Colonel Beck gave me, with this remark; and he assented with proper modesty, adding that a psychological change was indeed necessary, so that others than the Germans could speak of national prestige and living-space. Colonel Beck's account of his interview with Hitler in January of that year was along the same line. According to Beck, he decided to act like a colonel to this former corporal and was able to put it over, which perhaps was good for his conscience, troubled as it undoubtedly was because of his many concessions to the Nazis, but which also, perhaps, made even more violent the Nazi policy against the Poles.

Although Poland officially had refused to join the Anti-Comintern Pact of 1936, the Polish leadership—like that of the British and French —unconsciously adhered to it in their thinking and indirectly in many of their policies. We know now that Chamberlain's "collective security" proposal to the Soviets, which was then being discussed, restricted the Soviet Union, on Poland's own insistence, to placing military and material resources at the disposal of Poland and Romania when or if they asked for it. As Pertinax put it: The Soviet Union was to serve only as a storehouse into which Poland and Romania could dip to their hearts' content. Or, as a Polish leader blandly stated, what the Soviet Union should really do was to promise the Poles an area of Soviet territory of some 200 square kilometers to which they could retreat, if necessary, to reform their forces.

Every Pole with whom I talked, whether a fellow-teacher, a newspaperman, a porter carrying my luggage to the train, or a taxi-driver, said: "We will fight for Danzig if Germany tries to take it." And when, in view of my interest, I said, "Well, and what about help from the Soviet Union?" I was referred to Stalin's statement, in March of that year, to the effect that the Soviet Union would aid any country that resisted aggression. Then I would be very specific and ask: "Now, if that aid you want is airplanes, do pilots go with airplanes?" "Oh, yes," was the answer; it seemed to be the usual thing that the pilot and the tank-driver should go with their equipment wherever an airplane or tank was sold. But when I said: "What about outright Soviet military assistance?" they said, "Oh, no, we do not want Soviet troops in our territory."

One can understand this attitude in view of the fact that Poland was under Russian domination for years and also because of the fact that in 1920 Bolshevik troops were at the gates of Warsaw in a Soviet attack or counterattack on Poland. This attitude thus represented fear both of the old Russian imperialism and of new Soviet revolutionary effort. In arguments there would be the admission that both these former tendencies had been modified in the last years by the Stalin policy of "building socialism in one country." But the suspicion of Russia and Bolshevism was strongly traditional, as part of the old and new Polish nationalism. And the time when these two countries might come together and settle their grievances was fast running out.

The two weeks in Poland, June 5–20, terminated with a strained week-end when Goebbels visited Danzig. I wondered, for a moment, if I had delayed too long in my calculation to slip out through the Corridor. When the ship started to turn in the Gdynia harbor, we thought the Germans had decided to try another provocation by sending a battleship to Danzig to support Goebbels' harangues. But we were only testing a new compass. However, I could not avoid seeing swastikas, as I had hoped to do; the street corners and about 10 per cent of the apartments of Danzig displayed them in that part of the city through which our Warsaw-Gdynia train passed.

The German-Soviet Pact

There have been many guesses as to the exact date when preliminary negotiations of a political character started between the Soviet Union and Germany. In his outline of Soviet policy at the congress of the Party in March, 1939, Stalin indicated clearly that mutually beneficial commercial relations would be developed with all countries whose policies were not hostile to the Soviet Union. It would seem that in May of 1939 Molotov accepted a German suggestion that political matters might also be discussed in order to further the commercial negotiations. By that date the Moscow leaders were clearly disappointed in their negotiations with the British and the French, although still hopeful that an effective program of collective security could be worked out. The new state of mind of the Soviet leaders was clearly indicated in the significant leading articles of the *Izvestia* of May 11 and in Molotov's report to the Supreme Soviet on May 30. It was, then, from May of 1939 that negotiations for a nonaggression pact between Germany and the Soviet Union probably started. And it was in May that I was in Moscow.

For a specific turning-point in Soviet foreign policy the occasion of Litvinov's retirement will serve as well as any other. Litvinov was replaced by Molotov on May 3. Four days later I saw him in a theater lobby; friends of mine saw him on June 5, sitting in the Soviet parliament, of which he was a member. Why was he removed? Many reasons were suggested at the time; but in the light of present knowledge we can say that Litvinov's resignation was a warning to the democracies of Britain, France, and America that efforts at collective security were being deliberately sabotaged—were being jeopardized by the Chamberlains, Daladiers, and other men of Munich. Instead of being seen as such a warning, it was interpreted as a "purge"; and Chamberlain made a pretentious slap at Stalin for changing ministers during a crisis.

Litvinov's successor, Molotov, I had heard speak half a dozen times, though I had had no personal contact with him. I would not say he is a brilliant person; but he is a good, solid, common-sense Russian workman of peasant origin. I should imagine the British found it less interesting with Molotov and less active and less fiery than with the brilliant-minded Litvinov, but Molotov had long been one of the leading political figures in Russia. He was to report on Soviet foreign policy at a session of the Supreme Soviet, and the one big failure of my trip was being refused a ticket to attend this session. Although I had been admitted to the Soviet congress in 1936 and had heard Stalin's report on the new constitution, the changes in the Foreign Affairs Commissariat cost me this rather exasperating experience of being refused a fully legitimate request.

Although the British-Soviet negotiations were going on all this time (nothing was then known of the German-Soviet talks), it was impossible for me to talk freely with those directly concerned, some of whom I saw frequently. In a semijocular tone I kept asking them to keep in mind that I would like to talk the subject over as a historian after the signing of the pact with Britain. I did not push my request to be received by Molotov, because I realized that I could not raise with him the question that was of greatest interest at the moment. Because of the importance of these negotiations for the position of the Soviet Union in the world, I considered staying on another month in order to be able to have these "historical" conversations. But I decided, at the beginning of June, that I might have to stay on, not one, but many months; and my judgment proved to be correct at this point. As I left Moscow on June 5, my doubts as to whether the negotiations would terminate successfully were very definite. I allowed myself to say, both in Moscow and later in Warsaw, that in my opinion there would be no Soviet-British pact.

What factors led me to this conclusion, and why did the Soviets start turning to the Germans in May? On getting back to America in July of 1939, I summarized Soviet policy after Munich under three headings, as follows: (1) Munich will not bring peace or stop aggression, but aggression can be stopped by a genuine collective-security program. (2) The Soviets will collaborate in any such genuine collective-security program because it gives more security and is cheaper. (3) Unless such a program is forthcoming within a reasonable time, the Soviets will take their own steps for their own security—they will not impose themselves on others.

The Soviet Union condemned the Prague rape, in unequivocal terms, so that there could be no basis for London or Paris to doubt that Soviet leaders were ready to take whatever action would be necessary. From this point on, proposal followed counterproposal for five months. And yet, when August came around, no pact had been signed. Whose fault was this? The Soviet leaders claimed that the impasse had been deliberately caused by the artificial raising of obstacles on points of detail —such as the definition of "indirect aggression." Moscow suspected Great Britain of wanting to make only a meaningless, general declaratory arrangement under cover of which the policy of appeasement could be continued. Moscow also claimed that the original British proposal was far short of full reciprocity, that by refusing to broaden the scope of protection to actions concerning the Baltic states, as well as Belgium and Holland, a corridor was left open to Soviet frontiers. It was suggested that perhaps this was the British idea—the old idea of getting Nazi aggression directed toward the Soviets.

And, finally, Moscow insisted on an out-and-out military alliance between Great Britain, France, and the Soviet Union, with staff conversations simultaneous with the political arrangements. For let it be noted that there had been no staff conversations between the Soviet Union and France under the mutual-assistance pact of 1934. No loan had been made to Poland, though there was talk of a much larger loan to Germany. There were rumors of backdoor negotiations with Hitler and Mussolini; but when it came to negotiations in Moscow, no important "political leader" seemed to be available. When the British and French did finally accede to the Soviet demand and sent military missions to Moscow at the beginning of August, these traveled by the slowest route and had no authority to make definitive arrangements when they got there.

London, for her part, was afraid Moscow would try to take unfair advantage of the position in which England found herself as a result of her guaranties to eastern European countries, which she was in no position to fulfil by armed local assistance; would try to get the whip hand; and would try to be the one to determine the time to act if any agreement were reached. Also, Chamberlain, as we have suggested, may not have been sure whether the Soviet system, from a military point of view, was weak or strong; and sometimes he acted on the basis that it was weak, and then he acted on the basis that it was strong—perhaps too strong for comfort. This attitude vitiated the British approach in the negotiations and was mainly responsible for the dragging-out of these negotiations. As one British friend remarked to me (I quote exactly): "The trouble is you never can be *sure* that these Russians will let you down."

The initial mistake of the British prime minister, I believe, was that he thought the Soviet Union was in such a panic that its co-operation could be secured at a very low price. In my opinion, the situation was exactly the opposite. For the British Empire found itself threatened at many points; was less prepared for self-defense; and, in addition, had by its commitments in eastern and southeastern Europe to Poland and Romania made it advisable, if not indispensable, to secure the co-operation of the Soviet Union. And, yet, what Chamberlain and Bonnet wanted was to frighten Hitler with the Soviet Union without thereby committing themselves to anything.

The conclusion, in short, is that the negotiations between Britain and the Soviet Union failed because Chamberlain apparently did not really want the alliance with the Soviets which these negotiations presumably contemplated. In any case, he did not offer the Soviets anything that a responsible government of a strong power could accept.

It was from this conviction that Russia decided to look out for Soviet security on its own as best it could. There was only one alternative, once England and France would not offer the Soviets a program of full reciprocal collective security; the alternative was to accept Hitler's offer of a nonaggression pact.

Under the circumstances, therefore, it seemed to me fully understandable why the attempt to set up a new program of collective security had failed. I was prepared for such a failure, though I thought it would stop there and would mean simply the isolation of the Soviet Union. Back in Chicago, in my public and small-group talks, I dwelt on Chamberlain's policy, criticizing it without reservation. I overreached, for this line was interpreted as evidence of my alleged pro-Soviet, even pro-German, tendencies. On August 23 the Soviet-German Non-aggression Pact was signed. As I said at the time, quoting Louis Fischer, it took three men to make that pact: Hitler, Stalin, and Chamberlain—of the three, Chamberlain was by no means the least responsible.

Eight days after the pact the war broke out; and eight days after the war broke out (September 9, 1939) I had occasion to write my friend Loy Henderson as follows: "When Wheeler-Bennett the other evening said that the war must go on till Hitler and all his crowd are out, I answered: 'Who built up this crowd in Germany? Do you think you can overthrow them by paper from the air? When are you going to start fighting, now that the Soviet Union won't do it for you? Why don't you give the Poles some real help?' And the hell of it is that peace could have been secured, that is, real peace, last year, *before Munich*, I still believe."

In Russian history there was one particularly difficult period—when everything went wrong at once—which historians have always referred to as the "Time of Troubles" (1598–1613). And it would take a term like that to describe my own position during the twenty-two months from the signing of the Soviet-German pact on August 23, 1939, to the German invasion of the Soviet Union on June 22, 1941.

The Soviet imbroglio with Finland, coming after the pact with Germany and the invasion of Poland, brought to a culmination the anti-Soviet feeling in all Western countries. Nazi propaganda had always been based in large measure on "anti-Bolshevism," and it registered easily among such men as Chamberlain and Daladier. It was more surprising to find it a factor in the thinking and activity of a Blum or some of the socialists I saw in Poland. But what was most disturbing was to find that those whose profession it was to weigh the factors objectively —American students of international affairs and liberal journalists and commentators—should fall for this line as strongly as any others. Finland, in particular, was used by many of my liberal colleagues for an emotional upsurge, even though this played into the hands of Chamberlain and Daladier and kept their regimes going—to the cost of all of us.

The basis of this emotional appeal was to raise accusations to the level of facts. Thus it was insisted, despite the evidence at hand, that the Soviet-German pact was an alliance in the full sense of the word; that

Sovietism was just as aggressive as naziism; that the Soviets, like the Nazis, bombed civilian populations; that Nazis and Communists were actively co-operating in America and elsewhere; and that the Soviets industrially, as well as politically, were about to blow up. University colleagues and Washington politicians alike insisted on there being a "Stalin-Hitler alliance" and a "Communazi" *rapprochement*, the idea being to rally the liberals against Hitler and the conservatives against Stalin and thereby secure our own national unity.

On more than one occasion I told such people that the lie, as I allowed myself to call it, would come back on them like a boomerang, as, in fact, it later did. The accepted policy, as I phrased it at the time, was to "spit at the Bolsheviks"; and there was little concern when I asked: "Can't you be gentlemen? And how many lives and dollars will this cost us later on?" Many of my colleagues were saying that it was a duty of academic men as citizens to join in the emotional upsurge. I begged out of it by referring to the controversial character of my field of study—and, for my pains, was increasingly looked upon as a sort of Nazi-Soviet agent. My efforts to explain were taken as efforts to justify; and if I showed the least bit of impatience with the loose or prejudiced thinking I had to meet, or the least zeal in presenting the factual picture, I was considered an advocate—of the devil, of course.

If my own remarks at the time became increasingly bitter, the cataracts which were then developing on my eyes may have had something to do with it. One cataract was removed successfully; but the readjustment of the habits of a lifetime, such as walking, mounting stairs, and even eating, which is necessary after such an operation, was a considerable nervous strain. And, of course, this had to happen at the same time as the wave of public disapproval for all things Soviet. As time went by, my classes had grown smaller and I had reduced my outside lectures to a minimum. I had at first taken to avoiding discussions with colleagues; I even began to go to the office by the back door in order not to meet with them. But in the end I went on a rampage and got myself really ostracized—put in the doghouse, as I expressed it. I went about cutting off so many heads that my brother suggested that I should spend more time on the farm and apply myself to cutting off the heads of the thistles and burdocks. One result of this was a serious nervous breakdown, confining me to bed for some months, which took the form of what the doctors diagnosed as dermatitis—a type of shingles, but which I translated as "the doghouse mange."

CHAPTER XXXI

RUSSIA ACTS ALONE

The March into Poland

THE SOVIET UNION HAD ALWAYS SAID IT WOULD MEET ADVANCING troops on somebody else's territory than its own—and that is just where it did meet the Germans. When the pact with Germany was signed, Stalin knew that Hitler would soon take Danzig and the Corridor. He therefore immediately called certain classes to the colors and deployed them along his western frontier. And he added to these troops when he saw that Britain and France were doing nothing to aid Poland in the opening days of the war from September 1 to 17. Then when the fighting in Poland moved eastward into the Polish Ukraine, the Soviet Red Army crossed the frontier and pushed the Germans back. Except in the Lvov area there was no fighting; but there was maneuvering, and very skilful maneuvering, on the part of the Soviets.

That a detailed partition of Poland was not effected on August 23 at the time of the Soviet-German pact is indicated by the moving back and forth of the line dividing German and Soviet forces. It was good politics on Stalin's part to refuse Hitler's offer of a boundary (in September, 1939) which would have brought under Soviet control some of ethnic Poland. Instead, in the main he took the Curzon Line, which was ethnically the best and also politically what Versailles had settled on. Thus the Soviets annexed only that territory which Poland had seized by force in 1920 against the recommendation of the peacemakers of 1919.

A point of detail is of interest. While the Soviet government had no right to proclaim the end of the Polish state, on that September 17 there was, in fact, no Polish government in existence. The notification to other powers of the appointment of a new government by the former president of Poland came only on September 28, though it was dated September 15. Thus, on the seventeenth of that month one may say that the government of Poland was somewhere on the telegraph wire between Poland and Paris.

The process of sovietization in the areas taken over by the Soviet Union was carried out more or less along the pattern of the period of the New Economic Policy of 1921–28. Particularly, there was no immediate and forceful collectivization of agriculture. Also, small traders were allowed to continue business. Landlords, large manufacturers, large merchants, former officials, and some clergy were handled roughly, generally by local elements, and in many cases protected when the Soviet army units arrived on the spot. Some evacuation of industry, because of anticipation of Nazi attack, was carried on; other industries were speeded up, old plants reopened, new ones started. Writers and social workers of high caliber (albeit "Communist") were sent from Moscow to promote social and cultural development. The process had its questionable features, but at the same time the sovietization of these areas brought to the workman and peasant masses cultural institutions which they had not previously known and a form of participation in public life quite new to them and, of course, the elimination of what they were told, and may themselves have felt, were "exploiting elements."

In addition to the desire for military security, a principal basis for Soviet action was to liberate from Polish "imperialism" and "feudalism" the Ukrainians and White Russians. These groups had indeed suffered constant restrictions and even persecutions during the twenty years of Polish rule, and now they were drawn integrally into the corresponding Soviet republics of the Union. It is not clear what happened to the old Ukrainian nationalists, but their form of nationalism would be quite unwelcome under the Soviet system. Jews rushing in from German-occupied Poland were given nine months to get jobs and, if then unemployed, were sent east. No mass migration of Jews into the Soviet area was suggested by either Germany or the Soviet Union, however. Presumably the Soviet attitude was the same as that followed with respect to Jewish immigration during all those last years of increased Jewish persecution, namely, that these Jews, predominantly merchants and small traders, would not fit easily into the new Soviet economic order.

Among the Poles the Soviet action was characterized as sheer "aggression," not only by the leaders who set up a new Polish government in Paris and acted on the basis of a formal state of war existing between it and the Soviet Union, but also by Polish socialists, who inclined to the view that the Soviet Union was equally aggressive with Germany. Many Polish socialists who had been bitterly anti-Bolshevik sought refuge in the Soviet section, only to be arrested and in some cases executed. An underground appeal of a group of Polish socialists at that time indicated activity in the Soviet, as well as the German, portion of former Poland. Polish socialists have always been the bitterest of all socialists in their anti-Bolshevik stand.

The final settlement with respect to Poland was made on September 28, in a second pact between the Soviet Union and Germany, called one of "frontier and friendship." It was at this time that Germany and the Soviet Union announced that, as the two largest states on the Continent, they would, in the future, decide all matters in central and eastern Europe. This announcement aimed to put an end to the system of "client states" which Great Britain and France had developed as part of the Versailles settlement. Here was a very definite common interest of Germany and the Soviet Union—to put an end to a system that had aimed both at encircling Germany and at forming a *cordon sanitaire* against Sovietism.

Finland

Finland's history has been greatly influenced by her tragic geographic position. At the height of the intervention in the 1918–21 period the London *Times* described her as the military highway into Russia. "Finland," it said, "is the key to Petrograd and Petrograd is the key to Moscow." And, indeed, Finland was the jumping-off place for the first and last attack on the Soviet Union in this period. In the present period this relationship has been no less significant. The Mannerheim Line, for example, with its outposts only twenty miles from Leningrad, could be used for offensive, as well as defensive, purposes, serving as a shield for an attacking force. Finland's airdromes, built by Nazis to accommodate 2,000 planes at a time when Finland had only 150 planes of her own, can be understood only against the background of geographic realities.

Finland was long famous for her democratic tradition. She was the first country in the world to have a parliament with a socialist majority —in 1916, one year before the Russian revolution—and two years later her independence was conceded by the Bolsheviks. But this first, democratic Finland was soon suppressed by an extreme conservative regime under Baron Mannerheim, with the help of German military units led by General von der Goltz. Mannerheim was the first leader in Europe to have a private political army—the Civil Guards. Just as Finland had been first in having a socialist parliament, so now she was first in having an army of a fascist type.

Antagonism between Russians and Finns has been traditional for centuries. Of all the non-Russian groups of the old Empire, the Finns resisted Russification the most stubbornly, and they were also the most stubborn in resisting Soviet moves in 1939. After marching into Poland and imposing its protection on the three Baltic states, Moscow invited the Finnish government to discuss changes in their common frontier in return for increased trade (at a time when trade with Germany and Britain had been all but eliminated) and access to Murmansk (at a time when Finland's Baltic outlet had been cut off). And, at first, it seemed as though the Finnish government was not unprepared to go through with the negotiations.

But then, right in the midst of the negotiations, the attitude of the Finnish authorities changed. Pressures and promises from Britain and America, and in the first instance from Bolshevik-hating Chamberlain, were responsible for a sudden shift in the Finnish position. Demands that Moscow insisted were absolutely necessary to Soviet security were rejected. The Finnish army had already been mobilized, and large armed forces were sent to the borders. It is not clear to what extent there was Soviet mobilization in answer to this move, but the weak character of Russian military action in December would indicate that such mobilization was not extensive. And then came the inevitable "frontier incident."

There is no doubt but that Stalin grossly miscalculated in both the military and the political aspects of the Finnish campaign, though certain facts which were not then admitted have now generally been recognized. It is established, for example, that the Soviet air forces never deliberately bombed civilian centers—a fact which is confirmed by the official Finnish figure of 374 civilian casualties for the whole 105 days of extensive air fighting. Thus there was no real basis for the so-called "moral embargo" which the American government proclaimed against the Soviet Union. Also, it is now conceded that, when the Soviet military forces finally got into position, they showed great effectiveness, in view of the climatic conditions and the character of their task; in the opinion of many military experts the breaking of the Mannerheim Line was, indeed, a feat. And, finally, the rather decent peace which the Soviet Union gave to Finland tended somewhat to repair the damage which the Soviet leaders had done to their prestige by their unfortunate conflict with that country.

In its larger implications the Soviet-Finnish conflict fitted in with the plan of certain elements in the British and French military leadership to get the war into eastern Europe. Extensive aid to Finland was given by the British and French governments, of which they later boasted. The British government refused to act as mediator when the first steps were taken to re-establish peace, and when peace was, nevertheless, about to be signed, Chamberlain and Daladier publicly announced their offers to send expeditionary forces in Finland's behalf. The war on the Mannerheim Line seemed to have a popularity and an appeal that the war on the Siegfried Line lacked.

If Stalin's handling of the Finnish situation was something of a blunder, the question naturally arises: "Did Hitler egg him into it?" Even if Hitler didn't egg him on, the attack on Finland served Hitler well. For one thing, it tied Stalin to him. He got the trade treaty of February, 1940, this being the third and most important step in Nazi-Soviet relations. And, for another thing, the Soviets could not, and did not, object to Hitler's going for Denmark and Norway, in opposition to possible British and French moves there. In fact, on the day after the German invasion of Norway, the Soviet armed forces, acting under the terms of the Soviet-Finnish peace, were at last withdrawn from the Petsamo area. British, French, and American reaction to Finland, it seems, had convinced Stalin that, for the moment at least, his interests were on the side of Germany.

The Baltic States

Moscow's recognition of the independence of the Baltic States was always a contingent one. In the opening years of the Soviet period after 1917 these states had been the scene of considerable activity. Germany had pushed into the area in its advance on Petrograd. The Bolsheviks had tried to use it as a corridor to the west, both for trade purposes and for propaganda of revolution. And the Allied intervention had found in it a bridgehead, and later a section of the *cordon sanitaire* against Bolshevism. Consequently, when the situation had been stabilized and Moscow proceeded to recognize the independence of Esthonia, Latvia, and Lithuania in the treaties of 1920, it stated that it would respect their independence only so long as they did not again become centers of activity for other great powers.

In May of 1939, as I passed through Riga, I was told that as between the three "imperialists"—Germany, Poland, and the Soviet Union—the last would probably be the least onerous. In any event, the eventual reabsorption of these former provinces of the old Russia was regarded by many as inevitable. And with the partition of Poland and the German seizure of Danzig, the Soviets already moved to impose on the three states pacts of mutual assistance, garrisons of Soviet troops, evacuation of German residents, and other limitations on their strict independence.

Within each country, however, there still were groups which had aimed to build up political, as well as economic, relations with other countries than the Soviets. It was one of these groups that established a semidictatorial regime in Latvia in 1934 and in the other states also around that date. In 1940, with the taking of land by peasants in the Soviet part of Poland and the consequent unrest among the peasants in the Baltic area, landlord groups in this area sent a secret delegation to Hitler to invite his intervention in their behalf (as Hitler himself confirmed in his speech on June 22, 1941). Hitler at this time was just carrying through his seizure of the northern coast of Scandinavia, the Low Countries, and France; and the Soviets were not slow to intensify their own preparations against possible attack. In June and July of 1940, therefore, occupation and incorporation into the Soviet Union were carried through not only with respect to the Baltic States but with respect to Bessarabia and northern Bukovina as well. Thus, on the basis of the international situation, Moscow, did indeed, carry out its frank warning of some twenty years before, that it would respect the independence of its small neighbors only if such independence were genuine.

The Soviet technique in taking over these small countries was, as one writer has put it, "to combine invitation with pressure"—just as in their internal affairs the Soviets have combined educative with compulsive measures. The well-known methods of the Soviet purge of 1937–38 were resorted to, although now it was the liquidation of bourgeois elements, rather than of traitors or of doubters within the Party ranks, that was at issue. Between 200,000 and 300,000 recalcitrants are said to have been sent east. In the case of Latvia, there was specific reference to the coup d'état of 1934, and all state employees serving under this "fascist" regime were specifically designated for elimination as "enemies of the people." In the case of Bukovina, the class of landlord boyars was specified by the new regime as having been overthrown.

272

While the new pattern rested on the leadership of the Communist Party, there was no mention of the "dictatorship of the proletariat." The elements in whose name the new regime was being established were always indicated as "workmen, peasants, and toiling intelligentsia." This latter phrase was sometimes made more specific by referring to "employees" or to "writers," "teachers," and other members of the liberal professions. Liberal critics of the Bolshevik experiment have insisted that one lesson of the 1917 revolution was the need for the new authority to act in the name of all groups of toilers and not simply in the name of the workman class. The experience of the Baltic States would seem to indicate that the Moscow leaders have also, in the main, accepted this modification of their 1917–21 procedure.

This does not mean, of course, that all the Baltic intellectuals throve under the Soviets or, indeed, sided with the new system at all. I am inclined to believe that Anna Louise Strong's quotation of a remark made by a man at the American legation in Kaunas represented the view of many intellectuals, army officers, and others. What she quotes in *The Soviets Expected It* (p. 197) is: "It wouldn't have been so bad if the Red Army had merely seized the country and established a protectorate the way the Germans do. But they've started something going among the lower classes that is undermining the whole social structure. You should see my janitor!" And Miss Strong adds: "I didn't see this janitor, but I saw tens of thousands like him, workers and peasants who were experiencing the thrill of unwonted power."

Russia and America

I have already noted in connection with my 1936 trip that the Soviet leaders at that time hoped for two things from American foreign policy. First, the Soviets hoped that the great continental state of the Western Hemisphere would recognize its community of interest with the chief continental state of the Eastern Hemisphere—at least to the extent of advocating freedom of the seas as a means of maintaining intercourse between them. And, second, since they realized that close Soviet-American co-operation was out of the question for the moment, they hoped that America would, at any rate, co-operate closely with England and France as sort of go-betweens for the U.S.A. and the U.S.S.R.

And in 1939 I was impressed to find that President Roosevelt's foreign messages were being printed widely in the Soviet press and that the comment on them was most favorable. On a collective farm in the Ukraine, for example, the conversation at lunchtime turned to America; and it was interesting to hear a young peasant girl praise Roosevelt for his contribution to peace. But the second point on the program, the importance of England and France as go-betweens, was not working out so well—in fact, did not seem to be working out at all. I suggested, at the time, that the failure of America to implement Roosevelt's messages in some positive manner—a change in our neutrality legislation, for example—made the Soviet negotiators more careful as to what they would sign in the way of a pact with England and France. It was also possible, it seemed to me, that the delay in the negotiations with the Soviets contributed to the strengthening of isolationist tendencies in America, especially when it became clear that Chamberlain was holding back from signing the sort of alliance with the Soviets which might have had real meaning.

In the final analysis, therefore, the Soviet Union and considerable opinion in America shared, to a certain extent, the same doubt as to whether Chamberlain and Bonnet did even then mean business. The Soviet Union might well have hesitated to sign up with a Britain or France that could not secure material or even moral support from America, just as American public opinion might well remain skeptical of regimes in Britain and France which were unable or unwilling to bring into their programs of collective security the needed weight of the Soviets.

After the formal outbreak of the war in September of 1939, when Soviet-American relations were going from bad to worse, officials of each government went out of their way to criticize the policies of the other. Sumner Welles, for example, spoke of the Soviet absorption of the Baltic States as "predatory activities," and Molotov in his speech to the Supreme Soviet replied that Moscow was not interested in the opinions of "certain gentlemen" in Washington. A usual American interpretation of Soviet policy with respect to the war in Europe was, as we have seen, that it aimed to prolong the war as much as possible, so that there would be better soil for social revolution. And a Soviet interpretation of American policy with respect to the Far East was that it aimed to prolong the war between Japan and China, by helping both sides, in order to derive profit from war trade and reconstruction.

Moscow's bid for a peace settlement in the early stages of the war was, it may be noted, supported by Germany but refused by Britain and France. Then the Finns held out, bringing war to the Baltic, with the backing of the Western democracies (including America). As a result, Moscow found it expedient to put the blame for the continuation of the war on England and France. She knew there was no chance for agreement with these countries (or with America) so long as Chamberlain and Daladier were in power; she was disgusted with our Western intellectuals and liberals for falling for the anti-Soviet propaganda; and she wanted peace with Germany as long as possible in order to get ready for Hitler's attack in her own way. Thus, for the first year of the war the Soviet press repeatedly characterized the ruling groups in the Allied countries as the real "incendiaries of war"—being always careful, however, to hold responsible the ruling groups in these countries and particularly specific individuals within these groups.

The Western powers responded partly by expelling the Soviets from the League of Nations and partly by bringing economic pressure to bear on them. It had always been the Soviet policy to prefer American machinery to German, and American technical assistance to European in general. But with the coming of the war and the setting-up of a virtual blockade of the Soviet Union by Britain, the United States imposed its "moral embargo" on the Soviets because of alleged bombing of civilian centers during the Finnish-Soviet conflict. This, of course, meant a definite restriction on Soviet purchases in America and a consequent turning to Germany for needed machinery.

Moscow's miscalculations and mistakes in trying to deal with Finland on a "great-power–small-power" basis did greatly weaken its appeal among Americans; but we should not overlook the strong resemblance between the Soviet proposals to Britain and France on the "small-power" issue in the summer of 1939, under which the Soviets had urged that the proposed Anglo-French-Soviet pact should provide for automatic action with respect to any small neutral state, whether of eastern or of western Europe, in the event even of "indirect aggression," and the American proposals to the twenty Latin American countries at Havana in the summer of 1940. This was to be, as Carroll Binder aptly characterized the American policy sanctioned at the Havana meeting, "imperialism with benefit of clergy." It was interesting to note that many of the individuals who had most vehemently condemned what the Soviet Union had done in Finland now turned around and openly advocated that we be ready to do very much the same thing, in the event of emergency, in any one of the Latin republics, and particularly in Mexico.

In general, it can be said that in their foreign policies during this period the United States and the Soviet Union were by no means so far apart as they seemed to be at the time. The two largest neutrals were spitting at each other for months on end; and sometimes it was because each did not consider the actions of the other neutral, and sometimes it was because each wanted the other to become frankly belligerent. Moscow was at least doubtful of either the possibility or the usefulness of a British victory; and the United States was perhaps not too sure about the possibility or usefulness of a victory for China. But, as events have turned out, both countries did stand to benefit by the common victory of Great Britain and China. And as the crisis developed, this mutual benefit became more and more recognized even at the time.

Thus, until the debacle of France, Moscow had objected to America's failure to be strictly neutral with respect to the Allies. But with the French collapse in May of 1940 this attitude changed. By taking German aggression on her own back and by at last replacing Chamberlain with Churchill, England (with American approval) accomplished three things: she convinced Moscow that she was at last awake and fighting a real war; she indicated the grave danger of a Germany making a clean sweep in western Europe; and she abandoned her "economic war" involving the Baltic and Black seas. And Moscow responded to the new situation. Instead of objecting to our lack of neutrality, Moscow became almost anxious that America should give England every possible aid. In any case, the Moscow leaders emphasized to their people that such aid was being given; that, on this basis, England was going to fight it out; and that the struggle was likely to be long and arduous.

Russia and Germany; the German Attack

If it be accepted, as suggested in the preceding section, that Moscow was beginning to look with increasing favor upon a British victory, there are many who will still insist that Soviet policy in this period was very stupid. On many occasions commentators or analysts have suggested that the Soviets should, for their own good, have taken the offensive in the Balkans in the spring of 1941. When the British expedition became active in Greece, said the critics, the Soviets should have added their blow against Hitler. But from the Moscow point of view, this was still a will-o'-the-wisp. Moscow knew the military weakness of Great Britain. She was in touch with popular (leftist) forces in Bulgaria and Yugoslavia and was getting little encouragement from England in this connection. She saw that the British could not or would not even blow up the Romanian oil fields—that is, go in for a serious campaign in the Balkans. But, most of all, Russia must have remembered that she had once taken positive action in moving into Poland, Finland, the Baltic States, and Bessarabia, and that, except for Bessarabia, she had been severely criticized, perhaps by the same commentators, for aggression.

But Moscow had blocked Germany. During the twenty-two months of the German-Soviet pact the Soviet Union had blocked German expansion directly and indirectly as much as, if not more than, had the armed might of England and France together. This blocking of German aggression applied not only to the northeast of Europe—the Baltic direction. It applied also, though in a more limited sense, even to the northwest of Europe—the direction of England. For the Soviet march into Bessarabia in June, 1940, by Hitler's own admission one year later, disturbed his plan to invade England by forcing him to give attention to his Balkan front. No doubt, this Soviet move was carried through for the self-defense of the Soviet Union and was not thought of particularly as aid to Britain, even though it did, in fact, indirectly render such aid. In other words, there was no *objective* coming-together of Britain and the Soviet Union in the summer of 1940. But Moscow knew that Churchill wanted to fight Hitler, and there was thus basis for a *subjective* coming-together.

In the southeast of Europe, also, the Soviets must be considered substantially successful in blocking Germany, for their political pressure in the Balkan area was a basic factor in preventing Hitler's drive, if not into the Balkans itself, at any rate through the Balkans in the direction of Turkey and the Near East. Soviet-Nazi friction over the Balkans was developing already in the spring of 1940, when Soviet officials freely expressed their determination to "take on all comers to the Black Sea." In the following months the Soviets almost openly encouraged Turkey in resisting Hitler and censured Bulgaria for submitting to him. And in the case of Yugoslavia, Ribbentrop charged, on June 22, 1941, that the Soviets had secretly assisted her in arming against the Axis powers from November, 1940, on. In short, it was because the Soviet Union was really blocking him that Hitler finally turned on it. Churchill's public prognostications to this effect had proved correct.

Blocking Hitler in the European arena, however, was only one side of the Soviet coin—the other side was the home front. From August, 1939, on, there was a state of formal mobilization in the Soviet Union. But, as the Soviet leaders had anticipated, this entailed only a minimum of change because of the character of the Soviet society. True, difficulties in transportation and shortages in consumer's goods developed. Housing conditions became worse because of the abandonment of new construction. As a student returning in 1940 summarized the situation, it was hard on the people but not on the government.

What we didn't know at the time, but what became clear later on, was that big industrial building was going on east of the Volga. Appropriations for defense in the 1940 Soviet budget were 57 billion rubles out of a total of 179 billions, although expenditures for social and educational purposes also managed to increase over 1939. The increased drive for production brought measures involving still stricter enforcement of "production discipline," the official assertion being that these measures were directed against a small but disruptive minority and were therefore to be welcomed by the majority as protective and just. And in the field of management the Soviet system was still struggling and experimenting, apparently returning to earlier practices of greater centralization and more Party control.

Ranks had been re-established in the Red Army some years before, this having been done simultaneously with the more systematic fixing of ranks in the teaching profession. The explanation of these two moves had been the enhancement of the prestige of these two important professions in the "Toilers' State." Now, in 1940, a new law introduced the ranks of various grades of generals and admirals—two terms which had previously been deliberately avoided because the old regime had been designated as a "government of capitalists, landlords, and generals." The rank of political commissar, which had been re-established in 1937 just before the purge of the higher command, however, was again abolished and a single responsible authority in the military units restored—temporarily, as it later turned out.

With regard to the international situation, the Soviet press kept its readers very fully informed, with two exceptions. In the first place, during the early period of the fighting in Finland, when things were clearly going badly, the Soviet newspapers carried short, often one-line, official communiques to the effect that nothing essential was happening on the Finnish front, although later, when success favored the Soviet side, the press carried special articles. And, in the second place—and more important—there was no real exposure of Nazi methods in the regular Soviet press in that period; and the conclusion was therefore drawn by outside observers that this silence represented an actual state of Soviet acquiescence, if not approval.

In those years, as in 1937–38, it was again difficult, if not impossible, for foreigners to go down into the villages and factories and get the ordinary Soviet citizen to talk to them. The Soviets refused, in particular, to allow any foreign correspondents to cover their side of the Finnish fighting or to visit the provinces taken from Poland—all under the plea of military secrecy. And when it was suggested, as I took pains to suggest, that coverage by foreign correspondents would secure to the Soviets a better press abroad, the Soviet representatives generally smiled and then added that more consideration would have to be given to the lives of their soldiers than to the sentiments of outside readers. As a result, a very significant factor in the Soviet situation escaped the attention of the American and British publics. For, down in the factories and collective farms, in closed Party-unit meetings, or at general gatherings, and in wall newspapers, active defense propaganda directed against the Nazis was carried on all through this period. It would be surprising if the Germans themselves did not know of this; they probably did but couldn't do anything about it. But British and American diplomats and newspapermen apparently did not learn of it; or, if they did, the diplomats among them kept quiet and the newspapermen had their reports censored.

In general, it may be assumed that the Soviet people didn't like the Soviet-Nazi pact but that they understood the need for it. For they had been told of the negotiations with Britain and France. They had known in detail of Munich and the sellout of Czechoslovakia. Stalin's assertion in his speech of March, 1939, that the Soviets would not be a cat's-paw to pull other people's chestnuts out of the fire was constantly repeated. The Soviet leaders were seen to take energetic steps for the defense of the country. It was, all in all, a well-maneuvered race against time.

The situation had already been summed up by Joseph Stalin in a speech of his in February, 1931. "It is sometimes asked whether it is not possible to slow down the tempo a bit, to put a check on the movement," he said. "No, comrades, it is not possible. . . . . To slacken the

tempo would mean falling behind. And those who fall behind get beaten.
. . . . One feature of the history of old Russia was the continued beatings
she suffered for falling behind, for her backwardness. . . . . She was
beaten because to do so was profitable and could be done with impunity.
. . . . That is why Lenin said during the October revolution: 'Either
perish, or overtake and outstrip the advanced capitalist countries.' We
are fifty or a hundred years behind the advanced countries. We must
make good this distance in ten years. Either we do it, or they crush
us."

This statement was made in 1931. On June 22, 1941, ten years after,
Germany marched on Russia. The reprieve was now up. The time for
testing was at hand.